Debates in History Teachin

What are the key debates in history teaching today?

Debates in History Teaching explores the major issues all history teachers encounter in their daily professional lives. It encourages critical reflection and aims to stimulate both novice and experienced teachers to think more deeply about their practice, and link research and evidence to what they have observed in schools.

Written by a range of history professionals, chapters tackle established and contemporary issues enabling you to reach informed judgements and argue your point of view with deeper theoretical knowledge and understanding.

Debates include:

* What is the purpose of history teaching?
* What do history teachers need to know?
* Should 'academic history' be taught in the classroom?
* What is the role of evidence in history teaching and learning?
* How should you make use of ICT in your lessons?
* Should moral learning be an aim of history education?
* How should history learning be assessed?

With its combination of expert opinion and fresh insight, *Debates in History Teaching* is the ideal companion for any student or practising teacher engaged in initial training, continuing professional development or Masters level study.

Professor Ian Davies is based at the University of York, UK.

Forthcoming titles in the Debates in Subject Teaching Series:

Debates in English Teaching
Edited by Jon Davison, Caroline Daly and John Moss

Debates in Religious Education
Edited by Philip Barnes

Debates in Citizenship Education
Edited by James Arthur and Hilary Cremin

Debates in Art and Design Teaching
Edited by Nicholas Addison and Lesley Burgess

Debates in History Teaching

Edited by Ian Davies

Routledge
Taylor & Francis Group

LONDON AND NEW YORK

First published 2011
by Routledge
2 Park Square, Milton Park, Abingdon, Oxon, OX14 4RN

Simultaneously published in the USA and Canada
by Routledge
711 Third Avenue, New York, NY 10017

Routledge is an imprint of the Taylor & Francis Group, an informa business

© 2011 Ian Davies for selection and editorial material; individual
chapters, the contributors.

The right of the editor to be identified as the author of the editorial
material, and of the authors for their individual chapters, has been
asserted in accordance with sections 77 and 78 of the Copyright,
Designs and Patents Act 1988.

Typeset in Galliard
by Pindar NZ, Auckland, New Zealand

British Library Cataloguing in Publication Data
A catalogue record for this book is available from the British Library

Library of Congress Cataloging-in-Publication Data
A catalog record has been requested for this book

ISBN13: 978-0-415-57161-6 (hbk)
ISBN13: 978-0-415-57162-3 (pbk)
ISBN13: 978-0-203-83145-8 (ebk)

Contents

Illustrations

Figures

Tables

Contributors

Rosalyn Ashby has been a successful teacher of history, politics and economics, Essex LEA (Local Education Agency) History Advisor and Project Officer for Cambridge A-Level History Project (Option 2), and PGCE (Postgraduate Certificate in Education) and MA course leader and researcher at the Institute of Education, University of London.

Paul Bracey is Senior Lecturer in History Education at the University of Northampton. Prior to his current role, he taught in a range of schools for 19 years and was seconded to lecture PGCE students at Birmingham University for two years. His PhD examined diversity through exploring the significance of an Irish dimension in the English history curriculum.

Arthur Chapman is Reader in Education at Edge Hill University, Lancashire. He taught history in Surrey and Cornwall for 12 years and lectured in History Education at St Martins College/the University of Cumbria and at the Institute of Education, University of London, prior to joining Edge Hill. He is co-editor of *Teaching History*, a member of the editorial panel of the *International Review of History Education* and of the editorial board of the *International Journal of Historical Learning, Teaching and Research*. *Constructing History 11–19*, edited with Hilary Cooper, was published by Sage in 2009.

Christine Counsell taught in state schools for 10 years. Now Senior Lecturer at University of Cambridge Faculty of Education, she leads the History PGCE and teaches on Masters courses. She is also editor of the journal *Teaching History*.

Rachel Foster is a recently qualified teacher of history at Comberton Village College (11–16 comprehensive school), Cambridge.

Alison Gove-Humphries is an Adviser for School Effectiveness Division, Birmingham. A Head of Humanities for 17 years, she is now involved in teacher training, production of teaching materials and promoting an inclusive history curriculum.

Robert Guyver is Senior Lecturer and Teaching Fellow at University College Plymouth St Mark and St John. He was a primary teacher in three LEAs for 21 years. He was Chair of the Devon Association of Teachers of History in the late 1980s and a member of the DES (Department for Education and Skills) National Curriculum History Working Group (1989–90). He was an advisory teacher in Essex and now works in higher education with an interest in comparative perspectives on international history curricula. He has recently written two eCPD websites for the Historical Association on Tudors and Victorians.

Richard Harris is Lecturer in Education at the University of Southampton where he runs the history PGCE course and researches aspects of history education.

Terry Haydn worked for many years as a Head of History in an inner-city comprehensive in Manchester before moving to work in teacher education. He is currently Curriculum Tutor for History on the secondary PGCE course at the University of East Anglia.

Jonathan Howson is Deputy Head of Academic Department, Arts and Humanities at the Institute of Education, London. He is involved in research, writing and teaching history education.

Chris Husbands is Director of the Institute of Education, University of London.

Darius Jackson taught history in a range of schools in Gloucestershire and Birmingham before he became Lecturer in History and Citizenship in Education at the University of Birmingham. For his doctorate he is researching on the purposes of Holocaust education in history lessons.

Jenny Keating has degrees from Sussex and Monash universities. She worked in Australia as a commissioned historian, writing and researching on a variety of issues. Her latest book is *A Child for Keeps: The History of Adoption in England, 1918–45*. She currently works on the History in Education Project.

Peter Lee taught history in primary and secondary schools, but has misspent most of his life arguing about or researching history education at the Institute of Education, University of London.

Paula Mountford is Director of Initial Teacher Training at the University of York and Course Leader for the History PGCE programme.

Andrew Peterson is Senior Lecturer in Education at Canterbury Christ Church University. Previously to this he taught history, government and politics and economics to A-level students. He is the leader of three Citizenship Initial Teacher Education courses and has published academic work on the subjects of citizenship and moral education.

Ian Phillips is Senior Lecturer in History Education at Edge Hill University, Lancashire responsible for the History PGCE course. He is also the author of *Teaching History: Developing as a Reflective Secondary Teacher* (Sage, 2008).

Joanne Philpott is Deputy Head of City and Norwich School and was an Advanced Skills Teacher in Norfolk. She is regional adviser for Schools History Project and Historical Association and regularly delivers INSET (in-service education and training) on many aspects of teaching and learning. Joanne has published several articles, pupil materials and *Captivating your Class* – a book on A-level teaching skills.

Alan Sears is Professor in the Faculty of Education at the University of New Brunswick, Canada. He has written extensively about social studies, history and civic education in Canadian and international contexts.

Nicola Sheldon has degrees from Manchester and Oxford universities. She worked for 16 years in sixth-form colleges, teaching history and politics to A level and working in educational management. Her publications cover the history of truancy and institutional childcare. She currently works on the History in Education Project.

Denis Shemilt has taught history in secondary and higher education. From 1974–80 he was evaluator and then director of SHP, and co-director of the Cambridge A-Level project from 1985.

Helen Snelson has been Head of History at The Mount School, York, since 2006. Before that she taught history in two large and varied comprehensive schools in East and North Yorkshire.

James Woodcock is Assistant Headteacher at Sawston Village College (11–16 comprehensive school), near Cambridge. He is a former Head of History and a regular contributor to the journal *Teaching History* and to the Schools History Project annual conference.

Andrew Wrenn is General Advisor for History for Cambridgeshire County Council and a trustee of the Historical Association (HA). He co-wrote the 2007 HA report on teaching emotive and controversial history 3–19 and directed the HA's Key Stage 2–3 History Transition Project.

Series editors' introduction to the series

This book, *Debates in History Teaching*, is one of a series of books entitled *Debates in Subject Teaching*. The series has been designed to engage with a wide range of debates related to subject teaching. Unquestionably, debates vary among the subjects, but may include, for example, issues that:

- impact on Initial Teacher Education in the subject;
- are addressed in the classroom through the teaching of the subject;
- are related to the content of the subject and its definition;
- are related to subject pedagogy;
- are connected with the relationship between the subject and broader educational aims and objectives in society, and the philosophy and sociology of education;
- are related to the development of the subject and its future in the twenty-first century.

Consequently, each book presents key debates that subject teachers should understand, reflect on and engage in as part of their professional development. Chapters have been designed to highlight major questions, and to consider the evidence from research and practice in order to find possible answers. Some subject books or chapters offer at least one solution or a view of the ways forward, whereas others provide alternative views and leave readers to identify their own solution or view of the ways forward. The editors expect readers will want to pursue the issues raised, and so chapters include questions for further debate and suggestions for further reading. Debates covered in the series will provide the basis for discussion in university subject seminars or as topics for assignments or classroom research. The books have been written for all those with a professional interest in their subject, and, in particular: student teachers learning to teach the subject in secondary or primary school; newly qualified teachers; teachers undertaking study at Masters level; teachers with a subject coordination or leadership role, and those preparing for such responsibility; as well as mentors, university tutors, CPD organisers and advisers of the aforementioned groups.

Books in the series have a cross-phase dimension, because the editors believe that it is important for teachers in the primary, secondary and post-16 phases to look at subject teaching holistically, particularly in order to provide for continuity and progression, but also to increase their understanding of how children and young people learn. The balance of chapters that have a cross-phase relevance varies according to the issues relevant to different subjects. However, no matter where the emphasis is, the authors have drawn out the relevance of their topic to the whole of each book's intended audience.

Because of the range of the series, both in terms of the issues covered and its cross-phase concern, each book is an edited collection. Editors have commissioned new writing from experts on particular issues, who, collectively, represent many different perspectives on subject teaching. Readers should not expect a book in this series to cover the entire range of debates relevant to the subject, or to offer a completely unified view of subject teaching, or that every debate will be dealt with discretely, or that all aspects of a debate will be covered. Part of what each book in this series offers to readers is the opportunity to explore the interrelationships between positions in debates and, indeed, among the debates themselves, by identifying the overlapping concerns and competing arguments that are woven through the text.

The editors are aware that many initiatives in subject teaching continue to originate from the centre, and that teachers have decreasing control of subject content, pedagogy and assessment strategies. The editors strongly believe that for teaching to remain properly a vocation and a profession, teachers must be invited to be part of a creative and critical dialogue about subject teaching, and should be encouraged to reflect, criticise, problem-solve and innovate. This series is intended to provide teachers with a stimulus for democratic involvement in the development of the discourse of subject teaching.

Susan Capel, Jon Davison, James Arthur and John Moss
December 2010

Acknowledgements

I would like to acknowledge the highly professional efficiency of Jayne McCullagh who helped enormously with the administrative work associated with the early stages of producing this book.

I am very grateful to Christine Counsell, Peter Lee and Jerome Freeman who were good enough to offer discussion and to suggest themes and ideas for this book.

Of course, I am very grateful to all the authors who worked so hard – in the face of increasing professional pressures – to produce the excellent contributions to this book that will be of great value to all those who play a part in history education.

For practical reasons of space proper broader acknowledgements could not be made to very many excellent academics and professionals who exert a positive influence on history education. I would, however, like to acknowledge the very significant personal contribution made by Lynn, Hannah, Rachael and Matthew Davies who have created a very wonderful past and with whom there is a very positively anticipated future.

Ian Davies, University of York
March 2010

Introduction

Ian Davies

The purpose of this book is to highlight issues which are important in history education and which trainee and experienced teachers will have to address throughout their career. The book is designed, therefore, to encourage teachers to consider and reflect on issues relevant to history education in order to reach their own informed judgements. This will be of great value to beginning and experienced professionals as they work in the classroom with young people and in their current or future work as mentors and subject leaders.

The majority of trainee teachers learning to teach in secondary schools follow a one-year Postgraduate Certificate in Education (PGCE) course. The majority of secondary PGCE courses now offer up to 60 Masters level credits. Alongside this development for initial teacher education, a Masters in Teaching and Learning is being developed by the Training and Development Agency for Schools (TDA) which is designed to support the professional development of serving teachers in schools. Studying at Masters level requires trainee teachers to cover some issues in depth. This book, which covers many of these issues, provides a very useful resource to enable professionals to start developing a deeper understanding of important matters. This book will also be of use to more experienced professionals and others. The authors of this book wish to help teachers to reflect on the issues identified in order to reach their own considered judgement, so that they can discuss and argue their point of view and relate their professional work to key debates. The sort of history teacher that people are now and will become in the future will depend very much on their approach to the topics discussed in this book.

The book is divided into four main sections. In the first section ('Debates in history teaching: contexts and controversies') there is a historical overview of history education and phase-related reviews for primary, secondary and post-16. By the end of this section a reader will have a clear idea of the background to the development of history education and some of the current issues and controversies that are being faced by all teachers. In Section 2 ('Debating procedural concepts and history') there is detailed consideration of the nature of history education. Readers will be engaged by reflections on the fundamental building blocks of our professional work. A history teacher, obviously, needs a particular form of understanding and the detail of what this means is developed in Section 2. Key issues about the procedural concepts of history are explored and debated and through this process readers will have a clear idea of the complexities and necessities of history education. In Section 3 ('Debating the expression and purpose of history') there are three chapters that explore some of the uses to which history education may be put. In the contested terrain that characterizes debates not just about what history is but also about what it is for, there are chapters about moral learning, diversity and citizenship. Finally, Section 4 ('Debating the teaching and learning of history') explores some of the ways in which teachers and others use particular approaches in order to develop historical understanding.

Within these four sections each chapter will address a separate topic and readers are encouraged to consider issues from various viewpoints and to consider their own stance. It is hoped that through stimulating such consideration trainee history teachers and others will be able to argue their case in schools or elsewhere. Each chapter is supported by reference to further reading and other reference material which will enable readers to explore any of the issues in more depth.

No book can ever claim to be comprehensive. There are certainly topics and issues that could be explored in other publications that will be of use to beginning and experienced professionals. But the chapters of this book have been written by experts with vast experience and highly valuable expertise and it is hoped that this publication stands as a mark of respect to those who work in the vitally important history education profession and will support and strengthen their good work.

Debates in history teaching

Contexts and controversies

Chapter 1

History in education

Trends and themes in history teaching, 1900–2010

Jenny Keating and Nicola Sheldon

Introduction

The twentieth century has seen considerable changes in the way history is taught, and debates begun a hundred years ago continue over the importance of studying contemporary history, citizenship teaching and the relative priority of teaching facts over skills. We are working on a two-year research project tracing the development of history teaching in English state schools across the twentieth century.[1] This chapter considers the debates and policies described in this brief introductory chapter but will also look at the experience of history teaching in schools through archival sources and interviews with former pupils and teachers.

History teaching in elementary/primary schools, 1900–1960s

At the beginning of the twentieth century the vast majority of children received all their formal education in elementary schools. In the 25 years prior to 1900 there had been considerable variations in what was taught in response to changing funding regulations. History was particularly affected: from 1882, although pupils' reading books (readers) might include some history, the subject itself was optional. By 1890, out of 22,516 elementary schools, history was taught in only 414, compared with English in 20,304 and geography in 12,367 (Bd Ed, 1900: 116).

Alterations in the funding rules led to an increase in the number of elementary schools teaching history; by 1899 it was on the curriculum of 5,879 schools. From 1900 they were to include lessons 'on geography, history, and common things' (Ed Dept, 1900: 4), and by 1903 almost all were teaching history. The Board of Education provided guidance about how teachers should teach history in their 'Codes' and 'Suggestions for Elementary Teachers'. In the first 'Suggestions', in 1905, there was a great deal about what *might* be taught but it was stressed that 'the only uniformity of practice' the Board desired 'was that each teacher shall think for himself, and work out for himself such methods of teaching as may use his powers to best advantage and be best suited to the particular needs and conditions of the school' (Bd Ed, 1905: 5).

The Suggestions stated that 'the establishment of character' was a main aim of elementary education and strongly urged that history play a part in this. Younger pupils should be taught history orally 'through a series of biographies of typical heroes or heroines' (Bd Ed, 1905: 5). In geography, children learned that Great Britain was only 'one country among many others'. In contrast, in history:

> [T]hey should learn something about their nationality which distinguishes them from the people of other countries. They cannot understand this, however, unless they are taught how the British nation grew up, and how the mother country in her turn has founded daughter countries beyond the seas.
>
> (Bd Ed, 1905: 61)

The Board did not prescribe a particular pedagogical practice but said it would lie between the 'concentric', where different aspects of a historical period were looked at in turn, and 'chronological' (Bd Ed, 1905: 63). Teaching aids – maps, globes, pictures, lantern slides and teachers' own blackboard sketches and diagrams – and drama were to be used. Teachers were encouraged to organize school trips to museums, art galleries and historic sites. The importance of oral teaching throughout schooling was stressed but by the last three years (11–14) this was to be supplemented by a well-written and well-illustrated history book. Different schemes of study were suggested for these years but in the last year all included elements of 'citizenship' education, which was considered important for young members of the empire.

Over the next 55 years the government issued further Suggestions; there were no dramatic changes of direction but there were gradual changes. Teacher autonomy was always stressed, although considerable use of 'should' and 'must' somewhat detracted from this. In 1918 (when education was made compulsory for all pupils to age 14) it was stated:

> [T]he pupil has to acquire, by the time he leaves school . . . a tolerably connected view of the main outlines of British History . . . some knowledge of the government of the country, the growth of free institutions, the expansion of the Empire, and the establishment of our position among nations
>
> (Bd Ed, 1918: 92)

Recent history was to be taught, but was seen as problematic: treating it 'reign by reign' would never be 'really interesting and attractive', but studying constitutional and economic changes would be either too difficult for the children or potentially controversial. In 1927, studying the League of Nations and World history was recommended, but the latter would only include areas 'from which modern civilisation can trace a direct descent, i.e. Palestine, Greece and Rome' (Bd Ed, 1927a: 124). The last Suggestions before the Second World War recommended the study of modern history to the present day but only for 13- to 14-year-olds because of the complexities involved (Bd Ed, 1937: 425).

The learning of dates was an issue; in 1918 an HMI (His Majesty's Inspector) complained:

> The reaction against the 'dates of the kings and queens' has gone too far, and in many cases left the post-elementary school scholar without any dates at all, sometimes with very little appreciation of historical time.
>
> (Bd Ed, 1921: 54)

The 1927 Suggestions repeated this criticism and suggested the construction of 'time charts' by the children to provide a clear idea of dates and the duration of periods (Bd Ed, 1927a: 137).

A Board of Education inspectors' survey in 1926 of history teaching in 41 London elementary schools considered that most taught syllabuses were 'concerned too exclusively with the story of Britain and the British Empire'. World history was hardly taught, although in about a quarter of the syllabuses there was some reference to the League of Nations (Bd Ed, 1927b: 7). The inspectors criticized the junior class teachers' lack of narrative skills and the rare opportunities for children to participate in lessons. Even in the older classes, the inspectors estimated that most children spent at least 75 per cent of their time 'as passive listeners'.

Long before World War II, debate was beginning about the relevance of historical facts for younger children. The 1931 Hadow Report on 'The Primary School' suggested that the child should finish its primary education (i.e. at age 11) 'beginning to have a lively sense of the bearing of history upon his everyday life and environment', rather than attempting 'to acquire at the primary stage a knowledge of historical facts which properly belongs to the later stage' (Bd Ed, 1931: 171).

Nearly 30 years later, the 1959 Suggestions continued this discussion. They are fairly negative about history; the chapter on it is entitled 'The problems of teaching history to the young' (DES, 1959: 275) and it suggested, 'adult generalisations must not be forced too soon on children'. The best introduction to history would be through 'the magic of a well-told story'. Much is claimed for these stories; they stimulate the child's imagination and, 'in putting himself in another's place sympathy is born'. The Suggestions describe a process moving from myth and legend in the last year of infant school to stories of real people by the time children are 8 or 9, and a more chronological series of stories in the last junior school year (DES, 1959: 276, 277–8, 281).

History teaching in secondary schools, 1900–1960s

The beginning of the twentieth century saw considerable debate about how far technical and scientific teaching should be prioritized in secondary schools. Even before this, history had frequently not been well taught. A 1902 Board of Education report strongly criticized history teaching in boys' secondary schools; many had no libraries, no atlases and taught solely from one textbook throughout the school. Teaching was completely geared to examination syllabuses (Bd Ed, 1903: 65).

Over the next few years improvements were initiated. The 1904 Regulations for Secondary Schools included minimum hours for subjects judged necessary which included history. In 1907, schools were given more freedom to organize their timetables but history remained compulsory and was usually allocated two lessons a week. In 1908 the Board of Education issued a Circular on the 'Teaching of History in Secondary Schools' (1908b), which was extremely influential. The Circular recommended that 12- to 16-year-olds study 'a course of three or four years in which there should be a consecutive study of English history in the extended sense . . . i.e. English history with large digressions into foreign history. The whole of English history would then be divided into three periods, one of them being assigned to each year', with a year for revision (Bd Ed, 1908a: 3).

As with elementary school Suggestions, there was no compulsion in the Circular, but 'the experience of Inspectors, however, shows that in many schools there is clearly some need for help'. Learning dates should not be overemphasized 'but a few of the most important' should be known, together with the details of English monarchs, 'in connection with some of the important events of the reigns, and not merely by rote'. History should be brought alive by the study of sites and artefacts, books, maps, plans and pictures, specially prepared extracts and translations from historical documents. Well-chosen textbooks, regular written work and note-taking were all seen as essential (Bd Ed, 1908b: 2).

In the 1920s the Board of Education investigated the state of history teaching in the grant-aided secondary schools. Its inspectors confirmed that history was generally taught along the lines of the Circular, with most schools teaching it chronologically until the first external examination at 16. On the whole the Board's report was positive; teachers were more interested and knowledgeable than before, pupils' essay and note-taking skills much improved. Source books were now used, as the educationalist M. W. Keatinge had suggested in 1910 (Keatinge, 1910), and younger pupils were increasingly encouraged to draw and model and to act out historical scenes.

The report praised the introduction of both European and modern history in many schools although it was less happy about the accompanying neglect of the medieval period and potential inadequacy of teaching English history. It stated that 'the primary object of our main course must be to give the pupils a clear outline of the History of their own country' although between 15 and 18 they should also receive 'a series of special lessons, or lectures, on World History' (Bd Ed, 1923: 17, 19).

The teaching of World history was much discussed in the interwar years; it was suggested that with more global awareness disasters like world wars might be averted. In the mid 1930s the BBC Schools Broadcasting Service ran a World history course which over a thousand schools regularly listened to (CCSB, 1936). These years also saw debate over studying 'civics'. Should this be part of a modern history course, introducing pupils to current issues, or should it be a separate subject, teaching the rights and responsibilities of citizenship?

A survey of history teaching in English schools carried out in the mid 1930s described 'the lecture, rather formal in nature', as the most common method of teaching in secondary schools (Shropshire, 1936: 88–9, 123).[2] Teaching was usually chronological but with occasional use of topic-based work, which was attracting increasing interest by the late 1930s. The 'lines of development' teaching method was advocated by some teachers; an area such as 'the development of medicine and hygiene' or transport would be studied across the centuries (Jeffreys, 1935, 1936, 1937).

Since 1918 the previously complicated system of secondary school examinations had been organized into two main ones: the First School Examination (School Certificate), taken at about 16, and the Second School Examination (Higher School Certificate), taken at 18. To obtain the School Certificate pupils had to reach a required standard in five subjects; in 1937 history, one of the subjects, was taken by 82 per cent of candidates. For the Higher Certificate, history could be taken as either a main or subsidiary subject, with increasing emphasis on individual study in the library rather than using the teacher's notes and textbooks. In 1951 the Certificate Examinations were replaced by examination of individual subjects at 'O' and 'A' level, although the 1943 Norwood Report, which paved the way for the 1944 Education Act, had criticized the stultifying influence of public examinations and recommended their replacement by internal ones (Bd Ed, 1943: 33).

In fact the majority of pupils took no external history examinations before 1965. Prior to the implementation of the 1944 Act the vast majority of children left school at 14, having continued at elementary schools or moved to central schools, with a minority attending junior technical or trade schools. Generally all continued to study some history. The suggestions for history teaching in the 1926 Hadow Report, which looked at education for these children, were not dissimilar to those for secondary schools but recommended that, 'while the chronological order of events needs to be maintained, the presentation should be topical' (Bd Ed, 1926: 198).

The teaching of secondary school history did not really alter under the new system of grammar schools, modern schools and technical schools in the late 1940s and 1950s. The grammar schools continued to teach mainly by examination-oriented oral instruction, note-taking and textbooks, although some teachers used the 'lines of development' described above or began to teach 'patch' history – in which a particular period or subject is studied in depth, with the motive of 'finding out all it can about the character of life in some other age' (Min Ed, 1952: 18).

Less than a quarter of children went to grammar schools in the 1950s; most children attended secondary modern schools. The 1963 Newsom Report looked at the teaching of the children considered 'average' and 'less-than-average' in these schools. The emphasis was on work 'in depth for a short time rather than a little of everything all the time'. History was often grouped with geography and religious studies as humanities or social studies. Although pupils took no external examinations, other achievements were encouraged – 'the production of a class book, the making of a film strip'. Particularly in the last years of school there was an emphasis on studying contemporary history and citizenship issues (Min Ed, 1963: 166). In the technical schools there was sometimes an attempt to teach history in a way that was relevant to the different strands of technology studied in the school, using a lines of development methodology.

Challenges to history: the 1960s

While many history classrooms remained undisturbed in the 1960s, external changes underway in the organization of schools, in school examinations and the use of technology all had an impact on the teaching of history (Chitty, 1989: 19–48).

The Certificate of Secondary Education (CSE) was introduced in 1963 for pupils in secondary modern schools not able to reach O-level standard by age 16. Under the 'Mode 3' provisions, schools were allowed to devise their own syllabus and assessment, a practice which became popular with history teachers in secondary modern schools. Teachers could devise courses which tapped into the interests of pupils, such as local studies and class projects, but it also taxed their ingenuity to keep such pupils motivated (Bayne-Jardine, 1970: 215–19). Methods of delivery were therefore diversified by the study of documentary sources alongside museum visits and trips (Fines, 1968: 348–56). Partly, these developments were the outcome of increased school budgets which allowed teachers to buy more than just a class textbook, but publishers also responded to the desire for more 'authentic' materials (most famously the Jonathan Cape *Jackdaw* folders). They also resulted from initiatives by broadcast-ers, museums and archives to reach into the history classroom and engage children's imaginations. By the early 1960s, 30,000 radio sets had been provided to schools (Min Ed, 1963: 73). During the decade, TV became increasingly popular, especially at primary level where lessons could be fitted round the programme schedule. The use of filmstrips or 'radiovision', with a recorded soundtrack, was more popular at secondary level, as this could be fitted into timetabled lessons (Hayter, 1974: 21–2). Reprographic machines initiated the 'worksheet' revolution allowing teachers to produce their own materials.

In grammar schools, there was a growing interest in new history syllabuses, though this was always constrained by the O-level examination. Social and economic history increased in popularity, spurred perhaps by younger teachers who as undergraduates in the interwar period had been tutored in new areas of historical study (Strong, 1964: 74–9). Some teachers believed the Commonwealth and other contemporary international issues were more relevant to their pupils than British political history in the nineteenth century (LHTA, 1961–9: DES, 1967).

However, classroom learning was still dominated by dictation and board-copying due to the need to digest information for examinations which essentially tested fac-tual recall and essay writing (Booth, 1969: 66). A 1966 Schools Council Survey of 10,000 15-year-olds largely rated history as 'useless and boring' (Price, 1968: 343). In 1968, the journal *History* published the article 'History in danger', a clarion call to the history teaching community to save the subject from imminent threats to its survival on the school curriculum. More 'relevant' subjects such as social studies, integrated humanities and civics were introduced, while time for history was squeezed out (Moore, 1975: 109–12).

A new rationale for history: the 1970s

However, it could be argued that the major engine for change emerged from the internal existential questions which some history teachers and teacher trainers were beginning to ask (Steele, 1976: 1–61). As theories of child psychology gained popularity among educationists, history teachers faced a new challenge. Was history simply beyond the intellectual capacity of most children in school? Research into children's thinking in history along Piagetian lines suggested that only the most able were thinking in abstract terms about history before the age of 16 (Hallam, 1970: 162–78).

Placed on the defensive, history teachers and especially teacher trainers in the expanding colleges of education rethought the whole basis for history teaching to produce what has been called 'new history'. Many teachers and teacher trainers were already experimenting with the use of primary sources and active learning methods, such as drama and field work. However, a new rationale for school history was first fully explained in the Coltham and Fines' pamphlet, *Educational Objectives for the Study of History* (Coltham and Fines, 1971). Building on the theories of psycholo-gists Jerome Bruner and Benjamin Bloom, they tried to identify the characteristic practices associated with 'doing history' as an educational activity. The new approach aimed at developing children's skills in historical method as they encountered sources about the past. These skills included the appreciation of bias and different perspectives on past events as well as the use of 'empathy', but it was left to teachers to work out how this approach should be translated into the classroom (Coltham, 1972: 278–9).

The most significant 'new history' initiative, although one among several in the early 1970s, was the Schools Council History Project (SCHP), established in 1972 at Leeds University. It developed a new curriculum for the 13–16 age group, which would be examined via both O level and CSE (Sylvester, 1975: 105–8). SCHP's syllabus comprised a modern world study, a narrower depth 'patch' study, a development study over a long period of time and a local study. The Project thus wrapped together all the new syllabus ideas from the previous 30 years into one course. The Project did not ignore chronology or the need for children to be given secondary information, nor did it treat the choice of historical content as unimportant. However, it did offer a radical approach by explicitly building the course around fostering children's historical skills. Pupils revisited the key ideas of evidence, change and continuity, causation and anachronism at succeeding stages in the course. SCHP sought to justify its place in the curriculum on the basis of adolescent 'needs' and encouraged teachers to talk about the purpose of history in the classroom in order to engage pupils' commitment (SCHP, 1976: 11–12).

The contested ground of history: the 1980s

The influence of 'new history' was not limited to those history departments, in about a third of schools, which adopted the Schools Council History Project. Many others used their introductory 'What is History?' materials to teach the ideas of evidence and skills-based learning for pupils following other syllabuses. However, the single development which secured the influence of 'new history' over history teaching was the General Certificate of Secondary Education (GCSE) examination.

Dissatisfaction with O-level examinations had been apparent since the 1950s, but little had changed in 30 years (LHTA, 1955–61). The CSE, first examined in 1965, offered a variety of assessment including coursework. Thus, comprehensive schools had to divide their pupils at age 14 depending on which exam they would take at 16. In 1976, the Schools Council recommended a common system, but such was the caution among politicians that GCSE was not introduced until 1986 (QCA, 2009).

GCSE history exams included 20 per cent coursework and explicitly assessed students' skills in history according to a series of 'grade criteria'. Assessing such skills from written exam work was particularly challenging for teachers without an SCHP background. Most controversially, the assessment of 'empathy' was included, which critics claimed was unfeasible in school exams (Skidelsky, 1988; Low-Beer, 1989: 8–12). Yet GCSE was also a step towards the National Curriculum. It was the first nationally organized curriculum revision and marked the beginning of close government involvement in the school curriculum (Raban, 2008: 98). History GCSE provoked opposition from those who preferred traditional methods of assessment. Teachers at a school in Sussex questioned the rigour of the new exam and attempted to enter their pupils for an alternative Scottish examination. The issue became a *cause célèbre* in the press and was taken up by academic historians (Phillips, 1998: 22–3). It was a foretaste of the fierce debate over history in the National Curriculum.

History in the National Curriculum: the 1990s

Before 1990, Britain was unusual among developed nations in *not* having a national curriculum. Politicians began to take an interest in the outcomes of the education system when Britain's economic problems drew attention to the failing competitive position of British industry and the need for a better-educated workforce. In a landmark speech at Ruskin College, Oxford, in October 1976, Prime Minister Jim Callaghan declared, 'Public interest is strong and legitimate and will be satisfied. We spend £6 billion a year on education, so there will be discussion' (Callaghan, 1976). That discussion led eventually to the Education Reform Act of 1988 which introduced a National Curriculum for England and Wales. Prime Minister Margaret Thatcher preferred a core curriculum which specified only English, maths and science. Kenneth Baker, the education secretary, argued for a common curriculum up to age 16 which would fill most of the school timetable, with the core subjects supplemented by seven 'foundation' subjects, one of which was history. Baker's conception prevailed and working groups of academics, teachers, trainers and other experts were set up to draft the new curriculum during 1989 (Baker, 1993: 196–7).

There was apprehension about the government's plans but, on the whole, history teachers were willing to wait and see what the working group produced in the hope that a National Curriculum could tackle some of the weaknesses in the curriculum. In primary education, the advance of topic work had reduced the amount of time spent on history, with much work described by inspectors as 'superficial' (DES, 1989: 7). At secondary level, children experienced repetition or disjointed history education if they switched schools. Teachers often omitted periods in a race to cover everything in three years before pupils made their GCSE course choices (DES, 1978: 3–6, 59–62). Some local education authorities attempted to coordinate the syllabuses taught across their schools, but these experiments got no further than voluntary initiatives (DES, 1983: 1–17). *History in the Primary and Secondary Years: An HMI View* reflected the inspectorate's belief that innovation should be encouraged but there was 'no one way' to teach history nor content obligatory for all to learn (DES, 1985: 11–15). However, by 1988, inspectors' thinking had moved to establishing a basis for a common core of history which all children should be taught, in *History from 5 to 16* (DES, 1988: 12–13). They now strongly emphasized chronological understanding and the historical knowledge seen as essential to the transmission of a common culture and society's values.

History in the National Curriculum attracted more controversy and public attention than any other subject, although English came close. The History Working Group was aware of their critical role in selecting the content of the curriculum under the eye of a Conservative government committed to the primacy of British history (HiEP interviews, 2009). Press interest and academic discussion tended to focus on the debate about which historical incidents or personalities should be included (Elwyn Jones, 2000: 299–322). However, this was not the issue which strained most the relationship between the government and the History Working Group. All the working groups had been given an assessment structure which pictured progression through ten 'levels', each with a measurable target. The working group believed that progress in history could not be assessed on the basis of increased factual knowledge at each stage. They argued instead that attainment in history must be measured by testing the skills of the pupils, though naturally via the medium of factual information (Phillips, 1998: 68). In terms of content, the working group attempted to satisfy a wide range of interests, with a majority of the topics covering British history alongside study units in European and world history. They also stressed economic, social and cultural history alongside political events (DES, 1990: 31–3).

Two lengthy consultations followed the reports of the working group, receiving more than a thousand submissions markedly in favour of their approach, and the National Curriculum for History was implemented from March 1991. For primary schools in particular, it marked a radical departure placing tremendous demands on teachers without specialist expertise. The time required to cover the content had not been accurately estimated and it was clearly unmanageable. Moreover, the plans to test all ten subjects soon ran into trouble as teachers grappled with an unfamiliar assessment framework (Phillips, 1998: 115–17). Even before it was passed into law, the secretary of state, John MacGregor, decided to cut out much of the optional material. Following a review of the heavy curriculum load, his successor, Kenneth Clarke, made history and geography optional post-14. This compromised the coherence of the history curriculum, which had been designed to run chronologically to age 16 for all pupils. Key Stage 3 had to be hastily revised to include twentieth-century material (Hennessey HiEP interview, 2009; Phillips, 1998: 105). In 1993, with mounting opposition among teachers, a major revision was undertaken under Lord Dearing, resulting in a further slimming down of all subjects, but especially history and geography. Such reviews of the National Curriculum also brought to the fore those critics who demanded that certain essential factual detail should be specified for all children to learn (Lawler, 1993; McGovern, 1994).

History for the twenty-first century

Arguably, the position of history in schools was strengthened by the introduction of the National Curriculum. Much more history was taught in primary schools than had been the case before 1990 (Harnett, 2000: 32; HiEP interview, 2009). In addition, it was possible for publishers, media organizations, museums and the heritage sector to produce resources knowing that all schools covered broadly the same topics.

Under Labour governments since 1997, history has begun to face a number of challenges again. New priorities such as citizenship and vocational courses have squeezed teaching time at Key Stage 4 for traditional school subjects (Ofsted, 2007: 28–9, 32). Latterly, some schools have introduced a skills-based curriculum at Key Stage 3 and in primary schools 'cross-curricular' studies have been recommended (Opening Minds, 2006; DCSF, 2009). On the other hand, history is reportedly well taught and has been successful in maintaining candidate numbers at GCSE and A level in recent years (Haydn and Harris, 2007: 15). Perhaps it is sanguine to finish this chapter with the words of Dr Tim Lomas, whose 30 years' experience in history education prompted him to summarize the position thus: 'We have mostly been on the defensive and reacting to changes all the time. History is quite good at adapting; it has had to . . ... In many schools, history remains the most popular optional subject, despite everything that is thrown at it. It is resilient in that sense' (Lomas HiEP interview, 2009).

Chapter summary

- Until the 1990s, teachers in England were theoretically free to teach history as they chose. However, up to the 1960s, teachers generally followed recommendations in government 'Suggestions', 'Codes' and Circulars.
- For younger children these proposed using stories, moving from myth and legend to fact-based episodes. In the later years of elementary school (pre-1944) and in secondary school, teaching was generally chronological but with growing awareness in the interwar years of new approaches – uses of sources, 'lines of development', the 'patch' method.
- The emphasis was on British or English history but even before World War II there was considerable interest in teaching World history and aspects of 'civics' or citizenship. Comprehensive schooling and the raising of the school leaving age promoted new approaches for all-ability classes, such as the use of local studies and fieldwork.
- The 1970s saw a flowering of curriculum innovation promoted by expanding teacher training colleges. 'New history' advocated the learning of 'skills' in history, using sources to 'reconstruct' the past rather than a received narrative.
- The National Curriculum in history resulted in more teaching of the subject in primary schools and more consistency across schools in what was taught. British history was again given prominence. Revisions to the National Curriculum have allowed teachers more autonomy and prioritized diversity as well as the national story.

Further reading

Board of Education (1905) 'Suggestions for the Consideration of Teachers and Others Concerned in the Work of Public Elementary Schools'.
——(1908) 'Teaching of History in Secondary Schools', Circular 599.
DES. Department of Education and Science (1985) *History in the Primary and Secondary Years: An HMI View.*
——(April 1990) *National Curriculum History Working Group Final Report.*
Ofsted. Office for Standards in Education (2007) 'History in the Balance: History in English Schools 2003–07'.
Phillips, Robert (1998) *History Teaching, Nationhood and the State: A Study in Educational Politics.* London: Cassell.
SCHP. Schools Council History 13–16 Project (1976) *A New Look at History.* Edinburgh: Holmes McDougall.
Shropshire, Olive E. (1936) *The Teaching of History in English Schools.* New York: Teachers College, Columbia University.

Notes

1 The History in Education Project is based at the Institute of Historical Research under the leadership of Professor Sir David Cannadine, with funding from the Linbury Trust.
2 This continued into the 1960s. A respondent to our Pupil Survey described history teaching at her grammar school in the early 1960s: '[T]he teaching method consisted

basically of [the teacher] talking, then writing notes up on the board which we copied down . . . there was no encouraging us to think for ourselves, no independent learning' (RL/P48/HiE75, History in Education Project Archive, Pupil Survey, 23 November 2009).

References

Secondary works

Baker, K. (1993) *The Turbulent Years: My Life in Politics*. London: Faber & Faber.

Bayne-Jardine, Colin C. (1970) 'A Practical Approach', in Martin Ballard (ed.) *New Movements in the Study and Teaching of History*. London: Temple Smith.

Booth, M. (1969) *History Betrayed?* London: Longman.

Chitty, C. (1989) *Towards a New Education System: A Victory for the New Right?* Lewes: Falmer Press.

Coltham, J. (May 1972) 'Educational Objectives and the Teaching of History', *Teaching History* II, 7: 278–9.

Coltham, J. and Fines, J. (1971) *Educational Objectives for the Study of History*, Historical Association Pamphlet No. 35. Oxford: Clarendon Press.

Elwyn Jones, G. (Autumn 2000) 'The Debate over the National Curriculum for History in England and Wales, 1989–90: The Role of the Press', *Curriculum Journal* 11(3): 299–322.

Fines, J. (October 1968) 'Archives in School', *History* 53: 348–56.

Hallam, R. N. (1970) 'Piaget and Thinking in History', in Martin Ballard (ed.) *New Movements in the Study and Teaching of History*. London: Temple Smith.

Harnett, P. (2000) 'Curriculum Decision-Making in the Primary School', in James Arthur and Robert Phillips (eds) *Issues in History Teaching*. London: Routledge Falmer.

Haydn, T. and Harris, R. (September 2007) *Factors Influencing Pupil Take-Up of History Post Key Stage 3, Final Report*. Available online at: http://www.uea.ac.uk/~m242/qca3report%20_m242%20v1_.pdf (accessed 24 November 2009).

Hayter, C. G. (1974) *Using Broadcasts in Schools: A Study and Evaluation*. London: BBC/ITV.

Jeffreys, M. V. C. (1935, 1936, 1937) *History* 20: 233–4; 21: 230–8; 22: 219–27.

Keatinge, M. W. (1910) *Studies in the Teaching of History*. London: A. & C. Black.

Lawler, S. (ed.) (1993) *The Dearing Debate: Assessment and the National Curriculum*. London: Centre for Policy Studies.

Low-Beer, A. (1989) 'Empathy and History', *Teaching History* 55: 8–12.

McGovern, C. J. M. (1994) *The SCAA Review of National Curriculum History: A Minority Report*. York: Campaign for Real Education.

Moore, Roger F. (1975) 'History and Integrated Studies: Surrender or Survival?' *Teaching History* IV, 14: 109–12.

Phillips, R. (1998) *History Teaching, Nationhood and the State: A Study in Educational Politics*. London: Cassell.

Price, M. (October 1968) 'History in Danger', *History*. 53: 342–7.

Raban, S. (2008) *Examining the World*. Cambridge University Press: Cambridge.

SCHP. Schools Council History 13–16 Project (1976) *A New Look at History*. Edinburgh: Holmes McDougall.

Shropshire, Olive E. (1936) *The Teaching of History in English Schools*. New York: Teachers College, Columbia University.

Skidelsky, R. (1 March 1988) *Independent*.

Steele, I. K. (1976) *Developments in History Teaching*. London: Open Books.

Strong, C. F. (1964) *History in the Secondary School*. London: University of London Press.

Sylvester, D. (1975) 'Re-Thinking the Syllabus for 14–16 Year Olds', *Teaching History* IV, 14: 105–8.

Official documents and archival sources

Bd Ed. Board of Education (1900) 'Report, 1899–1900 (Elementary Education)', vol. III, appendix.

——(1903) 'General Reports on Higher Education with Appendices for the Year 1902'.

——(1905) 'Suggestions for the Consideration of Teachers and others concerned in the work of Public Elementary Schools'.

——(1908a) 'Memorandum in explanation and expansion of the Board's Circular on the Teaching of History in Secondary Schools', National Archives ED 22/36.

——(1908b) 'Teaching of History in Secondary Schools', Circular 599.

——(1918) 'Suggestions for the Consideration of Teachers and others concerned in the work of Public Elementary Schools'.

——(1921, although prepared in 1918) 'Humanism in the Continuation School'.

——(1923) Educational Pamphlets, No 37, 'Report on the Teaching of History'.

——(1926) 'Report of the Consultative Committee on the Education of the Adolescent' [The Hadow Report].

——(1927a) 'Handbook of Suggestions for the Consideration of Teachers and others concerned in the work of Public Elementary Schools'.

——(1927b) 'General Report on the Teaching of History in London Elementary Schools, 1927'.

——(1931) 'Report of the Consultative Committee on the Primary School' [The Hadow Report].

——(1937) 'Handbook of Suggestions for the Consideration of Teachers and others Concerned in the Work of Public Elementary Schools'.

——(1943) 'Curriculum and Examinations in Secondary Schools', Report of the Committee of the Secondary School Examinations Council [The Norwood Report].

Callaghan, J. (1976) *Towards a National Debate*. Available online at: http://education.guardian.co.uk/thegreatdebate/story/0,9860,574645,00.html (accessed 23 November 2009).

CCSB. Central Council for School Broadcasting (1936) Report to Central Council for School Broadcasting, History Sub-Committee [Minutes], 16 January.

Ed Dept. Education Department (1900) 'Code of Regulations for Day Schools'.

DES. Department of Education and Science (1959) 'Primary Education: Suggestions for the Consideration of Teachers and others concerned in the work of Primary Schools'.

——(1967) *Towards World History (Education Pamphlet No. 52)*.

——(1978) *Curriculum 11–16: Working Papers by Her Majesty's Inspectorate: A Contribution to Current Debate*.

——(1983) *Curriculum 11–16: Towards a Statement of Entitlement*.

——(1985) *History in the Primary and Secondary Years: An HMI View*.

——(1988) *History from 5 to 16 (Curriculum Matters 11)*.

——Her Majesty's Inspectorate (1989) *Aspects of Primary Education: The Teaching and Learning of History and Geography.*

——(April 1990) *National Curriculum History Working Group Final Report.*

DCSF. Department for Children, Schools and Families (2009) *Independent Review of the Primary Curriculum Final Report.* The results of the QCDA consultation can be found online at: http://publications.teachernet.gov.uk/eOrderingDownload/QCDA-09-4355.pdf (accessed 24 November 2009).

Min Ed. Ministry of Education (1952) 'Teaching History', Pamphlet No 23.

——(1963) 'Half of Our Future': A Report of the Central Advisory Council for Education (England) [The Newsom Report].

LHTA. Minutes of the London History Teachers Association (1953–76) Institute of Education Archives DC/LHT/A.1/3 and LHT/B.4.

Ofsted. Office for Standards in Education (2007) 'History in the Balance: History in English Schools 2003–07'.

Opening Minds: A Competency-based Curriculum for the Twenty-First Century (National Teacher Research Panel Report, 2006). Available online at: http://www.standards.dfes.gov.uk/ntrp/lib/pdf/boyle.pdf (accessed 24 November 2009).

QCA. Qualifications and Curriculum Authority (2009) *The Story of the General Certificate of Secondary Education (GCSE)*, Available online at: http://www.qca.org.uk/qca_6210.aspx (accessed 23 November 2009).

History in Education Project (HiEP) recorded interviews

Chris Culpin (22 September 2009)
John Hamer (1 June 2009)
Penelope Harnett (9 September 2009)
Scott Harrison (6 May 2009)
Roger Hennessey (11 November 2009)
Gareth Elwyn Jones (23 September 2009)
Ann Low-Beer (12 August 2009)
Tim Lomas (30 March 2009)
Michael Maddison (21 September 2009)
Peter Marshall (11 August 2009)

Chapter 2

Primary history

Current themes

Robert Guyver

Introduction

This chapter is about current themes in primary history. Primary history is contested and controversial. The period 1988–2010 has seen significant upheavals in the way in which history is contextualized and used in schools. The elusive concept of 'good primary practice' has not always been seen to have a secure and comfortable place sitting alongside centralized curriculum developments that have had strong elements of prescription. This is being written in mid 2010 as the long national curriculum period of the previous 20 years enters another phase after the general election of 6 May with another set of curriculum changes promised. A coalition of Conservatives and Liberal Democrats formed a new government and decided not to adopt the framework outlined in the Rose Review, promising to compensate schools who had already spent funds on extra related resources. A new commitment to a focus on 'the basics' and a stressing of subject disciplines seems to suggest that the Rose Review's emphasis on 'areas of learning' will not form a part of a new primary curriculum. The 2000 framework will stay in place until 2011–12 by which time a revision will have been written.

Key content and perspectives

This chapter examines a number of key issues across primary history education as it stands in 2010. Teachers need to be prepared to think outside the box as far as content is concerned because new units covering hitherto untaught periods or themes in history will inevitably emerge for the youngest to the oldest primary child. What is exciting about the future is the increasing availability of suitable and exciting source material online and access to a wide range of advice about creative and innovative approaches. One necessity is to remain in touch, through dialogue, with the wider academic world of history, despite a sense that historians may not fully appreciate the range of curriculum areas that primary teachers need to accommodate in their professional repertoire. There is a key role here for history teacher educators in higher education who with their knowledge of pedagogy can serve as a bridge between teachers and academics. The Historical Association, also with its growing website and its publication *Primary History*, is right at the centre of these debates.

Primary history developing its own identity within the wider curriculum

The history of the Rose Review (2009) is significant. In theory anyway it was accepted in full by Schools Minister Vernon Coaker and Education Secretary Ed Balls in November 2009, so that it could be moved to the White Paper stage before legislation. The results of the QCDA (Qualifications and Curriculum Development Agency) consultation can be found online (http://publications.teachernet.gov.uk/eOrdering Download/QCDA-09–4355.pdf). However, the legislation never happened; as has been seen, there has been a change of government and there are already indications of effects of this on the curriculum.

Despite concerns about content prescription, expressed at every stage when consultation has been invited (1989 after the interim report of the DES History Working Group (HWG); 1990 twice, both after HWG's final report and after the National Curriculum Council period of further consultation; 1993–4 at the time of the Dearing Review; in 1998–9 before the current version and in 2008–9 as part of the Rose Review), history in the primary classroom has remained vibrant and innovative, based on active learning and participation. Evidence for this can be seen in Ofsted (Office for Standards in Education) annual subject reviews and in individual school inspection reports, as well as in conference presentations and published work, for example in *Primary History.*

Defining quality in primary history needs to be seen almost like the two strands in the structure of DNA, and corresponds with two key questions, 'What is good history teaching and learning?' and, 'What is good primary practice?' There is, however, another question which transects these two, and that is, 'What makes a good primary history curriculum?' The temporary recontextualization of this within the Rose Review report in the wider synthesis of an *area of learning* that embraces historical, geographical and social understanding corresponded with the situation in many other parts of the world where history appears as part of social studies, for example in the individual state curricula in Canada and the USA, in a national curriculum programme in South Africa and – but with far less 'prescription' or advice in the content structure than in South Africa – New Zealand. These curricula can all be accessed on the internet and make for some interesting comparisons. Ironically, Australia, in its developing national curriculum, has opted for a single-subject approach with history alongside literacy and numeracy as part of the core. This underpins a central determination to get to grips with the interpretation of inclusion issues at the heart of controversies about Australian history.

Prescription and teacher autonomy

As has been noted the primary history curriculum is in a state of flux. The Rose Review final report included a piece of advice from the Historical Association:

> The Historical Association has always maintained that the National Curriculum as it stands is overprescribed, and this is detrimental to teaching and learning. We fully support a modified framework that supports the development of a less

prescriptive and a more flexible National Curriculum that draws upon subjects like history as tools for learning, as indicated in the interim report.

(Rose Review executive summary and recommendations 2009: 15)

Debates about prescription touch on wider issues of teacher professionalism and autonomy that have affected not only history but also the teaching and learning of literacy and numeracy, in particular. Recently, Hoyle and Wallace (2007) examined how teachers use irony and professional 'infidelity' to cope with overprescription in the curriculum. Having been a member of the original History Working Group and having read the responses to the interim report (August 1989) I am acutely aware of this problem. It is not a simple one, and notions of prescription and content per se can be intertwined, often confusingly, in related debates. These discussions can also be associated with teaching styles, especially bipolar identifications of transmission and discovery approaches. Content is essential in any sequence of primary history teaching and learning, especially as *context*. What is debated is the amount and nature of content and who decides on what it should be. There are undoubtedly also political considerations that transcend 'merely' pedagogical ones. Choice within the curriculum is, as can be seen above, a 'live' issue. The proposals in the Rose Review embedded a certain logic which is a response to some of the counter-logic in the original National Curriculum. The review allowed for previously unlisted periods or topics to be included (e.g. the Normans, the Middle Ages, the seventeenth and eighteenth centuries, the early nineteenth and early twentieth centuries, another 'ancient' society like China, some European history).

There was (indeed, 'is') choice in the 1999/2000 curriculum. Key Stage 1 history is full of choice around four framework content areas, based on the 'expanding horizons' curriculum (see the work of Kieran Egan, e.g. 1989). This means starting with the child and the locality and moving outwards and backwards in time and place. Of course there are flaws in this theory because even very young children will appreciate stories from the distant past, especially colourful ones with exaggerated characters as in myths and legends.

Key Stage 2 history has three sets of choice. The unit on *Romans, Anglo-Saxons and Vikings* embeds an assumption that an overview of all three 'settlements' will occur followed by a choice of one of these. Teachers can choose between *Victorian Britain* and *Britain since 1930*. Within the latter there is a choice between two distinct focuses, one of which is the war period. A choice is offered between seven non-European units, the most popular of which are Ancient Egypt and the Aztecs.

However, where choice is restrictive it can be seen to be unnecessarily prescriptive. For example, in the still extant 2000 curriculum there are areas of British (or national) history that are not included: British pre-Roman history, the Normans, the Middle Ages, the Stuart period, the eighteenth century, the early nineteenth century (1800–37) and the early twentieth century (1901–30). The Rose Review did get around this by suggesting under M12 (Middle Primary, Rose Review) (for lower Key Stage 2) that 'the movement and settlement of people in different periods of British history, and the impact these have had' can include, '*for example, the impact of the invasion and settlement of the Romans, Anglo-Saxons, Vikings, Normans or more recent immigration*'. Similarly under L13 (Lower Primary, Rose Review) (for upper primary or upper Key Stage 2), 'the effects of economic, technological and scientific developments on the UK and the wider world over time' might include *'the impact of changes in transport and technology in the last 200 years: the development and impact of roads, canals and railways in the eighteenth and nineteenth centuries; car manufacture and developments in aviation in the twentieth century; the impact of changes in transport on the local area'*. At a stroke some of the prescription of the previous curriculum seemed to disappear.

However, as this will not now be implemented there is likely to be a supplementary unofficial curriculum of worked units from which teachers might build their own curriculum. In the past these have been made available by the QCA/QCDA (Qualifications and Curriculum Authority/Qualifications and Curriculum Development Agency), although now we know that the QCDA will fall victim to government cuts after September 2010. Aspects of the unthinking use of schemes were criticized by Paul Bracey (2001). It was intended, even by the QCA, that teachers would construct their own using templates for planning. There would have been concern about the Rose Review that no *specific* national, regional or global history from any period in the past (even ancient) was highlighted. Nevertheless, one positive suggestion which would have addressed Ofsted concerns about connectedness was the inclusion of L14 (Lower Primary, Rose Review), 'to understand the broad chronology of major events in the UK, and some key events in the wider world, from ancient civilizations to the present day, and to locate within this the periods, events and changes they have studied'. It would be left to others to decide on what these would be, but situating whatever is chosen in wider frames to accommodate the big picture is regarded as good practice, and this is reflected in the writings of Peter Lee, Ros Ashby and Denis Shemilt. However, the issue of 'which narrative?' is a live one and even (as reported by Seumas Milne) raised by Colin Jones (president of the Royal Historical Society) in a *Guardian* article in June 2010.

Deciding on an emphasis will always be regarded as democratic if schools do it but overtly political if governments do it. The political aspects of curriculum choice are often about how the nation and concepts of nationhood are perceived and presented. This is a common issue around the world, but one that is being constantly revised especially in the light of the increasing movement of peoples and accelerated levels of travel. In the post–Cold War and largely post-colonial world there is a realignment of groupings of nation states and more of a sense of collaboration in what had been a competitive and often mutually suspicious atmosphere (Jörn Rüsen writes about this, in Macdonald, (2000)). One result of the change is the repositioning of national histories rather in the same way that a magician can turn a glove inside out to reveal something that was always there but was hitherto hidden.

In the Rose Review proposals for 'Late' primary, L12 suggests 'the characteristic features of and changes within two key periods of history that were significant to the locality and the UK', and adds *'as well as British history, one of the periods studied could be taken from European or world history'*. This promise of a sea change allowed for flexibility and the possibility of studying British history linked with either Europe or another part of the world, or the latter focus taken as free-standing (i.e. not linked with British history at all). This might raise eyebrows in some circles, the criticism being that this does not allow for enough British history (the opposite to having too much!). Many will see this as a welcome change, however. A worked example by Hilary Cooper of a whole-school plan for Key Stage 2 embracing all of Rose's proposals can be seen in *Primary History*, Autumn 2009, pp. 8–9. Interestingly the notion of 'my place' is set in local, national, European and global settings. But the status of these changes and rearrangements is now in doubt.

It is helpful in this debate to return to the nature of history. R.S. Peters, writing 45 years ago (in Archambault, 1965), asserted that curriculum subjects should have some kind of relationship with sets of public standards. Teachers of course have other standards to consider, especially in a world of ever-changing TDA (Training and Development Agency) and Ofsted regulation. The nature of history is an aspect of the discipline or process sometimes referred to as syntactic knowledge or syntactic understanding. But the quality of a teacher's subject knowledge is a matter of concern.

The 'senior subject' in this is academic university-based history, its professionals regulated through peer-reviewed journals and bodies such as the Royal Historical Society. The writings of historians take many forms, but often they are narratives or investigations which embrace a set of rigorously applied methods and principles, and among the most important of these is the verifiability of the sources or the evidence base. Two pedagogical approaches have been brought to bear on academic subject knowledge to help transform it into suitable matter for teaching. One is 'spiralling' and the other is 'transformation'. The work of Bruner (1960) and Shulman (1986) is useful here (Turner-Bisset, 2006).

Primary history as an academic subject in higher education

Through the experience of my own institution and as an external examiner at two other institutions in England, I have seen some fascinating cases where future primary teachers have undertaken dissertations in subjects where academic history and primary history have fused their horizons. In one course a particularly popular theme was the Second World War where opportunities were taken to study local documentary material in archives or oral material through live interviews, for example on the effects of the Blitz or the experiences of evacuees. The ability of primary teachers to identify, select, contextualize and present such sources of evidence would have a relationship not only to their own academic subject knowledge but also to their pedagogical understanding and ability. Where both are of a high standard good practice will emerge.

The growth of PhDs and a body of academic literature in books and articles related to primary history is a significant development for teacher training. PhDs in this area have been completed by John West (1981), Peter Knight (1988), Hilary Cooper (1991), Rosie Turner-Bisset (1996), Penelope Harnett (2001) and Paul Bracey (2008). I would include my own also (Guyver 2003). This also enables primary history to be available to students and tutors on an international scale. The work of the above as well as Grant Bage, Jon Nichol and Jacqui Dean (1997) and others has helped to create and sustain this publicly accessible knowledge base.

The Historical Association, HTEN (History Teacher Education Network) and HEIRNET (History Educators' International Research Network) have provided conferences as networking webs for lecturers as tutors and researchers to exchange ideas. EUROCLIO (European Association of History Educators) has also had annual conferences, and its board naturally includes some UK-based tutors. It is a Netherlands-founded organization (http://www.euroclio.eu/site/index.php) which has enabled an international dialogue to take place from which history teachers in emerging democracies in central and eastern Europe as well as Asia (e.g. Turkey) have benefited.

Citizenship issues: inclusion and identity in a diverse society

Citizenship and PSHE (personal, social and health education) in primary schools is approached in a practical way, with the intention not only of teaching new ideas but also putting them into practice in the way a school is run (see the *Crick Report*, DfEE, 1998). Teaching history with the objective of enhancing a sense of citizenship could suffer from the syndrome of over-determinism, in that the content of history could be chosen not for its own sake but to illustrate developments or landmarks in citizenship. This might also have features of 'exceptionalism', a term which applies to the sort of history which embeds an assumption that the developments being taught lead to a current citizenship model that represents the best possible situation in the modern world.

This is unlikely to happen in a primary setting. In England's curriculum PSHE and citizenship are firmly on the map with such initiatives as *Excellence and Enjoyment* (2003) and *Every Child Matters* (2003), and PSHE and citizenship being a non-statutory part of the primary curriculum (but nevertheless attracting the attention of Ofsted) since 2000.

Certainly there have been debates about Britishness. Gordon Brown, when he was Chancellor of the Exchequer in 2004 and 2006 gave two keynote addresses about this concept (they are available online: British Council, July 2004, at http://www.guardian.co.uk/politics/2004/jul/08/uk.labour1 and Fabian Society, January 2006, at http://www.fabians.org.uk/events/speeches/the-future-of-britishness). This issue is likely to be debated again in the light of the coalition government curriculum proposals after June 2010.

Brown attempted to synthesize a set of core values that epitomize the essence of Britishness, setting their development into a historical context. Some aspects of his selection and interpretation have been challenged, not least by Martin Daunton, in 2006 the president of the Royal Historical Society. An interview with him in 2008 has some interesting comments on schools and citizenship and he refers to Gordon Brown (see http://www.history.ac.uk/makinghistory/resources/interviews/Daunton_Martin.html).

A particular criticism about the way citizenship is used in schools focuses on the notion of 'presentism', a principle which promotes the philosophy of looking at the past through the lens of the present, e.g. seeing selected parts of history as illus-trating what Daunton calls 'the long march to liberty' (Daunton 2008). Similarly Jonathan Clark deplores presentism for its 'serious flaws of substance', one of which is an ignorance about the past and a neglect of the collective memory. Trenchantly he pulls apart the agenda of policies which masquerade as 'moderate, pragmatic and non-doctrinaire' identifying one of the features of this as the 'escape from history' (Clark 2003: 17).

One area of research that is lacking in the UK is an audit of the values of different communities. Sometimes these values are expressed in different languages. Such an audit has been completed as a literature review (*Values in the New Zealand Curriculum*) in NZ as part of a project undertaken for the government there by the University of Waikato (Keown *et al.*, 2005, available online). This kind of project is part of a wider set of objectives to see other people's histories and identities from the inside, not just in relation to a dominant national identity. The work of Leonie Sandercock is worth examining here in the context of the globalization of the movement of peoples and how this is reflected in the mix seen in cosmopolitan cities, or what she refers to as the cosmopolis (2003).

Creativity and innovation

Creative thinking is among the key skills listed in the 1999 curriculum. Among activities associated with this one idea promoted by the QCA is to use features of cultural authenticity in creative teaching. Although there is a difference between creativity and creative thinking, the ability to relate the past to the present after discussion can be related to almost any historical context. To support work on this the QCA published *Exploding Myths* in the context of the Gunpowder Plot as part of a set of *Creativity in Action* units, and the margin comments on the Year 2 children's activities and conversations revealed some significant features. However this is no longer available through the QCA/QCDA website after Government changes (post-May General Election).

Creativity is seen by the QCA as being imaginative; purposeful, directed at achieving an objective; original and valuable, in relation to its objective. To this end pupils will be seen to be questioning and challenging; making connections and seeing relationships; envisaging what might be; exploring ideas, keeping options open and reflecting critically on ideas, actions and outcomes. This ties in with the definition of creativity in *All Our Futures: Creativity, Culture and Education*, the National Advisory Committee's report (NACCCE 1999).

Rosie Turner-Bisset (2005) has written a practical and well-referenced commentary on creative teaching which discusses this topic in the context of several scenarios including the use of artefacts, written sources (e.g. she uses a letter written by Henry VIII), visual images, the environment, storytelling without a book, drama and role-play, music and dance and discourse. The cameos she includes are case studies of good practice. She develops effectively NACCCE's (National Advisory Committee on Creative and Cultural Education) notion of 'making connections and relationships between ideas and objects that have not previously been related' (NACCCE, 1999: 29 in Turner-Bisset 2005: 7).

The theories of R.G. Collingwood (1946) and Marjorie Reeves (1980) are still relevant (see also Marnie Hughes-Warrington 2003). Collingwood saw the job of a historian as imaginative reconstruction or re-enactment of the past. This was used in the 1970s and 1980s to promote *empathy* as a key part of teaching in humanities and social studies. The use of empathy began to have some ethical problems associated with it, some of which might be hinted at in the piece on Guy Fawkes (above, in the QCA publication). To what extent should children be allowed to have a free rein when empathizing with historical characters (like Guy Fawkes) whose activities are controversial? Nevertheless, Collingwood's concept of 'getting inside' an event (discussed by Hughes-Warrington 2003: 56–61) has features of *dualism*: while thinking (subjectively) the thoughts of the historical characters the student does not relinquish thinking objectively like a historian. There is evidence of this even in the words of the Year 2 children working (as reported by the QCA) on the Gunpowder Plot.

E.H. Carr in his classic *What is History?* (1961) and Richard Evans *In Defence of History* (1997) have chapters on history and morality which can be set against the work of Collingwood and even cross-referred to the evidence above. This corresponds with Peter Seixas's sixth benchmark for historical thinking, Understand Ethical Dimensions of History (see http://www.histori.ca/benchmarks/; see also Seixas 2006). Along the same lines in *Why History?*, Marjorie Reeves (1980), a past winner of the Historical Association's Norton Medlicott Medal, wrote about 'standing in another person's shoes' and using history to take children for journeys on a 'magic carpet'.

Another useful teaching and learning approach is clustered around Csíkszentmihályi's notion of the *zone of flow*, that children can be encouraged with the help of an open-minded teacher who can 'play' with ideas, to keep conversations open and flowing.

Social aspects of primary history: dialogue (including dialogic teaching and learning) and collaboration

Role play is clearly an excellent way to develop creativity and creative thinking in children and corresponds with the ideas of Collingwood and Reeves. It is important to empower children, and this can be done in stages. Role-play is a natural context for socially constructing knowledge and understanding, and although the teacher can don 'the mantle of the expert', especially in providing a meaningful context for the work, children need to have the opportunity to interpret and recontextualize the sources in their own way. This can, according to Dorothy Heathcote, best be done through discussion and social collaboration (for two sites, one on Heathcote and another by her, see http://www.mantleoftheexpert.com/community/about-us/dorothy-heathcote/ and http://www.mantleoftheexpert.com/wp-content/uploads/2008/11/dh-contexts-for-active-learning.pdf). In the context of history, a classic is the work on drama by John Fines and Ray Verrier (1974).

These approaches promote the active and experiential learning that is at the heart of the primary curriculum, and helps to give children ownership of the content through empowerment. The theories of Vygotsky and Bakhtin are useful here. Bakhtin believed in polyphony – truth being embedded in a multiplicity of voices – and in unfinalizability – that the last word can never be spoken, indeed that all topics are always open for comment and discussion. Robin Alexander has written extensively about dialogic teaching and learning, and in the final report of the Cambridge Primary Review (Alexander, 2010, but available in 2009) five key features are summarized showing the potential of talk in dialogic teaching. It is seen as collective, reciprocal, supportive, cumulative and purposeful. This sees teachers and children learning together, sharing ideas, allowing freedom in articulation, building on their own and others' ideas and chaining them 'into coherent lines of thinking and enquiry'. As with aspects of creative thinking this is best achieved with specific educational goals in mind (Alexander, 2010: 306). An example of this would be for the teacher to dress up as a character in the Great Fire of London of 1666 and get children to respond, after discussion, to a situation by answering the question, 'Who was to blame?'

Integration with other curriculum areas

History is being increasingly taught in combination with other subjects, and was, if only temporarily, grouped with geography and citizenship in the now shelved Rose Review. The debate about single subjects and curriculum integration has a long history, with the Hadow (1929–31) and Plowden (1967) reports having much to say about this. 'Topics' fell out of favour in the wake of the 1988–92 National Curriculum, having been seen by central government and HMI (Her Majesty's Inspector) as lacking in rigour and failing to offer opportunities to develop the knowledge, understanding and skills that were seen to be quite distinct for different subjects. Now, with key skills and other aspects of learning across the curriculum, and with a number of reports that see innovation through connection, it seemed that this agenda had changed, but this remains to be seen.

> As indicated in the interim report, the essential knowledge and skills all children should be taught, particularly in the middle and later phases of primary education, can be organised through clearly visible subject disciplines, such as history, geography and physical education. Subjects will be complemented by worthwhile and challenging cross-curricular studies that provide ample opportunities for children to use and apply their subject knowledge and skills to deepen understanding.
>
> (Rose Review final report executive summary
> and recommendations, 2009: 11)

The rich possibilities of cross-curricular work are exemplified in the Autumn 2009 edition of *Primary History* with examples of music and drama (with art/design and Design & Technology being used to support work on a banquet). A classic early work written even before the Plowden Report which reflects the excitement of discovery and innovation in primary teaching and learning is *An Experiment in Education* by Sybil Marshall (1963).

The use of ICT in the teaching and learning of history

No evaluation of the current state of play of primary history would be complete without an examination of the opportunities (as well as the possible negative potential) of the use of ICT (information and communications technology) and the internet. Significantly the internet can offer excellent resources – a good example of this can be found at The National Archives (TNA) – especially the Learning Curve sites, as well as at the British Library and the Imperial War Museum. The Historical Association's E-CPD (electronic continuous professional development) sites are flexible sources for teachers' subject knowledge.

Children's own ICT work can benefit from the latest technology, especially within a school's own networks, with wikis and discussion boards. Writing frames can be set up by the teacher but systems need to allow for initiative dialogue and collaboration.

Teachers increasingly use the IWB (interactive whiteboard) with all its flexibility. Schools can consider creating their own Learning Spaces with e-sources.

Chapter summary

Every aspect of primary history can be subjected to critical analysis. It seemed that opportunities had arisen for primary teachers to choose more of their own curriculum and relate it to an increasingly diverse population in meaningful ways, using exciting, creative and innovative approaches. But new proposals for the primary curriculum are in the very early stages after political changes in 2010. Nevertheless, despite the dangers of presentism with so many initiatives embedded into the curriculum, the past has a secure place in it, and teachers have increasing opportunities to enhance their own and children's subject knowledge. There are many ways in which good primary practice can thrive either in a more integrated curricular environment or, as might now happen, within a subject-based structure.

Key questions

1. Which is more helpful to teachers, an open curriculum or a specified framework?
2. Why might non-statutory units be counterproductive to teacher autonomy?
3. Should local, national, regional and global history all be equally weighted in curriculum design?
4. What would be the most practical way of reframing primary history and how could good primary practice be achieved in the teaching and learning of history within a new structure?

Further reading

Harnett, P. (2006) 'Exploring the potential for history and citizenship education with primary children at the British Empire and Commonwealth Museum in Bristol', *International Journal of Historical Learning Teaching and Research*, January, vol. 6. Available online at: http://centres.exeter.ac.uk/historyresource/journal11/journal-contents.htm (accessed 29 October 2010).

Phillips, R. (1998) *History Teaching, Nationhood and the State – a Study in Educational Politics*. London: Cassell. (This award-winning book gives an analytical background to debates about history teaching and the National Curriculum in the 1990s).

Primary History, Issue 53, Autumn 2009.

Shemilt, D. (2000) 'The caliph's coin – the currency of narrative frameworks in history teaching', in P. Stearns, P. Seixas and S. Wineburg (eds), *Knowing Teaching & Learning History*. New York and London: New York University Press, pp. 83–101.

References

Alexander, R. (ed.) (2010) *Children, Their World, Their Education: Final Report and Recommendations of the Cambridge Primary Review*. London: Routledge.

Bage, G. (1999) *Narrative Matters – Teaching History through Story*. London: Routledge.

——(2000) *Thinking History, 4-14: Teaching, Learning, Curricula and Communities (Primary Directions)*. London: Routledge.

Bracey, P. (2001) 'The implications of National Curriculum 2000 for initial teacher education: a primary perspective', in P. Goalen and C. O'Neill (eds), *Curriculum Change and History Teacher Education*. Lancaster: History Teacher Education Network, pp. 23–30.

——(2008) 'Perceptions of an Irish dimension and its significance for the English history Curriculum', unpublished PhD thesis, Birmingham: University of Birmingham.

Bruner, J.S. (1960) *The Process of Education*. Cambridge, MA: Harvard University Press.

Carr, E.H. (1961) *What is History?* Harmondsworth: Penguin. (More recent editions also.)

Clark, J.C.D. (2003) *Our Shadowed Present*. London: Atlantic Books.

Collingwood, R.G. (1946 [1989]) *The Idea of History*. Oxford: Oxford University Press.

Cooper, H. (1991) 'Young children's thinking in history', unpublished PhD thesis, University of London Institute of Education.

——(2007) *History 3–11: A Guide for Teachers*. London: David Fulton.

——(2009) 'In my view: planning for historical, geographical and social understanding – a conceptual framework: responding to the Rose Report through the lens of the Cambridge Review', *Primary History*, 53, 8–9.

Daunton, M. (2008) http://www.history.ac.uk/makinghistory/resources/interviews/Daunton_Martin.html (accessed 29 October 2010).

Department of Education and Science and the Welsh Office. DES and the Welsh Office (1989) *National Curriculum History Working Group – Interim Report*. London: DES and the Welsh Office.

DfEE (Department of Education and Employment) (1998) *The Final Report of the Citizenship Working Group (The Crick Report)*. London: DfEE.

Egan, K. (1989) Layers of historical understanding. *Theory and Research in Social Education*, 17(4), 280–94.

Evans, R.J. (1997) *In Defence of History*. Cambridge: Granta.

Fines, J. and Verrier, R. (1974) *The Drama of History*. London: New University Education.

Guyver, R. (2003) 'The development of knowledge bases for the effective teaching of primary history: case studies of postgraduates' reflections on initial teacher training', unpublished PhD thesis, Exeter: University of Exeter.

Harnett, P. (2001) 'The emergence of history as a subject within the primary curriculum during the twentieth century and its implementation in schools in the late 1990s', unpublished PhD thesis, Bristol: University of the West of England.

Hoyle, E. and Wallace, M. (2007) 'Educational reform: an ironic perspective', *Educational Management Administration and Leadership*, 35(9): 9–25.

Hughes-Warrington, M. (2003) *'How good an historian shall I be?' R.G. Collingwood, the Historical Imagination and Education*. British Idealist Studies Series 2 (Collingwood), Vol. 2. Exeter: Imprint Academic.

Keown, P., Parker, L. and Tiakiwai, S. (2005) *Values in the New Zealand Curriculum: A Literature Review on Values in the Curriculum*. Wellington and Hamilton, New Zealand: Ministry of Education and University of Waikato. Available online at: http://www.minedu.govt.nz/NZEducation/EducationPolicies/Schools/CurriculumAndNCEA/NationalCurriculum/ValuesInTheNZC.aspx (accessed 5 October 2010).

Knight, P. (1988) 'Children's understanding of people in the past', unpublished PhD thesis, Lancaster: University of Lancaster.

Marshall, S. (1963) *An Experiment in Education*. Cambridge: Cambridge University Press.

Milne, S. (2010) 'This attempt to rehabilitate empire is a recipe for conflict', *The Guardian*, Thursday 10 June.

NACCCE (National Advisory Committee on Creative and Cultural Education) (1999) *All Our Futures: Creativity, Culture and Education*. London: DfEE. Available online at: http://www.cypni.org.uk/downloads/alloutfutures.pdf (accessed 5 October 2010).

Nichol, J. and Dean, J. (1997) *History 7–11*. London: Routledge.

Peters, R.S. (1965) 'Education as initiation', in R.D. Archambault (ed.), *Philosophical Analysis and Education*. London: Routledge.

Reeves, M. (1980) *Why History?* London: Longman Group.

Rose, J. (2009) *Independent Review of the Primary Curriculum: Final Report*. (The Rose Review) Annesley, Nottingham: DCSF Publications. Available online at: http://web archive.nationalarchives.gov.uk/20100210151716/dcsf.gov.uk/primarycurriculum review/ (accessed 3 November 2010).

Rüsen, J. (2000) '"Cultural currency". The nature of historical consciousness in Europe', in S. Macdonald (ed.), *Approaches to European Historical Consciousness – Reflections and Provocations*, Eustory Series: Shaping European History, Vol. 1. Hamburg: Körber-Stiftung, pp. 75–85.

Sandercock, L. (2003) *Cosmopolis II – Mongrel Cities of the 21st Century*. London: Continuum.

Seixas, P. (2006) *Theorizing Historical Consciousness*. Toronto: University of Toronto.

Shulman, L. (1986) 'Those who understand: knowledge growth in teaching', *Educational Researcher*, 15(2): 4–14.

Turner-Bisset, R. (1996) 'Subject-matter knowledge and teaching competence', unpublished PhD thesis, Exeter: University of Exeter.

——(2005) *Creative Teaching: History in the Primary Classroom*. London: David Fulton.

——(2006) *Expert Teaching*. London: David Fulton.

West, J. (1981) 'Children's awareness of the past', unpublished PhD thesis, Staffordshire: University of Keele.

Chapter 3

Secondary history
Current themes

Terry Haydn

> What does history contribute to social literacy? What ways of thinking, writing and questioning would be lost if we eliminated history from the curriculum?
> —G. Leinhardt

Introduction

This chapter presents a brief summary of some of the issues and problems relating to the teaching of history in English schools. It draws on recent research and inspection findings, the work of eminent scholars in the field of history education and recent statements of politicians, and policymakers about the form, purpose and status of history as a school subject. At the end of the chapter, some further reading is suggested. I should stress that the views expressed in the chapter are my own and are not an attempt to summarize or aggregate the views expressed in other chapters in this volume.

Strengths and weaknesses?

The current state of history teaching in secondary schools in England is an uneasy mixture of positive elements and worrying developments and challenges.

In a presentation to the 2009 Schools History Project Conference, Ofsted's (Office for Standards in Education) specialist advisor for history, Michael Maddison, summarized the findings of recent Ofsted inspections, noting good teaching, good teacher subject knowledge, effective leadership and management of departments and good standards of pupil achievement as some of the strengths of history teaching which had emerged from inspection (Maddison, 2009). History teaching continues to attract large numbers of high-quality graduates and competition for places on courses of initial teacher education courses in history remains fierce. A recent study of pupil perceptions of history revealed that approximately half of them are actively interested in history outside the classroom, and there is some evidence to suggest that a smaller proportion of students are disaffected and disengaged from the study of history than was the case in previous decades (QCA, 2005; Harris and Haydn, 2006).

However, concerns and reservations have also emerged from recent inspection and research findings. Ofsted point to limitations in the effectiveness of assessment and feedback, inconsistencies in providing challenge for more able students and reductions in the amount of time dedicated to history in secondary schools (Ofsted 2007; Maddison, 2009).

Concern has also been expressed about the appropriateness of the GCSE (General Certificate of Secondary Education) examination for history (Culpin, 2002) and the effect of the 'levels' system of assessment (Counsell, 2003; Burnham and Brown, 2004; Haydn, 2004). The question of what it means 'to get better at history', and how to measure and record progression, remains a difficult issue and a source of tension not just between politicians and practitioners but also between departments and senior management teams in many schools (Counsell, 2010). Counsell (2003) also makes the point that although there is much good practice in teaching history to less able pupils, such practice is not universal. The use of ICT (information and communications technology) to improve teaching and learning in history is another area of history teaching where there are significant differences between departments. There are some departments which have transformed pupil attitudes to the subject through the adroit and creative use of ICT, and where pupils commit considerable amounts of time to learning history outside the classroom by using a range of Web 2.0 applications; there are others which either do not significantly exploit the potential of new technology or who use it in dull and unimaginative ways (Haydn, 2010).

There is also evidence to suggest that pupils emerge from schools lacking a 'usable' and coherent mental framework of the past, and are left with 'bits and pieces of knowledge that add up to very little and fail to validly inform or even to connect with their perceptions of present realities' (Shemilt, 2009: 142 – see also Howson, 2007, Foster *et al.*, 2008, and Lee and Howson, 2009, for further development of this point). Several recent studies indicate that there are many pupils who do not have a clear grasp of *why* they are obliged to study history at school, a finding which has obvious implications for pupil motivation and engagement with the subject (Adey and Biddulph, 2001; Fink, 2004; Harris and Haydn, 2010).

The balance of attention given to stories and sources and the relationship between these two facets of history also remains a contentious (and frequently misrepresented) issue in history education (Counsell, 2000; Lee and Ashby, 2000). These problems are exacerbated by the meagre time allocated to history under current timetabling arrangements in most English state schools (Historical Association, 2009): history teachers have to make hard choices about what to include in their lessons in the limited time available.

History's place on the school curriculum

Of even greater concern is history's place on the school curriculum. When the National Curriculum was introduced in 1991 it was envisaged that history would be compulsory for all pupils in state schools up to the age of 16 (Phillips, 1998), as is the case in most other European countries. Subsequent changes to the National Curriculum, the move towards a 'free-market' curriculum post Key Stage 3 – and the importance attached to schools' A–C pass rates at GCSE have combined to marginalize history as a school subject (Culpin, 2007; Historical Association, 2009; Harris and Haydn, 2010), with the Historical Association going as far as to argue that 'in a number of schools, history is disappearing as a discrete subject within the curriculum' (Historical Association, 2009: 1).

In a report redolent of Mary Price's landmark article 'History in danger' (Price, 1968), Ofsted's highlighting of the fact that only 30 per cent of pupils continue to study beyond Key Stage 3, and the title given to the report (Ofsted, 2007), attracted considerable media and political attention. A recent survey of 644 schools by the Historical Association revealed that in many schools, pupils are not obliged to study any humanities subject beyond Key Stage 3, so in the new 'free-market' Key Stage 4 curriculum (as compared with the Key Stage 4 curriculum instigated in the original National Curriculum of 1991) history has to fight for its place in the option pools against what have been termed the 'predator' subjects of business studies, psychology, media studies and citizenship. In some cases history is one of more than 20 options available to pupils (Harris and Haydn, 2010). As with many other markets, the playing field is not necessarily a level one. There is evidence to suggest that some schools are moving to a view that history, as a literary and academic subject, is not an appropriate subject for less able pupils, and so less scholarly pupils are being directed or encouraged towards a vocational curriculum post–Key Stage 3, or towards what one head teacher termed 'the latest GCSE fiddle' (quoted in Harris and Haydn, 2010 – see also Grimston and Warren, 2010). There are significant pressures on schools to optimize their GCSE A–C pass rates and it has been argued that some pupils have been guided or directed away from history with a view to improving the GCSE examination profile of the school (see, for instance, Culpin, 2007). This may go some way to explaining the paradox that whereas around 70 per cent of pupils reported that they enjoyed studying history at Key Stage 3, only 30 per cent are continuing to study it at Key Stage 4 (Harris and Haydn, 2006).

Nor is this the only challenge to history's position on the school curriculum. In a number of schools, history as a school subject is being replaced by competence-based curricula such as the RSA's 'Opening Minds'.[1] Out of 42 history teachers questioned about the impact of integrated or competence-based curricula, only four reported that the effects has been positive in terms of pupil progress in history (Historical Association, 2009: 2). Ofsted reports on the impact of such courses have also expressed reservations about their impact on pupils' historical knowledge and understanding (Ofsted, 2009).

To add to these concerns, the amount of time allocated to history in the school timetable has also been reduced in recent years, with many schools providing less than an hour a week for history education. This is perhaps one of the most widely held grievances of history teachers: the difficulty of teaching all the 'range and content' specified by the National Curriculum for history, while also paying due attention to all the key concepts and processes, the development of pupils' key skills and the ability to study elements of the past in depth, and in overview, in a way that leads to the development of meaningful gains in pupils' knowledge and understanding of history as both a body of knowledge and a form of knowledge. The option for schools to condense Key Stage 3 into two years further exacerbates this problem. Where a school has adopted a competence-based curriculum in Year 7, and chosen to cover Key Stage 3 in two years rather than three, this means that the Key Stage 3 programme of study might be reduced to as little as 38 hours of teaching (Historical Association, 2009).

Lomas (quoted in Keating and Sheldon, 2010) has argued that history has proved to be resilient as a school subject and that it has been 'in danger' before, but given these recent developments at Key Stage 3 and the fact that the proportion of young people choosing to take history to examination level has declined from 82 per cent in 1937 to around 30 per cent in 2009 (Keating and Sheldon, 2010), there would appear to be reasonable grounds for concern about the health and vitality of history as a school subject.

The political dimension

Politicians of all political parties have spoken very positively about the importance of history as a school subject in recent years (Osler, 2009), but this does not appear to have safeguarded history's position on the school curriculum. To at least some extent the diminution in the role of the humanities has been an unintended outcome of other developments (such as the elevation of the 5 A–C GCSE pass rate to a key indicator of school performance). The Conservative Party, which is the largest party in the new coalition government in the UK, has argued for the strengthening of history's place on the school curriculum, and expressed strong support for the teaching of traditional school subjects rather than competence-based approaches (Collins, 2005; Gove, 2010). The current schools' minister Nick Gibb (2010a) has stated that 'the thorough teaching of history is crucial for a broad and balanced curriculum'. There is, however, a tension between these statements and the belief that schools should be free to organize their own curriculum, free from government interference. Moreover, the model of school history which is extolled is very much the restoration of what Sylvester (1994) termed 'The Great Tradition' of history education. In the words of current secretary of state for education Michael Gove: 'I'm an unashamed traditionalist when it comes to the curriculum; most parents would rather their children had a traditional education, with children sitting in rows, learning the kings and queens of England.' There is also the suggestion that history should be about the transmission of traditional values (such as pride in the British Empire) rather than an enquiry-based subject (Gove, 2010). These developments resurrect some of the same dilemmas for history teachers and teacher educators as the introduction of the National Curriculum in 1991: a government that is keen to restore the status of history as a school subject but in a way which may differ radically from the views of many history education professionals (both in terms of history teachers in schools and those responsible for the training of history teachers).

In the light of these developments and uncertainties it could be said that these are 'interesting times' for school history. It is difficult to be certain how these uncertainties will be resolved, but there are things that history teachers and teacher educators might do in order to protect the health and utility of history as a school subject (see concluding section).

What is school history for?

There is a wide range of views about the purposes and potential benefits of school history (a collection of quotations about the purposes of school history can be accessed at http://www.uea.ac.uk/~m242/historypgce/purposes/purposesquotes intro.htm).

The History Working Group which formulated the original National Curriculum for history drew up a list of nine purposes of school history, which were an uneasy compromise or *modus vivendi*, which included some 'traditional' justifications – giving pupils a sense of identity and an understanding of their cultural roots and shared inheritances – and some elements which had come to prominence in more recent years – introducing pupils to the distinctive methodology of historians, and 'preparing pupils for adult life by imparting a critically sharpened intelligence with which to make sense of current affairs' (DES, 1990: 1–2).

In addition to this rationale for history, the overall aims and values of the National Curriculum (an often overlooked facet of the National Curriculum) stipulated that all subjects should develop 'enjoyment of and commitment to learning', and 'build on pupils' strengths, interests and experiences and develop their confidence in their capacity to learn and work independently and collaboratively.' The general aims of the National Curriculum also put significant emphasis on the development of critical intelligence, intellectual autonomy and active citizenship – school leavers were to be equipped to 'think creatively and critically, to solve problems and to make a difference for the better . . . to make informed judgements and independent decisions' (DFEE/QCA, 1999: 11).

History was also charged with responsibility for making a major contribution to citizenship education in the UK (MacGregor, 1995; DFEE/QCA, 1999), in terms of developing pupils' political literacy, enquiry and communication skills and, 'in particular, the ability to critically evaluate evidence and analyse interpretations . . . to reflect on issues and take part in discussions' (DFEE/QCA, 1999: 183).

Ofsted inspection reports also supported the general professional consensus which had emerged, that school history should support the development of pupils' critical faculties ('History needs to provide young people with the ability to make up their own minds' – Ofsted, 2007: 30), while also providing them with a broad and coherent overview of the past (Ofsted, 2005).

The list of things that school history is supposed to do has therefore expanded over the past three decades, as curriculum time for the subject has been eroded (Historical Association, 2009).

Although media reporting of 'knowledge versus skills' issues is often simplistic and misleading, this remains a difficult issue for many history teachers. In the words of former history HMI (Her Majesty's Inspector) John Hamer:

> Much is made of teachers focusing on the development of historical skills at the expense of what should be their proper concern; the imparting of historical content. Too often discussion has been too strident and ill-informed. But there are issues about getting the balance right; about ensuring that pupils have a secure grasp of events, without being over-loaded; that they are able to use the knowledge they have; and that they do not spend time on mechanical tasks rehearsing formulaic responses to snippets from sources.
>
> (Hamer, 1990: 24)

One of the biggest challenges facing history teachers in England is how to deliver all the benefits which the study of the past might bestow on young people, in the very limited curriculum time available.

The dangers of a return to 'traditional' school history

There have been some calls for a return to 'traditional' school history as an answer to perceived problems with current models of history teaching (Collins, 2005; Gove, 2010). As in many other countries, there are politicians (from all parties) who believe that school history should concern itself primarily with presenting a positive and celebratory transmission of the narrative of the national past (Haydn, 1996; Osler, 2009). It is argued that this will generate social cohesion and a shared sense of loyalty to the state among all elements of the population. There are several problems with this, not least that there is little evidence to suggest that it works in contemporary societies where there is easy access to alternative narratives (see, for instance, Grever *et al.*, 2008). It can involve selectively manipulating the record of the national past to excise 'dark pages' and history can become closer to a fairy story or moral fable than 'proper, rigorous history'. It also is at odds with the disciplinary rules of history, a discipline that is supposed to be based on the consideration of evidence before claims and judgements are made (see Shemilt, 2009, for a more developed explanation of this point).

It is important that school history gives pupils 'a grounding' (Letwin, 1989) in the development of Britain's political and constitution systems, and this is currently enshrined in current curriculum specifications as one of the key 'themes' to be addressed at Key Stage 3:

> The development of political power from the Middle Ages to the twentieth century. This includes power relationships and systems of government in Britain and how they have changed over time. Examples should include the changing relationships between crown and parliament, the nature and motives of protest over time, the historical origins and development of the British constitution, the development of democracy.
>
> (QCA, 2007)

However, there are some dangers in foregrounding political and constitutional history to the exclusion of other facets of the past. The nation state is not the only important issue confronting young people growing up in the twenty-first century. Many of the issues that confront them, that interest them and that are relevant to their lives are not national in nature – the environment, work, poverty, globalization, the role of the state, sex, gender, crime, poverty, the media, culture, migration and so on. History is about the study of the human past, not just the national one. As well as being intellectually very dubious, the temptation to use school history to tell positive and historically simplistic stories about the national past, to the exclusion of other facets of the past, risks rendering history meaningless and irrelevant to young people. Part of the problem again here is the sheer lack of curriculum time to do justice to the full range of ways in which knowledge and understanding of the past can be of use to young people. As well as presenting teachers with hard choices in terms of content selection, there is a need to use synoptic overviews rather than 'chapter and verse' chronologies in order to cover content in a pedagogically effective way (Shemilt, 2009).

History should be taught in a way which gives pupils a knowledge and understanding of the past which helps them to understand how society has developed in the way it has. Historical perspectives are one of the ways of understanding the world we live in. Is there any issue, question or problem into which we cannot gain more insight by looking at what has gone before? (see Aldrich, 1997a). But a historical education can and should also develop some understanding of history as a form of knowledge, with its conventions and procedures for ascertaining the validity of claims made for knowledge. Part of what makes school history useful to pupils is its role in helping them to handle information intelligently, using the procedures and conventions which historians use to make judgements on the reliability of information and the validity of claims made. For pupils growing up in the twenty-first century (and who now sometimes acknowledge provenance in terms of 'Google', or 'Wikipedia'), school history can help young people to make mature use of the internet, and to understand that the internet is not the ultimate repository of truth and wisdom. Husbands (1996: 81) makes the point that '[s]chool history provides a framework for pupils to discuss polemical and contentious issues within academic canons of reliability, explanation and justification.' In the words of former secretary of state for education Keith Joseph:

> The complicated interplay of evidence which is itself not certain and subject to interpretation gives history a particularly valuable part in the development of an adult understanding. It helps pupils to understand that there is a range of questions – be they political, economic, social or cultural – on which there is no single right answer, where opinions have to be tolerated but need to be subjected to the test of evidence and argument. As the pupil progresses in this encounter with history, he should be helped to acquire a sense of the necessity for personal judgements in the light of facts – recognising that the facts often be far from easy to establish and far from conclusive. And it should equally awaken a recognition of the possible legitimacy of other points of view. In other words, it seems to me that the teaching of history has to take place in a spirit which takes seriously the need to pursue truth on the basis of evidence
>
> (Joseph, 1984: insert)

The move towards school history giving consideration to developing pupils' understanding of history as a form of knowledge as well as a body of knowledge has sometimes been misrepresented as an 'either/or' approach to skills versus knowledge in the history classroom (see Byrom, 1996; Counsell, 2000), with loose talk of a 'fact-free' curriculum and 'knowledge panic' headlines in tabloid newspapers (Culpin, 2007). There is a very real and difficult issue here, but it is one of balance and time constraints, not disregard for the importance of pupils' developing a usable and coherent mental framework of the past which will be of use in terms of 'orientation' and identity. As former HMI John Slater (1989: 5) acknowledged, these changes were not 'cost-free' in terms of content coverage, but were necessary and beneficial (on balance) in terms of acknowledging that there was more to getting better at history than simply 'knowing more stuff', in terms of the aggregation of substantive historical knowledge.

Lee and Ashby (2000: 200) provide a useful clarification of this point:

It is important not to misunderstand this shift from substantive to second-order (structural, procedural or disciplinary) interests. Despite popular polarities (usually portrayed as 'skills' versus 'knowledge', there was no retreat from the importance of students acquiring historical knowledge. Instead, 'knowledge' was treated seriously as something that had to be grounded. It is essential that students know something of the kind of claims made by historians and what those different claims rest on. 'Something', because understanding is never all-or-nothing: the goal was not to produce miniature professional historians.

Those who argue for the restoration of 'the good old days' of British history teaching, '[w]hen we learnt by heart the names of the kings and queens of England, the feats of our warriors and our battles and the glorious deeds of our past' (Stokes, 1990), might keep in mind that a substantial majority of pupils regarded this form of school history as useless and boring (Aldrich, 1987). It would be a return to what Ball (1993) terms 'The Curriculum of the Dead'.

When should history end?

Another important consideration in persuading pupils that the study of the past is of relevance to their lives is to clarify the relationship between historical knowledge and the present. Aldrich (1997b) makes the point that history as an academic discipline is not just about the past: 'The task of the historian is twofold. First, to provide as accurately as possible a representation and analysis of the past: second, to provide as accurately as possible an explanation between that past, the present and the future.' It is important to be explicit about the idea of historical perspectives as one of the ways of understanding how and why things are as they are today, how the past relates to the present and what possibilities this might indicate for the future. There is still too often a reluctance to 'open up' historical issues and make connections from the past to the present. Husbands (1996: 34) notes:

> Learning about the concept of kingship (*or whatever*) frequently involves two sets of simultaneous learning: learning about power and its distribution in past societies, and learning about power and its distribution in modern society. The former cannot be given real meaning until pupils have some more contemporary knowledge against which to calibrate their historical understandings.

Van Boxtel (2010) has argued that 'students should be given the opportunity to apply the skills they have acquired in history education in out of school contexts.' If pupils are going to look at pictures of Queen Elizabeth I and Henry VIII in history lessons to learn about understanding pictures and images, shouldn't they also look at contemporary iconography, so that they can apply what they have learned about decoding and understanding images? If pupils are going to learn about how Britain became a democracy, shouldn't they also learn about what happened *after* ordinary people got the vote (did it stop wars, did it make everything better, did it make women equal, did it really turn out to be government 'of, by and for the people'?) If they are going to learn about the Holocaust, shouldn't they think about what issues relating to the Holocaust are relevant to life today? Shouldn't they learn that we lost an empire as well as gained one (and that not all historians or imperial subjects thought that the empire was 'a good thing')? 'Opening topics up' to relate to important contemporary issues can be both illuminating and engaging for pupils. Study of the Chartists can be done 'in isolation' or as something which leads into the issue of how methods of extra-parliamentary opposition have developed over time, and up to the present day. The study of the Industrial Revolution can be done as 'the coming of the factories', the steam engine and textile machinery or it can be related to broader patterns of change in modes of production and employment. This in not just a matter of trying to enhance pupil engagement in the subject 'overviews' also help to develop pupils' understanding of major changes and developments relating to elements of the human past. The historian John Kenyon (1984) makes the point that it is unhelpful to 'pull up the drawbridge' before the present if we are hoping that history will help pupils to understand the present in the light of the past.

Tosh points out the dangers of a historical education that is 'heritage based' and which encourages a view of the past which is 'superficial, nostalgic and conformist . . . not so much a means of education as an adjunct to tourism' (Tosh, 2008: 11). He also points to the paradox of a society drenched in a range of historical activity (family history, historical collections, visits to sites):

> Should not historians be grateful that their subject has become 'the new gardening?' The problem is that – with the exception of a few TV programmes – none of these activities brings historical perspectives to bear on issues of topical importance. Indeed, their very popularity diminishes the public space that is available for that kind of analysis. We are confronted by the paradox of a society which is immersed in the past and yet detached from its history.
>
> (Tosh, 2008: 6–7)

A common mistake which my students make is to teach history as if it is just about the past. The more connections that are made across time, and to the present, the more meaningful, useful and engaging the subject will be. It will also make it easier for students to acquire the 'big picture' of the past that many commentators are calling for.

Who is history for?

For over a century there has been a political and educational consensus that all pupils should receive a historical education (Conway, 2010). Recent changes and developments suggest a move away from this state of affairs, or at the least the significant dilution of that historical education for large numbers of pupils (Historical Association, 2009; Harris and Haydn, 2010). There are now schools in England where history is not timetabled for pupils over the age of 13, and secondary schools where pupils learn history as a discrete subject for just one year. Many less able pupils are being guided or directed away from the study of history after Key Stage 3 (Harris and Haydn, 2010).

The Historical Association's recent survey revealed that whereas the position of history as a school subject in independent and grammar schools was still strong, it was only taught as a discrete subject in 72.3 per cent of the comprehensive schools in the survey, and in only 59.1 per cent of the new secondary 'academies' which are to be expanded by the new government. We may be moving to a position where less able pupils, and those in academies and comprehensive schools, are offered a minimalist and 'cheap and cheerful' historical education, while those in grammar and independent schools receive a more extensive one. It was interesting but disconcerting to find that in the jobs section of *The Times Educational Supplement*, 30 April 2010, there were 17 advertisements of history posts in the independent sector but none for history teachers in state schools.

Counsell (2006) makes the point that the historical consciousness of all pupils, including the less able, matters 'because they are future citizens, because they are human beings'. There is no question that recent changes to history's position on the school curriculum mean that young people's entitlement to a historical education has slipped below what is offered in any other European country.

The importance of knowledge

There has always been a tendency in the UK for policymakers to underestimate the complexity of the processes influencing teaching and learning (Simon, 1981; Alexander, 2004). It has sometimes been implied that there is no need for 'theory' in teacher education, and that someone with a good degree is all that is required (see, for example, Gibb, 2010b).

I have a 2:1 honours degree in history, taught for 19 years and have worked for 15 years in history teacher education, but it is only after the recent Schools History Project Conference that I have acquired clearer and better ideas for how to teach pupils about change and continuity in history. There are still gaps in my knowledge about how to teach history effectively, about how to make best use of new technology, about how to make sure pupils retain the knowledge they have acquired and so on.

Those who argue for the importance of knowledge in history education should consider that, as well as the existence of a body of knowledge about the substantive historical past, there is a body of knowledge about history education, which can help history teachers to teach more effectively. Not all contributions to this body of knowledge are flawless but it is arrogant to be dismissive of all that has gone before in this field.

There is evidence to suggest that pupils do not leave school with a coherent 'big picture' of the past and that this is unhelpful (Ofsted, 2007; Howson, 2007). If there is a consensus that this is not a good thing (which appears to be the case), Shemilt (2009) offers some evidence and constructive suggestions about which teaching approaches might best rectify this problem. There also appears to be a consensus that chronology is important in school history, but what does it mean 'to be good at chronology': is it just how many dates you can remember? Time and chronology are complex (and different) concepts, and there are things that have been written about these concepts which might help history teachers to teach them more effectively (see, for example, Dawson, 2007; Barton, 2009). Lee (1994) offers important and helpful clarifications about the role of 'facts' in acquiring historical knowledge; Seixas (2007) points out the difficulties which notions of a historical 'canon' present for history teachers; Wineburg (1997: 257) raises the important problem of knowledge application and 'the chasm between knowing X, and using X to think about Y'. Counsell

(2003) suggests helpful and well-substantiated strategies for teaching history to less able pupils in a way that is rigorous and effective. Although it is generally accepted that there is more to getting better at history than just 'knowing more stuff', there is a substantial body of literature about progression in history which might be helpful for a history teacher to be aware of (for a brief summary of some of these ideas, see Haydn and Harris, 2009). The suggestion that 'historian x' will draw up a 'clear and simple list' of the content for a new National Curriculum (Collins, 2005) displays a degree of ingenuousness and suggests that the statement was made by someone who has not read Robert Phillips' work on the formulation of the first National Curriculum for history (Phillips, 1998). Similarly, it is possible that those arguing for a return to 'traditional' kings and queens history may not have read the Newsom Report (1963), 'History in danger' (Price, 1968) or the Hargreaves Report (1984).

It is also important not to underestimate the extent to which history teachers as a community of practice have helped to improve the quality of history teaching in schools in recent years. *Teaching History* has probably been the single most influential factor in improving the quality of history teaching in the UK in recent years, together with the annual conferences of the Historical Association and the Schools History Project, and the History Teachers' Discussion Forum (http://www.schoolhistory.co.uk/forum/index.php?showtopic=12980).

These communities have had a much more extensive (and beneficent) influence on history teaching than more expensive top-down 'national strategy' approaches. In the light of the decimation of LEA (Local Education Authority) advisory services for history, they provide the most cost-effective continuing professional development for history teachers and a wise administration would give some thought to how best to support these networks.

Nor is knowledge for effective teaching limited to subject-specific knowledge. It is important not to underestimate the importance that motivation and engagement plays in learning. Most experienced teachers would have reservations about the efficacy of Norman Stone's suggestion that children should have the national culture 'rammed down their throats' (quoted in Crawford, 1995). In the words of Sue Hallam (1996), 'They must want to learn, if you lose that, you lose just about everything.'

Teaching is not *just* 'a craft' (Gove, 2010); there are lots of things which teachers need to know if they are to teach effectively which go beyond 'craft' wisdom, important though that is. Wischut (2009) points to the dangers of policymakers generalizing from their own experience and allowing ideology rather than evidence to influence their decisions. In the words of Andrew Miller (2001: 104), 'It's difficult to change the way you see the world. We take on a certain view when we are young then spend the rest of our lives collecting the evidence.'

Chapter summary

- There are reasonable grounds for concern that under current arrangements not all pupils in England receive an acceptable historical education. If history is not to be compulsory up to the age of 16 there needs to be some consideration of what would constitute an acceptable minimum which would provide all pupils with 'a grounding' in history.

- An important weakness in current models of history teaching is that many pupils leave school without a coherent and useful mental map of the past.
- One of the biggest problems for history teachers is the limited time for history on school timetables in secondary schools. This makes it very difficult to teach all the things that the National Curriculum for history requires them to teach.
- This lack of time has implications for how much content can be covered. There is a danger that rushed coverage results in 'nothing beyond a set of imperfectly understood facts and ill-digested notions' (Fairley, 1967).
- The figure of 30 per cent take-up for the subject post–Key Stage 3 conceals massive variations across schools, with history constituting the biggest optional subject in some schools yet not being timetabled post–Key Stage 3 in other schools because of lack of demand (Harris and Haydn, 2010). It seems possible that some history departments are taking more time than others to try to make the purposes and possible benefits of school history explicit to pupils. In spite of 'school policy' pressures and effects, teachers and departments can make a difference.
- There is a professional consensus to support the idea that a historical education should include the development of pupils' knowledge and understanding of the substantive past *and* their understanding of disciplinary aspects of history. There is broad support for the role of the key concepts and processes outlined in the National Curriculum for history.
- There is considerable unease about the way that the National Curriculum 'levels' system is working and a widespread belief within history departments (but not necessarily senior management teams) that the assessment system at Key Stage 3 is not working well.
- All history teachers need to be able to answer the question posed by Lienhardt at the start of this chapter, both in terms of the usefulness of history as a whole and for all the themes, topics, events and people they teach. History teachers need to be able to articulate the purposes and benefits of studying the past, and particular elements of the past, not just to their pupils but also to parents, policymakers and senior management teams. They also need to be clear in their own minds why they are teaching particular topics and in what ways pupils will benefit from learning about that particular aspect of the past.
- The more that policymakers, history teacher educators and history teachers make discerning and intelligent use of the body of knowledge which has accumulated in the field of history education, the more likely it is that we will develop a more effective system of history education in schools which rectifies current weaknesses without damaging things that are working well.

Further reading

A collection of quotations about the purposes of school history can be accessed online at: http://www.uea.ac.uk/~m242/historypgce/purposes/purposesquotesintro.htm (accessed 26 May 2010).

Barton, K. (2009) 'The denial of desire: how to make history education meaningless', in L. Symcox and A. Wilschut (eds) *National History Standards: The Problem of the Canon and the Future of Teaching History*. Charlotte, NC: Information Age Publishing, 265–82.

Counsell, C. (2003) 'History for all', in M. Riley and R. Harris, *Past Forward: A Vision for School History 2002–2012*. London, Historical Association: 25–32.

Culpin, C. (2007) 'What kind of history should school history be?', *The Historian*, Autumn: 6–13.

Haydn, T. (2004) 'History', in J. White (ed.) *Rethinking the School Curriculum*. London: Routledge, pp. 87–103.

Joseph, K. (1984) 'Why teach history in schools?' *The Historian*, No. 2: insert.

Seixas, P. (2007) 'Who needs a canon?', in M. Grever and S. Stuurman (eds) *Beyond the Canon: History for the Twenty-First Century*. Basingstoke: Palgrave Macmillan, 19–30.

Shemilt, D. (2009) 'Drinking an ocean and pissing a cupful', in L. Symcox and A. Wilschut (eds) *National History Standards: The Problem of the Canon and the Future of Teaching History*. Charlotte, NC: Information Age Publishing, 141–210.

Slater, J. (1989) *The Politics of History Teaching: A Humanity Dehumanized*. London: Institute of Education, University of London.

Tosh, J. (2008) *Why History Matters*. Basingstoke: Palgrave Macmillan.

Note

1 The 'Opening Minds' Curriculum, promoted by the Royal Society for the Encouragement of Arts, Manufactures and Commerce (RSA), is based on a programme which eschews the teaching of specific subjects in favour of one that attempts to develop learner competence in five domains: citizenship, learning, managing information, managing situations and relating to people. Details of the programme can be accessed at http://www.thersa.org/projects/opening-minds (accessed 26 May 2010).

References

Adey, K. and Biddulph, M. (2001) 'The influence of pupil perceptions on subject choice at 14+ in geography and history', *Educational Studies*, 27(4): 439–47.

Aldrich, R. (1987) 'Interesting and useful', *Teaching History*, 47: 11–14.

——(1997a) *The End of History and the Beginning of Education*. London: Institute of Education, University of London.

——(1997b) Unpublished lecture, Institute of Education, University of London, September.

Alexander, R. (2004) 'Still no pedagogy? Principle, pragmatism and compliance in primary education', *Cambridge Journal of Education*, 34(1): 7–33.

Ball, S. (1993) 'Education, Majorism and "the curriculum of the dead"', *Pedagogy, Culture and Society*, 1(2): 195–214.

Barton, K. (2009) 'The denial of desire: how to make history education meaningless', in L. Symcox and A. Wilschut (eds), *National History Standards: The Problem of the Canon and the Future of Teaching History*. Charlotte, NC: Information Age Publishing, pp. 265–82.

Burnham, S. and Brown, G. (2004) 'Assessment without level descriptions', *Teaching History*, 115: 5–15.

Byrom, J. (1996) 'Working with sources: scepticism or cynicism? Putting the story back together again', *Teaching History*, 91: 32–4.

Collins, T. (2005) *Speech to the National Catholic Heads Conference*, London, 27 January.

Conway, D. (2010) Quoted in 'National Curriculum being dumbed down', *Daily Telegraph*, 4 January.

Counsell, C. (2000) 'Historical knowledge and historical skills: a distracting dichotomy', in J. Arthur and R. Phillips (eds) *Issues in History Teaching*. London: Routledge: 54–71.

——(2003) History for all, *Past Forward*. London: Historical Association: 25–32.

——(2006) Quoted in Culpin, C. (2007), *Times Educational Supplement*, February.

——(2010) *Teaching about Historical Change and Continuity*, address to Schools Council Project Conference, Trinity and All Saints College: Leeds, 4 July.

Crawford, K. (1995) 'A history of the right: the battle for control of National Curriculum history 1989–1994', *British Journal of Educational Studies*, 43(4): 433–56.

Culpin, C. (2002) 'Why we must change history GCSE', *Teaching History*, 109: 6–9.

——(2007) 'What kind of history should school history be?', *The Historian*, Autumn: 6–13.

Dawson, I. (2007) *Time for Chronology*, Available online at: http://www.thinkinghistory.co.uk/Issues/downloads/TimeforChronology.pdf (accessed 9 July 2010).

DES (1990) *National Curriculum History Working Group: Final Report*. London: HMSO.

DFEE/QCA. (1999) *The National Curriculum: Handbook for Secondary Teachers in England*. London: DFEE/QCA.

Fairley, J. (1967) *Activity Methods in History*. London: Nelson.

Fink, N. (2004) 'Pupils' conceptions of history and history teaching', *International Journal of Historical Learning, Teaching and Research*, 4(2).

Foster, S., Ashby, R. and Lee, P. (2008) *Usable Historical Pasts: A Study of Students' Frameworks of the Past*, End of award report, ESRC award number RES-000–22–1676.

Gibb, N. (2010a) Quoted in 'Academies "undoing good work" in boosting history studies', *Times Educational Supplement*, 11 June: 5.

——(2010b) Quoted in 'New minister Nick Gibb upsets teachers – already', *The Guardian* 17 May.

Gove, M. (2010) Quoted in 'Pupils to learn poetry by heart in Tory return to "traditional" school lessons', *The Times*, 6 March: 3.

Grever, M., Ribbens, K. and Haydn, T. (2008) 'Identity and school history: the perspective of young people from the Netherlands and England', *British Journal of Educational Studies*, 56(1): 76–94.

Grimston, J. and Warren, G. (2010) 'Exposed: the schools inflating their GCSE league results', *Sunday Times*, 13 June: 14.

Hallam, S. (1996) 'Differentiation', unpublished lecture, Institute of Education, University of London, January.

Hamer, J. (1990) 'Ofsted and history in schools', *The Historian*, 53: 24–5.

Hargreaves, A. (1984) *Improving Secondary Schools: Report of the Committee on the Curriculum and Organisation of Secondary Schools*. London: ILEA.

Hargreaves, D. (1984) *Research Studies* (companion volume to *Improving Secondary Schools*). London: ILEA.

Harris, R. and Haydn, T. (2006) 'Pupils' enjoyment of history – what lessons can teachers learn from their pupils?', *Curriculum Journal*, 17(4): 315–33.

——(2010) 'What happens to a subject in a "free market" curriculum: a study of secondary school history in the United Kingdom', *Research Papers in Education*, in press.

Haydn, T. (1996) 'Nationalism begins at home: the impact of national curriculum history on perceptions of national identity in Britain', 1987–1994, *History of Education Bulletin*, 57, April: 51–61.

——(2004) 'History', in J. White (ed.) *Rethinking the School Curriculum*, London: Routledge, pp. 87–103.

——(2010) 'History and ICT', in I. Davies (ed.) *Debates in History Teaching*. London: Routledge, pp. 423–48.

Haydn, T. and Harris, R. (2009) 'Children's ideas about what it means to get better at history: a view from the UK', *International Journal of Historical Teaching, Learning and Research*, 8(2): 26–39.

Historical Association (2009) *Findings from the Historical Association Survey of Secondary History Teachers, Spring 2009*. London: Historical Association.

Howson, J. (2007) 'Is it the Tuarts and then the Studors or the other way round? The importance of developing a usable big picture of the past', *Teaching History*, 127: 40–7.

Husbands, C. (1996) *What Is History Teaching?* Buckingham: Open University Press.

Joseph, K. (1984) 'Why teach history in schools?' *The Historian*, No. 2: insert.

Keating, J. and Sheldon, N. (2010) 'History in education: trends and themes in history teaching 1900–2010', in I. Davies (ed.) *Debates in History Teaching*. London: Routledge, pp. 15–37.

Kenyon, J. (1984) 'The lessons of history', *The Observer*, 4 March.

Lee, P. (1994) 'Historical Knowledge and the National Curriculum', in H. Bourdillon (ed.) *Teaching History*. London: Routledge, pp. 41–52.

Lee, P. and Ashby, R. (2000) 'Progression in historical understanding 7–14', in P. Seixas, P. Stearns and S. Wineburg (eds) *Teaching, Knowing and Learning History*. New York: New York University Press, pp. 195–220.

Lee, P. and Howson, J. (2009) 'Two out of five did not know that Henry VIII had six wives: history education, historical literacy and historical consciousness', in L. Symcox and A. Wilschut (eds) *National History Standards: The Problem of the Canon and the Future of Teaching History*. Charlotte, NC: Information Age Publishing, pp. 211–64.

Leinhardt, G. (2001) Quoted in Wineburg, S. (2001: ix) *Historical Thinking and Other Unnatural Acts*. Philadelphia: Temple Press.

Letwin, O. (1989) 'A grounding', in B. Moon, P. Murphy and J. Raynor (eds) *Policies for the Curriculum*. London: Hodder and Stoughton, pp. 70–3.

MacGregor, J. (1995) Quoted in Davies, I. and John, P., 'Using history to develop citizenship education in the National Curriculum', *Teaching History*, 78: 5–7.

Maddison, M. (2009) *An HMI View of History in Secondary Schools: Successes, Challenges and Opportunities*, address to SHP Conference, Trinity and All Saints College, Leeds, July.

Miller, Andrew. (2001) *Oxygen*. London: Spectre.

Newsom Report (1963) *Half our Future: The Newsom Report*. London: Central Advisory Council for Education.

Ofsted (2005) *Annual Report of Her Majesty's Chief Inspector of Schools 2004/5*. London: Ofsted.

——(2007) *History in the Balance*. London: Ofsted.

——(2009) 'Planning for change: the impact of the new Key Stage 3 Curriculum', Reference No. 080262. London: Ofsted.

Osler, A. (2009) 'Patriotism, multiculturalism and belonging: political discourse and the teaching of history', *Educational Review*, 61(3): 85–100.

Phillips, R. (1998) *History Teaching, Nationhood and the State: A Study in Educational Politics*. London: Cassell.

Price, M. (1968) 'History in danger', *History*, 53: 342–7.

QCA (2005) *Pupil Perceptions of History at Key Stage 3: Final Report*. London: QCA.

——(2007) *The National Curriculum for History: Key Stage 3*. London: QCA. Available online at: http://curriculum.qcda.gov.uk/key-stages-3-and-4/subjects/key-stage-3/history/programme-of-study/index.aspx?tab=4 (accessed 8 July 2010).

Seixas, P. (2007) 'Who needs a canon?', in Grever, M. and S. Stuurman (eds), *Beyond the Canon: History for the 21st Century*. Basingstoke: Palgrave Macmillan, pp. 19–30.

Shemilt, D. (2009) 'Drinking an ocean and pissing a cupful', in L. Symcox and A. Wilschut (eds) *National History Standards: The Problem of the Canon and the Future of Teaching History*. Charlotte, NC: Information Age Publishing, pp. 141–210.

Simon, B. (1981) 'Why no pedagogy in England?', in B. Simon and W. Taylor (eds) *Education in the Eighties: The Central Issues*. London: Batsford, pp. 124–45.

Slater, J. (1989) *The Politics of History Teaching: A Humanity Dehumanized*. London: Institute of Education, University of London.

Stokes, J. (1990) Speech in the House of Commons, quoted in *The Sunday Telegraph*, 1 April.

Sylvester, D. (1994) 'Change and continuity in history teaching', in H. Bourdillon (ed.) *Teaching History*, 9–26.

Tosh, J. (2008) *Why History Matters*. Basingstoke: Palgrave Macmillan.

Van Boxtel, C. (2010) *Something to Talk about: The Potential of a Dynamic Approach to Heritage Education*, address to the Euroclio Conference, Nijmegen, 26 March.

Wilschut, A. (2010) History at the mercy of politicians and ideologies: Germany, England, and the Netherlands in the 19th and 20th centuries, *Journal of Curriculum Studies*, 42(5): 693–723.

Wineburg, S. (1997) 'Beyond breadth and depth: subject matter knowledge and assessment', *Theory into Practice*, 36(4): 255–61.

Chapter 4

The history curriculum 16–19

Arthur Chapman

Introduction

This chapter provides a brief account of the current curriculum for history 16–19 and of its recent history and context. Criticisms of recent curriculum reform and practice are outlined and trends in results are considered. The discussion is necessarily brief and the intention is to raise and scope issues rather than to try to put them to bed.[1]

Courses and contexts: curriculum and assessment 16–19

The 16–19 curriculum and its discontents

The post-16 curriculum as a whole is currently much debated and has been the subject of numerous reforms and reform proposals since the 1970s (Hodgson and Spours, 2003, pp. 5–26).[2]

Curriculum debate and reform has been shaped by a number of concerns, including:

- concerns about the narrowness, overspecialization and incoherence of a curriculum that allows students to study a relatively small number of specialized subjects on a 'pick 'n' mix' basis;
- concerns about the vocational relevance, fitness for purpose, take-up and inclusiveness of education and training post-16 and, indeed, 14–19; and
- concerns about the effectiveness with which Advanced Level qualifications are performing their traditional functions of maintaining academic standards and preparing students for higher education.[3]

The current 16–19 curriculum for history has been shaped by these wider curricular debates and it is currently possible to study history post-16 by following one of a number of differently structured courses of study including, in descending order of candidature:

- AS and A-level courses of study including qualifications in history provided by five 'awarding bodies' for England, Wales and Northern Ireland, under a common rubric (QCA, 2006);[4]
- baccalaureate courses that combine specialist subject studies and non-specialist elements within an overarching curricular framework and that aim to ensure breadth and coherence of study;[5] and
- The University of Cambridge International Examination's Pre-U diploma – a non-modular course combining specialist subject studies which aims to provide students 'with the skills and knowledge they need to make a success of their subsequent studies at university' (CIE, n.d.).

It is likely that the range of history courses available will continue to increase and a Diploma in Humanities and Social Sciences is currently being prepared for delivery from September 2011 (CCS, n.d. (a)).

The remainder of this chapter concentrates on Advanced Level history.

Assessment regimes and regime change

Since its introduction in 1951, the Advanced Level qualification has been subject to periodic critique and revision but not, until Curriculum 2000, to large-scale structural reform. There have been three distinct Advanced Level 'regimes' since 1999/2000:

- a 'legacy' terminally assessed A- and AS-level regime, replaced from September 2000;[6]
- a modular six-unit assessment regime consisting of an AS qualification, intermediate in standard between GCSE and Advanced Level, and an A2 qualification at Advanced Level ('Curriculum 2000'); and
- a four-unit modular AS and A2 assessment regime operating under a new generic specification for advanced work (QCA, 2006) from September 2008.

The Curriculum 2000 reforms were intended to respond to a number of previous criticisms of Advanced Levels and set out, among other things:

- to enable breadth of study by encouraging students to study a broader range of subjects in their first year of 16–19 study than had hitherto been the case;
- to facilitate the transition from GCSE to GCE through an AS qualification at an intermediate standard; and
- to enable certification after one year of study.[7]

The reforms did not respond to more radical suggestions for reform of Advanced Levels – for example, to arguments for an overarching diploma to replace stand-alone advanced qualifications (Phillips and Pound, 2003). The Curriculum 2000 reforms generated problems of their own – in particular, controversies over assessment – and the 2008 reforms sought to address these problems by, for example, reducing the number of AS and A2 modules and assessments.

Advanced Level history: change and continuity?

Prior to the late 1980s history at Advanced Level largely focused on the essay as a vehicle for developing and assessing students' historical knowledge and understanding (Hill, 1972, p. 198). It both responded to and reinforced a traditional didactic pedagogy (Lang, 1990, pp. 14 and 26–34) where the teacher frequently took the role of a 'reliable and authoritative instructor' (Burston, 1957, p. 15) transmitting a received body of information. As the intention of the 'essay' was to develop argument, 'critical interpretation' (Burston, 1957, p. 16) and engagement with controversy, as much as factual grasp, however, Advanced Level pedagogy entailed 'encouraging pupils to express their views and to have confidence in their powers of judgment' as much as 'clear exposition and systematic explanation' (Burston, 1957, p. 14; Ministry of Education, 1952, pp. 62–73).[8]

The changes that had generated pressure for reform in the teaching of history to 5- to 16-year-olds in the late 1960s and early 1970s and that led to the setting up of curriculum reform projects such as the Schools Council History Project were also subsequently felt at Advanced Level (Hill, 1972, pp. 188–9). 'New history' approaches that aimed to make Advanced Level history simultaneously rigorously disciplinary and engaging for pupils were developed, notably the AEB (Associated Examining Board) 673 history syllabus, first examined in 1977, that included an historical methodology paper and that required students to produce their own small-scale dissertations on a historical topic of their own choice (Lang, 1990, pp. 46–7).

In 1983, a 'common core' of aims and objectives for Advanced Level qualifications in history was agreed (Fines, 1984, pp. 6–7, 26–8; Lang, 1990, p. 47) which recognized the centrality of second-order concepts such as evidence and interpretations of history to historical learning and in 1985 Her Majesty's Inspector looked forward to a future in which 'syllabuses will define more precisely what is to be examined; grades are likely to relate to agreed criteria' and '[f]actual recall is likely to be less dominant' (DfES, 1985, p. 28). The pressure for A-level history reform was significantly accelerated by the introduction of the GCSE in 1986–8.

By the early 1990s a diverse range of innovative A-level history courses had developed, alongside and as alternatives to more conventional exam-focused courses. These innovative courses included the Cambridge History Project, ETHOS and the London Syllabus E (Lang, 1990, pp. 46–7 and 52–4; Lewin, 1991, pp. 27–9; Fines and Nichol, 1994; Hibbert, 2006, pp. 26–43).[9] These courses were all focused, to one degree or another, on developing a conceptually informed understanding of history as a form of knowledge and on what ETHOS called 'doing history' or engaging students actively in historical research and argument beyond the traditional essay through teacher-designed coursework (Laver, 1991) and/or the 'personal study', a substantial student-led research project (Mantin, 1991). How far Advanced Level pedagogy and practice as a whole was impacted by these changes is a matter of debate (Lang, 1990, 26–34; Hibbert, 2006) but it is clear that innovations enabling disciplinary, student-centred and flexibly assessed models of curriculum post-16 were fully developed, tested and validated by the early 1990s.

In some respects innovation and diversity were casualties of Curriculum 2000, a reform programme that, among other things, reduced the number of specifications that could be offered and therefore promoted syllabus design focused on lowest common denominators in the A-level market.[10] There were a number of clear benefits in the new system, notwithstanding the criticisms that have been made of it, however, not least increased clarity about the topics that exam papers addressed.[11] In addition, the 2006 subject criteria for AS and A2 preserved key features of the innovative courses that preceded Curriculum 2000, generalizing these features to all Advanced Level specifications, as is apparent in the clarity with which procedural concepts are identified in the subject criteria (QCA, 2006, p. 5) and also in the requirement that 2008 AS and A2 specifications contain a compulsory coursework element focused on historical enquiry (QCA, 2006, p. 8). Some current specifications also preserve 'centre-designed' coursework options and thus enable curriculum innovation by teachers.[12]

How healthy is Advanced Level history? Assessing curriculum 2000

Trends in history numbers and results

The story of Advanced Level history since 1951 has, for the most part, been one of absolute growth in the numbers of candidates taking history and of relative decline in history's share of an expanding total number of A-level entries (Lang, 1990, p. 11). There are exceptions to this pattern, however, and, as Figure 4.1 shows, the story looked very different at the end of the 1990s when history numbers were in absolute decline (Husbands, 2001, p. 39). It is apparent, however, from Figure 4.1 that Curriculum 2000 had a positive impact on the number of candidates taking history, which increased year-on-year from 2000 reversing the absolute decline that occurred in the 1990s.[13] Figure 4.2 suggests that the introduction of the intermediate AS in 2000 played an important part in the 'recovery' in numbers between 2001 and 2008.[14] Absolute growth between 1992 and 2008 was, however, modest (an increase of 4.6 per cent) and needs to be set against the rapid growth in the candidature for other subjects.[15]

Figure 4.3 tells a very positive story also: 'results' have been riding a continuous upward curve of improvement since 1992 and history education is clearly getting better and better at 'delivery'. The story is even more remarkable in a long-term context: between the 1950s and the 1980s the history pass rate declined such that 'an examination which almost 80 per cent of candidates passed in 1951 was failed by more than 30 per cent in 1985' (Eric Evans cited in Lang, 1990, p. 11). This decline coincided with a considerable expansion in numbers post-16 and changes in the composition of the Advanced Level cohort – a trend that continues to the present, albeit one that now coincides with improving results.

Caution must be exercised in interpreting these statistical patterns, of course, but the pattern since the introduction of Curriculum 2000 is clearly a positive one in terms of both recruitment and results.[16]

Millennial bugs? Criticisms of Curriculum 2000

There is good reason to feel confident about the quality of teaching and learning in the contemporary post-16 history classroom:

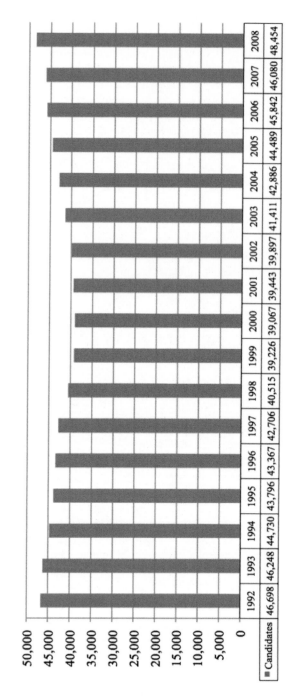

	1992	1993	1994	1995	1996	1997	1998	1999	2000	2001	2002	2003	2004	2005	2006	2007	2008
■ Candidates	46,698	46,248	44,730	43,796	43,367	42,706	40,515	39,226	39,067	39,443	39,897	41,411	42,886	44,489	45,842	46,080	48,454

Figure 4.1 Numbers of candidates sitting A2 examinations in history, 1992–2008.

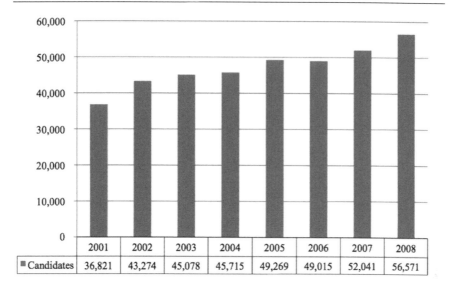

	2001	2002	2003	2004	2005	2006	2007	2008
▪ Candidates	36,821	43,274	45,078	45,715	49,269	49,015	52,041	56,571

Figure 4.2 Numbers of candidates sitting AS examinations in history, 2001–8.

- inspection evidence suggests that history is very well taught post-16 (Ofsted, 2007, p. 17);
- practitioner and much textbook literature provide evidence of a culture of innovative and engaging teaching and learning post-16.[17]

It seems curmudgeonly, in such a context and where statistical stories are so positive, to question the quality of student outcomes. Numerous concerns have been raised, however (for example, Tillbrook, 2002; Historical Association, 2005; Lavender, 2009), and it is important to register these concerns here. It has been suggested, for example:

- that examination processes have become increasingly self-referential, assessing historical competence through exercises that do not reflect real-world historical practice;
- that examination papers and mark schemes often reward 'criterion-compliant' answers that students can be coached to produce in order to maximize their marks rather than independence and originality of thought;
- that assessment is increasingly driving curriculum as evidenced, for example, by the rise of 'badged' textbooks tailored to particular assessment rubrics;[18] and
- that these developments have taken place in a context where examinations have increasingly replaced other more valid modes of recognizing and rewarding achievement (such as coursework or individual research) for bureaucratic or financial rather than educational reasons.[19]

Concerns about curriculum, rather than assessment, have focused on the narrow range of content that history specifications require students to study (for example, Tillbrook, 2002; Historical Association, 2005; Nicholls, 2007).[20] Notoriously, it was possible

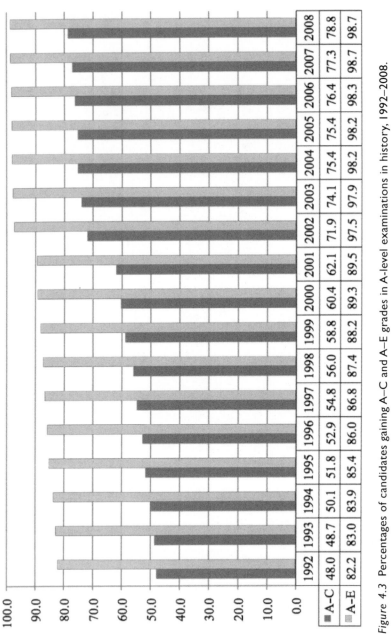

	1992	1993	1994	1995	1996	1997	1998	1999	2000	2001	2002	2003	2004	2005	2006	2007	2008
A–C	48.0	48.7	50.1	51.8	52.9	54.8	56.0	58.8	60.4	62.1	71.9	74.1	75.4	75.4	76.4	77.3	78.8
A–E	82.2	83.0	83.9	85.4	86.0	86.8	87.4	88.2	89.3	89.5	97.5	97.9	98.2	98.2	98.3	98.7	98.7

Figure 4.3 Percentages of candidates gaining A–C and A–E grades in A-level examinations in history, 1992–2008.

under Curriculum 2000 to gain an advanced qualification in history without in fact knowing very much history; as Tillbrook observed, 'one awarding body . . . permits 83% of its marks to be awarded for the study of twenty years of German history' (2002, p. 24). Discussions of curricular narrowing often centre on an undue focus on particular topics. Other forms of narrowness have also been noted, for example temporal and cultural parochialism, evident in the modern and Eurocentric nature of history topics (Lang, 1990, pp. 35–6; Chapman and Facey, 2004), and thematic narrowness and fragmentation (Roberts, 2003).

Research on the transition to higher education has also raised concerns about assessment-driven pedagogy and narrow thinking (Booth, 2005; Hibbert, 2006; Nicholls, 2007).[21] It has been suggested, for example, that students frequently come away from their Advanced Level studies in history with simplistic understandings of historical study and with dependent notions of their own roles as students consistent with a culture focused on advancing assessment success through didactic teaching and passive learning. Thus, for example, it has been reported that

> new undergraduates routinely report that in reading they are looking especially for 'facts' to use in their essays, with far fewer declaring that they look for interpretations or the position of the author, as might academic historians.
>
> (Booth, 2005, p. 16)

and that

> new undergraduates often see the tutor as the 'expert' who can (and perhaps should) provide them with 'the information'.
>
> (Booth, 2005, p. 17)

The criticisms and concerns discussed in this chapter section are largely historic and refer in the main to curriculum and assessment between 2001 and 2007. It is worth noting also that a number of them are anecdotal, that some of these concerns are likely to be perennial and that positive assessments of curriculum and assessment in this period have also been offered (Chapman, 2003; Freeman, 2005).[22] Furthermore, aspects of the 2008 curriculum reforms can be understood as addressing these concerns – for example, through a reduction in the number of assessments and the requirement that

> [a]ll . . . specifications must have internal assessment . . . comprising 15–20 per cent of the A level and assessing the skills of historical enquiry.
>
> (QCA, 2006, p. 8)

A stipulation that implies that it should no longer be possible to claim advanced understanding of history without some experience of 'doing history'.

Conclusions: advancing history post-16?

A number of conclusions are suggested by the foregoing discussion. First, it is apparent that there is much to celebrate about history post-16:

- The number of students taking Advanced Level history has expanded significantly since the 1950s.
- Remarkable and dramatic increases in examination pass and A to C rates have recently occurred.
- There has been substantial and significant curriculum innovation and renewal in history and 16–19 assessment frameworks for history are now clearly disciplinary in focus.[23]

Qualifications are necessary, of course, for example:

- Quantitative increases and real-world improvements are not necessarily the same thing (Power, 1999).
- It is too early to say if new assessment arrangements post-2008 will satisfy critics of Curriculum 2000.
- Developments pre-16 may threaten future recruitment post-16 (Historical Association, 2009).
- History numbers post-16 are smaller than they could and should be, given the powerful contribution that historical thinking can make to the personal and educational development of students and to democratic culture (Tosh, 2008).

Looking forward, there is much that can be done to broaden and develop the post-16 curriculum for history. Thus, for example, there is a great deal of scope for renewing and broadening the content of the curriculum:

- to reflect contemporary historical practice and culture – for example, contemporary concerns with memory (Wertsch, 2002) and contemporary modes and media of historical representation (Jenkins, *et al.*, 2007; Ofsted, 2007, p. 29); and
- to ensure that Advanced Level historical studies require students to engage with world history rather than with European or Atlantic perspectives on European or Atlantic aspects of modern history.[24]

The range of specifications available gives a great deal of scope for history teachers to actively shape the quality of the learning experiences available to pupils:

- by selecting the 'awarding bodies' and 'specifications' that provide the most robust opportunities for effective historical learning;
- by constructing learning experiences that reconcile the demands of assessment with challenging and engaging learning experiences for pupils;
- by selecting and combining 'specification' units so as to ensure breadth of study; and
- by developing innovative course content through centre-designed coursework where it is possible to do so (for example, Edexcel, 2007, p. 64).

There is a great deal of scope in all of these areas. It is apparent, for example, that different awarding bodies have interpreted QCA's stipulations about historical interpretations (QCA, 2006, p. 5) in different ways: Edexcel, for example, understand interpretations for assessment purposes largely as products (historians'claims) that students are required to assess (Edexcel, 2010, p. 50) whereas OCR's (Oxford Cambridge and RSA Examinations) Specification B understands interpretation as a process and intends candidates to develop methodological as well as substantive understandings of interpretations (OCR, 2008, p. 34); the choice of 'specification' is therefore clearly consequential for the ways in which students' historical understanding is developed.

It has always been possible, of course, to treat Advanced Level as an exercise in assessment more than an experience of education and it is perhaps harder now than it was in the past to resist the 'pressure to make examination success the sole aim' of history lessons (Burston, 1957, pp. 24–5). There is considerable scope, as of course there has always been, for engaging students in challenging and rewarding historical learning; we are particularly fortunate, it seems to me, in the quality and rigour of the models of practice available to inspire us.[25]

Further reading

Debates on the 16–19 curriculum in general and on curriculum change can be explored through the references to this chapter. Laffin (2009) models ways in which Advanced Level history can engage students and develop their historical thinking.

Notes

1 I am very grateful to Dr Katharine Burn, Chris Edwards, Dr Jane Facey, Jerome Freeman, Dr Barbara Hibbert and, in particular, Professor Jon Nichol for their comments on an earlier draft of this chapter. The infelicities and errors that remain are, of course, my own.
2 The recent Nuffield Review on education and training is comprehensive in its consideration of 14–19 curriculum and assessment (Nuffield, 2009) and sets an agenda for future curriculum reform. The review identifies a range of problems with current provision and argues, among other things, that the field is characterized by narrowness of educational vision, an 'Orwellian' jargon of performance management and restricted economies of power in which the voice of the learner and the expertise of the teacher are marginalized.
3 Many of these concerns have considerable vintage: proposals to address overspecialization were outlined by the Schools Council in 1973 and by the Higginson Report in 1988, for example (Phillips and Pound, pp. 13–14; Lang, 1990, pp. 45–6).
4 Oxford Cambridge and RSA Examinations (OCR) offer two distinct 'specifications' (A and B) and all awarding body specifications offer alternate content options that enable a wide variety of courses to be constructed.
5 Baccalaureate courses include the International Baccalaureate (IB), the Welsh Baccalaureate and AQA's Baccalaureate. Breadth and coherence is achieved, in the case of the IB, through components such as a 'Theory of Knowledge' course that requires students to reflect on the differing ways in which knowledge can be constructed.
6 Like the Curriculum 2000 AS levels, 'legacy' AS levels aimed to enable 'breadth' of study (Hodgson and Spours, 2003, p. 82); however, unlike post-2000 AS qualifications, they were examined at the same standard as A levels rather than at a level intermediate between GCSE (General Certificate of Secondary Education) and GCE (General Certificate of Education).
7 A flavour of the criticisms that these changes responded to is given by the following passage from the Higginson Report: 'Some students who set out on A Level courses

do not complete them, and, on average, about a third who take the examination in any subject do not receive an A Level pass grade in that subject' (cited in Lang, 1990, p. 45).

8 There are exceptions to this picture, of course, as is apparent from the fact that the 'personal study' (or 'project element') of Advanced Level has a very long history, dating back to 1966 (Fines, 1984, p. 32).

9 ETHOS built on the foundations laid by AEB 673 (Fines and Nichol, 1994).

10 Thus, for example, the London Syllabus E and more conventional syllabuses were merged into one new Edexcel specification. Earlier government policy changes, in 1993, led the AEB to abandon plans for rolling out ETHOS to all schools (Fines and Nichol, 1994, p. 142).

11 Although the definition of exam topics at Advanced Level became more detailed in the 1980s (Fines, 1984, pp. 12–14) there was still a considerable 'lottery' element to examination (Lang, 1990, pp. 50–1) prior to Curriculum 2000.

12 Curriculum 2000 constraints on exam boards offering more than one specification have also been relaxed and OCR's 'Specification B' represents a revival of innovative conceptual approaches developed in the 1990s (OCR, 2008).

13 The data presented in Figures 4.1–3 were provided by the Office of the Examinations and Qualifications Regulator (Ofqual) (Fisher, 2010).

14 Anecdotal evidence suggests that AS has been successful in engaging students who might previously, for example, have focused entirely on science and maths under the legacy A level in history at AS as a 'broadening' subject.

15 Psychology and law, for example, both grew more rapidly at A2 in the new millennium than history, the former growing by 69 per cent and the latter by 64 per cent between 2001 and 2008 (CCS, n.d.(b), p. 10).

16 An uplift in statistics tells us many things and not least that a culture focused on achieving statistical uplift has arisen: a key question to ask in such a context is always 'at what opportunity cost?' (Power, 1999).

17 Textbooks that exemplify these approaches include the Schools History Project's series of textbooks for AS and A2 – for example, Hite and Hinton (1998) and Mervyn (2001). Teaching strategies that develop rigour and engagement at AS and A2 are frequently exemplified in *Teaching History* (for example, Fordham, 2007) and elsewhere (Cooper and Chapman, 2009; Hibbert, 2009). Laffin (2009) is exemplary in developing active learning, eneagagement and rigour.

18 Textbooks whose titles begin with exam boards rather than their historical topics are legion. It would be invidious to cite examples.

19 Since 2008, marks awarded for coursework have been limited at 20 per cent of AS/A2, whereas it was possible, before 2001, to gain 50 per cent (and in the case of ETHOS 60 per cent) of A-level marks through coursework and personal study. These changes were driven by systemic, rather than history-specific, concerns about the validity of assessment.

20 The subject criteria for history require students to study 'a minimum of 25 per cent . . . of British history and/or the history of England, Scotland, Ireland or Wales' and 'change and/or development over a period of . . . at least 100 years' (QCA, 2006, p. 4).

21 See Alkis (2005) and Benjamin (2005) for student perspectives on these issues.

22 Complaints about "restrictive' syllabuses and 'hackneyed' questions' (Hill, 1972, p. 191) are, one suspects, as old as the concept of examination.

23 The understanding that progressing pupil learning entails scaffolding the development of metahistorical or second-order conceptual understandings is reflected in an explicit focus in specifications on conceptual learning across the range of post-16 qualifications (QCA, 2006, pp. 5–7; IBO, 2008, pp. 8–9; CIE, n.d., pp. 5–6) with the exception of the projected Humanities Diploma which appears weak in its articulation of disciplinary concepts (see, for example, CCS, n.d.(a), pp. 65–66).

24 Corfield (2009) indicates the scope that history can have and arguably needs to have.
25 Laffin (2009) is exemplary in this and other respects.

References

Alkis, C. (2005) 'A student's perspective'. Paper given at the Institute of Historical Research's conference History in Schools and Higher Education: Issues of Common Concern, 29 September 2005. Available online at: http://www.history.ac.uk/education/sept/alkis.html (accessed 24 May 2009).

Benjamin, T. (2005) 'Perceptions from a student in higher education'. Paper given at the Institute of Historical Research's conference History in Schools and Higher Education: Issues of Common Concern, 29 September 2005. Available online at: http://www.history.ac.uk/education/sept/benjamin.html (accessed 24 May 2009).

Booth, A. (2005) 'Worlds in collision: university tutor and student perspectives on the transition to degree level history', *Teaching History*, 121: 14–19.

Burston, W. H. (ed.) (1957) *Sixth Form History Teaching*. London: Historical Association.

Chapman, A. (2003) 'Camels, diamonds and counterfactuals: a model for developing causal reasoning', *Teaching History*, 112: 46–53.

Chapman, A. and Facey, J. (2004) 'Placing history: territory, story, identity – and historical consciousness', *Teaching History*, 116: 36–41.

Cooper, H. and Chapman, A. (2009) *Constructing History 11–19*. London: Sage.

Corfield, P. (2009) 'Teaching history's big pictures: including continuity as well as change', *Teaching History*, 136: 53–9.

Creative and Cultural Skills (CCS) (n.d. (a)) *Line of Learning Statement for the Diploma in Humanities and Social Sciences*. London: Creative and Cultural Skills. Available online at: http://www.humanitiesdiploma.co.uk/line-learning-statement-0 (accessed 7 March 2010).

——(n.d. (b)) *Market View for the Diploma in Humanities and Social Sciences*. London: Creative and Cultural Skills. Available online at: http://www.humanitiesdiploma.co.uk/line-learning-statement-0 (accessed 7 March 2010).

Department for Education and Science (DfES) (1985) *History in The Primary and Secondary Years*. London: Her Majesty's Stationery Office.

Edexcel (2010) *Specification GCE HISTORY: Edexcel Advanced Subsidiary GCE in History (8HI01); Edexcel Advanced GCE in History (9HI01) First examination 2010. Issue 2*. London: Edexcel. Available online at: http://www.edexcel.com/migrationdocuments/GCE%20New%20GCE/UA024847%20GCE%20in%20History%20Iss%202%20210510.pdf (accessed 28 October 2010).

Fines, J. (1984) *A Survey of A Level History*. London: Historical Association.

Fines, J. and Nichol, J. (1994) *Doing History 16–19: A Case Study in Curriculum Innovation and Change*. London: Historical Association.

Fisher, A. (2010) Email communication with the author, 15 February 2010.

Fordham, M. (2007) 'Slaying dragons and sorcerers in Year 12: in search of historical argument', *Teaching History*, 129: 31–8.

Freeman, J. (2005) 'The current state of the 4–19 history curriculum in England and possible future developments: a qualifications and curriculum agency perspective', *International Journal of Historical Learning, Teaching and Research*, 5(2). Available online at: http://centres.exeter.ac.uk/historyresource/journal10/papers/freeman.doc (accessed 8 March 2010).

Hibbert, B. (2006) *The Articulation of the Study of History at General Certificate of Education Advanced Level with the Study of History for an Honours Degree*. PhD thesis, Leeds: University of Leeds. Available online at: http://www.tactic-solutions.com/phd/bhibbert.htm (accessed 21 May 2009).

——(2009) 'Supporting sixth formers in their historical learning: developing the skills students need for transition to university'. Available online at: http://www.uk.sagepub.com/upm-data/29468_51_Supporting_Sixth_Formers.pdf (accessed 12 March 2010).

Hill, C. P. (1972) 'History in the sixth form', in W. H. Burston, C. W. Green (eds) *Handbook for History Teachers*. London: Methuen.

Historical Association (2005) *History 14–19: Report and Recommendations to the Secretary of State*. London: Historical Association.

——(2009) *Findings from the Historical Association Survey of Secondary History Teachers*. *London: Historical Association*. Available online at: http://www.history.org.uk/resources/secondary_news_415.html (accessed 12 March 2010).

Hite, J. and Hinton, C. (1998) *Fascist Italy*. London: Hodder Education.

Hodgson, A. and Spours, K. (2003) *Beyond A Levels: Curriculum 2000 and the Reform of 14–19 Qualifications*. London and Sterling, VA: Kogan Page.

Husbands, C. (2001) 'What's happening in history? Trends in GCSE and 'A'-level examinations, 1993–2000', *Teaching History*, 103: 37–41.

International Baccalaureate Organisation (IBO) (2008) *Diploma Programme: History Guide*. Cardiff: International Baccalaureate Organisation.

Jenkins, K., Morgan, S. and Munslow, A. (eds) (2007) *Manifestos for History*. London and New York: Routledge.

Laffin, D. (2009) *Better Lessons in A Level History*. London: Hodder Education.

Lang, S. (1990) *A Level History: The Case for Change*. London: Historical Association.

Lavender, L. (2009) *History in Schools – Present and Future. Event Report for the One-Day Conference Hosted at the IHR on 28th February 2009*. Available online at: http://www.heacademy.ac.uk/assets/hca/documents/events/History_in_Schools_report.pdf (accessed 19 March 2010).

Laver, J. (1991) 'Coursework at A level', in J. Fines (ed.) *History 16–19: The Old and The New*. London: Historical Association.

Lewin, J. (1991) 'A and AS level: present state of play', in J. Fines (ed.) *History 16–19: The Old and The New*. London: Historical Association.

Mantin, P. (1991) 'Some thoughts on teaching the A level personal study', in J. Fines (ed.) *History 16–19: The Old and The New*. London: Historical Association.

Mervyn, B. (2001) *The Reign of Elizabeth: England 1558–1603*. London: Hodder Education.

Ministry of Education (1952) *Teaching History*. London: Her Majesty's Stationery Office.

Nicholls, D. (2007) 'Building a better past: plans to reform the curriculum', *Teaching History*, 128: 60–6.

Nuffield Review of 14–19 Education and Training, England and Wales (Nuffield) (2009) *Education for All: The Future of Education and Training for 14–19 Year Olds. Summary, Implications and Recommendations*. Available online at: http://www.nuffield14-19review.org.uk/files/documents206-1.pdf (accessed 12 March 2010).

Office for Standards in Education (Ofsted) (2007) *History in the Balance: History in English Schools 2003–07*. Available online at: http://www.ofsted.gov.uk/Ofsted-home/Publications-and-research/Browse-all-by/Education/Curriculum/History/Primary/History-in-the-balance (accessed 14 August 2009).

Oxford Cambridge and RSA Examinations (OCR) (2008) *AS/A2 Level GCE, GCE HISTORY B Specification, Version 2, February 2008.* Available online at: http://www.ocr.org.uk/download/kd/ocr_9584_kd_gce_spec.pdf (accessed 28 October 2010).

Phillips, G. and Pound, T. (2003) *The Baccalaureate: A Model for Curriculum Reform.* London and Sterling, VA: Kogan Page.

Power, M. (1999) *The Audit Society: Rituals of Verification.* Oxford: Oxford University Press.

Qualifications and Curriculum Authority (QCA) (2006) *GCE AS and A Level Subject Criteria for History.* Available online at: http://www.ofqual.gov.uk/files/qca-06-2854_history.pdf (accessed 28 October 2010).

Roberts, M. (2003) 'AS and A2 history', in M, Riley and R, Harris. (eds) (2003) *Past Forward: A Vision for School History 2002–2012.* London: Historical Association, pp. 20–4.

Tillbrook, M. (2002) 'Content restricted and maturation retarded? Problems with the post-16 history curriculum', *Teaching History*, 109: 24–6.

Tosh, J. (2008) *Why History Maters.* Houndmills: Palgrave Macmillan.

University of Cambridge International Examinations (CIE) (n.d.) *Cambridge Pre-U.* Available online at: http://www.cie.org.uk/qualifications/academic/uppersec/preu (accessed 12 March 2010).

Wertsch, J. V. (2002) *Voices of Collective Remembering.* Cambridge: Cambridge University Press.

Section 2

Debating procedural concepts and history

Chapter 5

History education and historical literacy

Peter Lee

Introduction

An unfortunate division has developed in history education between a 'craft knowledge' approach, on the one hand, and reflection on the nature of history education, on the other. Reflection on history education without craft knowledge is likely to condemn itself to impotence, but craft knowledge without reflection on the nature of history education ends in miscarriage.

While classroom activities really do matter, they can be futile unless they fit into a clear conception of what a history education ought to be, which in turn rests on reflexive knowledge of the nature of history, and on empirical evidence about learning. It is time to construct a conception of historical literacy, nesting in the wider idea of historical consciousness.[1]

What is at stake in a history education?

History in England is being squeezed in three ways. It is losing its place in actual school curricula. It is being sold short in the current educational culture. Worse still, it is losing its own sense of purpose.

There is no space here to document the first claim, so readers might care to test it against their own experience of two-year Key Stage 3 courses, the revival of 'humanities' and cuts in timetables.[2]

The second claim refers to ignorance among some senior management teams about history, encouraged by initiatives that seek to replace school 'subjects' with generic 'skills'. Again, this cannot be pursued here, but two points must be briefly mentioned. First, assertions that history can be useful only if it provides information about the recent past rest on questionable assumptions about both history and learning. Second, while some school 'subjects' may be more or less arbitrary divisions of knowledge, not all are. Even leaving aside philosophical and historical arguments for treating disciplines seriously, empirical research over more than 30 years suggests that if students' knowledge is not to be inert and tied to the circumstances in which it was learned, specific disciplinary concepts must be grasped (Bransford, *et al.*, 1999; Boix-Mansilla, 2005).

The claim that history is losing its sense of purpose relates to two phenomena, fear and a need to be loved, which together are reminiscent of hostage behaviour.

First, there is the fear of having to argue for serious history, manifested in the desperate quest for 'fun' through 'activities' that have lost contact with thinking about aims (beyond 'interest' or 'fun' itself). Second, the need to be loved is displayed in 'me-too' responses to educational initiatives, which encourage heads and politicians to believe that arguments for history are weak, relying on its ability to help out with, for example, literacy and citizenship. History is important in its own right, as a way of seeing the world, not just for helping students to write, nor even for useful hints about proximate causes, and certainly not as fodder for politicians' (rival) conceptions of what it might mean to be a good citizen. History is the most sophisticated and rational way so far available of handling our experience of the fourth dimension.

A disastrous development in the past 30 years is the carelessness with which simple polarities have been allowed to become standard ways of thinking about history education. The most problematic of these is the pair 'skills' and 'knowledge'. Attempts to undermine this have regrettably accepted the terms in which the polarity is couched, and have had little impact. Once we slip into 'skills' language we are in trouble. Skills tend to be operations with agreed goals, learned by repeated practice (e.g. riding bicycles or writing neatly). History requires reflection and judgement, and historical abilities cannot be improved simply by practice. No matter how many 'source work' exercises or 'enquiries' students are set, if they have no grasp of the concept of evidence they will be doing something more akin to finding blemishes on apples in a supermarket in order to reject them, or compiling information in what used to be called 'projects'.

The point of history is to be able to say something valid about the past, often in thinking about the present and future, but not in such a way that our present interests and future desires determine how we organize and understand the past. We need *knowledge* of the past if we are to be able to understand our place in time: to assess the possibilities the past may have opened up or closed down. School history must, therefore, equip students with historical knowledge, but knowledge involves understanding, both of the past and of the basis of knowledge claims about that past. Achieving understanding means learning new concepts. Whereas 'skills' talk allows people to marginalize knowledge and understanding, and encourages some senior management teams to jettison history because other 'subjects' can teach 'analysis' or literacy or IT (information technology) skills, talk of concepts is unintelligible if separated from understanding and knowledge.

Moreover, while skills-talk tempts teachers into grandiose and indefensible claims about turning children into mini-historians, concept-talk encourages less pretentious but more serious ambitions, concerned with children acquiring understanding.

Towards historical literacy

History educators make bold claims about how well history is taught, but a sense of what history education should add up to seems curiously absent. We need a concept of *historical literacy* to enable us to tell others, and perhaps more importantly to remind ourselves, what is central to history education. What are the minimum requirements of historical literacy? As a tentative first approximation we might say that students should acquire the following.

1. An understanding of history as a way of seeing the world. This involves an understanding of the *discipline* of history and the key ideas that make knowledge of the past possible. Students should be helped to acquire a conceptual apparatus enabling them to understand the different kinds of claims made by history, and how these can be tested (including knowledge of how we know, explain and give accounts of the past).

2. A set of dispositions, including:

   a. A disposition to produce the best possible arguments for whatever stories we tell *relative to our questions and presuppositions*, appealing to the *validity* of the stories and the *truth* of singular factual statements. Acquiring respect for evidence is as important as acquiring a concept of historical evidence.

   b. Acceptance that we may be obliged to tell different stories from the ones we would prefer to tell (even to the point of questioning our own presuppositions).

   c. Recognition of the importance of according people in the past the same respect as we would want for ourselves as human beings.

   Together these imply that we should not *plunder* the past to produce convenient stories for present ends.

3. A picture of the past that allows students to orient themselves in time. This involves coherent *substantive* knowledge (sometimes called historical *content*) organized in the form of a *usable* historical past, on different *scales*. It means helping students abandon a view of the present as something separated from the past by a kind of *temporal apartheid*, so that they can locate themselves in time and see the past as both constraining and opening up possibilities for the future.

If students do not acquire knowledge and understanding of this kind, *and* the dispositions that must go with them, there is little to justify asking them to undergo a formal history education.

Awareness of the past and the claims we make about it come in many forms, and in a world where people wield stories about the past to defend themselves or to demand proper recognition of their communities, people are rightly cautious about claiming that any particular kind of story is better than the others. History education, however, is normative and must justify compelling children to study the past at school, rather than simply acquiring whatever is on offer from the family, the street and the media. (Since it is paid for by the state, it cannot fall back on 'fun' or even 'creating an interest': these aims can be met without public outlay in the local park or electronic game shop, not to mention other school subjects.) Characterizing the goal of history education as *historical literacy* may be rash, but it has the important merit of recognizing that students should leave education better able to understand the past than they could otherwise have done. But in what way does it offer something different from, and in important respects better than, other forms of historical consciousness?[3]

A notion of historical literacy implies that what students learn is *history*, not something else. The special character of the discipline of history as a form of historical consciousness is that it is a public form of knowledge, which attempts to meet standards of truth (at least with regard to singular factual statements) and validity (perhaps also truth) in its arguments and stories.[4] The questions we ask about the past are always asked from the present, and because we are human are likely to have practical implications, but it does not follow from this that they must impose an organization on the past that reflects our immediate practical ends, let alone that we can plunder the past for whatever we want to assert. Indeed, historians frequently go to some lengths to ensure that their questions do not simply reflect our present goals and desires; in a public form of knowledge questions, like claims, are judged by fellow historians, and they often arise from perceived defects in existing work, or opportunities created by the research of other practitioners. Individuals may have all sorts of reasons for asking questions and answering them in particular ways, but what they offer is weighed by the wider discipline over time. A discipline like history may be thought of as an organized metacognitive tradition: it insists on its practitioners reflecting on what they say, how they justify it and why.[5]

If this is accepted it should lead us to expect that history is not simply common-sense, and, indeed, we have empirical evidence gathered over several decades, and from several countries, that history is in fact counter-intuitive.[6] It requires understanding concepts that differ from apparently 'similar' everyday ideas. This is because some everyday ideas actually make knowledge of the past impossible.

Many students, for example, believe that we can only really know anything by directly experiencing it. Since the past has gone, history is not feasible. We weren't there so we cannot know what happened. Moreover, since there was only one past, and it happened in the way it did and not some other way, they are convinced that there can only be one true description of the past. We should not be surprised to find such ideas, because they work well enough in everyday life. Children typically learn how to 'tell the truth' by appeal to a fixed past. Mum asks her child, 'Did you break the window?', and the child sees the past as a fixed and known touchstone in terms of which the truth is measured: the choice is to tell the truth or to lie. Because adults and children share conventions on what is relevant to report in such circumstances, this view of a fixed past against which we can measure our assertions is workable in day-to-day affairs. But it fails utterly in history, where different views may exist about what questions to ask, the conventions of relevance may be contested, and what is asserted may not be something that could have been witnessed by anyone.[7]

History is counter-intuitive in other ways. Many students imagine that people in the past thought like us but wore strange clothes and did foolish things. Some are convinced that people in the past were less intelligent than us and perhaps morally inferior (Ashby and Lee, 1987; Barton, 1996). Students tend to assume that sensible behaviour in the past would have been what *we* would now accept as such, so the strange actions and practices of the past are a sign of backwardness, incapacity or idiocy. As Wineburg (2001) put it, history is an unnatural act.

Students left with these ideas untouched by teaching can hardly be said to have begun to understand history. This points to the second, much neglected, component of historical literacy. It is not enough to *know that* history can answer questions about the past, or that people thought differently in the past. To be historically literate, students must have acquired certain dispositions. As suggested above, these include a concern for truth and for valid argument, and respect for people in the past (as human beings just as real as we are). If students leave school without caring whether what they assert about the past is well founded, or asking if alternative accounts are better able to withstand criticism, they have not even begun to understand history. If they show no signs of concern for the grounds of historical knowledge, or of respect for people in the past, they are in a similar position to someone who claims to understand mathematics but pays no heed to the validity or the cogency of a proof. History education must make a difference to students' intellectual behaviour or it is nothing.[8] This is a matter not of indoctrinating students but of helping them understand that asking a serious question about the past implies subscribing to certain values. Teaching for historical literacy means taking seriously students' cognitive and rational ethics. It is unlikely to be an easy task. What kind of cognitive ethics do students subscribe to, implicitly or explicitly? How far and in what ways does teaching influence the development of students' attitudes to truth and validity, or their willingness to accord respect for people in the past? We know little about this area, and it demands the attention of researchers.

The third component of historical literacy is the acquisition of what the *How People Learn* project called deep understanding, which 'transforms factual information into usable knowledge' (Donovan, *et al.*, 1999: 12). This demands access to a range of concepts, in this case substantive concepts concerned with what is commonly called the *content* of history (as well as the second-order organizing or procedural concepts of the discipline).

The substantive concepts students should acquire are harder to specify than the second-order concepts, because they are much more numerous and are chosen according to the content of the history to be studied. Moreover, there are important differences between types of substantive concepts. Some, like *factory* or *peasant* or *democracy*, are helpful over long passages of history, although their meaning shifts with time, which means that students' understanding of them is likely to be closely related to their knowledge of what was going on in any particular historical period. Others, like *The Industrial Revolution, The Enlightenment* or *The Cold War*, are what Walsh (1967) called colligatory concepts, organizing specific phenomena in order to make sense of processes and events within a relatively defined compass. Colligatory concepts are in some respects like historical particulars (hence the definite article). They treat whole passages of the past almost as if they were coherent events, but of course understanding them also depends on understanding concepts like 'industry' and 'war'.[9]

Colligations play a central role in the organization of historical knowledge. They encapsulate historians' ideas about the changes that structure the historical field. Current emphasis on narrative (in both philosophy of history and history education) has allowed the role of colligations to be neglected, at a time when interest in the coherence and power of students' big pictures of the past is at last beginning to receive the attention it demands.[10] An ability to wield appropriate colligatory concepts may play a key role in students' access to usable historical pasts.

Use of the term 'historical *literacy*' begs clarification about how far it involves *writing* as well as *reading* knowledge. It should be plain already that students must understand the nature and status of claims made about the past, and know enough substantive history to follow what historians and others are saying (a reading knowledge). What, then, is a writing knowledge? What it does *not* mean is that students research and write historical works (becoming 'mini-historians').[11] Instead, it should be construed as the ability to actively make sense of the never stationary 'past-and-present', a historical perspective through which the world is interpreted and reinterpreted for what has been and is going on. This active historical consciousness is central to orienting oneself in time; there can be no *apartheid* separating the past from the present and future. Historically literate students know that the past is not 'dead and gone'.

For some purposes it may be appropriate to think of the present as the crest of a wave we are surfing. We are at the leading edge of a past which carries us with it on its face. Despite its faults, this analogy may help us avoid the temptation to assume that we live in an instantaneous present. We think we know about the present because we can directly experience it (or some parts of it, under some descriptions), and so wonder how we can really say anything secure about a past that is 'gone'. But in saner moments we know that this is a highly misleading picture of how things are. We know that 'contemporary' art, or 'politics nowadays', or 'current thinking about capitalism' are nothing to do with an instantaneous present. The 'present' seems to be longer or shorter, depending on what we are thinking of. We also know that we have intentions and policies, follow or try to escape from traditions, and are knowingly or unknowingly part of trends which may be long- or short-term. For all these, an instantaneous present is a nonsense.

The notion of 'temporal scale' is central to students' historical literacy. Students need a framework which enables them to construct a usable 'big picture' of the human past, but they also need more detailed knowledge of passages of the past studied on a finer scale.[12] They must be able to fit the more detailed studies into the big picture, and move back and forth between them. The depth studies test the large-scale picture, and the large-scale picture gives meaning to the depth studies. Relating depth studies to big pictures is not just a matter of fitting information together: students need to see how generalizations that are valid on one scale may break down at another, but that this does not invalidate their use at the larger scale.

Second-order concepts make a key difference. For example, students' assumptions about *change* can make history either unintelligible or useless. Take the reactions of two students, David and Danny, both aged 14, to the question, '*Would history help in deciding how to deal with race relations?*' (They were asked similar questions about politics and economics.)

DANNY: No – Because [. . .] times change and people change. Some races may have fallen out 10 years ago but are now good friends.

DAVID: Yes, definitely – Races are shaped, as are people, by events that occurred in the past. Tragedies would cause grudges between cultures and lead to tension. Being able to understand this, and possibly relate to it in a neutral way would help race relations in Britain.

(Lee, 2004)

For Danny, change means history has no use in thinking about the future, whereas David sees the present as related to the past and the future, making history valuable. There are different concepts of change at stake here. Kate, aged 15, made the same point as Danny: 'History is really useless because if things change as time goes on then there's really no need to learn about the past' (Lee and Howson, 2009: 240).

It might be thought that all Danny and Kate are lacking is content knowledge about how events unfolded, and so do not understand 'the nature of change'. But this is not the problem. Many students construe *changes* as equivalent to *events* or *actions*, usually taking place in a short space of time, and often very localized. Danny sees no use for history because for him change is random and fragmented, whereas David understands change as process-like, and hence can treat the present as the moving face of the past. Kate also recognizes that 'things change', but sees this as cutting off the past from the present and in so doing rendering history useless.

It is clear that second-order, procedural or disciplinary concepts provide an essential conceptual apparatus which students must acquire if they are to understand history. They are neither bolt-ons to historical knowledge nor substitutes for it. They make historical knowledge possible.

Thinking seriously about history education

Whereas in medicine aims tend to be agreed and the criteria of success are relatively straightforward (sometimes life or death), in history education they are up for debate. This is why appeals to 'best practice' are always inadequate, and why it is important in history education to develop a concept of historical literacy that fits into a wider conception of historical consciousness.

It is sometimes said that teaching is best thought of as craft knowledge. Craft knowledge is indeed central to teaching, but in thinking about what the point of an educational activity is, in specifying as clearly as possible the cognitive (or other) goals we hope to help students achieve, and even in thinking how to go about the activity, we need to have access to knowledge that goes beyond our own experience, and which may demand more systematic forms than craft knowledge. If history education is to get beyond recipes or instruction manuals, practices require coherent and well-founded justification. This means looking to disciplines that can elucidate history and learning: some that improve our conceptual clarity and others that provide empirical evidence about our students.

The consequences of setting 'practice' against 'theory' as an excuse for not doing the thinking (or even reading) required can be disastrous. We have seen this in the damaging teaching of *evidence* through notions of *bias*, or treating *reliability* as a fixed attribute of sources. A more recent example is the muddled treatment of *significance*, in which historical significance is assumed to be a fixed property of events, or is equated with human importance, and lists of criteria for the latter are given as if they elucidated the former. Currently, and more seriously, new ideas about 'frameworks' and 'big pictures' are elided with pre-existing notions of 'outlines' or 'overviews'. Howson (2009) rightly castigates such confusions, which completely muddle the very distinctions that offer some chance of learning how to rethink our teaching. Here and elsewhere apparently brilliant classroom activities can actually depress students' understanding if they encourage students to cling to lower-level ideas rather than to face up to the problems such ideas pose.

Teachers who wish to teach students more sophisticated ideas need to be treated as adult readers for whom advice on what to read, rather than sets of acronyms, is appropriate. More is at stake than craft knowledge: we also need reflexive and ordered thinking of the kind sometimes dismissed as 'theoretical'. Otherwise we are condemned forever to listen to the opinions of everyone who can claim 'experience', innocent of the way in which their own wisdom conflicts with that of their neighbour. Where such people are in positions of influence or authority they can do serious damage, muddling ideas which should be distinguished, or asserting as fact statements with no valid empirical support, offering spurious guidance to teachers. Maybe even something a little like the National Curriculum.

Further reading

Teachers wishing to go beyond recipes and think for themselves will want to sharpen their grasp of key historical concepts and acquaint themselves with research on students' ideas about history. The works in the References have been chosen to be helpful in this. For those wanting to go further a useful recent conceptual analysis is A. Megill (2007) *Historical Knowledge, Historical Error*, Chicago: University of Chicago Press.

Notes

1 My thinking about history education over many years has been inspired by historians and philosophers who have examined the presuppositions of history, and by psychologists who have uncovered the centrality of our presuppositions in learning. I owe a particular debt to R. G. Collingwood, whose work is at last receiving the serious attention it merits. Jörn Rüsen (1993) provides an impressive exegesis of historical consciousness, finding in it an important place for the discipline of history.

2 This was predictable several years ago, even if some commentators wanted to deny it. See Lee and Ashby (1999), and Riley's (2000) denial.

3 'Literacy' rather than 'consciousness' is used here to emphasize that, partly because it is normative, history education is narrower in scope than historical consciousness.

4 Lorenz (1994) argues that the temptation to deny that we can talk about the truth of historical narratives derives from residual positivism privileging claims for the truth of singular factual statements. We overdo the difference between narratives and singular factual statements because we fail to recognize that 'facts are small theories and true theories are big facts' p. 317 and *passim*.

5 This metacognition is internal to history, and not the same as philosophical reflection, to which historians are notoriously (if unjustifiably and unwisely) averse.

6 For a summary, see Lee (2005); for recent examples, see Dickinson *et al.* (2001), Ashby *et al.* (2005).

7 Changes in beliefs, birth rates or the business environment could not be directly witnessed like births or battles even if we were able to employ a time machine to go back and look. These things are inferred, not inspected.

8 'Intellectual' does not imply anything elitist unless we imagine that learning to think is elitist. Nor does it suggest impractical goals, since thinking historically is not an 'all-or-nothing' achievement. If it were, there would be little point in teaching it (or, by the same token, maths and science).

9 This does not mean that historical particulars in general (or individuals) can be treated as concepts. It is a mistake to assert that Napoleon or Henry VIII are historical concepts.

10 Philosophy of history became obsessed with natural science as a model for explanation in the 1950s and 1960s, and then shifted to literary theory for a model of narrative. Both these obsessions provided useful insights, but in the end they allowed philosophers to avoid having to get to grips with history. Much postmodern discussion of history is still stuck in this rut.

11 The reason for drawing back from characterizing school history as creating 'mini-historians' is not to privilege the views of individual professional historians over everyone else, but to recognize that they are embedded in a public form of knowledge. The historical past shares with other forms of so-called 'collective memory' the characteristic of being a collective construction, not just the production of individual historians. But it is unlike the others in its institutionalized metacognitive traditions which set standards – long-lived but not unchanging – that continuously subject it to critique. The past as constructed in history is never simply an individual story belonging to a particular person, or the sum of stories 'owned' by this or that social group. No one owns it, or could possibly own it, and summing everyone's personal stories does not make history.

12 See Shemilt and Howson in this book (Chapter 6), Lee (2004) and Shemilt (2009).

References

Ashby, R. and Lee, P. J. (1987) 'Children's concepts of empathy and understanding in history', in C. Portal (ed.) *The History Curriculum for Teachers*. Lewes: Falmer Press.

Ashby, R., Gordon, P. and Lee, P. J. (eds) (2005) *Understanding History: Recent Research in History Education (International Review of History Education, Vol. 4)*. London: RoutledgeFalmer.

Barton, K. C. (1996) 'Narrative simplifications in elementary students' historical thinking', in J. Brophy (ed.) *Advances in Research on Teaching Vol. 6: Teaching and Learning History*. Greenwich: JAI Press.

Boix-Mansilla, V. (2005) 'Between reproducing and organizing the past: students' beliefs about the standards of acceptability of historical knowledge', in R. Ashby, P. Gordon and P. J. Lee (eds) *Understanding History: Recent Research in History Education (International Review of History Education, Vol. 4)*. London: RoutledgeFalmer.

Bransford, J. D., Brown, A. L. and Cocking, R. R. (eds) (1999) *How People Learn: Brain, Mind, Experience and School*. Washington DC: National Academy Press.

Dickinson, A. K., Gordon, P. and Lee, P. J. (eds) (2001) *Raising Standards in History Education (International Review of History Education, Vol. 3)*. London: Woburn Press.

Donovan, M. S., Bransford J. D., and Pellegrino J. W. (eds) (1999) *How People Learn: Bridging Research and Practice*. Washington DC: National Academy Press.

Howson, J. (2009) 'Potential and pitfalls in teaching big pictures of the past', *Teaching History*, 136: 24–33.

Lee, P. J. (2004) '"Walking backwards into tomorrow": historical consciousness and understanding history', *International Journal of History Learning, Teaching and Research*, 4, 1. Available online at: http://centres.exeter.ac.uk/historyresource/journal7/7contents.htm (accessed 9 January 2010).

——(2005) 'Putting principles into practice: understanding history', in M. S. Donovan and J. D. Bransford (eds) *How Students Learn: History in the Classroom*. Washington DC: National Academy Press.

Lee, P. J. and Ashby, R. (1999) 'How long before we need the US Cavalry? The Pittsburgh conference on "teaching, knowing and learning"', *Teaching History*. 97: 13–15.

Lee, P. J. and Howson, J. (2009) '"Two out of five did not know that Henry VIII had six wives": history education, historical literacy and historical consciousness', in L. Symcox and A. Wilschut (eds) *National History Standards: The Problem of the Canon and the Future of Teaching History (International Review of History Education Vol. 5)*. Charlotte: Information Age Publishing.

Lorenz, C. (1994) 'Historical knowledge and historical reality: a plea for "internal realism"' *History and Theory*, 33(3): 297–327.

Riley, M. (February, 2000) 'Cavalry can stay at home', *Teaching History*, 98: 3.

Rüsen, J. (1993) *Studies in Metahistory*. Pretoria: Human Sciences Research Council.

Shemilt, D. (2000) 'The caliph's coin', in P. Seixas, P. Stearns and S. Wineburg (eds), *Teaching, Learning and Knowing History*. New York: New York University Press.

——(2009) 'Drinking an ocean and pissing a cupful', in L. Symcox and A. Wilschut (eds) *National History Standards: The Problem of the Canon and the Future of Teaching History (International Review of History Education Vol. 5)*. Charlotte: Information Age Publishing.

Walsh, W. H. (1967) *An Introduction to Philosophy of History*. London: Hutchinson.

Wineburg, S. S. (2001) *Historical Thinking and Other Unnatural Acts*. Philadelphia: Temple University Press.

Chapter 6

Frameworks of knowledge
Dilemmas and debates

Jonathan Howson and Denis Shemilt

Introduction

At best, references to 'frameworks of knowledge' are confused. At worst, the 'framework' label attaches to a diverse set of instruments, practices and ideas exhibiting tenuous family resemblances.[1] This chapter attempts to uproot usages for which more venerable terms should be preferred and to evaluate the utility of whatever survives semantic weeding.

Definitions and distinctions

A catalogue of 'frameworks' so-called in print and popular usage would overflow the boundaries of this chapter. It is, therefore, proposed to offer a stipulative definition that holds for most of the 'frameworks' used in schools or cited in scholarly papers and research reports.

A framework of knowledge

1. Serves to assist teaching and/or to facilitate learning about the past without representing the ultimate shape or substance of the learning intended.
2. Enables the contextualization, organization and evaluation of historical data with reference to high-level and chronologically ordered generalizations about 'what life was like' and/or 'how things were done' at different points in time.

This definition distinguishes 'frameworks' from 'summaries', 'outlines' and 'pictures of the past'. The latter are *objects* of learning, intended or actual, whereas 'frameworks' are *instruments* used by teachers and students to accelerate learning. In short, 'frameworks' are provisional factual scaffolds as adaptive to student constructions of the past as to teacher intentions for the demolition, reconstruction or extension thereof.

Semantic boundaries between 'frameworks', 'grids' and 'timelines' are more permeable. While all three instruments are used to facilitate learning, 'grids' serve to juxtapose and 'timelines' to sequence information; only 'frameworks' enable teachers and students to contextualize, organize and evaluate data against broad generalizations about human activity and experience.

Lacking a chronological dimension, 'grids' typically juxtapose information about states of affairs, processes or characteristics pertinent to different places, institutions or social groups. For example, the domestic and foreign policies, political ideologies and social systems of pre-war Italy, Spain and Germany may be represented in grid form for comparative purposes or to pre-empt confusion between them. 'Timelines', whether single or multi-stranded, sequence headline events, people or artefacts in time. In contrast, 'frameworks' enable students to organize material as instantiations of or exceptions to high-level generalizations. More sophisticated 'frameworks' may also require students to test and modify supplied generalizations or to produce new ones, i.e. to change the content or structure of the framework itself. Of course, these ideal-type distinctions don't always hold for real-life instruments and practices. Of necessity, teachers hybridize 'frameworks', 'grids' and 'timelines' to fulfil particular pedagogic purposes and meet group-specific learning needs.

Since exemplification of the pure and hybrid frameworks in print and popular usage is beyond the resources and remit of this chapter, 'framework' diversity will be analysed against five dimensions of difference (see Figure 6.1).

These include:

1. Organization of taught content

| Advance mapping and post hoc synthesis of data | Advance or post hoc linkage of blocks of data | Transformation, and evaluation of data |

2. Morphology and duration of use

| Fixed frameworks used over lesson – unit of work time spans | Aggregative frameworks used over unit of work – scheme of work spans | Progressive frameworks used over scheme of work – curriculum spans |

3. Temporal scale

| Intra-period time scales | Cross-period time scales | Species time scale |

4. Spatial scale

| From hamlets to nation states and overland empires | Overseas empires, trading networks, continents and 'civilizations' | Whole world (or representative elements thereof) |

5. Human scale

| Roles, groups, actions and artefacts (e.g. adolescents and/or music) | 'Peoples' and areas of experience (e.g. Polynesians and/or 'culture and praxis')* | Humankind and the totality of experience |

*   As used here 'praxis' refers to the unseen and unacknowledged elements of culture immanent in patterns of collective behaviour.

Figure 6.1 Five dimensions of difference.

Table 6.1 Framework grid for 'Magna Carta' unit of work

	WHAT'S THE STORY? What happened before and after Magna Carta?	CRIME AND PUNISHMENT What did Magna Carta have to do with getting a fair trial?	WHO'S THE BOSS? What did Magna Carta have to do with running the country?
Before Magna Carta: Anglo-Saxons to 1066			
Before Magna Carta: 1066–1215			
After Magna Carta: 1215–1500			
After Magna Carta: 1500–1837			
After Magna Carta: 1837–now			

The five dimensions chart shifts in framework use and purposes, from the traditional in the left-hand column, the adventurous and experimental in the centre column through to the speculative in the right-hand column. A good instance of transition from traditional (left column) to experimental (centre column) usage is offered by Rogers (2008) (see Table 6.1).

Rogers offers two parallel instruments: a planning framework containing high-level developmental generalizations and the empty framework for student use reproduced above.[2] Making a tacit distinction between format and use, Rogers refers to 'framework grids'. The 'framework grid' format is noteworthy in three respects: the use of key questions as headings for developmental generalizations, the distinction between topic-centred and thematic headings, and reservation of a chronological band for the Magna Carta 'back-story'. As these features suggest, Rogers' framework practices are even more radical than the instruments themselves.

Before introducing Year 7 students to their version of the 'framework grid', Rogers locates the story of Magna Carta within the context of King John's reign. He then presents a paradox: Magna Carta was repudiated by John, the rebellious barons and the Church within weeks of being signed and yet is one of the more important documents in British history. And even though America wouldn't be discovered by Europeans for more than 250 years, Magna Carta is arguably one of the more important documents in American history. How can something be more important centuries *after* it was signed than *when* it was signed? The paradox is sharpened when students are told that to answer this question they must know what happened hundreds of years *before* Magna Carta was written. Rogers then teaches the long back-story and after-story of Magna Carta from the eighth to the twenty-first centuries. Students consolidate their knowledge by completing the first column of cells in the 'framework grid'. In subsequent lessons the role of Magna Carta in the histories of judicial and executive government are explored and consolidated by means of framework entries. Students' own grid entries are then used to address problems of change and continuity, causation and development, to link generalizations in and through time and to extrapolate possible futures.[3]

Rogers' framework practice is *spatially* limited to a single kingdom (albeit with some reference to the USA and UN Universal Declaration of Human Rights), and its *human scale* focuses on a single artefact, the Magna Carta. His approach is, however, experimental with respect to a *temporal scale* that crosses periods, extends back in time, connects with the present and emphasizes that the history of Magna Carta ends not in the here and now but extends into the future. More radical still, the 'framework' is built up, in students' heads as well as on paper, over the entire unit of work and, in the last two lessons, serves as an object for whole-class teaching wherein blocks of period-specific data are fused into cognate lines of development and used to answer questions about how and why things happen in human affairs. In sum, Rogers' framework practice is both adventurous and ambitious: frameworks are used as means to new as well as to old ends.

As previously noted, *dimensions of difference* extend into the realm of proposed, but yet to be implemented, frameworks.[4] The most obvious feature of these speculative ventures is their scale: whole-world history from the dawn of biologically modern humans and all, or nearly all, aspects of action and experience. Shemilt (2009) has proposed the use of four *starter frameworks* pertaining to 'growth and movement

Table 6.2 Starter framework for 'Modes of Production' curriculum dimension

YEARS AGO	HOW DO YOU SPEND YOUR TIME?	WHAT DO YOU EAT?	HOW LONG DO YOU LIVE?
60,000	FORAGER: you look for roots and berries, small animals, shellfish, snails and grubs. This takes most of your time.	Whatever you can find that you can digest. Often you eat very little.	You may be killed at birth. If not, you are likely to die before 5 years of age and are unlikely to live past 30.
15,000	HUNTER-GATHERER: if female, you still look for roots and grubs. If male, you hunt big game in a group of 50–100 people. You all follow the big animals as they move around. This takes a few hours per day: you have lots of leisure time.	When lucky you eat meat. When times are hard, it's back to roots and snails. When unlucky, you starve or eat other people.	You're a bit more likely to get to 30. If sick or injured you're likely to be left behind to starve or be eaten.
7,000	FARMER: you herd animals and protect them; sow, weed and gather crops; bake bread; make porridge and weak beer. A *few* of you with specialist knowledge and skills make baskets, pottery and cloth. This takes nearly all your time: you have little leisure.	When lucky you eat meat and drink milk. Every day you eat bread, beans and porridge. You store food to get you through hard times.	More, but not many, of you live to 30 or 40. You may recover from injuries and sickness but are more likely to get sick or be killed in warfare or in house fires.

(continued)

YEARS AGO	HOW DO YOU SPEND YOUR TIME?	WHAT DO YOU EAT?	HOW LONG DO YOU LIVE?
150	INDUSTRIAL WORKER: you go to work in a factory or a mine (women and men, boys and girls). You make bricks, machines, clothes and other things we still have today. You have a few hours a week for leisure and a few days a year at the seaside. There are still lots of farmers *but* you're more likely to work in a factory than on the land.	*You eat meat, bread, fresh vegetables and fruit. You drink tea and eat a few things brought from other countries. As long as you can work and earn money you can always buy food and beer.*	*Most of you will live into your forties but disease is a big killer, especially of children under 5. If you get old or infirm and have no family willing or able to look after you, you're unlikely to live long.*
NOW	SERVICE WORKER: you go to work in a shop, office or restaurant. You teach, nurse, wait on tables, write, solve difficult sums or use computers. A few of you even get paid for telling jokes or playing sport. There are still lots of farmers who grow food and industrial workers who make everything from electricity to paper cups, but you're more likely to work in an office than on the land or in a factory. You have so much leisure you're often bored.	*You eat junk food and fun food which you buy from a take-away or heat up from frozen. You also eat (and drink) far too much. You rarely feel hungry and are more likely to be overweight than starving.*	*Most of you can expect to live past 70 or 80 . . . unless something goes wrong! We get almost all our food from overseas AND world population is growing fast. SO WHAT COULD GO WRONG? Will there be enough roots and grubs if we need them?*

of peoples', 'modes of production', 'socio-political organization' and 'culture and praxis'. A slightly modified *starter framework* for 'modes of production' is reproduced in Table 6.2.

This framework illustrates what might be in a teacher's head when planning to teach Year 7 and requires simplification or elaboration to match student characteristics and prior attainment. An introductory lesson preparatory to framework teaching would address key questions like, 'Had you been born 60,000 years ago, you would have been outside on your hands and knees grubbing for roots and snails to eat. Why aren't you doing that now? How did we get from grubbing for roots and snails to buying coke and crisps from a talking machine?'[5] Framework content may be taught within a single lesson and reinforced over two or three lessons by means of role play, simulations and written tasks. For future use, students then insert their own generalizations into an empty framework similar to that devised by Rogers. For less literate students a triple storyboard format may replace the text-based example.

Similarities with Rogers' 'framework grid' include use of descriptive and evaluative key questions as column headings. The text- or cartoon-based generalizations students enter into framework cells have the potential to link both horizontally and vertically, and may be seen as *moving pictures* of life through, not just in, the past. Differences from Rogers' 'framework grid' and practice include:

a)   Use of the framework to pose questions which, when answered by in-depth or thematic study, inform evaluation and modification of the framework structure as well as content. Questions pertaining to the transition from hunter-gathering to farming lifestyles may, for example, focus on human motivation, '*Why did big-game hunters choose to sacrifice leisure time and become farmers?*'; on gaps in information, '*When and why did people start living in cities?*'; and on information that begs important questions, '*Why did farmers but not hunters make cloth and pottery?*' Answers to such questions lead to modification and elaboration of framework structures by shifting the placement and increasing the number of temporal divisions, and by changing and augmenting key-question columns. Cycles of *framework analysis and evaluation ⇒ depth or thematic study ⇒ framework modification and elaboration ⇒ framework analysis and evaluation* continue for the duration of the history curriculum. Unlike Rogers' 'framework grid', which facilitates the production and linkage of generalizations, that above constitutes a generalization in and of itself, a generalization that mutates as student learning progresses – it is a *transformative framework*.

b)   The framework is not unit-specific but evolves across units and schemes of work, 11–14, 11–16 and ideally 11–19. The *starter framework* concerning 'Modes of Production' illustrated above is used to initiate a long-term and cyclical process of structural and substantive modification governed by student learning. Framework processes are both *emergent* and *progressive*, i.e. teachers might continue to engineer progression in the quality of learning outcomes, but must also work with whatever generalizations and judgements students make about the past.

c)   Rogers' 'framework grid' serves as connective tissue linking a Key Stage 3 topic to a more distant past and to the present. In the speculative *modes of production* framework this relationship is reversed: the whole of human history takes centre stage and a succession of thematic and in-depth topics play supporting roles. The name of the game becomes the study, progression and transformation of *starter* and *emergent frameworks* until students possess *pictures of the past* as big and sophisticated as time permits and pedagogical ingenuity contrives. Frameworks thus conceived differ from the instruments and processes used to contextualize and connect topic-sized segments of the past.

It must be emphasized that Rogers' use of framework instruments and processes remains the most radical to have been externally evaluated. Speculative frameworks designed for use over units and schemes of work are only of interest in so far as they suggest where history education could and maybe should be heading.

Debates about frameworks

Fifteen years ago 'frameworks' would not have merited a chapter in this volume. So why have they attained a modicum of celebrity? And why, for such a recent arrival at the history education disco, do they look and behave so variously? A single answer may be given to both questions: 'frameworks' have been offered as partial solutions to a range of problems and anxieties with respect to gaps and distortions in students' knowledge of our island story; to the seeming inability of most students to turn disconnected facts and stories into joined-up narratives of national glory, human rights or anything else; and to the questionable relevance of parochial history education agendas to future citizens of a world dependent on globalized economic and financial systems, threatened by common problems of climate change, resource depletion, population growth and mass migration, and looking for solutions to international treaties, accords and agencies.[6] It follows that 'framework' instruments and processes are diverse because they are optimized to address one or other of these issues. And because most issues relate to the aims and purposes of history education, debates about frameworks quickly reduce to matters philosophical or political. For instance, variations in the temporal, spatial and human scales of frameworks follow from debates not just about the balance of content coverage – recent versus distant, social versus economic, national versus world – but also about the desirability of teaching *lessons from history* versus the *lessons of history*, of teaching identity-shaping yarns and cautionary tales potentially applicable to possible futures versus teaching where humankind has been, by what means it has arrived at its present position and where, by choice or compulsion, it might go from here.[7] This and other debates are not particular to discussions about frameworks; they are common to most other chapters in this volume and, in consequence, extend beyond the bailiwick of this one.

Some debates, technical as well as philosophical, are particular to decisions about framework processes and formats. These are fuelled by gaps in our knowledge about optimal ways of enabling students to construct and use 'bigger pictures' of the past and, as might be expected, are most acute for large-scale frameworks with progressive structures and transformative outcomes. Three such debates are summarized below.

Joined-up history or grand narratives by stealth?

Grand narratives, however skeletal, are implicit in framework instruments and practices intended to enable 'bigger-picture' formation. Selection of one rather than another framework may impact on the substance as well as the quality of 'bigger-picture' outcomes. That students also learn iconic stories – about a murder in a cathedral, the disappearance of princes from a tower and so on – from framework-free teaching is neither here nor there; such stories are unlikely to form minds and attitudes unless connected to the present as constituents of greater and more significant narratives. The pointlessness of disconnected tales ripped from the past entails a collateral harmlessness; in contrast, joined-up accounts of the human past have greater potential for both good and evil.

This debate may move forward in one or both of two ways. First, it is necessary to determine whether, for reasons advanced by some postmodernist theorists, objection is taken to the learning of any and every 'grand narrative', or whether only narratives directly or indirectly imposed on students are proscribed. In the case of the former, the debate raises issues about the nature and logic of history too profound to be addressed here. If debate focuses on the extent to which 'grand narratives' emergent from framework-based teaching can and should be autonomously developed and wholly owned by individual students, technical as well as philosophical problems present. The latter pertain to the balance of risks and benefits attaching to students entering adult life with a chaotic collage of past facts and stories pasted onto consciousness as opposed to a grand narrative, or 'bigger picture', stealthily shaped by framework-based teaching. Risk-benefit calculations are contingent, first, on the degree to which 'bigger-picture' outcomes are moulded by frameworks and autonomous learning compromised; and second, on the certainty and quality of learning gains offered by framework-based teaching. These are empirical questions to which, as yet, we lack the technical means to offer satisfactory answers.

The diversity of 'bigger pictures' formed by students exposed to framework techniques is consistent with a high degree of autonomy in picture formation, but the parameters and extent of 'framework shaping' are impossible to define and quantify without comparative studies involving large student numbers (see Blow *et al.* 2008). Nor can learning gains from implementation of framework techniques be guaranteed. Small-scale experiments with 11- to 17-year-old students yield persuasive evidence that framework-based approaches can both enable and accelerate formation of usable 'bigger pictures' of the past, but exportation of techniques to the generality of schools and student populations has yet to be attempted.[8] Uncertainty also remains about the developmental potential of framework approaches. Frameworks have been used to teach 'bigger pictures' that trace narrow themes, cross periods or bridge topics, but formation of *big pictures* of the whole human past over one or more key stages has yet to be reported. In theory, approaches that work for narrow themes and temporally contextualized topics should be adaptable to *big-picture* teaching but, in the absence of empirical evidence, the fact and scale of educational benefits projected for framework-based *big-picture* teaching are speculative.[9]

One framework or many?

Debates about the quality, and hence value, of learning outcomes connect with others about the number and sorts of 'big' or 'bigger pictures' of the past students should possess, and hence with debates about the numbers and sorts of frameworks teachers should use. This impinges on aforementioned issues of intellectual autonomy. A student locked into a single interpretation of, say, the Holocaust, or only able to view it from a single perspective, is intellectually disabled and, it may be argued, has been unintentionally manipulated. The toxicity of monolithic perspectives on and interpretations of the entire course of human history may be much greater. This simplistic representation of complex arguments begs many questions, not least about the ways in which and extent to which accounts must differ for multiple perspectives and interpretations to be seen as other than variations on a single theme. Must alternative perspectives and interpretations be contradictory, contrary or merely inconsistent?[10]

A persuasive solution to this problem is offered by Peter Lee (1991) in the form of criteria for worthwhile and usable accounts, or 'pictures', of the past.[11] Lee demonstrates that it is theoretically possible for a *big picture* of the past to be open, flexible and self-updating without losing coherence or exhibiting multiple personality disorder. The key property implied by Lee's criteria is variation in the temporal resolution and content focus of *big pictures* in response to shifts in the questions posed about the past. In sum, the ideal learning outcome is a single *big picture* of the past with sufficient flexibility to accommodate new information, including new ways of looking at existing content, and to generate new 'big', 'bigger' and 'little' pictures of the past on demand. This ideal presents significant technical challenges for framework approaches. Should teachers work with a single comprehensive framework or a few complementary ones? Is it easier to teach students how to generate *bespoke frameworks* by decomposing and rearranging elements from a single framework or by fusing elements drawn from complementary ones? These and other challenges are more likely to be met by framework approaches designed to progress *big-picture* formation over the long term, i.e. over Key Stage 3 as a minimum and through end-of-key-stage break points at best.[12]

Concept-based or concept-free frameworks?

Should teaching of second-order concepts particular to history as an academic discipline be integrated with framework approaches? Or should frameworks focus solely on content?[13] Philosophical debates aside, research evidence suggests that the ways in which students construe *change and development, cause and consequence* and, less directly, the nature and status of historical *accounts* both limits and enables *big-picture* formation (Blow *et al.* 2008). For example, the facility with which students evaluate and synthesize the generalizations on which framework use and *big-picture* formation depend increases as they distinguish *continuity* from *persistence* and *repetition in time, development* from *progress, turning points* from *trends*. More basic still, a student's ability to make appropriate sense of developmental generalizations depends on the realization that events have *historical* as well as *intrinsic significance* and may change the lives of people who know nothing of them decades or centuries hence to a sometimes greater extent than of people who directly experience and report them. Mastery of causal concepts also signifies in this connection. Students who construe causation in history as akin to human agency in everyday life assume that things happen because a cause, or causes, 'do' or 'make' these things. Events like storms and such 'factors' as religion and economics, fate and luck, are anthropomorphized such that it is thought to be in their character to do what they do, to make what happens happen. Agency-based causation is short-range, unmediated and unproblematic – much like common-sense conceptions of intentional action. Events are explained by ascertaining who or what 'done it'. The idea that causal processes can span generations is counter-intuitive because, contrary to experience, this is not how things happen in the real world wherein people do things and what's done happens.

Although evidence of the role played by second-order concepts in *big-picture* formation is accumulating, ways of accommodating concept development within framework practices and instruments have only recently begun to be debated (Rogers, 2008). As yet, we know how a few cogs spin but not how the whole machine works.

Conclusion

Were this volume to be published 15 years from now would a chapter be reserved for discussion of 'frameworks'? It is impossible to say but an affirmative answer could be given were the construction and use of 'bigger pictures' of the past to remain on the history education agenda, and troublesome technical problems about the nature and use of 'frameworks' to have been resolved. For present purposes, it is prudent to view 'frameworks' as a theoretical and technical project of great promise but uncertain delivery.

Further reading

A searching analysis of the background concerns and problems that inform framework experiments is offered by Lee and Howson (2009). A review of framework and alternative approaches to *big-picture* teaching is contained in Shemilt (2009) but readers should note that, since this is a published version of a conference paper given in 2006, the review is more dated than might be supposed. For an example of experimental practice in UK schools, see Rogers (2008); and for an instance of current framework controversies and debates, see Howson (2009).

Notes

1 The promiscuous use of terminology has been condemned by a number of authors, e.g. by Ian Dawson (2008) who offers '*thematic studies*' as an alternative.
2 Rogers' instruments were flanked by eight cartoons illustrating the story – and back-story – of Magna Carta through time.
3 Further information about teaching procedures, assessment instruments and learning outcomes is contained in Rogers (2008) and in Blow *et al.* (2008).
4 This statement must be qualified. In 2009 Rick Rogers used frameworks with Year 7 and Year 9 students that exhibit some, though not all, 'right-hand' characteristics of the five *dimensions of difference*, but outcomes thereof have yet to be evaluated.
5 The authors are indebted to Ros Ashby for these key questions.
6 Research by Lee and Howson (Howson, 2007; Lee and Howson, 2009) demonstrates that many graduate historians and most secondary students struggle to articulate taught content into a coherent conspectus of the past.
7 Debates about 'historical consciousness' and 'historical literacy' signify in this connection. See Peter Lee in this volume (Chapter 5) and Lee (2004).
8 See Rogers (2008); Blow *et al.* (2008); and Shemilt (2009).
9 In this connection, at least one attempt to achieve framework ends by other means has met with qualified success. Staff in a selective grammar school reverse-engineered a framework by using graph axes as retrospective organizers (see Shemilt, 2009). About two-thirds of students were able to map transfers of political power, rights and freedoms across a motley collection of Key Stage 3 topics. This success was, however, qualified by the frequency with which facts and chronologies were adjusted to fit prescribed themes. In addition, the conceptual demands of the approach render it unsuitable for use in non-selective schools. It should also be noted that 'bigger pictures' of the past composed from topics selected on the basis of presumed relevance to national or ethnic identities, citizenship concerns or whatever are partial and distorted in so far as connections forged between them reproduce and magnify biases implicit in topic selection.
10 These questions are debated with clarity and cogency by Arthur Chapman in Chapter 8 of this volume.
11 See also the magisterial paper by Lee and Howson (2009).

12 Outcomes from School History Project Studies in Development indicate that students able to conceptualize lines of development for sub-themes have difficulty in doing more than switching from one sub-theme to another, i.e. most students able to compare and contrast point-like events on lines of development cannot do likewise for the sub-thematic lines of development themselves (Shemilt, 2000; 2009).

13 Peter Lee (2005) has made the definitive case for concept-based history, arguing that our ability to make sense of historical content is constrained by our understanding of the concepts intrinsic to the nature and logic of History as a *form of knowledge*. A case more closely focused on framework practices and instruments is made by Jonathan Howson (2009).

References

Blow, F. J., Rogers, R. and Shemilt, D. J. (2008), 'Framework working group report', unpublished report of a QCDA-funded research and development group established at the Institute of Education under the direction of Jonathan Howson.

Dawson, I. (2008) 'Thinking across time: planning and teaching the story of power and democracy at Key Stage 3', *Teaching History*, 130: 14–23.

Howson, J. (2007) '"Is it the Tuarts and then the Studors or the other way round?" The importance of developing a usable picture of the past', *Teaching History*, 127: 40–7.

——(2009) 'Potential and pitfalls in teaching big pictures of the past', *Teaching History*, 136.

Lee, P. J. (1991) 'Historical knowledge and the National Curriculum', in R. Aldrich (ed.), *History in the National Curriculum*. London: Routledge.

——(2004) '"Walking backwards into tomorrow": historical consciousness and understanding history', *International Journal of History Learning, Teaching and Research*, 4, 1. Available online at: http://centres.exeter.ac.uk/historyresource/journal7/7contents. htm (accessed 9 January 2010).

——(2005) 'Putting principles into practice: understanding history', in M. S. Donovan and J. D. Bransford (eds), *How Students Learn History in the Classroom*. Washington DC: National Academy Press.

Lee, P. J. and Howson, J. (2009) '"Two out of five did not know that Henry VIII had six wives": history education, historical literacy and historical consciousness', in L. Symcox and A. Wilschut (eds), *National History Standards: The Problem of the Canon and the Future of History Teaching (International Review of History Education Vol. 5)*. Charlotte: Information Age Publishing.

Rogers, R. (2008) 'Raising the bar: developing meaningful historical consciousness at Key Stage 3', *Teaching History*, 133: 24–30.

Shemilt, D. (2000) 'The caliph's coin', in P. Seixas, P. Stearns and S. Wineburg (eds), *Teaching, Learning and Knowing History*. New York: New York University Press.

——(2009) 'Drinking an ocean and pissing a cupful', in L. Symcox and A. Wilschut (eds), *National History Standards: The Problem of the Canon and the Future of History Teaching (International Review of History Education Vol. 5*. Charlotte: Information Age Publishing.

Chapter 7

What do history teachers (need to) know?

A framework for understanding and developing practice

Chris Husbands

Introduction

- All teachers need to draw on a range of knowledge to teach successfully; the range of knowledge on which they need to draw is extensive and complex.
- This chapter draws on classroom research to explore the range of knowledge; of content, of the nature of the discipline, about pupils and about resources and strategies, and to consider how they relate to each other.

AD 43, 1066, 1381, 1485, 1649, 1660, 1789, 1815, 1832, 1914, 1939, 1979. Familiar enough: the punctuation marks of a conventional and mainly English history. Slightly less familiar: 1317, 1331, 1453, 1538, 1683, 1821, 1878, 1913: punctuation marks in the history of the Ottoman Empire. Of course, punctuation marks do not make a language, just as a sequence of dates does not make history. Language depends on grammar, vocabulary, syntax, structure, as history depends on narrative, explanation, analysis and causation. History teachers 'know' their dates, though the two lists at the opening of this paragraph should prompt reflection on which dates – which punctuation marks – history teachers need to be familiar with if they are to teach successfully in increasingly diverse schools. But these lists also prompt other questions about the relationship between these punctuation marks and the other elements of historical discourse: what is it that history teachers need to know in order to teach history, and how is that knowledge base best understood?

There is an everyday answer to this question: history teachers need to know a lot of history, and – crude as they are – some selection of dates might be a place to start. It is difficult to mount an argument against the proposition that teachers should know the subject they teach. To teach successfully, teachers must be intellectually capable and well informed. There has been increased worldwide emphasis on recruiting well-qualified candidates into teaching (see McKinseys, 2007). This is such an obvious proposition that it seems absurd to disagree. And yet, the teachers have always been somewhat suspicious of those who are 'merely' academically well qualified: it's argued that teachers need most to be able to relate to young people, that knowledge of 'the world' makes them better at working with demotivated or less able learners. Knowledge might be less important than the ability to communicate, to understand kids and make learning real. Moreover, it's been argued that one can know 'too much'. Detail can clutter; good teaching needs a clear, coherent overview (Shemilt, 2009: 144). Recent research has emphasized the importance of teachers' ability to provide pupils with an overarching 'map of the past', rather than an acquaintance with detail (Foster *et al.*, 2008). Knowledge, it seems, is not straightforward after all.

Contemporary interest in the nature of subject knowledge for teaching derives from the model of pedagogical content knowledge (PCK) initially proposed by Lee Shulman, who saw it as a mechanism for connecting distinct bodies of knowledge for teaching. 'It represent[ed] the blending of content and pedagogy into an understanding of how particular topics, problems, or issues are organized, represented, and adapted to the diverse interests and abilities of learners, and presented for instruction' (Shulman, 1986: 8). PCK requires teachers to be able to use analogies, illustrations, examples, explanations and demonstrations as conduits for their subject knowledge to engage and enthuse pupils. Studies since 1986 have suggested complex relationships between subject knowledge and pedagogic knowledge (Wilson and Wineburg, 1988; Turner-Bisset, 1999; Brown *et al.*, 1999), but the essence of the concept is captured in Figure 7. 1. Shulman's model of pedagogic content knowledge provides a way of relating subject-matter knowledge to pedagogic knowledge.

Shulman himself has outlined a variety of models to explore the different sorts of knowledge on which teachers draw, and the rather schematic relationship between them has been widely questioned. Critics have argued that Shulman sees knowledge as a fixed and external body of information which teachers 'know', and generates a teacher-centred pedagogy which focuses primarily on the skills and knowledge that the teacher possesses, rather than on the ways teachers interact with pupils (see, for example, Moon, 2007). In the United Kingdom, studies of effective teachers have frequently taken subject-matter expertise for granted, and have focused equally on the importance of teacher knowledge of classroom practices and techniques as a

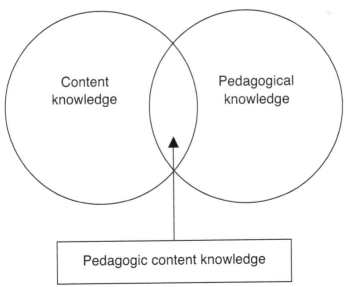

Figure 7.1 A simple representation of Shulman's model of pedagogic content knowledge.

principle – perhaps the principal determinant of classroom success (e.g. Muijs and Reynolds, 2005).

All this makes it worth investigating history teacher knowledge in more detail. This chapter draws on, but also extends, a study undertaken in history classrooms in schools in England (Husbands *et al.*, 2003) to construct a framework for thinking about the relationships between the different sorts of knowledge deployed by teachers. In that study, teachers were observed over the course of a full teaching day, and at the end of the day interviewed in some detail about the lessons they had taught. A follow-up interview explored the observed lessons in the wider context of the history curriculum as taught and interpreted in the school. Knowledge in this study encompassed teachers' beliefs, since, 'in the mind of the teacher components of knowledge, beliefs and intuitions are inextricably intertwined' (Verloop *et al.*, 2001: 446). The study led us to consider three types of teacher knowledge: knowledge about *history*, knowledge about *pupils* and knowledge of *classroom practices, resources and activities* that they could use to realize their goals in lessons. This typology of teachers' knowledge resonates with many other studies, although it is simpler than some other models. In this chapter, I draw on this research to set out a framework for understanding history teachers' knowledge and to consider some implications of both learning to teach and enhancing the quality of teaching.

Unpacking history teachers' knowledge about history

A critical foundation of teachers' knowledge is their substantive or content knowledge, which is often detailed, deriving from either their degree or their continued engagement with reading or television and DVD documentaries. Successful teachers deploy this knowledge in both planning and action. One teacher, working with a class of 14-year-olds, modelled historical interpretation, talked in detail about the Munich crisis of 1938 and then added, 'but my interpretation – and this is controversial – is different. I think . . .' Teachers are able to tell engaging narratives, often highly polished through years of telling to engage pupils (Bage, 2000). Teachers draw on this knowledge extensively: a teacher introducing a class of pupils to the Roman Empire draws on other ideas about empire; a teacher talking about the Battle of Hastings links it backwards and forwards to other critical turning-point battles. When we discussed content knowledge with teachers, they tended to either take it for granted or even dismiss it. One teacher said, 'I haven't actually done a lot of reading. I think it's *something that's built up over time*', while in relation to Northern Ireland, 'well I suppose I do *but I don't have to make an effort* because it's something I'm very interested in' (Husbands *et al.*, 2003: 71, emphases added). The implications of very detailed content knowledge are often clear in successful history lessons, and especially in extended classroom questioning where teachers used knowledge to ask closely focused questions and to probe pupils' responses, to correct or explore misconceptions.

This account of teachers' detailed knowledge is misleading; detailed content knowledge is characteristic of successful teaching but it is not sufficient. Teachers' knowledge about history is not defined by their knowledge of the historical past alone. Moreover, history teachers' own content knowledge is almost certainly too limited for the classroom. Just occasionally, it is possible for teachers to pursue their

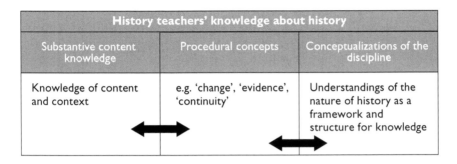

Figure 7.2 History teachers' knowledge about history.

own enthusiasms in classrooms, but the demands of the curriculum are diverse, and most history teachers at some time or other need to build up new knowledge about unfamiliar topics; for example, the English history graduate required to teach about the history of the Middle East. On Shulman's model, what should happen is that teachers would 'acquire' knowledge from engagement with the subject and then derive from that pedagogic content knowledge. In practice, something different seems to happen in the relationship between substantive and procedural knowledge.

Experienced teachers operate with confidence in discussing the substantive and procedural dimensions of school history. Lee and Ashby (2001) put the distinction in this way:

> [S]ubstantive history is the content of history, what history [is] 'about' . . . procedural ideas about history . . . concepts like historical evidence, explanation, change are ideas that provide our understanding of history as a discipline or form of knowledge. They are not what history is 'about' but they shape the way we go about doing history.

Teachers in our study made reference to the substance, or content, that they wanted their pupils to understand but this was almost invariably seen in terms of procedural concepts such as evidence, change, continuity or causation. A lesson on nineteenth-century public health, for example, might be about specific developments, but was also about pupils' understanding of change over time. A teacher told us that a lesson about medieval castles 'isn't really castles at all, it's getting the kids to appreciate that things are not going to stay the same across five hundred years'. The emphasis on procedural concepts closely linked to substantive history appears to be characteristic of teachers' discourse about their lessons. Not surprisingly, a distinction between novice and experienced teachers lies precisely in their different approach to procedural concepts: a lesson might be 'about' the Battle of Hastings, whereas for experienced teachers the lesson is 'about' the procedural concept. One important way of thinking about learning to teach a subject is, therefore, that it involves the acquisition of increasingly sophisticated understandings of procedural concepts.

This is particularly the case in approaches to one procedural concept – namely, the use of historical evidence. The understanding of historical evidence was a feature of the so-called 'new' schools' history associated with the SCHP (Schools Council

History Project) (SCHP, 1973), and involved a sophisticated set of approaches to the idea that historical knowledge was constructed rather than received. Indeed, David Sylvester, the first director of the Project argued that what differentiated the Project from earlier practice was not the use of evidence – which had been advocated as long ago as 1910 by M. W. Keatinge – but its conceptualization of history as 'constructed' knowledge based on approaches to the place of evidence in history (Sylvester, 1994). In the 30 years since the beginning of the SCHP, there have been criticisms of some of the classroom practice generated by a concern with evidence. Grant Bage, one of the most sophisticated of such critics, argued that concern with evidence neglects the intimate relationship between the evidential base and the provisional narratives which can be built upon it: concentration on source work 'narrows time-horizons and prohibits grand narrative' (Bage, 1999: 18). There is some truth in this, but successful practices integrate knowledge about evidence into classroom enquiry; questions about bias, provenance, utility, reliability are less important than the relationship between evidential material in the context of a real historical question: What does this show us? Why does it show us that? What doesn't it show us? 'Doing history' is the focus of good lessons – not 'doing sources'.

A third feature of subject knowledge relates to the notion of history as a discipline. For many history teachers this has a particular prescience given the pressure on their subject in the curriculum. For one of the teachers in our study, 'history is riddled with uncertainties, history is up in the air'. For another, 'the question I ask is "am I enabling those children to do good history?" . . . history for me is setting questions, finding out, coming across the problems of methodology, patterns being thrown up that then raise finding out more'. Successful teachers draw on an overall conception of history as a discipline. Recent work has emphasized the importance of organizing ideas and frameworks – what Foster *et al.* (2008) have called 'usable historical pasts', and this sense of the epistemological frame for history is a critical component of teachers' subject knowledge.

What teachers know about pupils

A second dimension of history teachers' knowledge related to pupil learning, and can be understood in two ways: first, teacher knowledge about how pupils learn in general, and, second, though less pronounced knowledge of how students develop understanding *in history*. It is a truism to argue that teachers need knowledge about pupils in order to generate learning for pupils, but more detailed scrutiny of the way teachers explain and deploy this knowledge offers insights about successful history teaching.

All teachers have a theory of learning, though their ability to articulate it with clarity is not necessarily linked to the sophistication of the understandings they possess. Teachers have practical theories about how pupils engage with material, about how pupils process, store and deploy what they have learned. These theories shape the way teachers teach. One of the most important developments of the last 30 years in history classrooms has been a movement away from largely transmission-based approaches in which pupils were assumed to be 'empty vessels' to be filled with knowledge towards social constructivist models of learning in which pupils engage actively with learning through discussion, peer learning and so on. In some schools, there has been explicit attention to (often modish) frameworks for developing thinking about these approaches: multiple intelligence theories (Gardner, 1999), neurolinguistic programming, visual, auditory and kinaesthetic learning. Claims are made for the potential of discoveries in neuroscience to change the way teachers think about pupil learning, though we found little evidence that such theories loomed large in teachers' thinking. Instead, we found grounded, practical theorizing about classroom learning expressed in terms of motivation and engagement. One teacher said: 'I'm always trying to think what is motivating the pupils? Just a straight question is not very motivating. It's motivating for those who know the answer, but for the others it's very easy to switch off, and I'm thinking, in what way can you keep people on board?', and translated this theoretical question into practice through classroom quizzes, which 'get them really hooked'. Other teachers working from practical theories used video extracts to grab attention and set up the conditions for engagement, and this could not be taken for granted – 'tricks', incongruities, problems needed to be set to engage; once that was done, learning might be possible. If motivation and engagement were prerequisites for learning, teachers in our study also talked about the importance of learners' confidence. One said: '[T]hey need to feel comfortable . . . they mustn't all collapse at the beginning . . . they have to be made to feel confident, there's no doubt about that. They've become increasingly confident and don't think twice about writing an essay now.'

These ideas about pupil learning relate to general assumptions about how pupils engage with new material and the conditions necessary for engagement. What was apparent in our study was that teachers deployed knowledge about differences between pupils in sophisticated ways in classrooms. There is increased policy interest in personalization and differentiation, and these ideas are often seen as 'additional', 'bolt-on' elements of classroom teaching. Our study suggested that teachers had internalized

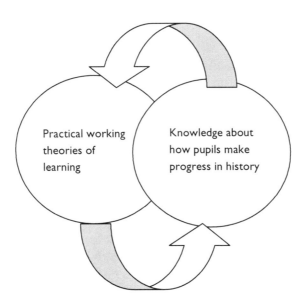

Practical working theories of learning

Knowledge about how pupils make progress in history

Figure 7.3 Knowledge about pupils.

ideas about differentiation; they knew that pupils learned in different ways and that classroom planning and action needed to take account of this. One teacher said, 'some students – they all learn differently – some need a more concrete approach to some aspects'. Another teacher deliberately planned her lesson in the light of this: 'I want to give them some space. It's their opportunity to verbalise their views in their own way. Some will respond to visual things, some respond to hearing it from other people and some of them respond to independently formulating it through an activity that's actually doing something themselves.' At the same time, our study found extensive evidence of deep knowledge of individual pupils – their interests, their preoccupations, their dislikes, their family situation and so on – and that such knowledge was used to shape interventions and classroom strategies.

There has been extensive research over the last 20 years on the way pupils learn history. Understandings have become detailed and sophisticated (Shemilt, 1984, 1987, 2009; Lee and Ashby, 2001). One question is the extent to which teachers deploy this knowledge in the course of their day-to-day work; the evidence is ambiguous. Some teachers were explicit and sophisticated in their management of the relationship between procedural and substantive knowledge. Others were aware of the importance of using procedural concepts to structure lessons. Others were confident in the deployment of these procedural concepts as frames for the assessment of pupil understandings. It was more difficult to track the ways teachers used knowledge about pupil understanding in history to shape thinking about the learning they wished to stimulate. For some this was explicit, but was sometimes more difficult to find. This is not a new finding. In an exceptionally thorough study of teachers' work in empathy, Cunningham (2003) suggests that at least some history teachers have clear ideas about how pupils' conceptual grasp develops, but to unearth these she had to dig deep in her questioning with teachers over an extended period of time. Our own work suggested that teachers have strong images of pupils' understanding in history, and that in some cases there is an awareness of the results of recent research which suggest that pupil learning is not stage-related, that structures of learning depend on engagement and revisiting. It may be that for experienced history teachers this is so interlinked with their knowledge of school history and their knowledge of how pupils learn that it does not make sense to try and disentangle them. Nonetheless, there is evidence to suggest that *in addition to* general ideas about how pupils learn, successful history teachers have a developed understanding of progression in learning history.

Knowledge in action: knowledge about resources and approaches

History lessons in twenty-first-century classrooms have become resource-rich. Some lessons exhibit many and varied resources – print, screen, commercial, school-produced – while others are exceptionally simple in their resourcing. In one lesson, the only resource deployed was the teacher and her voice, used to stimulate a lengthy, sophisticated debate about the arguments for and against putting Charles I on trial in 1648. Nonetheless, published resources continue to play a significant part, although the traditional – and in some ways continental – model of 'working through the text' appears to have declined markedly: teachers control textbooks rather than the other way around. Some teachers talk about using tried-and-tested resources: in one school, a teacher drew out a 35-year-old, dog-eared pile of textbooks to be used alongside a very recently published text because, he explained, 'nothing since this has set the issue out so clearly'. However, the reprographics revolution of the 1980s allowed history teachers to produce their own resources, tailoring materials to the school's circumstances and pupil needs, and digital technologies have allowed teachers to go much further, affording access to a bewildering array of resources written, visual, aural and oral. Many relish the opportunity to experiment. Some school-produced resources are used to provide information, but others are used for specific images or sources of evidence that the teacher wished to use. Mostly, school-produced and web resources are used alongside published textbooks, to supplement, extend, focus or structure the use of published resources, often around a school-designated enquiry. What this variety does do, however, is to place a premium on teachers' knowledge of, and ability to deploy, resources which enable them to realize their classroom aims and aspirations.

This knowledge tends to be focused on and expressed in terms of activities and resources. It is worth remembering, however, that the most important resource in any classroom remains the teacher. History lessons are if not always teacher-led, in what is sometimes referred to as the 'traditional' transmission model, then certainly teacher-orchestrated. Teachers talk in history lessons. They tell stories, they ask questions; they probe pupil contributions; they offer judgements. They enable pupils feeding back to the class to clarify their ideas so that they can become accessible to other pupils. They check pupils' understanding and correct errors. They give information. They help pupils make judgements. They assess pupils' progress. They work with individuals and groups. We have already seen that in discharging these different activities teachers draw on their knowledge about history and their knowledge of pupils, but they also draw on their knowledge of when and how to deploy themselves as a resource – now intervening, now holding back; now allowing a classroom activity to run on, now closing it down. This is not simply situational skill but demands knowledge about the range of resources *of which teachers themselves are a part*.

Video clips are common – the web makes possible the use of short, perhaps 3-minute' clips to make a key point; where teachers used to show videos for an entire lesson, multimedia resources can now stimulate more active enquiry. The easy access to visual resources on the web have made some history lessons extraordinarily rich in colour images, allowing pupils to build up a sense of Renaissance architecture or Ancient Rome. These resources have placed at history teachers' fingertips a luxuriant variety of stimuli: the history teacher with the time and interest to do so can mount rich exhibitions. What is more difficult – and perhaps a work in progress – is to subject these resources to the critical knowledge-based scrutiny which conventional resources have been subject too. It is easier for a group of pupils to pore over a textbook illustration and to compare it with a written text than it is for a class to subject a projected image to detailed scrutiny.

However, the point here is that resources, and the classroom activities which they support, constitute an arena for the deployment of teacher knowledge. In one lesson, pupils were shown a series of very short clips from different films featuring Robin Hood, and used them to consider different ideas about the legend. In another lesson, pupils were shown – three times – a very short clip from the film *A Man for All*

Seasons, and were asked at each showing to explore different aspects of the encounter between Henry VIII and Thomas More. In these instances the teacher had made a decision about the purposes of the lesson and used knowledge about the range of material to produce a rich, but focused, learning experience for pupils. In other lessons, *sections* of text were used specifically as a source of information, with pupils asked to read and extract what was required before going on to use this in another activity resourced in a different way.

In our study, then, we found a deliberative matching of resources and activities to goals, as teachers drew on a wide repertoire to make decisions about what would be most appropriate. Even the teacher who said, 'I've taught this material so many times now, I know how it's going to go down and what the best way of doing it is' revealed the ways in which he was making adjustments to activities and trying things out: '[I]n the past I've done that in groups but I thought I would do it as a whole class', 'I don't normally do a question after but I just thought, let's see what they think, because as I was watching it I was reminded of how it does show the features we'd talked about' and 'there's a follow up here that I've done in the past'. Another teacher referred to activities associated with this particular lesson that he had used with other classes in the past, and also that in choosing to use one particular task he had chosen from a range of possibilities: '[A] straight list would have done its job'. It is not surprising that this broad repertoire was most evident in the talk of the most experienced teachers: they have had the time both to develop and use a wide range of strategies and also to see their different effects with a range of different classes and individuals. They have become adept at making choices that represent a best fit of the potentially competing demands of the needs, abilities and interests of their pupils, the ideas of history, their own interests and preferences, the time of day, what is available.

I have framed this discussion about teachers' classroom knowledge in terms of resources and activities because this is how teachers described their practices, but something more fundamental is at stake. Although teachers' descriptions of their practice are often couched in terms of activities, what is often clear is that profound understanding of pedagogy underlying these. In a recent study in American high schools, Westhoff and Polman identify tensions between novice teachers' understandings of general and subject-specific pedagogy, which they traced back to a paucity of subject knowledge (Westhoff and Polman, 2007). In English school classrooms we found no such tensions; instead, we found a close relationship between teachers' understandings of general pedagogy and its working out in the subject, but strongly expressed through the classroom implications of pedagogic issues.

A framework for thinking about knowledge: history, pupils and resources

We began with a common-sense proposition about subject knowledge in teaching, but teachers' knowledge is more complex – and more interesting – than that. Three dimensions to teacher knowledge have been explored, and they are summarized in Figure 7.4. As the discussion above has suggested, these three are not separate: they inter-relate and draw off each other. However, as a schematic representation of the argument, Figure 7.4 has some merits: it draws attention to the multidimensionality

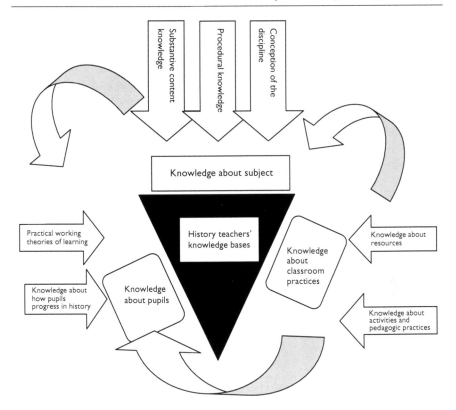

Figure 7.4 A framework for history teachers' knowledge.

of history teachers' knowledge; it suggests that each element in the model then draws on other components, and, at the centre, it suggests that they sit in a dynamic relationship to each other. Approaches which place subject-matter knowledge itself at the core fail to capture the inter-relationship and dynamism of the different sorts of knowledge we found teachers routinely deploying.

There are some potentially profound implications of this model for teacher learning and teacher development. Teacher education programmes – whether initial or in-service – frequently construct artificial barriers between different sites of learning – between library, seminar room and the classroom. This chapter suggests that these boundaries are artificial: understanding flows between the different sources and forms of knowledge, as each becomes a lens through which the others are perceived. For novices, the model here has implications too. The model reminds us that learning to teach involves the acquisition of diverse knowledge. It points to the school, and the classroom as the critical site in which learning is acquired, and provides foci for knowledge development. Equally, it reminds us that while the school is a critical site for knowledge development, focused support is needed to maximize the potential of schools to support teacher development.

Chapter summary

History teachers' knowledge is complex, rich and dynamic.

History teachers make active connections between their content knowledge and the other sorts of knowledge they need to deploy in order to work successfully: 'knowing more history' is not a secure basis for developing classroom practice.

Much of teachers' expertise and knowledge is grounded in classrooms and classroom practice, which suggests that classrooms are the most effective site for developing expertise.

Further reading

Husbands, C., Kitson, A. and Pendry, A. (2003) *Understanding History Teaching*. Milton Keynes: Open University Press.

Barton, K. C. and Levstik, L. S. (2004) *Teaching History for the Common Good*. Mahwah, NJ: Lawrence Erlbaum Associates.

References

Bage, G. (1999) *Narrative Matters: Teaching History Through Story*. London: RoutledgeFalmer.

——(2000) *Thinking History 4–14: Teaching, Learning, Curricula and Communities*. London: RoutledgeFalmer.

Brown, T., McNamara, O., Hanley, U. and Jones, L. (1999) 'Primary student teachers' understandings of mathematics and its teaching', *British Educational Research Journal*, 25(3): 299–322.

Foster, S. *et al.* (2008) *Usable Historical Pasts: A Study of Students' Frameworks of the Past: Full Research Report*, ESRC End of Award Report, RES-000–22–1676. Swindon: ESR.

Gardner, H. (1999) *Intelligence Reframed: Multiple Intelligences for the 21st Century*. New York: Basic Books.

Husbands, C., Kitson, A. and Pendry, A. (2003) *Understanding History Teaching*. Milton Keynes: Open University Press.

Lee, P. J. and Ashby, R. (2001) 'Progression in historical understanding among students ages 7–14', in P. Stearns, P. Seixas and S. Wineburg (eds), *Knowing Teaching and Learning History*. New York: New York University Press, pp. 306–25.

Cunningham, D. (2003) 'Professional practice and perspectives in the teaching of historical empathy', unpublished D Phil thesis, Oxford: University of Oxford.

Moon, B. (2007) *Curriculum, Domain Knowledge and Pedagogy: TLRP Thematic Seminar Series*. Available online at: http://www.tlrp.org/themes/seminar/moon/papers.html (accessed 27 November 2009).

McKinseys (2007) *How the World's Best School Systems Come Out on Top*. London and New York: McKinseys.

Muijs, D. and Reynolds, D (2005) *Effective Teaching: Evidence and Practice*, second edition. London: Sage.

SCHP (Schools Council History Project) (1973) *A New Look at History*. Edinburgh: Holmes MacDougall.

Shemilt, D. (1984) 'Beauty and the philosopher: empathy in history and the class-room', in A. K. Dickinson, P. J. Lee and P. Rogers (eds), *Learning History*. London: Heinemann.

——(1987) 'Adolescent ideas about evidence and methodology in history', in C. Portal (ed.), *The History Curriculum for Teachers*. Lewes: Falmer, pp. 39–61.

——(2009) 'Drinking an ocean and pissing a cupful: how adolescents make sense of his-tory', in L. Symcox, and A. Wilschut (eds), *National History Standards: The Problem of the Canon and the Future of Teaching History*. Charlotte, NC: Information Age Publishing.

Shulman, L. (1986) 'Those who understand: knowledge growth in teaching', *Educational Researcher*, 15: 4–14.

Sylvester, D. (1994) 'Change and continuity in history teaching, 1900–1993', in H. Bourdillon (ed.), *Teaching History*. London: Routledge, pp. 9–25.

Turner-Bisset, R. (1999) 'The knowledge bases of the expert teacher', *British Educational Research Journal*, 25(1): 39–55.

Verloop, N., Van Driel, J. and Meijer, P. (2001) 'Teacher knowledge and the knowledge base of teaching', *International Journal of Educational Research*, 35: 441–61.

Westhoff, L. M. and Polman, J. (2007) 'Developing preservice teachers' pedagogical con-tent knowledge about historical thinking', *International Journal of Social Education*, 22(2): 1–28.

Wilson, S. M. and Wineberg, S. S. (1988) 'Peering at history through different lenses: the role of the disciplinary perspectives in teaching history', *Harvard Educational Review*, 89(4): 527–39.

Chapter 8

Historical interpretations

Arthur Chapman

Introduction

A great deal has been written about the pedagogy of historical interpretations and much of this work is very helpful and practical.[1] This chapter does not aim to supersede or reprise existing work but rather to focus attention on historical, theoretical and logical dimensions of interpretation and to raise a number of considerations relevant to the task of developing students' abilities to think critically, comparatively and evaluatively about historical interpretations.[2]

What are historical interpretations and why should pupils study them?

The nature and importance of historical interpretation

Unlike, say, cows, molluscs or monkeys, human beings are temporal beings (Nietzsche, 2008; Heidegger, 1978): to be human is, among other things, to be conscious of time and to live by manipulating temporal constructs – identity, origin, destination, memory, trace, story, past/present/future and so on (Ricoeur, 2004; Rüsen, 2001). Human groups and communities come and continue to exist, at least in part, through the stories that they tell themselves about who they 'are', where they 'began' and where they 'are going' and through other memory practices, such as anniversaries, memorials and monuments, that embed these narratives in social life through ritual (Lowenthal, 1985; Samuel, 1994).

These narratives and memory practices aim to manage the passage of time, to construct and stabilize identity through time and to understand the limits and possibilities that the past creates for the present and future (Rüsen, 2001, 2005). These narratives and practices are interventions in the present, since they shape the self-understandings of individuals and communities, and historical interpretations are, therefore, potentially both consequential and controversial.

Understanding historical interpretations involves thinking critically about the diverse ways in which human groups and societies make sense of time and change. Subject disciplines exist to enable us 'to approach questions of importance in a systematic and reliable way' (Gardner, 2000, p. 144) and the study of historical interpretations should aim to provide pupils with tools that they can use to systematically compare and evaluate claims about the past if not in order to establish total and definitive 'truth' then certainly to move beyond the view that 'anything goes' and towards an understanding of how the validity of claims about the past can be assessed.

Many good arguments have been advanced for the study of historical interpretations – citizenship arguments, political arguments and so on – and it is plausible to suggest that the study of plural historical interpretations is important to the health of democratic culture in a diverse and complex world. The most compelling arguments for the study of historical interpretation are, however, historical: there is no alternative to studying historical interpretation, if we want to help students think reflectively and critically about a key dimension of their humanity and about the ubiquitous and often competing history stories and memory practices that clamour for attention in the present.

Historical interpretation in the history curriculum

Historical interpretations are a key component of the history curriculum in England and Wales, from Key Stage 1 to AS and A2 (QCA, 1999, pp. 16–17, 2006, p. 5, 2007a, pp. 112–13, and 2007b, p. 5). Simplifying the various curricular statements, we can say that it is intended that the study of 'interpretations' will enable students to:

1. *Understand that* the past has been interpreted in different ways;
2. *Understand how* the past has been interpreted in different ways;
3. *Explain why* the past has been interpreted in different ways; and
4. *Evaluate* different interpretations of the past.

The curriculum also requires that students engage with a broad range of historical culture and study the work of 'historians and others' (QCA, 2007a, p. 113).

The remainder of this chapter explores some of the issues raised by these curricular aims.

Understanding what historical interpretations are

Students' preconceptions about historical interpretation

Research suggests that, prior to asking students to identify, explain and evaluate variant interpretations of the past, we should focus on developing understandings of what interpretations are. Students often hold tacit assumptions, based on everyday epistemologies that are likely to impede the development of their understanding of historical interpretation; a primary and ongoing pedagogic task is to challenge these assumptions and help students develop more powerful ideas (Lee 1998, 2001; Lee and Shemilt, 2004).

Students often think in naïve realist ways about historical interpretations and assume (a) that the past has a fixed identity and meaning, (b) that interpretations should ideally mirror this fixed past and, therefore, (c) that historical accounts should be singular and that there will, in principle, be one 'best' account (Lee and Shemilt, 2004; Shemilt, 2000). Students who think in these ways tend also to view variation in interpretation with suspicion and explain it in terms of subjectivity and 'bias'. Naïve realist assumptions do not work in history: the meaning, and in many cases the basic identity, of things that 'have happened' is not fixed and is more aptly described as 'fluid' and historical interpretations are more like theories proposed in response to particular questions or problems than they are like pictures (Lee and Shemilt, 2004). We need to help students understand why this is and also to help them understand that we can deal rationally with plural accounts of a fluid past.

The fluidity of the past and the plural nature of historical interpretation

In so far as it exists at all, the historical past only exists in the present and in the form of:

- traces of the past (relics and reports)
- interpretations of the past constructed subsequent to its passing.

What we can say about the past results from an ongoing *dialogue* between traces and present questions and purposes and is shaped by a range of factors including:

- our orientation towards the past and understanding of what history is;
- our purposes in engaging with the past;
- our awareness and identification of traces of the past;
- decisions we make about which traces have relevance to the issues we are interested in;
- the questions that we ask of the traces we select for analysis;
- the assumptions, concepts and methods that we deploy as we interrogate and interpret these traces;
- the forms in which we express the answers to our questions.

These factors shape all attempts to engage with the past, to one degree or another, since even the most straightforward description implies theoretical commitments. Disciplined historical thinking is characterized, however, by an effort to make practices of interpretation explicit and available for scrutiny and an important purpose of history education is to make it clear to pupils that interpretation is open to rational discussion and evaluation. Engagement with the past is also a dynamic process: we are not stuck where we started and interpreting the traces of the past frequently involves the revision of questions and preconceptions (Megill, 2007).

In addition, all histories are in history: the ways in which we become conscious of the past, the ways in which we aim to interpret the past and the tools available for this task are as much reflections of who we are and of our particular place in time as they are of the traces of the past itself. Engagements with the past are always authored, driven by particular purposes or questions and undertaken by particular people or groups of people with particular beliefs and assumptions and even where 'facts' can be clearly and non-controversially established their meaning is inherently debatable (Koselleck, 2004, p. 149; Samuel, 1994).

The past is, therefore, inherently fluid and historical interpretations are inherently plural and variable: they are in history, have historicity and continually change as the present changes.[3]

Why do interpretations differ?

It is one thing to acknowledge that histories always and inevitably emerge from particular contexts and another to claim that histories are arbitrary expressions of their authors' subjectivities: maintaining the former does not entail accepting the latter. As Jörn Rüsen has shown, through his articulation of a 'disciplinary matrix' for historical study (Rüsen, 2005, p. 132) it is possible to acknowledge and model the ways in which historical practice 'is influenced by and related to practical life' but also to defend disciplined historical practice as a 'cognitive strategy for getting knowledge about the past' (Rüsen, 2005, p. 135).[4] Building on Megill's reading of Rüsen (Megill, 1994, p. 58), we can think of interpretations as structured by:

1. the *practical contexts* that they emerge from;
2. the *conception of history* that they express;
3. the *interpretive frameworks* they deploy; and
4. the *textual forms* in which they are expressed.

Practical contexts of interpretation

History arises from the experience of time, all history is located in time and historical interpretation can be thought of as addressing the practical needs of groups and communities for orientation in time (Rüsen, 2005, p. 10). Interpretive practice is inherently various: orientation in time is relative to the conceptions of time and questions that interpreters deploy, to the time in which an interpretation occurs and also to the groups and interests that the interpretation seeks to orient.

All histories are practically located in a number of other senses. Academic history operates within particular disciplinary practices and conventions, developed by scholarly communities to enable methodological rigour and rationality (Lorenz, 2001), and these practices differ from those found in other contexts of practice. Although it is not uncommon, for example, for computer games (Ferguson, 2006) or filmic constructions of the past (Harlan, 2007) to be scrupulously researched, they are also shaped by a range of practical considerations that typically have priority in these contexts (Fernández-Armesto, 2002, pp. 159–60; Rose and Corley, 2003). Interpretation involves the construction of meaning and interpretations are also, therefore, shaped by the conventions and the ethical and normative horizons of their social and cultural contexts of origin (Lorenz, 1998).

Historical interpretations are positioned and self-positioning, therefore, and must be historicized and located in the contexts from which they emerge and in relation to the purposes that they serve.

Conceptions of history

Constructions of the past are profoundly shaped by the 'stance' or mode of relationship to the past that they express. A number of authors have developed typologies of modes of relationship to the past: Barton and Levstick, for example, contrast *identification*, *analytic* and *moral* stances towards the past (Barton and Levstick, 2004, p. 7); Seixas and Clark (2004) distinguish between *monumental*, *antiquarian*, *critical* and *modern* conceptions of history and Rüsen (2005) identifies *traditional*, *exemplary*, *critical* and *genetic* forms of historical consciousness. Terminology is secondary to the essential point: we can approach the past in fundamentally distinct ways and the mode of orientation towards the past characteristic of the discipline of history is, in principle, distinct and distinguishable from those associated with, for example, collective memory (Wertsch, 2002).

Simplifying somewhat and for example, we can distinguish between approaches to the past:

- that aim to *identify* the present with the past (or to assert *continuity* between them) or that aim to *differentiate* the present from the past (or to assert *discontinuity*); and
- that aim to *affirm* the value of aspects of the past or that seek to *negate* them.

Thus, for example, *traditional* orientations towards the past assert continuity of identity between the past and the present and aim to ensure that the future is shaped by adherence to past values or practices through monuments, heroic narratives and so on. By contrast, *critical* orientations towards the past disrupt continuity, effect a breach between the past and the present and model the past as something to be negated and overcome, for example through iconoclasm and critique.

The discipline of history characteristically emphasizes difference, specificity and context in its orientation to the past and construes the past as strange rather than familiar, 'another country' rather than 'home' (Lowenthal, 1985; Tosh, 2008) and historians characteristically aim to engage with the past on 'its own terms', rather than to judge it in present-minded terms or to abolish the distance between past and present through 'identification'.[5]

We can distinguish between interpretations, then, in terms of their orientation towards the past. We can also argue about the relative merits of different modes of orientation. Footnotes and the critical assessment of testimony are not usually welcome at family gatherings (Wineburg, 2007, pp. 6–7); however, the wisdom of grounding collective identities on 'what we like to believe' about the past (Dasgupta, 2005) rather than on claims we can sustain is clearly open to question (Mukherjee, 2005).

Interpretive tools: concepts, questions, theories and methods

All engagement with the past is inherently theoretical: there is no perception without presupposition.

> No empirical activity is possible without a theory . . . All historians have ideas already in their minds when they study primary materials – models of human

behaviour, established chronologies, assumptions about responsibility, notions of identity and so on. Of course, some are convinced that they are simply gathering facts, looking at sources with a totally open mind and only recording what is there, yet they are simply wrong to believe this.

(Jordanova, 2000, p. 63)

Historians' interpretive frameworks are frequently discussed in historiographic literature and have been systematically analysed by Fulbrook (2002, pp. 31–50). Such frameworks shape how meanings are constructed but they also shape the questions or problems that interpretations pose. Explaining what people did, at Agincourt or on *Big Brother*, involves theoretical assumptions and answers to questions such as, '*Why do people do the things that they do?*' Answers to questions of this nature have consequences for the identification of archives, the choice of research methods and so on – if we think material interests determine human action, for example, we will pursue questions that we might not ask if we assume that culture and belief have priority. Methodological questions, such as the relative merits of 'microhistorical' and 'cliometric' approaches to the study of slavery, can be readily made accessible for students, as a recent report of teaching strategies adopted with 13- to 14-year-old students suggests (Hammond, 2007); and as Howells has observed, a focus on historians' questions and methods can focus students' attention on 'genuine historical controversy' and place 'the process of historical research and evaluation at the heart of . . . investigation' (Howells, 2005, p. 33).

Three points are worth stressing, given the fact that students often model differences in interpretation in terms of the subjective distortion of a fixed past (Lee and Shemilt, 2004). First, an interpretive framework is not an avoidable 'bias': there can be no interpretations without questions, categories and assumptions. Second, assumptions can be rationally debated, and historical controversies often turn on such issues as much as on substantive matters (Chapman, 2006). Third, different interpretive forms place differing degrees of importance on methodological debate: the discipline of history is distinguished from other forms of interpretation of the past by the fact that historians are expected to make their assumptions, concepts and methods explicit, so that they can be critically assessed by an academic community of practice, and to present *arguments* for interpretive decisions that they make.

Textual forms

There are impressive examples, in the pedagogic literature, of strategies that seek to engage students in the analysis of historical interpretations as 'deliberate' and 'crafted' artefacts (Moore, 2000, p. 36) designed to achieve particular effects (e.g. Banham and Hall, 2003; Lang, 2003; Ward, 2006).

It is useful to think about interpretations as working to persuade their audiences in a number of ways. As Grafton has argued, interpretations can be analysed in terms of 'rhetorics of narration', that work on various levels, from plot structure to surface features of a text, and in terms of 'a rhetoric of annotation' that works through 'citation and quotation' to support the claims that historians make (Grafton, 2003, pp. 231–3). We should think of historical texts as logical as well as rhetorical objects, however, and as organizing claims into arguments intended to establish warranted conclusions (Ginzburg, 1999). Understanding how an interpretation works as a text, therefore, is likely to involve considering some or all of the following:

* *narrative structure*, or how the text works as a story (Lang, 2003; Megill, 2007)
* *argument structure*, or how an interpretation works to justify its claims
  — through citation and annotation (Grafton, 2003) and
  — through logical argument (Chapman, 2006; Coffin, 2006; Fordham, 2007).

How do interpretations differ?

We need to distinguish between factors that may shape interpretations and what interpretations claim – it is possible, for example, for texts with radically different forms to advance essentially identical claims, and vice versa.

It is likely to be helpful when comparing interpretations to ask questions about:

* what different texts are *doing* and
* what different texts are *saying*.

In other words, it is likely to be helpful to ask questions about the kinds of claim about the past that different texts make and also about the logical relationships that exist between the claims advanced in different interpretations.

Table 8.1 develops an analysis by Allan Megill of the things that historical interpretations can be understood as doing.

Megill argues that, although it is often difficult to disentangle them in practice, all forms of historical writing engage in these four 'tasks' to one degree or another.[6]

The distinction between tasks is analytically useful and provides a way of thinking about how interpretations differ – whereas one interpretation might be primarily descriptive, for example, another might be primarily explanatory. Analysing interpretations in terms of the tasks they perform is a useful way of modelling the questions that interpretations can be understood as answering – descriptive questions (*Who? What? When? How?*), explanatory questions (*Why?*), evaluative questions (*So what?*) and so on. Focusing on tasks also draws attention to the *types of claim* that different

Table 8.1 The four tasks of historical writing[7]

Task	Explanation
1. Description	Describing an aspect of historical reality – telling what was the case
2. Explanation	Explaining why a past event or phenomenon came to be
3. Evaluation	Attributing meaning, value and/or significance to aspects of the past
4. Justification	Justifying descriptive, explanatory or evaluative claims by supplying arguments to support them

Source: Based on Megill, 2007, pp. 96–8, and adapted from Chapman, 2009, p. 58.

interpretations may be making: explanatory claims, for example, differ from descriptive claims and are validated in different ways. Task analysis can also allow differences in interpretive *logic* to be identified – two interpretations, for example, may articulate identical descriptive claims about what was the case in the past but derive differing evaluative conclusions from these claims. The analysis is also a way of distinguishing differences in interpretation type: academic history, for example, consists of a *superstructure*, of descriptive, explanatory or evaluative claims about the past, and an *infrastructure* that aims to justify those claims (Goldstein, 1976; Grafton, 2003): monographs typically justify their claims in ways that monuments do not.

Identifying differences in what interpretations do and identifying differences in what interpretations say are different things, however, and thinking comparatively about what interpretations say entails thinking about logical relationships that obtain between claims. Like propositions in general (Copi and Cohen, 1998), claims about the past can be considered as *complementary*, *contrary* or *contradictory* to each other.

Two interpretations may advance differing claims about the same aspect of the past without actually coming into logical conflict with each other, which is to say that we can accept the claims articulated in both interpretations simultaneously and describe them as *complementary*. Two interpretations may advance claims about the same aspect of the past that are *mutually exclusive*, which is to say that they cannot both be maintained at the same time in the same sense, but which do not *exhaust* the defensible claims that could be made, in which case we can describe the claims as *contrary* to each other: although only one claim can be true it is possible that both are false.[8] Two interpretations may advance claims that are *contradictory* if they understand terms in the same sense and make claims about the same aspect of the past that are *mutually exclusive* and *exhaustive*; thus, for example, one interpretation might articulate descriptive claims about a event, and thus presuppose that this event occurred, whereas another interpretation might deny that the event occurred – either it occurred or it did not and one account must be true and another must be false on the question of existence/non-existence.

A logical analysis of interpretive differences can be combined with an analysis of interpretive tasks to specify how interpretations differ; it is possible, for example, that two accounts may be complementary in their descriptive claims, contrary in their explanatory claims, and so on. Engaging students in logical analysis need not be a terminologically complex undertaking and is a matter of asking questions like, '*Can we accept both of these claims at the same time?*'

Evaluating historical interpretations

The fluidity of the past and the plurality of interpretation does not mean that interpretation is an arbitrary or subjective process – the contexts from which interpretations emerge are, after all, interpersonal contexts of practice and objectivity is a matter of adherence to interpersonal standards (Megill, 2007). It is possible, therefore, to assess the validity of interpretations of the past in terms of their formal properties, using 'rules of thumb' or norms of practice (Bevir, 1994; Husbands, 1996).

A number of authors have developed criteria for comparing and evaluating historical interpretations (Bevir, 1994; Megill, 2007; McCullagh, 1984). Disciplined historical interpretation, Goldstein has argued, is in the business of 'explaining the evidence' or traces of the past that remain in the present (Goldstein, 1976) and we can evaluate competing constructions of the past by asking questions such as the following:

- Do the interpretations *accurately* refer to the archival traces to be explained?
- How *comprehensive* are the interpretations in explaining relevant archival traces?
- How *consistent* are the claims that interpretations advance
  — in themselves and
  — with other claims that we already have good reason to accept?
- How far does an interpretation open up new possibilities (e.g. raise new questions)?[9]

Other questions can and should be asked, of course: we can, for example, debate the logic of historical arguments or question the conceptual or criterial assumptions that authors make (Chapman, 2006). The key point is that we should help students understand that histories can be evaluated criterially through debate rather than by 'checking' interpretations against a 'fixed' past and that, in principle, we may end up accepting more than one competing account provided that evaluation criteria are met.

Interpretations serve many purposes and many of these purposes are not concerned with the production of interpersonally defensible knowledge claims about the past. Just as apples are not spectacles and should not therefore be assessed using optical criteria, so monuments are not monographs and differing modes of constructing the past should be assessed in different ways. Because histories deal with human action they raise ethical questions, for example (Lorenz, 1998), and we can assess evaluative claims about the past in terms of the ethical principles they depend on. It is possible also, of course, to argue that interpretations should be assessed as texts rather than claims and against aesthetic criteria. These arguments are plausible but not entirely persuasive: if a monument (or film, or comic strip and so on) makes or implies claims about what 'was' then we should assess these claims using the best available principles for assessing claims of this type. We can assess the value of a film as a film, of course, but filmic considerations have no implications for the historical validity of the claims that a film advances (Rose and Corley, 2003).

Further reading

As has been suggested, it is imperative that we make use of research findings on how students learn history if we are to help students progress: Lee and Shemilt (2004) provide a concise summary of what is known about progression in the understanding of interpretations and accounts and a fuller exploration of key research on accounts that is readily accessible online is Lee (2001). Seixas and Clark (2004) is a fascinating discussion of historical consciousness that explores student thinking in depth and is a good way into this literature and Nemko (2009) is a recent practical application of these ideas. The polychronicon feature in *Teaching History* explores interpretation questions and provides useful practical teaching suggestions (see, for example, Donaldson, 2009, and Poole, 2009).

Notes

1 For example, Banham and Hall, 2003; Counsell, 2004; Davies and Williams, 1998; Fordham, 2007; Hammond, 2007; Howells, 2005; McAleavy, 1993; Mastin and Wallace, 2006; Sinclair, 2007, and Ward 2006.
2 This chapter make no claim to originality and depends heavily on existing work; this is a work of synthesis, therefore, and one that I hope does not do too much violence to the work that it depends upon.
3 See Chapman (2007) for a discussion of the historicity of interpretations of Stonehenge.
4 A number of very useful models of factors to consider when exploring differences in interpretation have been proposed (for example, Haydn *et al.*, 2008)
5 The degree of success with which history can achieve this is, of course, open to debate (Jenkins, 1997).
6 Many historical descriptions are also evaluations, for example, as phrases like 'The Indian Mutiny' or 'The Great Reform Act' indicate.
7 The table is based on Megill's work but adapts it: Megill uses 'interpretation' to refer to what I am calling 'evaluation' here, for example.
8 'Truth' is understood here as a formal property of propositions rather than in terms of the correspondence between propositions and states of affairs.
9 These questions are inspired by Bevir's arguments but (a) do not reproduce them fully and (b) modify and simplify them in a number of ways.

References

Banham, D. and Hall, R. (2003). 'JFK: the medium, the message and the myth'. *Teaching History*, 113: 6–12.

Barton, K. C. and Levstik, L. S. (2004). *Teaching History for the Common Good*. Mahwah, NJ, and London: Lawrence Erlbaum Associates.

Bevir, M. (1994). 'Objectivity in History'. *History and Theory*, 33(3): 328–44.

Chapman, A. (2006). 'Asses, archers and assumptions: strategies for improving thinking skills in history in Years 9 to 13'. *Teaching History*, 123: 6–13.

——(2007). 'Relics rock: constructing Stonehenge'. *Teaching History*, 126: 20–1.

——(2009). 'Making claims you can sustain: the importance of historical argument'. *Teaching History*, 135: 58–9.

Coffin, C. (2006). *Historical Discourse: The Language of Time, Cause and Evaluation*. London: Continuum.

Copi, I. M. and Cohen, C. (1998). *Introduction to Logic*, 10th Edition. Upper Saddle River, NJ: Prentice Hall.

Counsell, C. (2004). *History and Literacy in Year 7: Building the Lesson around the Text*. London: Hodder Education.

Dasgupta, S. (2005). 'What we like to believe – the debate over *The Rising* is about India's perception of itself', *Telegraph*, 26 August 2005. Available online at: http://www.telegraph india.com/1050826/asp/opinion/story_5155618.asp (accessed 15 January 2010).

Davies, I. and Williams, R. (1998). 'Interpretations of history: issues for teachers in the development of pupils' understanding'. *Teaching History*, 92: 36–40.

Donaldson, P. (2009). 'The Great War and cultural history'. *Teaching History*, 134: 24–5.

Ferguson, N. (2006). 'How to win a war', *New York Magazine*, 16 October 2006. Available online at: http://nymag.com/news/features/22787/ (accessed 18 September 2008).

Fernández-Armesto, F. (2002). 'What is history *now*', in D. Cannadine (ed.) *What is History Now?* Houndmills: Palgrave Macmillan.

Fordham, M. (2007). 'Slaying dragons and sorcerers in Year 12: in search of historical argument'. *Teaching History*, 129: 31–8.

Fulbrook, M. (2002). *Historical Theory*. London and New York: Routledge.

Gardner, H. (2000). *The Disciplined Mind*. New York: Penguin Group (USA).

Ginzburg, C. (1999). *History, Rhetoric and Proof*. Waltham, MA: Brandeis University Press.

Goldstein, L. J. (1976). *Historical Knowing*. Austin and London: University of Texas Press.

Grafton, A. (2003). *The Footnote: A Curious History*. London: Faber & Faber.

Hammond, K. (2007). 'Teaching Year 9 about historical theories and methods'. *Teaching History*, 128: 4–10.

Harlan, D. (2007). 'Historical fiction and the future of academic history', in K. Jenkins, S. Morgan and A. Munslow (eds) *Manifestos for History*. London and New York: Routledge, Taylor & Francis Group.

Haydn, T., Arthur, J., Hunt, M. and Stephen, A. (2008). *Learning to Teach History in the Secondary School: A Companion to School Experience*. London: Routledge.

Heidegger, M. (1978). *Being and Time*. Oxford: Blackwell.

Howells, G. (2005). 'Interpretations and history teaching: why Ronald Hutton's *Debates in Stuart History* matters'. *Teaching History*, 121: 29–35.

Husbands, C. (1996). *What is History Teaching? Language, Ideas and Meaning in Learning About the Past*. Buckingham: Open University Press.

Jenkins, K. (1997). 'Introduction: on being open about our closures', in K. Jenkins (ed.) *The Postmodern History Reader*. London: Routledge.

Jordanova, L. (2000). *History in Practice*. London: Arnold.

Koselleck, R. (2004). *Futures Past: On the Semantics of Historical Time*. New York: Columbia University Press.

Lang, S. (2003). 'Narrative: the under-rated skill', *Teaching History*, 110: 8–14.

Lee, P. J. (1998). '"A lot of guess work goes on": children's understanding of historical accounts'. *Teaching History*, 92: 29–35.

——(2001). 'History in an information culture', *International Journal of Historical Learning, Teaching and Research*, 1(2). Available online at: http://centres.exeter.ac.uk/historyresource/journal2/journalstart.htm (accessed 21 August 2009).

Lee, P. J. and Shemilt, D. (2004). '"I just wish we could go back in the past and find out what really happened": progression in understanding about historical accounts'. *Teaching History*, 117: 25–31.

Lorenz, C. (1998). 'Historical knowledge and historical reality: a plea for internal realism', in B. Fay, P. Pomper and R. T. Vann (eds) *History and Theory: Contemporary Readings*. Malden, MA, and Oxford: Blackwell Publishers.

——(2001). 'History: theories and methods', in N. J. Smelser and P. B. Baltes (eds) *International Encyclopedia of the Social and Behavioural Sciences, Vol. 10*. Oxford: Elsevier.

Lowenthal, D. (1985). *The Past is a Foreign Country*. Cambridge: Cambridge University Press.

McAleavy, T. (1993). 'Using attainment targets in Key Stage 3: AT2, interpretations of history'. *Teaching History*, 72: 14–17.

McCullagh, C.B. (1984). *Justifying Historical Descriptions*. Cambridge: Cambridge University Press.

Mastin, S. and Wallace, P. (2006). 'Why don't the Chinese play cricket? Rethinking progression in historical interpretations through the British Empire'. *Teaching History*, 122: 6–14.

Megill, A. (1994). 'Jörn Rüsen's theory of historiography between modernism and rhetoric of inquiry'. *History and Theory*, 33(1): 39–60.

——(2007). *Historical Knowledge/Historical Error: A Contemporary Guide to Practice*. Chicago: University of Chicago Press.

Moore, R. (2000). 'Using the internet to teach about interpretations in Years 9 and 12'. *Teaching History*, 101: 35–9.

Mukherjee, R. (2005). Clio is not for worship – history is best freed from nation-building, *Telegraph*, 4 September 2005. Available online at: http://www.telegraphindia.com/1050904/asp/opinion/story_5188782.asp (accessed 15 January 2010).

Nemko, B. (2009). 'Are we creating a generation of "historical tourists"? Visual assessment as a means of measuring pupils' progress in historical interpretation'. *Teaching History*, 137: 32–9.

Nietzsche, F. (2008). *On the Use and Abuse of History for Life*, originally published 1873, Ian Johnston, trans., Available online at: http://records.viu.ca/~johnstoi/Nietzsche/history.htm (accessed 7 December 2009).

Poole, R. (2009). 'Bringing space travel down to earth'. *Teaching History*, 137: 50–1.

Qualifications and Curriculum Authority (QCA) (1999). *National Curriculum for History, Key Stages 1–3*. Available online at: http://curriculum.qcda.gov.uk/uploads/History%201999%20programme%20of%20study_tcm8-12056.pdf (accessed 28 October 2010).

——(2006). *GCE AS and A Level Subject Criteria for History*. Available online at: http://www.ofqual.gov.uk/files/qca-06-2854_history.pdf (accessed 28 October 2010).

——(2007a). *History Programme of Study for Key Stage 3 and Attainment Target*. Available online at: http://curriculum.qcda.gov.uk/uploads/QCA-07-3335-p_History3_tcm8-189.pdf (accessed 28 October 2010).

——(2007b). *GCSE Subject Criteria for History*. Available online at: http://www.ofqual.gov.uk/files/qca-07-3454_gcsecriteriahistory.pdf (accessed 28 October 2010).

Ricoeur, P. (2004). *History, Memory, Forgetting*. Chicago and London: University of Chicago Press.

Rose, V. E. and Corley, J. (2003) 'A trademark approach to the past: Ken Burns, the historical profession and assessing popular presentations of the past', *Public Historian*, 25(3): 49–59.

Rüsen, J. (2001). 'History: overview', in N. J. Smelser and P. B. Baltes (eds) *International Encyclopedia of the Social and Behavioural Sciences, vol. 10*. Oxford: Elsevier.

——(2005). *History: Narration, Interpretation, Orientation*. New York and Oxford: Berghahn Books.

Samuel, R. (1994). *Theatres of Memory: Past and Present in Contemporary Culture*. London and New York: Verso.

Seixas, P. and Clark, P. (2004). 'Murals as monuments: students' ideas about depictions of civilization in British Columbia', *American Journal of Education*, 110(2): 146–71.

Shemilt, D. (2000). 'The caliph's coin: the currency of narrative frameworks in history teaching', in P. N. Stearns, P. Seixas and S. Wineburg (eds) *Knowing, Teaching and Learning History, National and International Perspectives*. New York: New York University Press.

Sinclair, Y. (2007). 'Teaching historical interpretations', in M. Hunt (ed.) *A Practical Guide to Teaching History in the Secondary School*. Abingdon: Routledge.

Tosh, J. (2008). *Why History Maters*. Houndmills: Palgrave Macmillan.

Ward, R. (2006). 'Duffy's devices: teaching Year 13 to read and write'. *Teaching History*, 124: 9–15.

Wertsch, J. V. (2002). *Voices of Collective Remembering*. Cambridge: Cambridge University Press.

Wineburg, S. (2007). 'Unnatural and essential: the nature of historical thinking'. *Teaching History*, 129: 6–11.

Chapter 9

What do we want students to do with historical change and continuity?

Christine Counsell

Introduction

How are school students to engage with the second-order concept of historical change? This chapter outlines some problems and possibilities, especially those arising from recent work by history teachers. In particular, I will explore the value of the 'enquiry question' as a way of enshrining and directing a change/continuity challenge.

I also argue that while traditional notions of rate, extent, speed, type and nature are useful in characterizing the analytic demand of change/continuity, and while these attributes form valuable starting points for shaping enquiries, activities or learning goals, nonetheless, a more subjective, experiential dimension is often missing. Without this missing element, both historical scope and student engagement may be impoverished.

Causation and change: very different beasts

Change and continuity are elusive prey. By contrast, cause and consequence are easier to trap. History teachers from all stables invariably know what a causation *question* looks like: Why was there a Russian revolution? How important was Islamic scholarship in shaping the Renaissance? The analytic imperative of a causation question is clear. Moreover, because the validity of any causal explanation is relative 'to the questions posed as well as to what is known about the past' (Lee and Shemilt, 2009: 47), such explanations can be neither definitive nor exhaustive. Students have a reason to experiment. They can select, classify, connect or prioritize their causes until they find explanatory power. The cognitive challenge readily reveals itself. Because students must construct *their own* causal explanation, their own argument, it is self-evident that there is something for them to *do*.

An abundance of research explores students' causal reasoning (e.g. Lee and Ashby, 2000; Lee *et al.*, 1996; Lee and Shemilt, 2009) and there are numerous practical models (e.g. Howells, 1998; Chapman, 2003; Counsell, 2000a, 2004a; Woodcock, 2005). Causation has a pedagogic tradition, stemming back at least 35 years. It translates easily into practical, interactive, lively tasks. Debates on the best approaches proliferate (e.g. Pate and Evans, 2007) but at their centre are shared reference points concerning the *kind of analysis* that engaging with a 'Why . . .?' question involves.

This is not the case with change and continuity. Change does not harness or enshrine a set of reasoning processes in quite the same way. As Stanford (2008) points out, the 'knowledge transforming' (Bereiter and Scardamalia, 1987) to be done by the student is much less obvious. We do have abundant theory concerning the nature of historical change and continuity (e.g. Koselleck, 2002) and we do have research into how students' ideas about change can develop and gain more power. Lee, for example, reminds us that students need to move from a concept of a change as an event to the idea of change as a 'process' and change in 'states of affairs' (Lee, 2005). Shemilt (1980), in the original SCHP (Schools Council History Project) evaluation, elaborated possible goals and these have been taken up by teachers such as Banham (2000: 28–9; see Figure 9.1). But while there is discourse and some consensus about historical ideas of change *versus* common-sense ideas, there has been much less sustained *professional* discourse about the analytic demand of a change question or about the kinds of activities students might undertake. Only recently have we seen a spate of bold efforts to theorize from classroom practice about what constitutes a 'change' activity and the emergence of a discourse arising from teacher-constructed professional knowledge (e.g. Foster, 2008; Gadd, 2009; Jarman, 2009; Jones, 2009).

The current National Curriculum framework in England (QCA, 2008) offers a more direct account than its predecessors of what students should be doing with change/continuity, and it is possible to see this as daughter (perhaps granddaughter) of the original SCHP concept of change (Shemilt, 1980). By referring to 'change' rather than changes and by keeping her conceptual opposite – 'continuity' – in view, the rubric makes clear that students are expected to make judgements. Students are required to consider the 'nature' or 'extent' of change. Also, the word 'analyse' is explicitly used in relation to 'change'. The National Curriculum in England has, in fact, made change/continuity an explicit demand since 1991, although this was somewhat watered-down in 1995 when a reference to 'changes' rather than 'change' seemed to obscure its role as a second-order concept (DES, 1991; DfE, 1995). Indeed, the former National Curriculum's section on change and continuity was 'infuriatingly difficult to make historically rigorous' (Stanford, 2008). In the current 2008 version, change as concept returns and the analytic demand is (a little) more explicit (QCA, 2008).

But few history teachers, in my experience, feel confident in creating activities that involve students in *problematizing* the idea of change/continuity, let alone in designing enquiries. One reason for this might be an ambivalence concerning what is meant by 'change' as a focus for analysis. It is easy for 'change over time' to collapse into a content imperative rather than a conceptual demand. If studying 'change over time' simply means reciting or organizing a lot of events chronologically then there is little for students to do other than to regurgitate. Even where there is a desire to foster conceptual understanding, 'it is all too easy to assume that we are teaching students about change by telling them about it' (Stanford, 2008: 6). Conceptual analysis and acquisition of substantive knowledge are, of course, related (Counsell, 2000b, 2003), but a focus *only* on the latter will deny both access and challenge to many (Lee, 2001; Howson, 2009).

In order to advance our discourse about historical change, it may be helpful to turn to the activities and questions with which history teachers try to elicit pupils' thinking. It is therefore to teachers' contributions and the possibility of theorizing from them that I now turn. The disparate offerings by creative practitioners give us many useful starting points.

Activities fostering reflection and analysis

So, how can students engage in 'knowledge-transforming' activities concerning historical change and continuity? What kinds of change/continuity problems or questions

---

When discussing Shemilt's point on change, think about the following issues:

1. Pupils need explicit reference to these ideas. They need a chance to linger and reflect on the ways in which they use the word 'change'. What makes 'historical' change different from other kinds of change?
2. Which enquiry questions in your work schemes are best suited to teaching Shemilt's objectives? As you review your Key Stage 3 plans, think about the types of enquiry that lead to explicit reflection on change. Try this as a 10-minute INSET(in-service education and training) activity:

'QUICKIE' INSET activity on planning:

Which of Shemilt's points on change might be teased out by enquiries built around the questions below? Match them up:

- Did sixteenth-century religious change happen more quickly in Scotland or in England?
- What changed and what stayed the same in Britain between 1642 and 1660?
- How big a turning point was the Russian Revolution in the last two centuries?
- Only change? What kinds of continuity has the computer age seen?
- What did Tony Blair's attack on 'The Forces of Conservatism' tell us about attitudes to change at the end of the twentieth century?
- Why was the discovery of germ theory a crucial turning point?
- Was medicine in the Middle Ages really worse than it had been Roman times? (showing pupils that progression, stagnation and regression are all at work).

Such questions lend themselves to fun and thought-provoking activities, such as:

- analytical timeline activities;
- parallel timelines charting and comparing different issues;
- living graphs plotting different types of change on each axis, as in the work of Peter Fisher and the Newcastle thinking skills team;
- imaginative role plays, bringing key figures back to life.

Figure 9.1 Extracts from in-service training activity developed by Banham (here Banham is inviting the reader to consider the points raised by Shemilt (1980: 35–6, 80)).

Source: Banham, D. (2000).

might they try to solve? What should we encourage in their judgement-making and what kinds of practical activities might best nurture this?

Banham's (2000) Shemiltian-derived activities (see Figure 9.1) have had some professional influence. For example, as a trainee history teacher Michael Fordham, drawing upon the practical theorizing of Banham, asked a mixed-ability class of 11- to 12-year-olds to characterize change in the degree and mode of harshness deployed by William Duke of Normandy (see Figure 9.2). After making their own judgements about degree of 'carrot' and 'stick' deployed by William, students were then able to plot the fluctuations in Norman policy. They produced graphs to show changing patterns of harshness between 1066 and 1072. They soon realized that their starting generalizations about Norman harshness were unsatisfactory; rather, it was becoming clear that Norman brutality *fluctuated*. The word 'fluctuate' was new to the students and they enjoyed the new analytic power it gave their arguments. For example, by the end of the lesson sequence, and after building secure chronological knowledge, one student concluded, 'long-term continuity fluctuated around short-term change'. The analytic focus on change/continuity was thus achieved.

More recently, Gadd (2009) in a published study used hermeneutic methodology to uncover principles in her own practice. She drew upon aspects of Shemilt (1980) and Banham (1998, 2000) in order to show how overview and depth can interact to provide more 'storied' (and memorable) knowledge and how this, in turn, could interact with analytic thinking about change.

Foster (2008) illustrates a further strand of professional theorizing. Working with Year 9, Foster developed the winning idea of a 'road map' to civil rights as an effort to help students reflect on the underlying processes in the course of the American civil rights movement. Foster was determined that her students should avoid slithering into

---

Did William I change how he ruled over time?

Fill in 'carrot' and 'stick' boxes for each of the events below:

1066   William burns land around London, but doesn't kill Edgar the Aethling. Instead he sends him to France.
1067   To secure London, William gives the city its freedom, but does give it a Norman noble.
1068   William makes peace in the north by allowing English nobles to keep their positions.
1069   To secure the south, William replaces English nobles with Normans and builds castles to defend them.
1070   William burns the north, killing many people and destroying towns and villages.
1071   William defeats the Danes but lets them go in peace.
1072   William makes peace with King Malcolm of Scotland.

With thanks to Michael Fordham, Hinchingbrooke School, Huntingdon, for permission to publish his work.

Figure 9.2 Activity sheet preparing pupils for analysis of change.

a simple account of the *causes* of change. Teachers often invite discussion concerning change/continuity only to become frustrated as the activity collapses into students merely considering *why* that 'change' occurred. They thus turn it into a causation problem and the work of characterizing change and/or continuity evaporates. Foster deliberately sought to obviate this through a metaphor encouraging students to play with speed, nature, extent and interplay of change/continuity:

> Initially, I toyed with the idea of a marble maze . . . or with a snowball going down a mountain. However, I wasn't happy with the restrictions these metaphors imposed. The downward pull of gravity seemed to suggest a deterministic view of change. Finally, I hit on the idea of a car journey. It was flexible enough to accommodate all the aspects of change and continuity that I wanted students to consider: it represented change as a process rather than as an event, it represented the rate, pace and direction of change.
>
> (Foster, 2008: 5)

For Foster, the analytic measures of speed, rate, nature and direction of change gave her the conceptual framework to shape her learning goals and her pedagogy. This is how she initiated student discussion:

> I [asked] students to brainstorm factors . . . that would slow down or speed up a car journey. . . . After wondering aloud how the civil rights movement was a bit like a car journey, students were asked to take each factor that affected the speed, rate, nature and direction of change (for example white violence, federal government intervention, media attention, leadership, non-violent tactics) and to see if they could match it to one of the ideas on the board. . . . most were quick to make connections between ideas such as the driver of the car and leadership of the campaigns, and to realise the scope for argument . . . – was Martin Luther King the driver, the engine, the fuel, or the 'Google map' of the campaigns? Students could then decide how far each campaign had travelled in terms of progress towards civil rights and how fast the change was.
>
> (Foster, 2008: 5)

Foster also noted the assessment potential of the activity:

> [The students] wanted to explain their metaphors . . . Ben took to giving me regular status reports every few minutes ('. . . and now the NAACP [National Association for the Advancement of Colored People] is a dead end, so the Montgomery boycott has to begin on a new road . . .'). I learned more about his thinking in those frequent short conversations than I had done in all my previous lessons with him.
>
> (Foster, 2008: 5)

Another approach explored by many teachers is to give pupils challenging choices from collections of similar-sounding words that could be used to describe a process. Students choose from 'refresh, renew, revise, rework, restore or reform' to capture what is meant by the change that was (say) the Renaissance. Working with smaller-scale topics, students have enjoyed reflecting on distinctions between 'transform, translate, transmogrify and transfigure'. In his work on Jewish experience in England, Jarman defended his use of 'change vocabulary' as an effort to help students see change as a process rather than as an event (2009: 9).

My hope is that such efforts will signal the beginning of a widely rooted, practitioner-led, critical discourse about change, with potential to match that which we have on causation. In addition, if a consideration of change/continuity is to enliven the historical thinking of all school students, we need the various parallel discourses – teacher experimentation and resultant theorizing, research into children's ideas, national statutory demands – to find themselves in increasingly productive relationship.

Enquiry questions fostering reflection and analysis

For the remainder of this chapter I want to tease out one dimension of the above using the popular planning tool, the 'enquiry question' (Riley, 2000). I use 'enquiry question' in a strictly 'Rileyesque' sense – that is, a single question that will knit together a sequence of about three to eight lessons and which students will think about directly in *each* lesson, as they prepare to construct *their own answers* to that question in the final lesson. An enquiry in this sense lends structure and direction to a series of activities. It provides the goal for a final, substantial and motivating activity through which students demonstrate understanding gleaned in the prior lessons. By trying to pose a true 'change' *question*, we can start to approach its meaning for pedagogy and to reflect the distinctive analytic demand of the account students might typically construct.

I recently published a textbook on Islamic history for 11- to 12-year-olds (Byrom et al., 2007). Prior to writing and subsequently, various classroom activities were trialled. One collection of interlocking stories that offers scope for a consideration of change and continuity is that in Enquiry 6: 'A place to pray: What does the story of Cordoba reveal?' I had been attracted by the learning potential of a study of al-Andalus, and of Cordoba in particular, from the eighth to the sixteenth century. In that remarkable city Muslims, Jews and Christians built a culture together (Menocal, 2002). Periods of toleration and fruitful cooperation merged with darker periods of conflict and persecution. What strands of continuity moved through those developments? What forms of 'change' took place? And what kind of change shaped the

---

When was Cordoba most peaceful?
What stayed the same in Cordoba?
When was it safest to be a book in Cordoba?
When did Muslim Cordoba end?
When did Christian Cordoba begin?
When did the Christians change Cordoba?
When did Cordoba change most quickly?

Figure 9.3 Possible enquiry questions for shaping students' investigations of medieval Cordoba.

extraordinary mosque – large enough to hold 10,000 people – by the tenth century? What patterns of change did it see?

The enquiry questions in Figure 9.3 capture my early thinking about how 'big-picture' understanding of Cordoba might be processed through a more analytic 'change' lens. With these questions I was drawing upon classic analytic properties of change/continuity, namely extent of change, speed or pace of change, nature or type of change and interplay between change and continuity (Shemilt, 1980). Through such questions, students can explore ways of characterizing change as well as engaging with issues such as progress and regress – realizing that change is not necessarily synonymous with either of these. The questions require them to identify and seek warranted generalizations about shifts in ways of working and living, seeing and being. These enquiries generated the usual activities of analytic timelines, graphs and debates about the extent to which a particular moment constituted a turning point. The enquiry question, 'When was it safest to be a book in Cordoba?' resulted in the liveliest concluding activity which students enjoyed immensely. They made their own 'little book' in which they wrote the story from the perspective of an actual book. Melanie (aged 12) creatively explored the extent and nature of changes within patterns of toleration and persecution:

> How exciting it is to be living under Al-Hakan II! I was written in Arabic but I have been translated into Greek and Latin!! The copyists in the workshops can hardly keep up. There are so many people who want to read me. Everyone wants to read me and everyone wants me in their own language!

150 years later:

> My Muslim owner has hidden me. Although I contain noble Muslim thoughts, the Almohads have come from North Africa and they do not like me. I fear I am to be burned . . .

Through enquiries that invite judgement, students can tease out patterns, trends and exceptions and so reach their own characterization of the degree or extent of change. In each of the enquiries in Figure 9.3, students must make the temporal dimension visible in their analysis. This explicit temporal dimension foregrounds the change and continuity focus in their reasoning. Working with enquiry questions such as these, students are unable to treat Muslim Spain as static, and instead have to structure an account that discerns and characterizes human activities or experiences that were shifting, while distinguishing these activities and experiences from those that were more stable.

A further specific genre of enquiry questions fits into this approach – one that links change and continuity with notions of periodization, thus allowing students to problematize a traditional period label. Consider the questions in Figure 9.4. These highlight the arbitrary and constructed character of labels, even those that appear to be fixed by absolute chronology, such as a particular decade. Once these take on iconic or mythic cultural significance, even these become open to question. For example, 'What shall we call the Middle Ages?' contains significant intellectual challenge. Calling the Middle Ages 'middle' is as unsatisfactory as calling the middle

When was the Reformation?
Who had the quickest Reformation – Scotland or England?
When were the 1960s?
When did the French Revolution end?
Were the Dark Ages always dark?
What shall we call the Middle Ages?
When did the 'emancipation of women' end?
When did the 'emancipation of women' begin?
What was a Victorian? Were all Victorians Victorian?
What belongs in 'The story of multi-cultural Britain'?

Figure 9.4 Enquiries requiring students to challenge or reinvent labels.

child 'Middle' – the name offers no intrinsic account of distinctiveness. So how then could we characterize 'the Middle Ages' more powerfully? To tackle this, students must reflect on what (if anything) could be said to knit the Middle Ages together. If it is to warrant a label at all then that warrant must be found in states of affairs that might be judged relatively stable or enduring across the medieval period and what might be said to distinguish from what came before and after, a distinction drawn by a true 'change'. The enquiry has become a fascinating question, one which curious students relish tackling, and one which will force them explicitly to foreground problems of change and continuity.

Helping students explore the temporal, subjective qualities of change and continuity

For all the strengths of the approaches in Figures 9.3 and 9.4, however, my experience of working with teachers and students on these enquiries suggests to me that something is still missing. Attempts to characterize change and continuity through dispassionate analysis of its extent, type, speed or interplay still leave students at one remove from deep engagement with the *experience* of historical change and/or continuity. The study of change cannot, surely, be left at the abstract, distanced level of states of affairs – those large, discernible patterns in institutions and governments, in ideologies and beliefs, that history textbooks concern themselves with. It is the notion of 'experience' that interests me, not in the 1970s/1980s pedagogic sense of 'empathy' (although that is part of it), but rather in the sense of meaning-making – the structures of meaning held and continuously transformed by the people who were active and responsive agents living at the time. How did the citizens of Cordoba in the eleventh century actually experience change and what did it mean for them? A few paragraphs in a work of scholarship on the eleventh century or in a standard textbook might give the impression (for example) of mounting despair and terror at the encroachments of the Christians to the north, of the terrifying sacking of the city of the Berbers in 1013, of the desperate pleas to the Almoravids and then to the Almohads for help later in the century followed by the mixed benefits of the latter's rule. We hear from scholars that the population of Cordoba collapsed in that year, as did the size and the wealth of the city. But these are the necessary generalizations of the historian. How is an 11- to 12-year-old in the twenty-first century to make meaning out of these generalizations about change and continuity at the level of human experience *at the time*? If all school students are to be intrigued and compelled by enquiry into such broad historical developments, they will need a deeper engagement with and a curiosity about the way people at the time experienced these developments.

My contention is that judgements about degree or nature of 'change' or 'continuity' must be at least partly constructed out of the time orientation in which people lived. Humans can only ever make meaning temporally. We remember the past and anticipate the future. Memory and anticipation frame all our action and the meaning of our acts. It is possible to incorporate this emphasis on the temporal quality of human experience into students' enquiries. We would need to reflect on how (say) eleventh-century Cordobans positioned themselves temporally and historically. What did change and continuity mean to them? How did it *appear* to them in their consciousness? Their knowledge (or lack of knowledge) of their own past will be intricately involved here. Pain at seeing trade collapse, population fall or art destroyed must have emerged from the collective memory, from the collective historical consciousness of what Cordoba had once been. If this was constructed out of past experiences, was this mainly from their own living memory or from the collective memory of custom and oral stories?[1] What forms did fears, hopes and longings take? How did they envision the future? Were they resigned to eventual Christian conquest? If so, what image of this might they have held in their imaginations and was it, for some, equal or even preferable to the experience of Almohad or Berber invasion? And what did this psychological reality mean for the market-stall holder, the worshipper in the mosque, the Jewish doctor? Whatever forms it took, theirs was a mental reality shaped by temporal projection. These would have been both individual and collective memories through which experience of continuity was enacted and sustained and against which experience of change was encountered or measured.

This has implications for the kinds of enquiry questions we might frame for students. To the questions in Figure 9.3 we might add questions such as: Who noticed Cordoba changing? In 1013, what might Cordobans have remembered about their city? What might have been the hopes and dreams of different Cordobans in 850? I am not suggesting that students attempt original research into these enormous challenging questions, but rather that the intellectual effort to consider such issues involves a useful effort of *imagination* focused on the temporal dimension – memory, nostalgia, fear, projection, anticipation and hope. These were the mental tools by which people in the past collected and made meaning of their own pasts and constructed projections of the future.

Here I want to draw a key distinction. I am not arguing that we abandon the analytic perspective of the historian's bird's-eye view, nor am I merely making the obvious point that we need to complement 'bird's-eye-view' analytic work with other dimensions of study – the micro and affective dimensions such as the empathetic engagement with an individual, the depth to complement the overview, thinking and feeling to complement the cognitive. My interest here is in developing the properties of a problematized reflection on change and continuity.

To illustrate what a students' enquiry might look like with this subjective perspective on temporally constructed experience and meaning built into it, I will use another historical setting, that provided by Duffy (2003) in *The Voices of Morebath*. This moving work is built up entirely from the church accounts kept by Sir Christopher Trickay, between 1520 and 1574 – the duration of his tenure as priest in the tiny parish of Morebath in Devon. Living through the bewildering vicissitudes of Henry VIII, Edward VI, Mary and Elizabeth I, the parish priest chronicles the changes in doctrine, outward observance and financial arrangement experienced by the people of Morebath. We hear of struggles to adapt, sorrow at lost practices, defiance (secret and public), compliance, adaptation and accommodation. Through it all, we make sense of Sir Christopher Trickay and the 400 or so people of Morebath as they lived through the interaction of change with more enduring tradition.

Armed with the unusual (and pedagogically convenient) tool of a priest whose tenure spanned 54 years across some of the most rapid developments in religious and political governance in history, teachers can ask students: What changed in Morebath? Did Sir Christopher Trickay change? What stayed the same in Morebath?

So far, these are the obvious change/continuity questions requiring an analytic focus on degree, nature or speed of change. If emphasizing contemporary temporal projection, however, they might ask: What would the people of Morebath have remembered in 1574? What might the people of Morebath have feared in 1558? How did people in Morebath try to keep things the same? Why did candles matter to the people of Morebath in 1550? (A theme of the book is the changing policy of lights in front of the saints, the financial arrangements for securing these and the growing doctrinal pressure to abandon them).

To some extent, this is simply a further adaptation of Banham's notion of small stories illuminating bigger ones, the 'overview lurking in the depth' (Banham, 1998, 2000). Many teachers adopt Banham's approach (e.g. Gadd, 2009) because they feel that if overview studies lose touch with small detail and human experience, this may hold twin dangers for students' learning: first, the danger of imposing crassly simplistic generalizations on a period (a historical danger); second, the danger of putting off the younger teenager who is not invited to engage at the level of individual human experience in a particular place at a particular time (a motivational or pedagogic danger). But there is more to my rationale than the importance of using the small story of individual, family, village or local place. Such singularities provide a necessary setting and foothold for students' engagement, working knowledge and reflection but, as such, they are merely medium and means. My point is rather that temporally charged enquiries focusing on human experience necessarily have a phenomenological quality to them – a reflection on how people's own past and future *appeared to them*, calling dearly held practices and customs to mind, both in presence and absence. When no longer present, they remembered or lamented them, sought to recreate or preserve them, or somehow managed the future prospect of change that would obliterate such practices for ever.

How are children to embark on this without allowing modern preconceptions and proclivities to distort their reading of the past? This is the Wineburgian conundrum: the need both for distance and for familiarity; the need both to involve our human selves and to let ourselves go, lest we merely see the past in our own image (Wineburg, 2001). Wineburg discusses the conundrum that we must bracket out our own world view and yet, at the same time, not lose our humanness, for it is our own humanness that allows us to 'reach across the distance' and make meaning. The history teacher's task is always riven with that tension (Counsell, 2004b).

Yet this is precisely where the second-order concept of change/continuity has such potential, for the kind of enquiry we carry out in its name must balance a historical distancing with a closer encounter. Thinking about change and continuity forces the student to locate that close encounter within a much broader enquiry. When engaged on a change/continuity enquiry, *why* is the student contemplating the collective memory of the Morebath villagers? They are doing it in order to build up a fuller characterization of patterns of change and continuity over a 50-year period. *Why* is the student considering how a Cordoban citizen might have beheld the artistic wonders of the mosque in 980? In order to reflect on whether the Cordobans would have seen their mosque as static or changing. The wider perspective pulls us back and creates a larger context for the small-scale effort of imagination.

So, while I welcome the recent more explicit emphasis on change and continuity as a second-order concept and its power in giving students something to tussle with, argue about and be puzzled by, I think we should look at rubrics that attempt to enshrine that concept (e.g. QCA, 2008) with caution. They do not exhaust the possible pedagogic foci. A focus on the highly analytic – the type, speed or nature of change – is not enough.

If history teachers are to take on the subjective temporal dimensions of change/ continuity in the tasks that they create for student reflection, they are likely to need a range of sources of stimulus. For me, as a practising history teacher, then as a teacher educator supporting others' practice, inspiration came first from two novels. The first is Naipaul's *The Enigma of Arrival* which hinges on an account of the interior world of the narrator as he gradually makes meaning out of change itself:

> I lived not with the idea of change, of flux, and I learned, profoundly, not to grieve for it. I learned to dismiss this easy cause of so much human grief. Decay implied an ideal, a perfection in the past. . . . Wasn't the place, now, for me, at its peak?

Four hundred pages later, the author is less sanguine. This time, it was not 'their' ending, a process of decay that the narrator had merely observed and from which he had felt detached. At this point the change becomes his own and so is experienced differently. This was an ending *for him*:

> Philosophy failed me now. Land is not land alone, something that is simply itself. Land partakes of what we breathe into it, is touched by our moods and memories. And this ending, this end of a cycle, in my life, and in the life of the manor, . . . caused me grief.
>
> (1987: 452)[2]

Crossley-Holland's *The Seeing Stone* is a novel for children about a village on the Anglo-Welsh border in 1199. I once developed an activity (Counsell, 2004a) for Year 7 using chapter 16 (see Figure 9.5). There is a rhythm to imitate here, a 'tune on the page' (Barrs and Cork, 2001). The teachers trialling the activity reported that asking students to imitate the 'I have three sorrows . . . I have three joys . . .' pattern proved invaluable in enabling them embrace the complexity of a past situation. The

Three sorrows, three fears, three joys

My first sorrow is Serle, who is unfair and mean to me. My second sorrow is my tail-bone. I am almost sure it is growing. My third is the secret Lady Alice told me, and the pain she feels. These are the sorrows of my heart and body and head.

My first fear is that my father will never agree to let me go into service away from home. And my second is even worse. I'm not all that good at my Yard-skills, my tilting especially, so what if my father doesn't mean me to be a squire at all? I know Grace likes me and I do hope that we will be betrothed. But my third fear is that my parents may want her to be betrothed to Serle and not to me.

My three joys . . .

Figure 9.5 Extract from Crossley-Holland's novel. This was used as a template to help pupils write a similar account in a different setting.

Source: Crossley-Holland, K. (2000).

repetition and chant-like quality of the passage make it memorable. It can be used as a framework for unlocking thinking and reshaping knowledge. It has a special value in the context of a change/continuity enquiry because sorrows, fears, hopes and joys have a temporal dimension, a necessary projection forward and back. A development of this idea for medieval Cordoba would be for students to make a 'little book' of sorrows, fears and joys. Figure 9.6 illustrates activities students might undertake. In each one, although an analytic account of degree or type of change/continuity remains indirect, students must make reference back to a range of longer-term contextual features in order to make sense of the remembrance or projection.

Conclusion

Since 1991, the National Curriculum in England has made historical change part of its rubric, but with patchy impact. Its latest incarnation (QCA, 2008) may or may not result in more teachers teaching it explicitly. What history teachers and history teacher educators can do, however, is debate the attributes of mature historical thinking and develop practices for how these might best be nurtured (Counsell, 2004c). For now, and very tentatively, these are mine. If students are to get better at reflecting upon and analysing change and/or continuity, they seem to need a blend of the following:

- opportunities to carry out *explicit, direct analysis* of change and continuity (employing extent, nature/type, speed/rate properties);
- a growing repertoire of fascinating, remembered stories, large and small (overview and depth) so that they create the working knowledge that *a story* leaves behind (Counsell, 2000b); they need to move about within this knowledge in order to become curious about apparent patterns, trends and aberrations;

---

1. **Abdul Rahman I's dream, fear and sorrow before the mosque is built**
   (Use pages 43 and 44 of Byrom *et al.* (2007) *Meetings of Minds.*)
   My dream is . . .
   My fear is . . .
   My sorrow is . . .

2. **Abdul Rahman I's joys after the mosque is built**
   My first joy is . . .
   My second joy is . . .
   My third joy is . . .
   These are the joys of my . . ., and my . . . and my . . .

3. **Al Hakan II's three hopes**
   My first hope is . . .
   My second hope is . . .
   My third hope is . . .
   These are the hopes of my . . ., and my . . . and my . . .

4. **Maimonedes' sorrows**
   Maimonedes has fled to Egypt but as he remembers his time in
   Cordoba what are his sorrows? What Cordoba traditions and joys
   would Maimonedes have remembered? Why is he now sad?
   My first sorrow is . . .
   My second sorrow is . . .
   My third sorrow is . . .
   These are the sorrows of my . . ., and my . . . and my . . .

5. **The archbishop's sorrows**
   The cathedral is built and Emperor Charles I has rebuked you. What
   are your sorrows? What are your fears? How will you still find joy in
   your work in Cordoba?

Figure 9.6 Activities on Cordoba using Crossley-Holland's sorrows, fears and joys
idea.

- active reflection upon *types of question* about change; for example 'When . . .?' questions; questions about beginnings or endings; questions about labelling of periods; questions about speed or nature of change. Do students start to recognize these question styles and the reasoning associated with them?
- intriguing encounters with the *subjective experience* of people in the past and opportunity to speculate how people made *meaning* of that experience through their own temporal lenses.

Notes

1 See Cubitt for a discussion of the function of memory in creating continuity through the 'transgenerational consolidation of certain bodies of knowledge and practice' (2007: 121)
2 See Jones (2009) for an example of an enquiry and accompanying activities influenced by Naipaul's emphasis on the temporality of subjective experience.

References

Banham, D. (1998) 'Getting ready for the Grand Prix: learning how to build a substantiated argument in Year 7', *Teaching History*, 92.

——(2000) 'The return of King John: using depth to strengthen overview in the teaching of political change', *Teaching History*, 99.

Barrs, M. and Cork, V. (2001) *The Reader in the Writer: The Links between Literature and Writing Development at Key Stage 2*. London: Centre for Literacy in Primary Education.

Bereiter, C. and Scardamalia, M. (1987) *The Psychology of Written Composition*. New York: Lawrence Erlbawm Associates.

Byrom, J., Counsell, C. and Riley, M. (2007) *Meetings of Minds: Islamic Encounters c.570 to 1750, Students' Book*. Harlow, UK: Pearson Education.

Chapman, A. (2003) 'Camels, diamonds and counterfactuals: a model for causal reasoning', *Teaching History*, 112.

Counsell, C. (2000a) 'Using history to help students sort, classify and analyse: why was Becket murdered?' *Teaching Thinking*, Issue 1, Spring 2000.

——(2000b) 'Historical knowledge and historical skill: the distracting dichotomy', in J. Arthur and R. Phillips (eds), *Issues in History Teaching*. Abingdon: Routledge.

——(2003) 'Fulfilling history's potential: nurturing tradition and renewal in a subject community', in R. Harris, and M. Riley (eds), *Past Forward: A Vision for School History, 2002–2012*. London: Historical Association.

——(2004a) *History and Literacy in Year 7: Building the Lesson Around the Text*. London: Hodder Murray.

——(2004b) Editorial, *Teaching History*, 117.

——(2004c) 'Putting knowledge, concept and skill back together again: reflections on tradition and renewal in the history teaching professional community in England', Euroclio Conference, University of Bologna, March 2003. *Euroclio* Bulletin 19.

Crossley-Holland, K. (2000) *Arthur: The Seeing Stone*. London: Orion.

Cubitt, G. (2007) *History and Memory*. Manchester: Manchester University Press.

Department of Education and Science (DES) (1991) *History in the National Curriculum (England)*. London: HMSO.

Department for Education (DfE) (1995) *History in the National Curriculum (England)*. London: HMSO.

Duffy, E. (2003) *The Voices of Morebath: Reformation and Rebellion in an English Village*. New Haven: Yale University Press.

Foster, R. (2008) 'Speed cameras, dead ends, drivers and diversions: Year 9 use a "road map" to problematise change and continuity', *Teaching History*, 131.

Gadd, S. (2009) 'Building memory and meaning: supporting Year 8 in building their own big narratives', *Teaching History*, 136.

Howells, G. (1998) 'Being ambitious with the causes of the First World War: interrogating inevitability', *Teaching History*, 92.

Howson, J. (2009) 'Potential and pitfalls in teaching "big pictures" of the past', *Teaching History*, 136.

Jarman, B. (2009) 'When were Jews in medieval England most in danger? Exploring change and continuity with Year 7', *Teaching History*, 136.

Jones, H. (2009) 'Shaping macro-analysis from micro-history: developing a reflexive narrative of change in school history', *Teaching History*, 136.

Koselleck, R. (2002) *The Practice of Conceptual History: Timing History, Spacing Concepts*. Stanford University Press.

Lee, P. (2001) 'History in an information culture: Project Chata', *International Journal of Historical Learning, Teaching and Research*, Vol. 1 (2).

——(2005) 'Putting principles into practice: understanding history', in M. S. Donovan and J. D. Bransford, *How Students Learn: History in the Classroom*. National Academies Press.

Lee, P. and Ashby, R. (2000) 'Progression in historical understanding among students aged 7 to 14', in P. N. Stearns, P. Seixas and S. Wineburg, *Knowing Teaching and Learning History: National and International Perspectives*. New York: New York University Press.

Lee, P., Ashby, R. and Dickinson, A. (1996) 'Progression in children's ideas about history', in M. Hughes (ed.), *Progression in Learning*, Multilingual Matters, BERA.

Lee, P. and Shemilt, D. (2009) 'Is any explanation better than none? Over-determined narratives, senseless agencies and one-way streets in students' learning about cause and consequence', *Teaching History*, 137.

Menocal, M. R. (2002) *Ornament of the World: How Muslims, Jews and Christians Created a Culture of Tolerance in Medieval Spain*. Boston: Little, Brown & Company.

Naipaul, V. S. (1987) *The Enigma of Arrival*. Picador.

Pate, G. and Evans, J. (2007) 'Does scaffolding make them fail? Strategies for developing causal argument in Years 8 and 11', *Teaching History*, 128.

QCA, (2008) *The National Curriculum*. London: DCSF and QCA.

Riley, M. (2000)'Into the Key Stage 3 history garden: choosing and planting your enquiry questions', *Teaching History*, 99.

Shemilt, D. (1980) *History 13–16 Evaluation Study: Schools Council History 13–16 Project*. Edinburgh: Holmes McDougall.

Stanford, M. (2008) 'Redrawing the Renaissance: non-verbal assessment in Year 7', *Teaching History*, 130.

Wineburg, S. (2001) *Historical Thinking and Other Unnatural Acts*. Philadelphia: Temple University Press.

Woodcock, J. (2005) 'Does the linguistic release the conceptual? Helping Year 10 improve their causal reasoning', *Teaching History*, 119.

Chapter 10

Causal explanation

James Woodcock

Introduction

Understanding why things happened as they did is at the heart of historical understanding. More than this, it is 'indispensable in both our personal and our collective lives: it is a precondition for making sense of experience and for acting to shape it effectively' (Chapman, 2008: 3). Philosophers, historians and history teachers have all considered how and why things have happened; their thoughts and advice can and should inform our teaching of causality in the history classroom.

This chapter has three purposes. First, it attempts to summarize the current state of the art of teaching historical causation. Second, in so doing, it hopes to offer an introduction to the central aspects of teaching historical causation. Finally, to those teachers more experienced in this area, it is intended to offer fresh inspiration. The range of literature and the ubiquity of causal analysis in history classrooms in the UK means it is tempting to presume that there is nothing more to say about teaching causation. However, there are plenty of avenues yet to explore, at a minute, human level and at the macro, epochal level. Some of these possibilities will be identified in this chapter.

This chapter is structured as follows:

WHAT IS GOOD CAUSAL ANALYSIS? This section examines what professional literature has to say about the features of good causal analysis, drawing upon practical examples to illustrate how this might be taught. Each sub-section considers one aspect of causal reasoning and understanding. For example, the roles of chronological understanding and counterfactual analysis each have their own sub-sections.

WAYS FORWARD? This section explores new ways of approaching causal analysis in the classroom. In particular, it identifies how we might use historians' own models of causation, how we might consider more non-human causes, such as geographical factors, and invites readers to reconsider how we discuss 'luck' in history lessons.

What is good causal analysis?

If our planning is to be coherent, accessible and challenging we need to decide upon the success criteria for an explanation and analysis of a causal process. These criteria, gleaned from professional, historical and philosophical literature are familiar to modern history teachers:

- pertinent selection and deployment of evidence and examples;
- sorting and categorizing evidence and ideas into broader themes and factors;
- informed and logical explanation of how a particular point answers the question;
- drawing causal links between events and themes;
- deciding upon a hierarchy of causes;
- sustaining an argument which is consistent, persuasive and logical;
- addressing alternative views and interpretations of events or particular pieces of evidence.

(Evans, 1997, 129, 142; Carr, 1984, 89–90;
Chapman, 2003; Leonard, 1999; Woodcock, 2005)

Chronology and connections

The order of events is fundamental to any causal analysis: errors in chronology will lead to confused, unsustainable explanations. However, ordering events only takes us so far. Events have multiple causes: nothing in history is so simple as to have a single, isolated cause. Nor does history happen through a series of events acting on each other in a linear chain. Nor does history happen through a series of factors acting in parallel isolation towards a key event. History as it happens is an infinitely tangled web of cause and effect, of reinforcement and negation, reflection and refraction, acceleration and hindrance (Woodcock, 2005). Consequently, our teaching must allow students to perceive, explore, comprehend and unravel this complexity.

What is a 'cause'?

Chapman (2008) highlights an important misconception: 'causes are not things'. Rather, to identify something as a cause is to ascribe to it a relationship with another thing (Shemilt, 1983). Just as information is only 'evidence' when applied for a purpose, to support a particular case, so things (beliefs, actions, events and circumstances) are identifiable as causes only when one can identify a resulting consequence.

In the history classroom, when we talk of causes we are referring to events, circumstances, actions and beliefs which have a direct causal connection (whether intended or not) to a consequential event, circumstance, action or belief. Such causal connections might be direct or indirect, and might take many different forms, necessitating the need for a range of vocabulary (Woodcock, 2005; see 'The "language of causation"', p. 127) to delineate between, for example, 'motivating' or 'facilitating' factors. As considered below, causes might be human (e.g. actions influenced by personal beliefs) or non-human (e.g. the weather or physical geography).

Which event's causes do we want students to explain?

It is a truism to say that history teachers ask students to explain the causes of events. However, Goldstein warns that we must be careful here. Historians often talk of explaining why X happened, as though X has some special, separate existence. While identifying and highlighting X in this way is a necessary function of developing causal understanding, we must nevertheless remain aware of this 'artificial separation of [X], creating the impression that in history there are [Xs] waiting around to be explained' (Goldstein, 1996: 84). To isolate and label an event or collection of events as X is to create an interpretation, based upon a judgement about the historical significance of those events and circumstances. Another historian studying the same period could conceivably decide that the more pressing need is actually to explain the causes of a different event, Y – Y being in their mind more significant. A third historian might then decide that the label X is inappropriate, and that Z is a more suitable name. Subsequently, a fourth historian might accept the label X is in fact appropriate, but assert that X should contain additional events and circumstances to those suggested by our first historian.

If this sounds too theoretical, consider this: what was the Holocaust? (Or should that be Shoah?) If students are to explain why the Holocaust happened, a common challenge at Key Stage 3 and 4 (students aged 11–16), we, or they, have to make some, perhaps provisional, judgement as to what the Holocaust was. Similarly, consider the question: 'Why did the Second World War break out?' What do we mean by 'the Second World War'? Conventional explanations would presume that World War II had a definite starting point of 11 a.m. on 3 September 1939. But was it at that point a world war? This is certainly a question we could ask at Key Stage 3. If we decide it was only a European (or European imperial) war in September 1939, then we must continue our causal explanation of what caused the thing we call World War II until the war reaches a global scale. Alternatively, the invasion of Poland was not the first conflict that would ultimately be labelled part of World War Two. Japanese imperialist expansion into China, beginning in 1931 or at the latest 1937, could be considered part of World War Two; if so, an explanation of the causes of 'World War II' must also explain the causes of that conflict. A different problem is posed by another question entirely appropriate at Key Stage 3, 'How did Charles I lose control?' 'Loss of control' is not an easily identifiable 'event' that has a defined, undisputed date. Any answer to this enquiry must therefore actually consider not just how but also when Charles lost control. Students would therefore need to decide what constitutes a loss of control in this context and could then identify challenges to this control from cards or a narrative of the events 1625–49.

Identifying specific consequences

As a cause is not a thing but a relationship between things, then students cannot identify causes without considering their consequences. Precision is particularly important here: students need to be able identify the specific *consequences* of each cause, and they need to be able to show how and why event A led to event B in particular. Then, students need to answer the question. If the question is, 'Why did C happen?' and two of the causes of C are A and B, it is not enough to explain how A led to B: students must explain how A, B or A and B together actually led to C. Similarly, it would be inadequate for students to say that A led to C without also explaining the role of B (Woodcock, 2005). This is well illustrated by common simplifications of why famous events have happened. It is a popular but *incomplete* explanation to say that the enactment of direct taxation from London or the special treatment afforded to East India Company tea merchants caused the American War of Independence. The War of Independence began in 1775, yet the Stamp Act and Townshend Acts took effect in 1765 and 1767 respectively. While such events are clearly significant, a complete explanation of why the war broke out must include what happened during those crucial, intervening 8–10 years.

How important is each cause?

Having identified the caused event or circumstances and gone on to identify potential causes of that event, students must then decide upon the relative importance of those causes. This is hard. In essence, importance in a causation exercise means deciding which cause had most influence on the other causes and on the 'final' event itself, and justifying that decision. To do this, we need to decide on the degree and nature of the influence: is it direct or indirect, transformative or simply providing momentum? Here, the 'language of causation' and counterfactual analysis are both invaluable. (Woodcock, 2005; Chapman and Woodcock, 2006)

The 'language of causation'

Sophisticated causal analysis requires subtle, precise claims and distinctions. Crucially, therefore, we must consider how students express their understanding of historical causation. This does not have to be achieved through verbal means; Foster (2008) and Stanford (2008) have both written persuasively about the validity and importance of visual means of communicating historical understanding. Nevertheless, verbal communication is an essential part of our society and educational system, and can offer a particular, perhaps peculiar, means of expressing understanding. (Note that this does not have to be restricted to written expression; for example, see Fullard and Dacey, 2008.) Further, language is not just for expressing an understanding. It also informs and shapes that understanding. Words are tools not just for speaking and writing; they are tools with which we think, imagine, speculate and organize our ideas. 'Thought is not merely expressed in words; it comes into existence through them' (Vygotsky, 1986: 218). Conscious reflection upon the deeper, multifaceted meanings of words and, crucially, what they can add to students' historical understanding, analyses and explanations can play a central role in developing students' conceptual understanding. Ultimately, if students have a refined and diverse vocabulary, and develop expertise and confidence in its use, they will be able to think and communicate in a more precise, refined, nuanced manner (Woodcock, 2005). Activities such as those explained in Woodcock (2005) provide students with new ideas about historical causation and new means of expressing ideas; both are essential for progression. The central activity described by Woodcock (2005) involves students reconsidering the precise meanings of a range of words to use instead of the blunt word 'cause'. For example, students would decide whether the words such as 'trigger', 'latent' or 'exacerbate' implied chronological timing, speed or importance. From this, they could apply such words in analysing and explaining the causes of World War Two. For example, students could be given a series of sentences purporting to explain how one event caused the war; students would be asked to 'choose and improve' such answers by refining the choice of cause word to more accurately reflect the role of that cause. Typically, students might consider whether the Nazi–Soviet Pact 'provoked' Hitler's invasion of Poland or whether some alternative form of words would be more appropriate.

Counterfactual analysis

Counterfactual analysis means asking students to consider, 'what if . . .?' in order to consider how events might have turned out differently, but for one event or action. For example, one might ask Year 9 students (aged 13–14), 'What if Franz Ferdinand had not been assassinated?' Such questions perhaps provide their most helpful function when considering the relative importance of causal factors. Counterfactual questions require a (re)consideration of the role of the various events and factors in the causal process. They can lead to fresh insight into how and why a particular event or process was caused and into how important particular causes were. For example, if we ask the question, 'Would Elizabeth have defeated the Spanish Armada if the weather had been better?' we are asking students to consider the importance of the weather in the failure of the Armada. Was it essential to Elizabeth's 'victory' or did it merely facilitate it?

There is, however, an intrinsic danger with counterfactual analysis. By its nature we are asking students to consider, 'create' or speculate about events which did *not* happen (or at least did not happen there, or then, or in that way). This seems to cut against what history should actually be about – i.e. things which did actually happen – so it has not always been a popular means of analysis (Wrenn, 1998). Certainly, we must be aware of this potential danger and ensure that students see this form of counterfactual analysis as a tool, a means to an end – that end being to make more sense of what *actually* happened. Used with caution, counterfactual analysis is a very powerful tool. It is also interesting how students are often inclined to use counterfactual analysis as an 'instinctive' means of explaining how or why something happened (Woodcock, 2005; Chapman, 2003). When Year 7s (aged 11–12 years) are asked why they believe the Battle of Stamford Bridge helped William to win at Hastings, it is remarkable how many responses begin with words to the effect of, 'Well, if Harold hadn't had to fight Harald Hardraada, then . . .'

Games and analogies

A causal process is abstract and complex, so it can benefit from physical, practical and visual representation. Games and analogies can be helpful, fun and engaging.

When searching for analogies, we can find inspiration from the causal processes which happen around us all the time. We could use the lighting of a fire, the firing of a gun, the baking of a cake, a timebomb, the scoring of a goal, the building of a house and so on. Students are often highly imaginative and creative, and can relate a historical process to a particular analogy, or devise their own analogies.

Games too are a fertile area. Dominoes are a common image used to explain causal processes. Buckaroo has been used successfully (Chapman, 2003). Marble Madness, has many parallels with a causal process (Chapman and Woodcock, 2006) and Jenga has a lot of potential. Because many such games are built around decision-making and ruing errors they can be very enlightening when embarking upon counterfactual analysis.

Even the flaws of games and analogies as models of a causal process can be exploited. Is Buckaroo really a valid model of how the First World War was caused? How useful is Jenga for explaining how Charles I lost control? Such a question has produced surprisingly sophisticated responses from Year 8 (aged 12–13) students who were beginning to explore the nature of the causal process, which might be far more difficult to draw out without an analogy such as Jenga to stimulate and provoke thought. For example, one student suggested that the blocks at the bottom of the Jenga tower should represent the longer-term causes of the Civil War. A peer challenged this, arguing that placing them at the bottom would make them the most important causes (how could the tower stand up without them?). Yet, the second student argued, just because a cause was long-term did not mean it had to be the most important; importance, he implied, was more to do with impact than timing.

Ways forward?

Using historians' models of causation

Historians and philosophers have long theorized about the nature of causality. Such models can, and should, inform our own understanding and practice. Further, they can be used, tested and challenged by our students. Here, I explore one historian's model in depth, as an example of how one might deconstruct and employ in our classrooms other historians' models of causality.

Human causes and causes of human action

Many of the causes that students consider are human actions. Clearly, humans make decisions, follow whims, take actions and make mistakes. Their decisions have reasons and the resulting actions have consequences, intended and unintended, predictable and unforeseeable. Historian C. Behan McCullagh (2004) offers an overview of different theories about the causes of human actions, which we could use to inform our planning, to guide students' analysis and/or to be challenged by students. McCullagh draws upon a wide range of philosophy, historical writing and psychology to categorize the causes of human actions, providing intriguing structures and lenses with which to analyse the past. (Llewellyn and Snelson (2009) have already shown that psychology can be successfully deployed in the history classroom.) Below, I have summarized McCullagh's commentary, and recast it for use in the history classroom:

(a) Mental causes:

    (i) Mental causes of which people are conscious:
        (1) actions taken after deliberation;
        (2) actions taken due to the influence of strong emotion;
        (3) actions taken through habit, or by following convention, or by following instructions;

    (ii) Mental causes of which people are unconscious:
        (1) actions taken to meet their basic needs;
        (2) actions taken to achieve power;

(3) actions taken due to the influence of the subconscious (Freudian analysis).

It would be fascinating to consider in such terms Elizabeth I's decision to execute Mary, Queen of Scots, particularly given her long deliberation over a very personal, emotive and politically explosive dilemma, and her subsequent apparent regret, retraction and denial. We must, however, be very cautious pursuing some of these ideas. There is a real danger of making anachronistic judgements, (ill-)informed by cod-psychology. The most obvious danger area is using Freudian analysis, not least because it is hard to evidence claims about subconscious influences (McCullagh, 2004: 88). Certainly, any psychological analysis must be rooted in and tempered by the available evidence and a wider understanding of the social and cultural context of the relevant parties. If we do allow our students to explore such routes they must, therefore, also be taught how to recognize the strength of their claims, the degree to which they are speculating, how to qualify their claims and how to express provisionality.

(b) Cultural and social causes:

    (i) Social practices:
- Actions taken in a particular context can be explained in part by reference to the conventions and beliefs of the society in which they were taken. Crudely, one might be able to argue that in a particular set of circumstances X did Y because that's what people in X's community would do in those circumstances if they had the same beliefs as X. This perspective could be very useful in helping to explain the apparently strange actions of people from the 'foreign country' that is the past (Lowenthal, 1985, quoted in Chapman, 2008: 7).
- A Year 7 student recently asked the author why Harold did not just pretend to be killed and run away from the Battle of Hastings; an understanding of Anglo-Saxon notions of kingship and masculinity would help to answer such questions. Similarly, through a lens of 'social practices' students are more likely to understand the peculiar medical treatments proposed for dealing with the Black Death.

    (ii) Social roles:
- Some actions are taken because the actor has a particular responsibility or duty, which either specifically requires that action or which can be fulfilled by taking a particular action. This can offer insight into how social hierarchies such as the feudal system functioned. Considering social roles and concepts of duty might also help students to explain Charles I's actions and attitude towards parliament.
- Someone might do something because they are influenced by someone else, who has power over them in some way. This power and influence could be the result of threats or enticements, or because the powerful person is impressive and thus persuasive or inspirational. This could help students to explain why people acted according to the wishes of despots such as Stalin. While fear was undoubtedly a powerful factor, it is an incomplete explanation; the above ideas might spark students to

reconsider and broaden their understanding of how dictatorships have functioned.

(iii) Social functions:

- Some people serve a particular function in society due to the effect of their personality, behaviour or mere presence. This function can help to explain the actions of others: people with a social function might be said to set the tone for others' actions, or create a culture in which certain actions are more likely to take place. The effectiveness of leaders can be enlightened thus, such as when considering Hitler's role in Nazi Germany. Did he play an active, decision-making, controlling role; or, was it his image, aura and symbolic presence (his 'social function') that most influenced the actions of others?

McCullagh's work could help our students to produce very sophisticated causal analysis. The various means of explaining human actions which he considers in many ways reflect what Lee *et al.* (2001) found to be the hallmarks of 'higher-level' historical analysis. Lee *et al.* have shown that students tend to move from (a) explanation in terms of personal wants and purposes, to (b) explanation by role or stereotype, to (c) explanation by reference to the logic of the situation (explaining it in everyday, possibly anachronistic terms), to (d) explanation by reference to the way in which people at the time thought and ultimately to (e) explanation in terms of the wider context of ideas. The similarities between Lee *et al.*'s findings and the different forms of explanation identified by McCullagh are clear, particularly at stages (d) and (e). McCullagh's various models could therefore guide our planning, steering our students away from anachronistic explanations towards higher levels of analysis, which are rooted in a deep sense of person, place and period.

Before we plan lessons that provide such a context to inform students' causal explanations, we must first decide what we mean by 'context'? All events, thoughts, actions occur in a variety of discrete, overlapping and concentric contexts. For example, if we want students to explain the actions of Charles I 'in context', we need to decide which context and how deeply to immerse students within it. Do we consider his actions in the religious and political context of 'Reformed' England; or, in the context of seventeenth-century Europe more widely; or, in the context of political and religious radicalization and the growing assertiveness of parliament? Similarly, while it would be good to see students interpret Charles' actions in the context of his role as a king, would it not be better for them to interpret his actions specifically as a seventeenth-century king, or an English king, or both? The answer to the question, 'which context?' lies in the purpose of the enquiry within your wider curriculum. For example, if your enquiry about the causes of the 'English' Civil War stands within a unit charting the changing monarchical power in the British Isles 1066–1750, then central to the enquiry should be the causal role of changing contemporary conceptions of monarchy and government. But if you are considering the 'English' Civil War in the context of the European legacy of the Reformation, then you need to set his actions in that different geographical, temporal, religious and political context. Clearly, in order for students to engage with such explanation, we would need to bring them to a point of deep contextual knowledge and empathetic understanding.

Only then would they have the necessary understanding of the intellectual, emotional, social, political, cultural, institutional and philosophical contexts within which the individuals were acting. Without such understanding, which needs to be planned for explicitly, students would probably explain actions and reactions in terms of 'what they themselves would do'. (See Barton and Levstik (2004), chapter 11, and in particular their commentary on Ashby and Lee's model of progression in empathetic understanding.)

Having decided upon a context in which to place your causal enquiry, we could plan to challenge students further, by requiring them to consider how McCullagh's different factors *inter-relate*. Individuals within a society have social functions, are influenced by contemporary conventions and beliefs and are driven by conflicting desires and fears. Where alternative courses of action were available, students should consider the influence and relationship between each of those factors and on the final outcome. To avoid anachronism, students could use social convention to narrow down all the theoretically possible courses of action to those options plausibly available to contemporaries. Then, students could consider the beliefs, desires and fears of the individual actor to consider which of those plausible options was more likely to be followed by *them*. Henry II and Thomas Becket's quarrel, often considered in Year 7, would certainly be illuminated by such analysis.

Further light can be shone on disputes, civil wars or revolutions if we explore diverse and *conflicting* beliefs and the influence of (a) the beliefs themselves and (b) the conflict over the beliefs. For example, Charles I's views of his own social role and the function of parliament differed from those of his opponents, leading ultimately to his execution. Here, we can take students on a journey. We can explain many of Charles' actions by his belief in the Divine Right of Kings, but why should that doctrine appeal to him in particular? Why should such a doctrine would appeal to Charles' supporters, and why did others reject it, or at least reject that Charles himself was divinely appointed? With the right level of scaffolding and differentiation there is no reason why Year 8s could not begin to engage with this at some level. Something as simple as a card-matching exercise could help. For example, a series of cards could describe the beliefs or attitudes of selected key players of the period (such as Charles, Cromwell, Laud, Hampden and Pym). A second set of cards could describe various possible motives for holding such beliefs. Students would then be asked to decide which motives would apply to which character. These motives could reflect McCullagh's different classifications of type of motive (e.g. some cards might describe how some were motivated by the desire to follow convention and tradition; others might be motivated by personal ambition and so on).

Significant challenge could be offered if you explicitly ask students to explain Charles' actions and events in their many different contexts. Here we would be exploring the interface between interpretation and causal explanation (and significance), as identified by Chapman (2008). A biographer might be inclined to explain an individual's actions by emphasizing personal factors; a cliometrician would want to explain those actions by reference to a much broader socio-economic context; a student of the Reformation would highlight the politico-religious factors (Hammond (2007) shows how cliometricians and micro-historians are within the grasp of Year 9 (aged 13–14 years)). If you did want to ask students to consider how to explain actions in different contexts, a layers of inference diagram (Woolley, 2003) could be devised, with Charles' actions described in the centre of the page, and a series of layers extending outwards. In the inner layer students could explain his actions by reference to his personal beliefs and circumstances; in the next layer out students would explain his actions by reference to the social role of seventeenth-century monarchs; further out, students could explain how the particular political and/or religious circumstances of the period influenced his actions. The author's colleague Matthew Stanford has also proposed a more visual way of encouraging students to contextualize actions by placing a character in a scene. Students would have to decide on the costume, the setting, the foreground and background, the wider surroundings and so forth in order to represent the various personal, social and cultural factors influencing their behaviour.

Finally, if we are to base lessons and activities around McCullagh's ideas, we would need to decide on the degree to which the philosophical and historiographical background to such ideas is made explicit to students. For example, an ambitious teacher might ask a class to test Nietzsche's claim that '*Not* for pleasure does man strive, but for power' (quoted in McCullagh, 2004: 91). To do this, one could take a historical example (a revolution might be ideal; Henry VIII's rule could also be examined in such terms) and ask students to identify the reasons why people acted as they did: was it for pleasure or power? Or something else entirely?

Non-human causes

Geographical factors

We have so far considered the many ways in which *human* actions can be explained. However, it is insufficient only to consider human actions, or circumstances of human origin, as causal agents. Many an A-level student would have referred to bad harvests as a cause of revolution and Year 8 might well be familiar with the role of the storm in the failure of the Spanish Armada. Similarly, the role of disease in the European conquest of Latin America is well documented. In all such events, the relationship between natural events and human action and reaction is a core part of the causal process.

In contrast to searching the depths of the human mind, through the McCullagh model, why not ask students to consider sweeping, macro events at an epochal level? Pulitzer Prize–winning geographer Jared Diamond (1997) takes a 13,000-year view of human history, exploring the role of geographical factors in shaping human history. While historians often focus on the ambitions of man, Diamond considers, for example, how crop type and the domseticability of animals gave Eurasian cultures sufficient advantage to become the dominant powers since the last Ice Age. In the classroom, Lambert (2004) shows how geographical concepts and analysis can offer revealing new insights into historical questions. Just as place, space and scale can reshape our understanding of the Holocaust so too could they provide new ways of contextualizing and explaining causal processes.

Reconsidering luck, chance and accident

Aristotle (350 BC) identified chance as one of seven factors that explain people's actions, and 'luck' is ever popular with Year 7 students explaining why William won the Battle of Hastings. Philosophers, theologians and Shakespearean protagonists debate the role of chance, fortune and fate in human affairs. Fate might be outside the historian's realm, but luck is commonly considered, certainly in the classroom. To the author, however, 'luck' has always sat awkwardly in historical causal analysis. Considering the role of 'luck' can lead students to group otherwise unrelated factors into an incoherent 'luck' category, leading to murky explanations. Also, labelling a factor as 'luck' can devalue the role of particular events and circumstances, dismissing them as though they were random and without cause, thus obviating the need for deeper analysis. More fundamentally, we are perhaps mistaken if we treat 'luck' as a causal agent at all. A Year 9 student helped to clarify the author's thinking on this matter. 'Luck' is so problematic because it means very different things, accident, or good fortune, which can lead to confusion and obfuscation. The student's implicit argument was that describing something as 'lucky' is a way of *interpreting* consequences; but luck does not *cause* those consequences. 'Accident' might, however, help us to resolve this difficulty. Accidents, or unintended consequences and coincidences, have causes, and, in turn, consequences, and those consequences might be described as 'lucky' for a beneficiary. This points towards far more refined analysis than, 'William won because he was lucky.' For example, we could instead say that 'William's victory was *facilitated* by accidents.' William could *consider* himself lucky that the wind prevented his invasion until after Harald Hardraada's invasion in the north. But, William did not *decide* to invade England simply because the wind was blowing in the right direction (only a peculiarly aggressive king would do that). Instead, his decision to invade was driven in part by personal ambition. Thus, 'luck' does not really provide *causal* enlightenment here, but 'accident', considered alongside personal motivation, perhaps does: William's victory could be *described* as lucky because it was *caused* in part by an accident.

Conclusion

What is the future for the teaching of historical causation in our classrooms? What areas have not yet been explored? Provided we are cautious of anachronism, psychology could provide inspiration. Why not also consider philosophical and historiographical writings on the nature of causation? Does McCullagh's model stand up to scrutiny in the context of the causes of the French Revolution? Since Wrenn (1998) has encouraged us to be less sniffy about counterfactuals, are we now ready to ask students to explore alternative futures, or at least richly imagined alternative pasts in the mould of Robert Harris (1992), informed by deep counterfactual analysis? With cross-curricular learning increasingly discussed in schools, can we exploit the fact that many other subjects look at causal processes, not least science and geography? (Indeed, much of the 'language of causation' is scientific: latent, precipitate, evolve, catalyst.) Why not ask students to compare the nature of causal process in each subject? Or, join your geographers in exploring how the role of place and the domestication of animals has shaped our world. Cows as causes, anyone?

Further reading

Chapman, A. (2003) 'Camels, diamonds and counterfactuals: a model for causal reasoning', *Teaching History*, 112: 46–53.

Diamond, J. (1997) *Guns, Germs and Steel: The Fates of Human Societies*. New York: W. W. Norton.

Lee, P., Dickinson, A. and Ashby, R. (2001) 'Children's ideas about historical explanation', in A. Dickinson, P. Gordon and P. Lee (eds) *Raising the Standards in History Education*, vol. 3, pp. 97–115. London: The Woburn Press.

McCullagh, C. B. (2004) *Putting Postmodernism in Perspective*, chapter 4, pp. 70–115. London: Routledge.

References

Aristotle (350 BC), 'Rhetoric', (I.1369a5). W. Rhys Roberts, trans., Available online at: http://classics.mit.edu/Aristotle/rhetoric.mb.txt (28 November 2009).

Barton, K. C. and Levstik, L. S. (2004) *Teaching History for the Common Good*, Chapter 11. New Jersey: Lawrence Erlbaum Associates.

Carr, E. H. (1984) *What is History?* London: Penguin.

Chapman, A. (2003) 'Camels, diamonds and counterfactuals: a model for causal reasoning', *Teaching History*, 112: 46–53.

——(2008) 'Cause and consequence: developing historical explanation' (unpublished), Institute of Education, University of London.

Chapman, A. and Woodcock, J. (2006) 'Mussolini's missing marbles: simulating history at GCSE', *Teaching History*, 124: 17–27.

Diamond, J. (1997) *Guns, Germs and Steel: The Fates of Human Societies*. New York: W. W. Norton.

Evans, R. J. (1997) *In Defence of History*. London: Granta Books.

Foster, R. (2008) 'Speed cameras, dead ends, drivers and diversions: Year 9 use a "road map" to problematise change and continuity', *Teaching History*, 131: 4–7.

Fullard, G. and Dacey, K. (2008) 'Holistic assessment through speaking and listening: an experiment with causal reasoning and evidential thinking in Year 8', *Teaching History*, 131: 25–9.

Goldstein, L. J. (1996) 'The what and the why of history: philosophical essays', Lieden. The Netherlands: E. J. Brill.

Hammond, K. (2007) 'Teaching Year 9 about historical theories and methods', *Teaching History*, 128: 4–10.

Harris, R. (1992) *Fatherland*. London: Hutchinson.

Lambert, D. (2004) 'Geography in the Holocaust: citizenship denied', *Teaching History* 114: 42–7.

Lee, P., Dickinson, A. and Ashby, R. (2001) 'Children's ideas about historical explanation', in A. Dickinson, P. Gordon and P. Lee (eds) *Raising the Standards in History Education*, vol. 3, pp. 97–115. London: The Woburn Press.

Leonard, A. (1999) 'Exceptional Performance at GCSE: what makes a starred A?', *Teaching History*, 95: 20–3.

Llewellyn, A. and Snelson, H. (2009) 'Bringing psychology into history: why do some stories disappear?', *Teaching History*, 135: 30–8.

Lowenthal, D. (1985) 'The past is a foreign country', in A. Chapman (2008) 'Cause and consequence: developing historical explanation' (unpublished), Institute of Education, University of London.

McCullagh, C. B. (2004), *Putting Postmodernism in Perspective*, chapter 4: 70–115. London: Routledge.

Shemilt, D. (1983) 'The Devil's Locomotive', *History and Theory*, 22(4): 1–18.

Stanford, M. (2008) 'Redrawing the Renaissance: non-verbal assessment in Year 7', *Teaching History*, 130: 4–11.

Vygotsky, L. (1986) *Thought and Language*. Cambridge, MA: MIT Press.

Woodcock, J. (2005) 'Does the linguistic release the conceptual? Helping Year 10 to improve their causal reasoning', *Teaching History*, 119: 5–14.

Woolley, M. (2003) '"Really weird and freaky": using a Hardy short story as a source of evidence in the Year 8 classroom', *Teaching History*, 111: 6–11.

Wrenn, A. (1998) 'What if . . . what if . . . what if . . . we had all been less sniffy about counterfactual reasoning in the classroom?', *Teaching History*, 92: 46–8.

Chapter 11

Understanding historical evidence

Teaching and learning challenges

Rosalyn Ashby

Introduction

It is essential to history education in an open and democratic society that school students come to understand the nature and status of the curriculum knowledge they acquire. Developing students' concept of evidence is central to a disciplinary approach to knowledge and essential for understanding the relationship between the material that the past has left behind and the claims history makes about the past.

This chapter begins with a brief discussion of the importance of historical evidence to a history education. It goes on to explore the nature of this concept by picking out some relationships and distinctions that bear on students' understanding. Students' propensity to treat history as a copy of the past and historical sources as 'face-value' information poses a serious challenge for teachers. Those most able to meet this challenge will need a developed understanding of what is involved in learning this concept and some knowledge of their students' likely misconceptions about it.

The importance of evidence to a history education

If history as a body of knowledge and history as a form of knowledge are to maintain a symbiotic relationship it is imperative that the concept of evidence is not detached from knowledge goals. Treating evidence as a skill, focusing only on the routine interrogation of sources and limiting historical enquiry to the construction of personal opinions have left history justifying its place on the curriculum in ways that underplay its value as knowledge. In a climate where skills are increasingly seen as generic and given a central role in the curriculum it is worth restating some of the arguments that stress the importance of evidence to knowledge.

Understanding the grounds on which knowledge claims rest has been at the heart of academic arguments justifying a disciplinary approach to history education. The Schools Council History Project (SCHP) pressed for the independent existence of history on the curriculum by stressing the importance of concepts that make history a distinct form of knowledge. It was felt that 'whilst children can be more or less *well informed* about the conclusions of expert enquiries into the past, they are only *educated* to the extent that they possess understanding of the methods, logic and perspectives proper to these enquiries' (Shemilt, 1980: 26). Rogers, writing in support of this approach, was also concerned with the inadequacy of knowledge accepted only on the basis of 'good authority' arguing for an understanding of 'the grounds upon which our claims to knowledge rest' (Rogers, 1978: 5). He wanted a history education that enabled students to distinguish a 'judicious and well-informed opinion as opposed to a silly, ignorant and prejudiced one' (Rogers 1984: 22). For both Shemilt and Rogers the focus for history education was knowledge but knowledge accompanied by some understanding of how it had been established and recognition of the status implications of this.

Lee was also concerned that when students 'learn the products of historian's research, they still do not know any history unless they understand something of what counts as good grounds' (Lee, 1994: 45). He claimed 'the ability to recall accounts without any understanding of the problems involved in constructing them or the criteria involved in evaluating them has nothing historical about it' (Lee, 1994: 45). Like Shemilt and Rogers, Lee's 'good grounds' argument is not suggesting that all history lessons begin from scratch with 'sourcework' dominating classroom activities.

> They [students] cannot be historians (if 'historian' means 'professional historian') and it would be absurd to insist that pupils test everything they are taught by direct recourse to the relevant sources, let alone produce all their history from the sources themselves. It is equally absurd, however, to say that schoolchildren know any history if they have no understanding of how historical knowledge is attained, its relationship to evidence, and the way in which historians arbitrate between competing or contradictory claims.
>
> (Lee, 1994: 45)

The importance of the 'good grounds' argument is directly related to students' being in a position to distinguish history from other forms of knowledge that relate to the past. 'Without an understanding of what makes an account historical, there is nothing to distinguish such an ability from the ability to recite sagas, legends, myths or poems' (Lee, 1994: 45). Few teachers would argue with the following statement:

> Concern with the evidential basis of claims to knowledge, with the developmental logic of historical accounts, and with the modal logic of causal explanation is not [mere] pedantry; on the contrary, it is a moral concern fundamental to the maintenance of an open tradition, and, thereby, of an 'open society'.
>
> (Shemilt, 1991: 7)

The concept of evidence

Defining the concept of evidence in history is the work of philosophers and demands some serious study. What is undertaken here is a limited discussion of the terms used in connection with evidence frequently encountered in classrooms. Some attempt to demonstrate the relationship evidence has with what the past has left behind and history has been attempted and explored in the context of students' learning.

A concept not a skill

Perhaps the first thing to stress is that evidence is a concept and not a skill. Evidence is not something we do or practise doing; it is something we understand, or come

to understand. It is this understanding that is at work in our minds when we con-
template the value of a historical source in relation to a specific enquiry, examine
the basis on which a historical particular might rest or consider the ways in which
facts are used within historical accounts. It is not that skills play no part in handling
sources and understanding evidence. Students' generic skills play a role in teachers'
decisions about, for example, how many variables a student can handle, or how different levels of literacy impact on the length and language of source material. History
specific skills are important but the effective application of these skills is likely to
depend on the conceptual understandings students are working with. In identifying
evidence as one of the concepts crucial to the historical enterprise, the SCHP rightly
gave recognition to the attendant skills of 'enquiry, hypothesis formation, analysis,
inference, judgement and synthesis' but stressed it was the 'fundamental structural
concepts' that were 'the objects of understanding', while making clear that their
'associated skills function as mechanisms of understanding' (Shemilt, 1980: 7). A
problem arises when 'doing history', seen as important in developing the skills of
the historian, takes precedence over developing an understanding of the nature and
status of historical knowledge through a developed concept of evidence.

The past and history

The past is everything that ever happened and history is what we claim about it.
This is a straightforward distinction that we often take for granted. However, many
school students work with the assumption that the past and history is one and the
same thing and see history as a copy of the past. This assumption has implications for
students' understanding of historical evidence in several ways. For students who think
like this history is just a fixed and static picture of what was, has little to do with now
and is interesting but useless. A jigsaw image of the past – sometimes encouraged by
teachers – assumes that the only problem history faces is in finding the missing bits
of a jigsaw puzzle. Differences in historical accounts are then seen as a consequence
of historians not having access to all the bits and inventing things to fill in the gaps.
A Lego view of history might be a better image to encourage than a jigsaw version
of the past, where the evidence available or the singular factual statements available
can be put together in different but perfectly valid ways.

Sources and evidence

The distinction between sources and evidence ought to be a straightforward matter
but there is reason to believe these words are used interchangeably as though they
are the same thing. One example of this is a published wallchart found in many classrooms headed 'Kinds of Evidence' setting out what are actually 'Kinds of Sources'.
This is a serious category mistake and one that encourages students to believe that
evidence is a category of objects, which it is not.

Historical sources, on the other hand, are categorized by historians and some of
these categories make important distinctions that indicate their relationship with the
potential evidence. Distinctions between records and relics are useful for students
in developing a concept of evidence. They are suggestive of other categorizations
such as intentional and unintentional that can indicate the caution needed in treating

them as evidence. Examining sources for what they intended or did not intend to reveal helps students to move beyond a face-value response towards an understanding of inference and deduction. Diaries that were kept for personal reflection need to be treated in different ways to those kept by politicians with a view to 'setting the record straight'. Going beyond eyewitness reports is important in helping students to understand the complexities attached to source evaluation and in challenging assumptions that the only way of knowing about the past is through a 'truthful eyewitness'. Medieval rubbish tips for example were not created to fool the historian, and castles don't present problems of bias.

Evidence is not a category of objects or anything physical in the world. Sources yield evidence but only when they are used as such, to support a claim, back up a theory, establish a fact or to generate a hypothesis. Jordanova makes clear this distinction and the complexity of the relationship.

> Sources are simply 'raw' materials of whatever kind. They have the potential to bear on a historical problem, but it is always necessary to show precisely how they do so. To call something evidence implies that the case for its relevance has been made – evidence bears witness to an issue. In a sense evidence is a philosophical concept – if I ask for evidence of something, I have a set of logical problems in mind, to which this thing we call 'evidence' will speak.
>
> (Jordanova, 2000: 96)

Where school students treat sources and evidence as though they are the same thing they are likely to assume these sources will speak for themselves. Before sources can be persuaded to yield up the evidence they have to come under scrutiny, and not be taken as authority or accepted without question. 'Sources have no absolute value, however enchanting they might be' (Jordanova, 2000: 184), nor as Walsh warns do such things 'bear their meaning' or 'their authenticity on their face' (Walsh, 1961: 18).

Students, however, do have a propensity to treat historical sources as face-value information. This is particularly true when using written sources, where the focus is on 'What does it say?' 'What is it about?' Activities designed to offer some cognitive challenge to this position encourage students to shift their focus to 'What is it?' through questions that ask 'Who wrote it?' 'Why did they write it?' Who was it written for? What was it written for? 'When was it written?' 'Are the authors in a position to know what they claim?' These questions help students to look not at a source but through it, to the circumstances surrounding its production. Although these questions are the backbone of sourcework in many classrooms some warning is necessary. These questions can lead students to conclude that particular sources should be rejected for their bias and unreliability. Attempts to shift students away from naïve responses to testimony have been attempted through questions that ask whether a source, despite its problems, might nevertheless be useful for a specific enquiry.

Objects and artefacts can have some advantage over written sources. Not just because they avoid problems of literacy but also because students often respond to encounters with these sources with the question 'What is it?' rather than 'What does it say?' While problems of bias and reliability are less likely to get in the way of learning, other problems come to the fore. Teachers are often left without important contextual information that would allow this question to take student thinking forward. For example, if students are to decide whether a particular object is a cult object or a cooking pot, a spoon or a digging tool, a chair or a throne, it is important for them to have some knowledge of where it was found and what else it was found with.

The point of source interrogation is to encourage material the past has left behind to answer our questions about that past. It cannot do this in any direct sense but student questioning of it can move them into a closer association with how it came into being and what this means about how it might be treated. This step is not always taken and the point of source interrogation is lost along with the interest of the students. The ultimate question about a source is not about bias or reliability but will it, and how might it, bear the weight I want to place on it as evidence for the claim I want to make, or the hypothesis I want to test. A range of contexts are important in making these decisions.

Sources and contexts

The questions picked out above help students to consider how a source came into existence. Helpful also is a sense of what any given source 'meant in the world from which is survives' (Dickinson *et al.*, 1978: 9). Modern-day examples can help demonstrate to students why this matters. 'Is it a shoe or a trainer?' 'Is it the *Sun* or a newspaper?' It is not that a serious newspaper is a better source than the *Sun* but that knowing the difference actually matters in terms of how each might be used. Three contexts are important to this.

The question or enquiry

The question or enquiry we are pursuing determine how we might use any given source as evidence. It is not possible to determine the value, usefulness, utility or reliability of a source, or its category as primary or secondary, independently of the use to which we want to put it as evidence. This was a common classroom mistake in the early days of the School History Project (SHP) but quickly remedied by most thinking teachers. The relationship between the material the past has left behind and the focus of our historical enquiry is central to an understanding of evidence. Developing students' understanding of this relationship can be approached through a focus on the nature of the question.

Questions or enquiries set parameters for what can count as evidence in answering them. Given the nature of the question what evidence is needed? What sources might generate this? How do the evidential implications of a particular kind of question relate to the likely status of the claim we then make? Some questions have less complex relationships with the evidence than others. For example, questions about what happened and questions about why something happened offer a clear distinction between what might count as evidence in the first and what counts in the second. A description of an action can be witnessed, whereas the intention behind the action has to be understood within the complexities of the context of that action, and inferred through the range of possibilities that might attach themselves to it in this context. Claims about intentions will be less certain than those about actions. An enquiry question asking for the intentions behind an action would need to be broken down further. What does this person have to gain by this action? What might this person by trying to prevent or defend? What might they be reacting to? Why react in this way and not another way? Further, the intentions behind an action might be difficult to ascertain if the outcome of that action is one that was not intended. Distinctions might need to be made about the stated intentions of the historical character and those the historian perceives.

Source sets

A great deal of historical knowledge might be built on the evidence generated by a single source. Sources may yield even more when examined in relation to other sources. Students need to understand how this works to fully appreciate the relationship between sources, evidence and knowledge claims. What other sources are available that might shed further light on a particular source? Attempts to teach students the importance of treating sources as a set was at the heart of the SHP 'unseen' examination paper. The creation of source sets is not an easy task. Poorly thought through or misunderstood examples led to ridicule about the 'tyranny of sources A – G' and easy jibes about the use of short sources. While source sets are important for teaching students about the nature of historical evidence, a diet of these is not helpful to student motivation. These source sets, often accompanied by 'background information' to provide a knowledge context of established facts, bring into view a third context. What is already known that bears on the question being pursued and the sources under evaluation?

Prior knowledge

The knowledge context for sourcework in the classroom probably needs more emphasis and tighter focus. For example, knowing that the Licensing Act lapsed in 1695 is crucial to differences in the interpretation of popular printed material prior to and following 1695. Students need to recognize the relationship and paradox that exists between the interpretation of sources and history's existing knowledge base.

> The resolution of this paradox lies in recognizing once more that history is an ongoing public tradition. Historians do not labour in solitary confinement, but come to their evidence with a range of accepted knowledge, standards and procedures based on the work of their colleagues down the years. This shared knowledge is not fixed and unchallengeable, but equally it is not a matter of *faute de mieux* knowledge or profitable short cuts. The works of other historians are not just second-best sources of information, but part of a common framework in terms of which historical questions, interpretations and evidence are given meaning. It is not simply information which is at issue here, but a whole way of looking at the world.
>
> (Dickinson *et al.*, 1978: 10)

The use of sourcework at the expense of access to well-established facts and historical accounts can undervalue the work of historians. Students come away from some lessons with the belief that 'primary sources are better than secondary' and historians are seen as providing 'second-rate' knowledge because their accounts are 'second-hand'.

Different kinds of claims

Historical claims differ in nature in much the same way that questions do: descriptions, explanations of actions or events, accounts of change. They can be presented to students as hypotheses to be tested, as singular factual statements, as historians' accounts.

Testing hypotheses

As with questions, exploring the nature of a hypothesis encourages students to consider what might count as evidence in its support and what might disconfirm it. However, when using sources to test hypotheses the number of variables involved can, for many students, put their conceptual understanding of evidence under pressure. Over-learned routines in the treatment of sources also cause problems. For example, when the following hypothesis was set against a set of six sources in the context of a given background of knowledge, many students tended to focus on the first two statements and ignore the last.

> About the year 500 a leader of the Britons fought the Saxon invaders and defeated them several times. One of his battles was at Badon Hill. He became a hero.

For these students, the sources supporting the third statement were rejected as having no relevance for the time period of the hypothesis. The sources that could have provided evidence for this third statement were rejected because of their failure to witness the events of the first two statements. Few students recognized that these rejected sources provided evidence for the third statement. In planning for, and testing, students' conceptual development, it is also important to consider how to systematically extend students' conceptual achievements within increasingly complex skills contexts.

More complex challenges for hypothesis testing might ask: How might different statements within a hypothesis relate to one another? How might differences between hypotheses be understood? Are they contradictory or complimentary? Are some more risky than others? What scale and scope do they encompass?

Singular factual statements

In treating some statements as accepted fact students might consider them as evidence for higher-level claims. For example, take the fact that 'Hitler entered the Rhineland in 1936'. The evidence base for this factual statement is straightforward in relation to the evidence, although the existence of film footage suggests it had more import at the time than the statement on its own implies. However, the interest in this fact, both at the time and for the historian, moves beyond the fact itself. What meaning does this action have? What were the intentions behind it? What was Hitler up to in taking this action? What else does this action fit into?

It is possible to describe this action as an intention. 'Hitler challenged the Treaty of Versailles'. The evidence of the action, however, is not sufficient and will not bear the weight on its own of this intention. The details of the Treaty of Versailles are needed to demonstrate the action is inconsistent with its terms. The fact that Hitler entered the Rhineland in 1936 is also used as evidence of his policy of aggrandizement. But to legitimize this claim it is necessary to expand the evidence base further. The dilemma for those having to interpret the intentions behind this action at the time reflects the weakness of its evidence base. Eyewitness reports do not help and statements of intent by political figures are difficult to interpret. The historian, however, is privy to what happened subsequently and is therefore able to make this claim on the basis of subsequent events. In a longer temporal span some historians' accounts might use this action as 'marking the end of peace in Europe', or 'the beginning of the road to war'.

Historians' accounts and explanations

Historical knowledge tends to be shaped by 'scholarly traditions and by the concerns historians find around them' (Jordanova, 2000: 174). These traditions generate further questions and open up new arguments. History education needs to develop students understanding of this and curriculum choices ought to give some recognition to this community of scholarship. These matters require extensive discussion in their own right. The points made here are limited to the relationship between knowledge building and evidence. Complex understandings can be developed from limited starting points.

For example, students might be given two singular factual claims and the evidence base for these discussed. 'The Romans had good weapons' and 'The Romans conquered Briton'. Students need to understand that the first of these statements rests on much more than the examination of Roman weapons. The statement implies a context comparison with other weapons. A relationship between the first and second statement is therefore implied. As a consequence a third statement might be ventured: 'The Romans were able to conquer Briton because they had good weapons'. These statements are now given a causal relationship. How does the evidence requirement shift for this? Where does it shift to? The level of certainty attached to this causal statement differs from the previous two. What might challenge the validity of this causal statement? Explanatory adequacy might come into question and additional or alternative factors considered.

Working with these ideas in classrooms helps students to relate evidence work more clearly to knowledge, and consequently to their understanding of the nature and status of that knowledge.

Developing an expertise

As it is not possible to ignore evidence in history, a history education should not ignore it either. Teachers who recognize the conceptual complexity of the challenge their students face and the misconceptions they might be working with will be more able to provide appropriate learning experiences than those who do not.

Teaching complex ideas in simple ways needs to replace the teaching of simple ideas in complex ways.

Developing a sense of purpose

Best practice in the classroom cannot be determined by any given approach to the teaching of evidence seen as 'good' or 'bad'. 'Fitness for purpose', though a well-worn phrase, remains crucial to lesson design. 'Good grounds for knowing' is central to that purpose. Wineburg reminds us of the dispositions this approach to knowledge can generate.

> [H]istory teaches us to resist first-draft thinking and the flimsy conclusions that are its fruits. This kind of history cultivates caution and teaches us we must engage in a sober accounting of what we do not know. Without this capacity, we are destined to be history's victims rather than its students.
>
> (Wineburg, 2007: 11)

Understanding history

Wineburg also provides an appropriate starting place for understanding the concept of evidence in the context of the teaching challenge.
Wineburg, S. (2007) 'Unnatural and essential: the nature of historical thinking', *Teaching History*, December, 129: 6–11.

He gets to the heart of the relationship between what a source is *about* and the *circumstances of its production*, and the shift in focus necessary for treating sources as evidence.

Do not neglect reading from philosophy of history. The following are straight-forward and thought-provoking.
Walsh, W. H. (1961) *An Introduction to Philosophy of History*. London: Hutchinson.
Atkinson, R. F. (1978) *Knowledge and Explanation in History*. London: Macmillan.
Collingwood also deals with *inference* and *testimony*, what he calls *scissors and paste* history, *evidence*, and *questions* and *evidence*.
Collingwood, R. G. (1946, new edition 1993) *The Idea of History*. Oxford: Oxford University Press.

Understanding learning

Knowledge of learners is essential. The misconceptions that many students work with about evidence can impede their progress. They require targeted intervention.

A publication by the US National Research Council is essential reading.
Donovan, M. S. and Bransford, J. D. (eds) (2005) *How Students Learn: History in the Classroom*, National Research Council. Washington DC: National Academies Press.

The first chapter by the editors discusses the importance of the three key principles of *How Students Learn* based on an analysis of decades of work in the cognitive and developmental sciences, which has provided the foundation for an emerging science of learning. The second chapter, written by Peter Lee explores these ideas in the context of learning history, and a close reading of this will support an understanding of the key concepts that are essential to a disciplinary approach to historical knowledge. The third chapter, by Ashby, Lee and Shemilt, presents two case studies. Each involves a specific task – comprising teaching materials and questions – in the context of how the task might be used in developing students' ideas about historical evidence. Students' ideas are discussed alongside attempts to offer the kind of cognitive challenge that might help to replace less with more powerful ideas about evidence. This third chapter is built on a body of research, dating back decades, about students' understanding of historical evidence. In chapter 4, Baines, building on his research and considerable teaching experience, examines the demands on history teachers and the intellectual challenges students face in attempting to understand historical accounts.

See, also, Shemilt's Evaluation Study of SCHP for valuable insights into the nature of the difficulties teachers and students face, as well as two of the relevant published findings from the Economic and Social Research Council funded *Chata* (Concepts of History and Teaching Approaches) Project (a project that built on earlier small-scale classroom-based research by Lee, Dickinson and Ashby).

Shemilt, D. (1980) *Evaluation Study.* Edinburgh: Holmes McDougall.
Ashby, R. (2005) 'Students' approaches to validating historical claims', in R. Ashby, P. Gordon and P. Lee (eds), *Understanding History: Recent Research in History Education (International Review of History Education*, Vol. 4). London: RoutledgeFalmer.
Ashby, R. (2004) 'Developing a concept of historical evidence: students' ideas about testing singular factual claims', at Jon Nichol (ed.), *International Journal of Historical Learning, Teaching and Research*, 4(2).
Shemilt and Lee make specific reference to evidence and an agreed model of progression in students' understanding based on cumulative research knowledge.
Lee, P. and Shemilt, D. (2003) 'A scaffold not a cage: progression and progression models in history', *Teaching History*, 113: 13–23.

References

Ashby, R. (2005) 'Students' approaches to validating historical claims', in R. Ashby, P. Gordon and P. Lee (eds), *Understanding History: Recent Research in History Education (International Review of History Education*, Vol. 4). London: RoutledgeFalmer.
——(2004) 'Developing a concept of historical evidence: students' ideas about testing singular factual claims', at Jon Nichol (ed.), *International Journal of Historical Learning, Teaching and Research*, 4(2). Available online at: http://centres.exeter.ac.uk/history resourcejournalstart.htm Click on Archive, then click on Volume 4, No. 2 July 2004. (accessed 7 September 2010).
Atkinson, R. F. (1978) *Knowledge and Explanation in History.* London: Macmillan.
Collingwood, R. G. (1946, new edition 1993) *The Idea of History.* Oxford: Oxford University Press.
Dickinson, A. K., Gard, A. and Lee, P. J. (1978) 'Evidence in history and the classroom', in A. K. Dickinson and P. J. Lee (eds), *History Teaching and Historical Understanding.* London: Heinemann.
Donovan, M. S. and Bransford, J. D. (2005) *How Students Learn: History in the Classroom*, National Research Council. Washington DC: National Academies Press.
Jordanova, L. (2000) *History in Practice.* London: Arnold.

Lee, P. J. (1994) 'Historical knowledge and the National Curriculum', in H. Bourdillon (ed.), *Teaching History*. London and New York: Routledge.

Lee, P. and Shemilt, D. (2003) 'A scaffold not a cage: progression and progression models in history', *Teaching History*, 113: 13–23.

Rogers, P. (1978) *The New History*. London: Historical Association.

——(1984) 'Why teach history?', in A. K. Dickinson, P. J. Lee and P. J. Rogers (eds), *Learning History*. London: Heinemann.

Shemilt, D. (1980) *Evaluation Study*. Edinburgh: Holmes MacDougall.

——(1991) Preface in P. Lee, J. Slater, P. Walsh and J. White (eds), *The Aims of School History: The National Curriculum and Beyond*. The London File: Papers from the Institute of Education. London: Tufnell Press.

Walsh, W. H. (1961) *An Introduction to Philosophy of History*. London: Hutchinson.

Wineburg, S. (2007) 'Unnatural and essential: the nature of historical thinking', *Teaching History*, December, 129: 6–11.

Chapter 12

Significance

Andrew Wrenn

Introduction

This chapter will explore recent definitions of historical significance as used in history education. First, it will do so by reference to research and examples of practice in schools, which consider what pupils might mean by the term without the concept having necessarily been directly taught to them. It goes on to cite the major contributions of Rob Phillips and Christine Counsell who propose two useful models for direct teaching about historical significance. These have helped teachers scaffold pupils' understanding of the concept and develop frameworks for them to analyse the reasons why events or people were or are considered significant. Additionally, the chapter refers to history teachers who have extended the ideas of Counsell in supporting pupils to develop independent criteria of their own for ascribing historical significance. It concludes with an exemplary case study based on the teaching of the historical significance of the Holocaust.

Judging the historical significance of an event, issue or a people plays an important role in public life but until recently has not been widely taught in schools history. It was first introduced in the revised National Curriculum for History in 1995 but only took its place as a concept in its own right in 2007. The 2007 definition states:

> 1.5 Significance
> a. Considering the significance of events, people and developments in their historical context and in the present day.

In addition further explanation is given in the accompanying 'gloss':

> Significance: This includes considering why judgements about the significance of historical events, issues and people have changed over time; identifying the criteria and values used to attribute significance and assessing how these have been used in past and present descriptions and explanations. Statements about significance are interpretations that may be based on contestable judgements about events, issues and people, and are often related to the value systems of the period in which the interpretation was produced.

As can be seen there is a strong overlap with the separate 'process' of historical interpretation but an essential point to grasp is that the way significance is ascribed is a fluid and subjective business that can change over time.

Asked about the historical effect of the 1789 French Revolution, Chou en-lai (a Chinese communist prime minister and revolutionary 1898–1976) replied, 'Too early to tell.' His answer acknowledges that the significance of this particular event will be subject to change depending on later events. Understanding historical significance includes an appreciation that it is not fixed or a 'given' even in relation to the French Revolution.

How do pupils ascribe significance to historical events, issues and people without necessarily being taught about the concept beforehand?

A number of researchers have investigated how pupils ascribe historical significance while in the process of studying history as a subject. Seixas (1997) devised the following questionnaire which was given to some Canadian pupils to complete.

Two-part student questionnaire

Part I

On this page, create a diagram of the history of the world. Choose the most significant events. If there are important trends, developments or themes which extend over a number of years, also include them. Arrange these events, trends, developments and themes on the page in a way which makes sense to you. Where one event is connected to another event, or a theme or trend, draw lines or arrows showing the connection or influence.

(A blank page follows.)
This is why I chose these events:
This is why I organized them on the page in this way:

Part II

A.   Put an X next to the events listed here that you have heard of before
  - ☐   Writing of the Bible
  - ☐   Gupta dynasty in India
  - ☐   Writing of the Koran
  - ☐   The invention of movable type
  - ☐   European exploration of the Americas
  - ☐   Industrial Revolution
  - ☐   *Common Sense* by Thomas Paine
  - ☐   French Revolution
  - ☐   The end of slavery in the British Empire
  - ☐   Development of the germ theory of disease
  - ☐   The beginning of free public school
  - ☐   Canadian Confederation

- [ ] End of Manchu dynasty in China
- [ ] World War I
- [ ] World War II
- [ ] The dropping of the atomic bomb
- [ ] Widespread use of birth control
- [ ] Development of rock music
- [ ] Murder of John F. Kennedy
- [ ] The end of the Soviet Union

B.   Of the ones you have marked with an X, which is most significant?

C.   Why do you say it is most significant?

D.   Of the ones you have marked with an X, which is least significant?

E.   Why do you say it is least significant?

F.   If someone wanted to argue that your answer to D is really the most significant, how might they do so?

G.   How would you respond to their argument?

H.   Is there an event which is not on this list which you think is very significant for world history? If so, what is it, and why do you think it should be on the list?

The responses varied widely. Some pupils took the questions to be asking about what they could remember of what they had been taught. Others interpreted the term as significance in what seemed important to them as individuals. For example, a pupil of Chinese origins chose Chinese-related events. Some chose according to whether they liked or disliked something, for example rock music. One pupil highlighted significance on moral grounds: '[C]rushing of the world's aboriginal peoples'. The exercise revealed different degrees of understanding about what was being asked of pupils and of the very meaning of the word significance itself. Seixas drew the following conclusion from the variety of responses to the same question: '[S]tudents do not swallow whole what this year's teacher and textbooks tell them is historically significant. Rather they filter and sift and remember and forget, adding to, modifying and reconstructing their frameworks of understanding, through their own often unarticulated values, ideas and dispositions' (1997: 24). So pupils' understanding of what historical significance means may well be dynamic, diverse and subject to change. The pupil who understands significance as recall will remember different details at different times of their schooling. The pupil who chose Chinese-related events may widen their view as they mature. 'Crushing of the world's aboriginal peoples' may become less significant to the individual over time. Seixas also found that pupils from the two main language-speaking groups in Canada, Francophone and Anglophone, also assigned significance to past people and events using different criteria (1997: 24).

Cercadillo has also found evidence of a variety of pupil responses in answer to questions about historical significance. Her conclusions, based on research in England and Spain, indicate that pupils' thinking about significance is influenced by their culture and the way they are taught history. Cercadillo compares the responses of two Year 8 pupils. The English pupil writes, 'we've been learning that (the Spanish Armada) wasn't really an English victory but a Spanish mistake . . . I think in the long term it was more important for the English . . . .' (2006: 24). The Spanish pupil wrote, 'This source is written long ago . . . maybe they haven't decided yet what is right'! Cercadillo concludes that '[t]he first one [i.e. student quotation] suggests that the Armada meant more to the English in the long term. The second one sought a "right" answer – a fixed meaning of the Armada' (2006: 24). She claims that these two pupil responses reflect the different traditions of teaching history in each country. English pupils are not taught history as 'given', while in Spain and most European counties curriculum and assessment systems still tend to emphasize the pursuit of facts and details over questions of historical significance, evidence and interpretation.

Despite Cercadillo's praise for the English model of teaching history, reasoning about significance among English pupils is not necessarily sophisticated. Conway reports that his pupils had blinkered ideas about significance: 'A significant number equated "important" with "good" and reasoned accordingly' (2006). In addition, 'I discovered that the two dominant ideas present among my pupils seemed to be that "important" corresponds either with "good" or "frequent".' In considering the significance of factors in the Industrial Revolution one pupil used a simple value judgement. 'I think the changes are bad because late on in the 1890s pollution was caused'. In Ceradillo's terms this pupil response shows a 'fixed' understanding of significance; that is, changes were judged to be wholly negative by reference to one consequence alone.

How did Rob Phillips help to scaffold pupil understanding of the concept of historical significance and how it can be ascribed?

So research and practice tends to show that many pupils in different settings have an inadequate grasp of what might constitute historical significance and how it can be ascribed. They may think of it as a matter of recall, as given or 'fixed' or define it very narrowly. Arguably, this puts the onus back on teachers of history to improve their understanding. The influential thinking of Rob Phillips (2002) has encouraged history teachers to build in more opportunities for teaching about historical significance in their planning. He drew on the foundational definition of Geoffrey Partington, who claimed that assigning significance to an event or person was dependent on the factors below.

1. Importance – to the people living at the time.
2. Profundity – how deeply people's lives have been affected by the event.
3. Quantity – how many lives were affected.
4. Durability – for how long people's lives have been affected.
5. Relevance – the extent to which the event has contributed to an increased understanding of present life.

Table 12.1   An acronym for helping students to think about the significance of the First World War

G	Groundbreaking
R	Remembered by all
E	Events that were far-reaching
A	Affected the future
T	Terrifying

Phillips (2002) created an acronym, GREAT, for pupils to assign to the First World War in answer to the enquiry question, 'Why was the First World War called the Great War?' Table 12.1 shows how the acronym reflects Partington's definition of significance.

Pupil responses were also shaped by earlier enquiry questions that directed pupils to consider each of Partington's factors in relation to the First World War in turn.

1. Importance – who was affected by the war?
2. Profundity – how were people's lives changed?
3. Quantity – how many people were affected by World War I?
4. Durability – why is it important to remember World War I?
5. Relevance – why is it important to study World War I?

Phillips' practice bears many of the hallmarks that characterize effective history teaching. Each lesson in the sequence built up pupils' knowledge of events so that they could draw on prior learning in the final activity. Activities were arranged in an engaging and accessible variety around specific enquiry questions in the style pioneered by Michael Riley. Teachers, such as Geraint Brown of Cottenham Village College in Cambridgeshire constructed enquiries of their own using Phillips' GREAT criteria. As part of a study of World War I in the schools village pupils were given 'the GREAT criteria [and asked to use] the database (of the local dead) to find evidence to support or challenge this definition of the First World War as the "Great War" for local people' (Brown and Woodcock, 2009: 7). Teachers using Phillips' acronym have the opportunity to lift the responses of their pupils to questions about significance beyond some of those quoted by Seixas, Cercadillo and Conway. The acronym scaffolds a nuanced understanding of significance for pupils. However, its use can only take them so far, as Brown and Woodcock (2009) have found. 'We were failing to move pupils' on from applying "given criteria"' (p. 7). In other words, pupils could find evidence to show the extent to which an event might be Groundbreaking, Remembered by all, Events that were far-reaching, Affected the future and were Terrifying. But they were being told what significance was by the teacher not devising criteria to apply to an event or person themselves. The acronym risked hobbling pupils developing a greater understanding of significance as a concept and the processes by which it can be ascribed.

How did Christine Counsell help scaffold pupil understanding of the concept of historical significance and how it can be ascribed?

In 2004 Counsell took the exploration of historical significance further. Noting Phillips' acronym as 'extremely useful', she also commented that he did not intend

Table 12.2 Events and consequences

The First World War	The Tolpuddle Martyrs
The Russian Revolution	The Children's Crusade
The Glorious Revolution	The poetry of Walt Whitman
The emergence of the railways	The Jarrow March

his criteria for universal application – that is it was devised with the First World War specifically in mind. 'He did not go so far as to suggest that pupils should test the model by applying it to other events, nor that they should explore whether it matches others reasons for attributing significance'! (p. 30) Counsell identified three red herrings or common distractions when asking pupils to think about historical significance.

> One red herring is the view that teaching historical significance of a particular event (or person or situation) as though this were a matter of fixed consensus . . . This would suggest that the significance of an event is something uncontested, something about which we all agree. It also suggests that pupils just have to know why something is significant, rather than engage with the very idea of significance itself!
>
> (p. 11)

Counsell goes on to say, 'A second red herring is easy appeal to "relevance to today".' She claims that 'if our conception of historical significance is intrinsically or necessarily related to this . . . we lay ourselves open to charges of presentism.' Pupils might get an anachronistic view of history, seeing too much through a present-day lens.

As Counsell says a single, fixed link to the present 'does not explain why many events and developments are judged so that they live on in the history books, in scholarly debates, in T.V. history, in a theme park, or in a heated, sensitive argument in a pub.'

Lastly, Counsell claims 'a third distraction occurs when we fail to get beyond "consequences" or "results".' There is a real danger that historical significance comes to be judged mainly or even solely because of what flows from an event, a situation or a person's life. Table 12.2 lists on the left-hand side events Counsell suggests have plenty of consequences, short-term and long-term. On the right-hand side are listed some that she argues have negligible short-term results.

She claims that the significance of the right-hand events cannot be adequately explained by reference to what happened as a result of them; 'Why did these things end up discussed in public domains long after the event?'

As Martin Hunt (2003) wrote: 'There is a danger in what may be an apparent overlap with the "second order" concept of consequence. Greater understanding is more likely to be achieved if there is a clear distinction between the two.' Unlike Phillips, Counsell makes no direct reference to Partington but instead draws heavily on the thinking of Tim Lomas (1990) which she characterizes as 'the most theoretically consistent and practically realistic'. Counsell slightly adapted Lomas' original 'key ideas' to propose the following.

1. to understand that history operates on the basis that some events are more important than others;
2. to establish criteria for assessing the significance of events, people and issues in the past;
3. to understand that some events, which may have seemed significant at the time, were not, while the significance of other events is only recognized later;
4. to understand that different people will have different ideas about which people, events, changes and issues are significant;
5. to be able to understand why people may hold different ideas about what has been significant;
6. to understand that the significance of an event is determined by the nature of the historical enquiry;
7. to understand that relatively minor events can be highly significant (e.g. they have symbolic significance);
8. to be able to distinguish between the consequences of an event and its significance;
9. to understand that an event or change usually becomes significant because of its connection with other events.

Counsell goes on to suggest four kinds of activities that pupils should be undertaking in relation to historical significance:

1. Applying given sets of criteria for judging historical significance.
2. Devising (and applying or testing) sets of criteria of their own.
3. Discerning implicit criteria in other's judgements about historical significance.
4. Using any of the above to challenge or support others' judgements about significance.

In devising criteria that pupils might apply 'across a range of events and developments' Counsell proposes five 'Rs' that she claims are firmly rooted in the process of writing history itself.

*   Remarkable
    — (The event/development was remarked upon by people at the time and/ or since.)
*   Remembered
    — (The event/development was important at some stage in history within the collective memory of a group or groups.)
*   Resonant
    — (People like to make analogies with it; it is possible to connect with experiences, beliefs or situations across time and space.)
*   Resulting in change
    — (It had consequences for the future.)
*   Revealing
    — (Of some other aspect of the past.)

She states that this is intended as a pedagogic model . . . 'not as a pure philosophical statement about the nature of historical significance.' Also unlike Phillips' GREAT criteria, the five Rs are a formula 'that a pupil could apply to the First World War, to the Children's Crusade, to Josephine Butler (a leading nineteenth-century campaigner against the Contagious Diseases Act) and to the pyramids of Ancient Egypt alike.'

How have history teachers tested out and developed the models of teaching about historical significance proposed by Phillips and Counsell?

Since Phillips' (2002) work in this area a number of history departments have tested out and developed their approaches further. Osowiecki (2004) devised an enquiry based on the study of the Renaissance. The overarching enquiry question – 'What was remarkable about the Renaissance?' – deliberately directed pupils towards one of Counsell's five Rs, partly in an effort to shift their thinking away from defining historical significance in terms of consequences alone. Bradshaw (2006) introduced Phillips' GREAT criteria into a lesson sequence on the First World War.

- Was it Gavrilo Princip's bullet which started the GREAT war?
- Why did some people think the war was going to be GREAT?
- Did the allied Generals make GREAT mistakes?
- How GREAT was the difference between WWI and previous wars?
- How GREAT was the effect of the war on the people back home?
- How has the GREAT war been remembered?
- Does WWI deserve to be called the GREAT war?

Pupils also applied the five Rs to 'a catchy song called Enola Gay which recalled the mission of the plane carrying the first atomic weapon dubbed "Little boy"' (McCluskey, 1980). Bradshaw suggests that pupil understanding of historical significance can be deepened and built upon by revisiting the five Rs over the three years of Key Stage 3.

- Year 7: Should Thomas Beckett be remembered?
- Year 8: What was remarkable about the Renaissance?
- Year 8: What does Josephine Butler reveal about nineteenth-century Britain?
- Year 9: What is so resonant about the Vietnam War?

Bradshaw (2006) proposes a hierarchy in developing pupil understanding of historical significance.

I. Building any consideration of significance on a foundation of substantive knowledge about the event, person or situation.
II. Understanding GREAT and the five Rs.
III. Applying these criteria to events, people or situations.
IV. Identifying criteria ascribed to events or people or situations by others.
V. Criticizing, developing and using criteria of their own.

(p. 31–2)

Table 12.3 The structure of an enquiry to develop understanding of significance

Sub-question	Activities	Role of significance
1. What can Cottenham war memorial tell us about the significance of WWI locally?	Pupils examine local war memorials and names of the local dead. They create their own questions for and interrogate a database of the local war dead.	Pupils are introduced to the idea of the 'impact 'of the war locally. Through analysis of the database and rich personal stories they begin to use their own provisional significance criteria for the significance of the war locally – 'e.g. the age of victims, the number of victims, the emotional impact of particular events, etc.'
2. In what ways have people judged WWI to be the 'Great War'?	Pupils compare differing definitions of the term 'great' e.g. very large in size (a great tower); very skilful ('he is great at maths'); superior character, noble ('he was a great and good man'). They analyse E. H. Gombrich's judgements about WWI from an extract of his writing and create their own GREAT criteria afterwards, comparing them with the views of another author (text/audio/video, etc.).	Examining different definitions of the label 'great ' should help pupils understand the different criteria for significance that might be used in judging WWI. This consideration of possible criteria is extended by analysis of the E. H. Gombrich quotation. In creating their own criteria for why WWI is significant, to match the acronym GREAT, they draw on their conclusions from Gombrich (e.g. 'T' stands for 'Terrifying Technology'). Lastly, they compare Gombrich with the views of another author whose criteria for judging WWI might differ.
3. So, how far does the local experience support claims for WWI being the 'Great War'?	Pupils research local evidence which supports or contradicts Gombrich's judgements about WWI. Given different views about WWI from different periods since 1918, pupils match local evidence that might support or contradict that view. They then complete a piece of extended writing in answer to the enquiry question.	Pupils test out Gombrich's criteria for the significance of WWI against a range of local evidence. They repeat the same activity for a variety of other views of the significance of the Great War. They begin to realize that evidence can be used selectively to support or contradict particular criteria. They also begin to realize that significance is a label, a judgement, an assertion that could vary depending upon another place, time, culture and purpose, etc.

Brown and Woodcock (2009) have developed an existing Year 9 Local History unit on the First World War having decided that in imposing Phillips' GREAT acronym 'we were failing to move pupils on from applying "given criteria"' (Counsell, 2004: 32). In their planning, they deliberately aimed at the most advanced features of Bradshaw's proposed hierarchy; 'Identifying criteria ascribed to events, people or situations by others' and 'criticising, developing and using criteria of their own'. Table 12.3 summarizes the structure of the enquiry.

Teaching historical significance: a case study on the Holocaust

An effective way of deepening pupil understanding about historical significance is to teach the event, issue or people concerned in a wide-ranging chronological context.

One of the most important pieces of teacher planning on the Holocaust was by Hammond (2001), who was working prior to the published thinking of both Phillips and Counsell. She contends that 'only by placing the Holocaust in a variety of important and contrasting overviews can we achieve . . . a proper understanding of the historical significance of the event' (p. 18). The work of her department took place in the context of an enquiry question that was chronologically wider than the Holocaust itself. 'Why was WWII even more devastating than WWI?' Its events are taught as part of a comparison between the First and Second World Wars initially which is one overview. Pupils are then given a range of date cards describing historical incidents of anti-Semitic persecution from the fourth century AD to the present. Pupils then have to peg the cards on a washing line according to whether they judge that the persecution was more religiously or racially motivated. This is the second and chronologically wider overview to be visited. Lastly 'the washing line' completely changes its meaning as one end has 'minor persecution' on it and the other 'major persecution'. Pupils peg the same cards up but judge the placing of events according to what they decide to be the degree of persecution. The second chronological overview is therefore revisited but from a different perspective. Through the debate, pupils not only become more familiar with substantive historical knowledge about anti-Semitism but also deepen their understanding of the significance of particular events. Following more study in depth of the Holocaust itself, pupils return to the enquiry question, 'Why was WWII even more devastating than WWI?' Their responses can refer to a bigger picture than just the world war because they have considered the Holocaust's significance in a wider anti-Semitic context.

Futher reading

Brown, G and Woodcock, J (2009). 'Relevant, rigorous and revisted: using local history to make meaning of historical significance'. *Teaching History, 134.* London: Historical Association.

Lyon, G (2007). 'Is it time to forget Remembrance?'. *Teaching History, 128.* London: Historical Association.

'Historical significance', in *A Guide to the New Key Stage 3 Programme*, Available online at: www.history.org.uk.

References

Bradshaw, M (2006). 'Creating controversy in the classroom: making progress with historical significance'. *Teaching History, 125*. London: Historical Association.

Brown, G and Woodcock, J (2009). 'Relevant, rigorous and revisited: using local history to make meaning of historical significance'. *Teaching History, 134*. London: Historical Association.

Cercadillo, L (2006). 'Maybe they haven't decided yet what is right: English and Spanish perspectives on teaching historical significance'. *Teaching History, 125*. London: Historical Association.

Conway, R (2006). 'What they think they know: the impact of pupils' preconceptions on their understanding of historical significance'. *Teaching History, 125*. London: Historical Association.

Counsell, C (2004). 'Looking through a Josephine-Butler shaped window: focusing pupils' thinking on historical significance'. *Teaching History, 114*. London: Historical Association.

Gombrich, E H (2005). *A Little History of the World*, London: Yale University Press.

Hammond, K (2001). 'From horror to history: teaching pupils to reflect on significance'. *Teaching History, 104*. London: Historical Association.

Hunt, M (2003). 'Historical Significance', in R. Harris and M. Riley (eds) *Past Forward: A Vision for School History 2002–2012*. London: Historical Association.

Lomas, T (1990). *Teaching and Assessing Historical Understanding*. London: Historical Association.

McCluskey, A (1980). 'Enola Gay', recorded by Orchestral Manoeuvres in the Dark (OMD). London: Dindisc.

Osowiecki, M (2004). 'Seeing, hearing and doing the Renaissance (Part 1): Let's have a Renaissance party!'. *Teaching History, 117*. London: Historical Association.

Osowiecki, M (2005). 'Seeing, hearing and doing the Renaissance (Part 2): Let's have a Renaissance party!'. *Teaching History, 118*. London: Historical Association.

Phillips, R (2002). 'Historical significance-the forgotten key element?'. *Teaching History, 106*. London: Historical Association.

Seixas, P (1997). 'Mapping the terrain of historical significance'. *Social Education, 61*(1).

Section 3

Debating the expression and purpose of history

Chapter 13

Moral learning in history

Andrew Peterson

Introduction

This chapter will explore:

- the place of moral learning within history curricula in England;
- arguments for and against moral learning as an aim of history education;
- the key challenges of including moral learning within history education.

The development of moral learning has often been cited as a fundamental purpose of history education. However, its place in history learning today is, for a number of reasons, contested. There are some commentators who would reject the idea that a foremost aim of the subject is to develop pupils' moral understanding, and who would suggest that to pursue moral aims undermines the true goals of history education. Even where there is agreement as to the importance of moral outcomes, there is not necessarily consensus about the form which such learning should take. This chapter takes the view that it is both important and necessary for teachers of history education to consider the place of moral learning within their subject and to engage in careful reflection as to the ways in which pupils encounter values within their classrooms. The issues involved are explored in the following way. First, the arguments advanced against the place of moral learning within history education are considered, and these are rejected in light of positions which view moral exploration as a key element of the subject. Second, on the premise that moral learning does and should possess an integral place within history education, a number of challenges are raised regarding the possible form and focus which this might take. Within both the second and the concluding section some suggestions are offered for further research and discussion in this area.

Morals and morality can be understood as referring in a broad sense to particular codes of conduct. Moral actions and judgements relate to standards of good and bad behaviour, and are usually framed around particular concepts such as fairness, justice and honesty. The following categorization provided by Arthur *et al.* (2001: 88) is a useful starting point for defining what the term 'moral learning' might be taken to mean in relation to history education. They propose three elements of pupils' moral engagement within history, each of which fundamentally relates to discourse. These are an understanding of the moral vocabulary of any historical period, the forming of moral judgements on the basis of historical evidence and investigation, and the use of current moral vocabulary in order to understand and discuss historical periods. In other words, pupils' learning of history involves moral thinking and the use of moral vocabulary in order to arrive at reasoned moral judgements. The importance which Arthur *et al.*'s classification places on the moral outcomes of history accords with curricular documents relating to history education over the past 25 years (DES, 1985; NCC, 1993; Ofsted, 1994a, 1994b; QCA, 1998, 1999). More recently the National Curriculum programme of study for Key Stage 3 history, for teaching from August 2002, intimated at the role of history in promoting pupils' moral development 'through helping pupils to recognize that actions have consequences by considering the results of events and decisions, and to explore how different interpretations of the past reflect different viewpoints and values' (QCA, 1999: 8). In defining the importance of history, the same document makes clear that what pupils learn in history 'can influence their decisions about personal choices, attitudes and values' (QCA, 1999: 14). However, the revised curricular programme of study for Key Stage 3, taught from September 2008, is less clear in its treatment of moral values. While it suggests that the curriculum decisions made by schools should provide pupils with the opportunity to 'explore the ways in which the past has helped shape identities, shared cultures, values and attitudes today' (QCDA, 2007: accessed online 1 November 2009, http://curriculum.qca.org.uk/key-stages-3-and-4/subjects/key-stage-3/history/index.aspx), it is notable for its lack of explicit reference to the subject's moral dimensions.

These curricular references are important, and suggest that although there may be a place for moral learning within history the extent and form of this may not always be explicitly clear for teachers. Current curricular arrangements do not provide teachers with any specific or detailed guidance as to the nature of moral learning nor how they might provide for this in their classrooms. As Barton and Levstik (2004: 106) point out, the importance of pupils' moral engagements within history is 'generally unacknowledged and, as a result, unanalyzed'. This is despite the fact that the manner in which teachers interpret the place of morals within their curricula and classrooms is fundamental to how they and their pupils understand the nature of the subject. As such, this raises significant questions for history teachers about whether, and if so how, moral outcomes should form part of their work. The next section of this chapter outlines the arguments which have been advanced against the moral aims of history education and offers some suggestions as to why these should be discounted.

Moral learning and history: critical perspectives

Despite Maxwell's (2008: 79) claim that those against moral learning in history education represent a 'somewhat radical, purist minority', there is an important body of work which questions and critiques the promotion and exploration of values within the subject. The idea that historians should be wary of developing a moral focus within their work developed largely in the 1950s, and can be understood as a reaction to the strong *moral judgements* made by prominent historians of the time. The position of Knowles (1955: 4–5) highlights this critical stance. He argued that 'the historian is not a judge, still less a hanging judge'. The historian Edwin Fenton (1966, cited in Smith, 1986: 82) prioritized the moral neutrality of the historian, and went so far as to suggest that 'we must not teach that democracy is better than totalitarianism, that religion is a good thing, that the family is the basis of society, or that money is more important than anything else'. Central to such arguments is the view that in seeking to make moral judgements, the rationality and objectivity of the historian was compromised. According to Butterfield (1951, cited in Lee, 1992: 41), '[I]t is not clear that moral indignation is not a dispersion of one's energies to the great confusion of one's judgement'. In advancing their arguments, historians such as Knowles, Fenton and Butterfield were essentially seeking to preserve what they believed to be the true scope and skills of the historian; namely, rational, critical and detached investigation. Such skills were perceived to be undermined by the development of moral judgement and values.

Although written half a century ago, these critical viewpoints have influenced more recent discourse on history education. Drawing on the work of Fenton (1966), Smith (1986) asks us to distinguish between three types of values. Smith understands *behavioural* values as those which are necessary for a productive learning environment, and he includes, for example, the requisite behaviour for classroom discussion and debate within this. *Procedural* values are those skills and techniques central to the pursuit of the historian, such as critical thinking and enquiry, the interpretation of evidence and a desire for rigorous interrogation of arguments and ideas. The third type of values is *substantive*. Substantive values frame, define and give meaning to actions, thoughts and feelings and generally involve a value judgement. Although Smith does not define the scope or content of these values in a meaningful way, he makes clear that history teaching should restrict itself to behavioural and procedural values while omitting those that are substantive. Instead, Smith prioritizes the impartiality and neutrality of the teacher who has respect for the moral autonomy of pupils to develop their own perspectives on substantive issues.

Another particularly strong contemporary proponent of the view that history should not be used for moral purposes is Lee (1992). Advancing fears similar to those of Butterfield, Lee is concerned about the detriment that moral exploration may have on the objectivity and rational detachment of historians. In his thought-provoking analysis, Lee distinguishes between the aims of history as a subject and the aims of education per se, arguing that the former should have priority within the history classroom and should not be subordinate to the latter. In other words, while the aims of education might have a moral purpose, the subject itself does not and should not be used in pursuance of such aims. Some critics go even further in their indignation. In a controversial stance on learning about the Holocaust, Kinloch (1998, 2001) has bemoaned the fact that history teachers have tended to focus on its moral issues and lessons at the expense of more 'historical' outcomes, arguing that pupils' study of the Holocaust was only capable of producing 'the most banal of moral conclusions' (2001: 104). His critique centres on his belief that history education should be concerned primarily with historical questions such as what happened, why it happened and how it happened, rather than on moral questions of action or inaction and right or wrong. Similarly to Smith and Lee, Kinloch's position is aimed at creating a distinction between the critical faculties required by historians and the more complex and affective capacities of moral thinking.

Those who question the place of moral learning within history education clearly have the integrity of the subject at heart, and are concerned with the detrimental effect that integrating a moral lens may have on the subject's rational status. However, there is a tendency in these arguments to understand the exploration of moral values in a narrow way and as referring primarily to *uncritical* moral judgements. History teachers must remember that there is an important difference between, on the one hand, crude moralizing and, on the other, the rational and critical exploration of moral values, actions and events leading to the making of a considered moral judgement. The examination of historical periods, including its people, cultures, ideas and beliefs, will unavoidably involve pupils in thinking about and questioning ethical and moral values and principles. This said, few involved in history teaching would accept that crude moralizing, in terms of uncritical judgements based on poor evidence and interpretation, has a place in history education. Much more acceptable is the development of pupils' abilities to consider moral relationships between actors, to critically engage with the decisions taken through a sound interrogation of the evidence at hand, and to seek to make judgements about the topic at hand. Central to this is pupils' critical appreciation of the similarities and differences between the moral vocabulary and values of historical periods and those of contemporary society. Indeed, the ability of pupils to reflect critically on moral questions and issues as part of their studies is not just integral to history education but also to the discipline of history itself. As Arthur *et al.* (2001) remind us, 'no one can effectively study history without some form of moral deliberation or judgement' (Arthur *et al.*, 2001: 96), and as Walsh (1993: 180) argues, 'the refusal of an ethical encounter with the past is a denial of spontaneous expectations, a methodical exclusion of a range of responses that naturally seem appropriate'. This does not necessarily mean that that pupils' moral learning will always be certain and clear. Just as is the case with historical enquiry and interpretation more generally, the exploration of moral issues and the making of moral judgements within history classrooms are just as likely to be tentative and cautious as they are likely to be certain and assured.

It is also worth considering whether it is necessarily the case that moral reasoning and judgements cannot be objective in the same sense as historical enquiry (see Walsh, 1993: 180). Commentators such as Lee and Kinloch mistakenly distinguish historical judgement, which is viewed as detached and reasoned, from moral judgement, which they view as subjective and emotive. This distinction is over-simplistic and does not recognize the complexities involved. In his classic text *What is History?*, E. H. Carr (1961: 79) asserted that 'historical facts . . . presuppose some measure of interpretation; and historical interpretations always involve moral judgements'. As Salmons (2003: 143) explains, through their engagement in rigorous historical enquiry pupils come to understand 'the complexities of the world in which choices were actually made and decisions taken; only then can people's actions (and inactions) be judged within the context of their time, and only then can we begin to draw meaningful lessons for today', and as Arthur *et al.* (2001: 98) point out 'moral judgements need as much scrutiny as historical evidence'. In other words, history learning does involve moral reasoning and judgement. That these must be based on sound historical enquiry in order to be significant and effective is no argument against their place within the history curriculum. Recognition of the complexity involved in exploring moral issues and making moral judgements, and how these may benefit from sound historical enquiry, strengthens rather than weakens the nature of history as an academic discipline. This said, even where history teachers are in agreement as to the importance of developing moral learning within history there is still room for a great deal of discussion, debate and disagreement as to what this means. There is a need, therefore, to clarify the way in which pupils encounter moral values within history classrooms, as well as the purpose of their doing so. The next section considers these issues in the context of the challenges faced by teachers in developing moral learning within history.

Developing moral learning in history: the challenges

This section highlights three challenges upon which current discourse concerning the nature and process of moral learning within history might usefully focus; namely, the values which underpin history curricula, the selection of appropriate themes and topics for developing moral learning and the pedagogical approaches appropriate for supporting pupils in exploring moral issues. For the purpose of clarity these issues are presented separately but it is important to remember that in practice they are likely to be interconnected.

The first challenge facing teachers in including moral learning within their history curricula concerns *which values are to be explored and promoted*. No straightforward list of values exist for history teachers to refer to, and, were there to be one, it is likely that discussion would still remain about how such values could be interpreted. In establishing the basis for a consideration of the substantive moral values which might be explored within history, and perhaps more importantly how such values might be understood, Walsh (1993: 180) makes the following useful suggestion:

> In pluralist societies history writing will be better for taking account of the pluralism of contemporary values, laying special emphasis on the values that are shared, being explicit about relevant more 'personal' values, and so forth – in other words, for adopting the manners and procedures of everyday ethical discourse in this kind of society.

This reminds us that substantive values have an important place within history and that teachers should seek to be cognisant as to their form and meaning in order that they support pupils' explorations. Walsh's suggestion that the consideration of values within history education should take account of the pluralism of contemporary values also suggests that their expression within the classroom should be balanced and should recognize and engage with those of the wider communities in which pupils live. This includes the school, the locality and society as a whole. Barton and Levstik's (2004: 107) suggestion that 'some aspects of morality will vary among groups' while 'others are rooted in the nature of . . . democracy' highlights both that the promotion of core values is generally acceptable and that moral exploration necessarily involves history teachers and their pupils in engaging with values upon which there may be conflicting definitions and to which there may be different levels of commitment. Without recognition of controversial and sensitive issues there is a danger that teachers may embrace history education's moral dimension in a narrow way, emphasizing a limited set of values over and above others. We should also remember that the question of which moral values should be promoted or explored is not particular to history. In other curriculum subjects and across education as a whole there is a great deal of discussion as to which values should be taught (Halstead and Taylor, 2000). Although a *National Forum for Values in Education and the Community* produced a Statement of Values for schools and teachers which featured within the 1999 National Curriculum, it is not clear that teachers actively engage with this Statement in a meaningful way. History teaching does not stand in isolation from these debates, and it is important that teachers not only familiarize themselves with them but also engage and seek to shape discussions about the values of the curriculum.

A second challenge for developing our understanding of moral learning within history concerns the *selection of topics and themes* appropriate for such purposes. Just as with any other element of historical learning, effective moral exploration requires careful planning. This includes a thoughtful selection of topic or theme to act as a stimulus. It is important to recognize that such selections, and the learning which results, can be implicit or explicit. Indeed, this distinction is useful in framing our thoughts. It has been suggested that any history curriculum necessarily involves *implicit* moral learning by virtue of the values which have informed the selection or rejection of the topics to be studied. Walsh (1993: 182) makes this point when he cites the importance of 'our *ethical* beliefs about the rights of people and the value of democracy' in underpinning curriculum construction. We might also consider decisions regarding the percentage of curricula time allocated to British and non-British history, the treatment of sensitive and controversial issues such as empire, the recognition of the role and importance of women, and the inclusion of black and minority ethnic representations within the curriculum, as all also being determined by particular moral values.

While the implicit structuring of the curriculum by values is important, for real moral learning to take place history teaching must go further. Of particular challenge is the *explicit* development of moral learning. While it could be argued that the study of any historical topic has the potential for developing moral outcomes, careful thought must be given as to which topics and themes are most the suitable for this purpose (see Historical Association, 2007: 41). At times such consideration can seem fairly straightforward. The study of the civil rights movement in post-war America and the role of Martin Luther King by necessity involves pupils in considering core democratic values such as justice, tolerance and freedom. When studying the civil rights movement, pupils are likely to be engaged with moral questions about particular decisions made, and about actions taken or not taken on by groups and individuals. Similarly, in their study of the Holocaust pupils will be engaged with questions of morality in the form of particular values, issues and dilemmas. Indeed, recent empirical research commissioned by the Holocaust Education Development Programme (HEDP, 2009: 73) into teachers' understandings of teaching about the Holocaust suggests that a high number of teachers do think about pupil outcomes in moral terms. Interestingly, however, the research seems to suggest that such moral thinking remains implicit in history teachers' minds. When questioned about the subject specific aims for teaching about the Holocaust, the aim 'to reflect upon the moral and/or ethical questions raised by events of the Holocaust' was ranked by history teachers only eighth out of the eleven aims given in terms of its importance. However, those aims considered by history teachers to be the most important when teaching about the Holocaust where 'to develop an understanding of the roots and ramifications of prejudice, racism, and stereotyping in any society', 'to learn the lessons of the Holocaust and to ensure that a similar human atrocity never happens again' and 'to explore the roles and responsibilities of individuals, organizations, and governments when confronted with human rights' violations and/or policies of genocide'. Each of these is essentially moral in nature. This suggests both that moral aims often remain implicit rather than explicit within the work of history teachers and that more work might be needed to make sure that pupils are aware of the moral learning taking place.

Even when the moral imperative of a particular topic appears clear, as in the case of the Holocaust, critical voices exist which raise reservations that are of interest to history teachers. One such warning is provided by Maxwell (2008; see also Kinloch, 1998, 2001). Adopting a different perspective from the critical viewpoints cited in the previous section, he questions the development of personal and social skills as the 'primary justificatory grounds for the intimate study in schools and universities of genocide and other forms of systematic, politically motivated extreme cruelty' on the basis that this '*instrumentalises* such events for the sake of supporting young people's interpersonal skills and well-being' (Maxwell, 2008: 76). Maxwell ultimately suggests that the use of particular historical events for essentially moral purposes 'is highly ethically problematic, if not actually morally offensive' (Maxwell, 2008: 76). While we need not let such comments detract from the moral purpose of history, they should be taken into account when planning for teaching and learning. In other words, in selecting topics from which to develop moral learning, history teachers must carefully consider the ethical suitability for doing so.

The distinction between '*weak*' and '*strong*' curricular justification suggested by Maxwell (2008: 83) is helpful in focusing our thinking here. According to Maxwell, weak justification refers to instances where the focus and form of learning required to meet an educational end can be readily substituted. In contrast, strong curricular justification refers to instances when the focus and form of learning are the 'exclusive means to some educational achievement' (p. 83). The relevance of this distinction to history teaching is the extent to which curricular content and processes are the sole means through which pupils engage in a particular form of moral learning. Where history education provides the only means to this end, the curricular justification can be said to be strong. Where other, perhaps better, opportunities exist the justification can be considered as week. In the current educational context, the statutory intro-duction of citizenship education has provided particular opportunities and challenges for history education. A fundamental question facing teachers of history is the extent to which the moral learning outcomes which are at the core of the subject may be similarly developed, or even better developed, through topics or themes covered in other subjects. To suggest that other subjects are capable of producing certain moral outcomes does not mean that similar moral outcomes cannot or should not be developed within history. It does suggest, however, that, at the very least, pupils' moral learning within history should relate to that within their other lessons. This calls on teachers of history to look beyond the confines of their subject area and reminds us that history education is unlikely to be the only form of moral education experi-enced by pupils. It also requires teachers to critically engage with the contribution to the moral development of pupils which their subject makes in combination with other areas of the school curriculum and, indeed, of schooling itself.

A third issue in need of clarification is the particular *approach*, or to be more precise *approaches*, to moral learning which history education can adopt. This question is particularly prescient because as Maxwell (2008: 80) suggests, 'most values-educational initiatives . . . tend to muddle through without much in the way of a theoretical base'. It is also noteworthy that there is little evidence that those involved in the discourse around moral learning in history have sought to explicitly defend or critique a particular approach to moral education. This lack of reference is perhaps surprising given that the three main forms of learning prevalent in the literature on moral education – values clarification, moral reasoning and character education – each finds potential expression within history. Moreover, there are important differences between each approach with regard to the specific purposes and processes of exploring moral values within the classroom that are likely to impact on the content of history lessons.

A *values clarification* approach is built on the notion that pupils' moral education should take the form of clarifying the content of their own *personal* values, with the goal of internal consistency (Raths *et al.*, 1966). A different approach to moral education is provided by Kohlberg (1981, 1984), who argued that pupils should be taught the skills of *moral reasoning*, including the ability to reflect on their moral positions, to take perspectives and to make rational and reasoned autonomous decisions. A third approach is that of *character education*. Character education is a diverse field, and character educators can be generally defined as those who advocate an approach to moral education which centres on the teaching of virtue (see McLaughlin and Halstead, 1999: 132). Often these approaches to moral education can be seen within the work of historians even if they are not openly mentioned. For example, when Musgrave (1983, cited in Arthur *et al.*, 2001: 97) wrote that 'the stories of national heroes, Nelson and Florence Nightingale, have been taught in the hope that they would be seen as moral exemplars', he references a technique central to character education. Similarly, Smith's (1986: 83) suggestions that history teachers should 'insist on fair-play and impartiality', 'on the moral autonomy of each student' and should provide 'the classroom conditions within which individuals may shape their own views on particular substantive issues' are suggestive of a values clarification approach. However, in neither case is a particular approach endorsed *explicitly*. This lack of specific clarity should be of professional concern, not least because each approach is underpinned by certain aims and necessitates particular pedagogical processes. Indeed, the relationship between moral approach and pedagogical process is extremely salient. At a basic level, all moral learning shares certain pedagogical principles, including those necessary for pupil engagement in discussions, debates and reflective analytical writing. For this to occur successfully requires a particular, positive classroom climate. However, beyond these central principles each approach has its own nuances. An important example of such nuances concerns the relationship between moral learning and action. The values clarification and the moral reasoning approaches are both essentially concerned with thinking in line with particular processes through the exploration of values, issues and questions. In contrast, character education additionally seeks to develop moral actors who possess and act in accordance with certain moral dispositions. By necessity character education provides pupils with an opportunity to demonstrate their understanding in practice. This requires particular forms of pedagogy within classroom, school and community settings. In other words, approaches to moral learning within history education based on character seek to produce not just good historians but also good people. While for some history teachers this particular approach to moral learning may be a step too far, it does serve to highlight how moral approaches can, and indeed should, impact on the work of history teachers. At present it is not clear that those interested in history education have sought to interrogate and clarify the subject's relationships to particular approaches to moral education in a clear and sustained way, and as such this remains a key issue for history teachers.

Recognition of these three forms approaches to moral education should provoke important reflection on the part of history teachers concerning the practical methods and strategies which they might employ within their classrooms. While many published professional resources contain some form of moral focus for pupil learning, there is currently a scarcity of resources available which explicitly seek to help history teachers to this end. In developing resources and activities history teachers will necessarily be involved with deep questions regarding purposes and aims, as well as more expedient issues concerning time pressures, curriculum coverage and providing assessment opportunities and judgements.

Conclusion

The arguments and issues considered here provide an insight into the contested place and nature of moral learning within history education. While there is disagreement as to the form that such learning should take, history education must not lose sight of its moral purposes; to do so would detract from one of the key characteristics of the subject. Moral learning does not lie at the periphery of history but at its core. As such the questions and debates discussed in this chapter should be at the forefront of history teachers' minds. A recurring theme is that much of the moral learning which occurs within history education is too often implicit and that, for this reason, further dialogue and critical reflection aimed at making such learning explicit would be beneficial. While there is a corpus of work that engages with the question of pupils' moral learning within history, it is striking that at present there is very little published literature available which makes use of empirical research into how pupils encounter morals within their study of history or which seeks to interrogate the views of history teachers concerning the place of moral learning within their classrooms. There is a need for academics and school teachers to engage in this area, and for more empirical work to be undertaken within schools. The lack of clarity concerning the place of moral values within history teaching also raises pertinent issues for the education of history teachers. This includes the extent to which new entrants to the profession are prepared for handling moral questions and issues with their pupils, as well as the themes and pedagogical approaches which might sustain and develop these. Such questions are not only significant in the developing professional identity of new history teachers but also pertinent to all teachers of the subject. For this reason it is a professional prerequisite that we all engage in further dialogue in order that pupils' moral learning be clear, considered and informed.

Further reading

Arthur, J., Davies, I., Kerr, D. and Wrenn, A. (2001) *Citizenship Through Secondary History*. Routledge: London.
 Includes a chapter on the extent to which history can support pupils' moral learning and development which provides a sound and useful introduction to the issues and an analysis of the moral role of both subjects.
Lee, P., Slater, J., Walsh, P., and White, J. (eds) *The Aims of School History: The National Curriculum and Beyond*. Tufnell Press: London.
 A collection of critical essays which include reference to the moral purposes of history education and which are written in an intellectual yet accessible way.
The Historical Association (2007) *Teaching Emotive and Controversial History 3–19*. Historical Association: London.
 Written by experts in the field, this report considers the nature of emotive and controversial issues which clearly relate to moral learning within history education. The issues raised and the recommendations made are interesting and thought-provoking.

References

Arthur, J., Davies, I., Kerr, D. and Wrenn, A. (2001) *Citizenship Through Secondary History*. Routledge: London.
Barton, K. C. and Levstik, L. S. (2004) *Teaching History for the Common Good*. Mahwah, NJ: Lawrence Erlbaum Associates.
Butterfield, H. (1951) *History and Human Relations: Moral Judgement in History*. London: Collins.
Carr, E. H. (1961) *What is History?* London: Penguin.
Department for Educational and Science (DES) (1985) *History in the Primary and Secondary Years: An HMI View*. London: HMSO.
Fenton, E. (1966) *Teaching the New Social Studies in Secondary Schools*. New York: Holt, Reinhart & Winston.
Halstead, M. and Taylor, M. (2000) 'Learning and teaching about values', *Cambridge Journal of Education*, 3(2): 169–202.
Historical Association (2007) *Teaching Emotive and Controversial History 3–19*. London: Historical Association.
Holocaust Education Development Programme (HEDP) (2009) *Teaching About the Holocaust in English Secondary Schools: An Empirical Study of National Trends, Perspectives and Practice*. London: HEDP.
Kinloch, N. (1998) 'Learning about the Holocaust: Moral or historical question?', *Teaching History*, 93: 44–6.
Kinloch, N. (2001) 'Parallel catastrophes? Uniqueness, redemption and the Shoah', *Teaching History*, 104: 8–14.
Knowles, D. (1955) *The Religious Orders in England. Volume II: The End of the Middle Ages*. Cambridge: Cambridge University Press.
Kohlberg, L. (1981) *Essays on Moral Development: The Philosophy of Moral Development*. Vol. I. San Francisco: Harper & Row.
Kohlberg, L. (1984) *Essays on Moral Development: The Philosophy of Moral Development*. Vol. II. San Francisco: Harper & Row.
Lee, P. (1992) 'History in schools: Aims, purposes and approaches. A reply to John White', in P. Lee, J. Slater, P. Walsh and J. White (eds) *The Aims of School History: The National Curriculum and Beyond*. London: Tufnell Press, pp. 20–34.

McLaughlin, T. and Halstead, M. (1999) *Education in Morality*. London: Routledge.

Maxwell, B. (2008) 'Justifying educational acquaintance with the moral horrors of history on psycho-social grounds: "Facing History and Ourselves" in critical perspective', *Ethics and Education*, 3(1): 75–85.

National Curriculum Council (NCC) (1993) *Teaching History at Key Stage 3*. York: NCC.

Ofsted (1994a) *Spritual, Moral, Social and Cultural Development: An Ofsted Discussion Paper*. London: Ofsted.

Ofsted (1994b) *Framework for the Inspections of Schools* (revised edition). London: Ofsted.

Qualifications and Curriculum Authority (QCA)(1998) *Education for Citizenship and the Teaching of Democracy in Schools* (Crick Report). London: QCA.

Qualifications and Curriculum Authority (QCA)(1999) *National Curriculum for England* (Key Stages 3 and 4). London: HMSO.

Raths, L., Harmin, M. and Simon, S. (1966) *Values and Teaching – Working with Children in the Classroom*. Columbus, OH: Merrill.

Salmons, P. (2003) 'Teaching or preaching? The Holocaust and intercultural education in the UK', *Intercultural Education*, 14(2): 139–49.

Smith, R. I. (1986) 'Values in history and social studies', in P. Tomlinson and M. Quinton, (eds) *Values Across the Curriculum*. London: Falmer Press, pp. 77–86.

Walsh, P. (1993) *Education and Meaning: Philosophy in Practice*. London: Cassell.

Chapter 14

Teaching diversity in the history classroom

Paul Bracey, Alison Gove-Humphries and
Darius Jackson

Introduction

Considering diversity within the history curriculum is timely. This chapter will explore the significance of current developments related to diversity and then address the following questions: What is the relationship between history and contemporary issues? What is the relationship between diversity as a concept and its substantive content? Developing a big picture of the past: What are the implications for diversity? This will be followed by a series of guiding principles which we hope will support the development of diversity in the history curriculum.

Since 2007 there have been several key developments associated with diversity within the history curriculum. The *Curriculum Review Diversity and Citizenship* (2007) recommended that history could 'provide opportunities to study 'how movement of diverse people to, from and within the British Isles have shaped the UK through time' (Ajegbo *et al.*, 2007: 53). It also regarded Britain as a multinational state made up of England, Northern Ireland, Scotland and Wales, as well as considering the significance of immigration, commonwealth and the legacy of empire and the European Union. The Historical Association report entitled *Teaching Emotive and Controversial History 3–19* (Wrenn *et al.*, 2007) strongly emphasized the need to explore multiple narratives and perspectives of the past as a means of teaching emotional and controversial issues. The Her Majesty's Inspector report *History in the Balance* (Ofsted, 2007) challenged teachers to consider 'big issues' in history and made specific reference to regional and multicultural diversity.

It is, therefore, hardly surprising that diversity has a prominent place in the secondary curriculum. The Key Stage 3 curriculum (DfES, 2007) emphasized diversity as a strand of knowledge and as a second-order context. *The Independent Review of the Primary Curriculum: Interim Report* (DfCSF, 2009) included reference to diversity and proposed a history curriculum which included local, British and world history. The report also proposed that schools should teach about 'the movement and settlement of people in different periods of British history'. The National Curriculum (2010) based on the Rose Report would have implemented these proposals in 2011. A change of government following the United Kingdom general election in May 2010 led to the abandonment of plans to implement a curriculum based on the Rose Report. Nevertheless we will consider diversity within the current 5–14 curriculum where history is both compulsory and explicitly defined within the school curriculum. We will start by defining the place of diversity in the national curriculum.

How is diversity defined in the National Curriculum?

The 2008 Key Stage 3 programme of study 'Importance of History' statement says that history 'encourages mutual understanding of the historic origins of our ethnic and cultural diversity'. Diversity is also explicitly defined as a statutory key concept entitled *Cultural, ethnic and religious diversity* (1.2) which includes understanding the diverse experiences and ideas, beliefs and attitudes of men, women and children in past societies and how these have shaped the world. However, the explanatory notes go further than this statement and indicate that pupils should also explore racial equality. It gives a broader explanation of diversity as a concept which includes regional, linguistic, social economic and technological, political and religious differences. It also indicates that the concept should be taught through the range of groups and individuals investigated, including minorities and majorities, European and non-European people. It makes reference to how people and societies from different contexts will interpret the past in different ways.

Diversity is either implicit or explicit within the range and content of British and world history. Examples of explicit reference to diversity include, for example, 'the different histories and changing relationships through time of the peoples of England. Ireland, Scotland and Wales' (3e), 'the impact through time of the movement and settlement of diverse peoples to and from and within the British Isles' (3f) and 'the British Empire and its impact on different people in Britain and overseas' (3h). Elsewhere it is implicit, such as in 'the development of political power' (3d), which includes 'the nature and motives of protest over time.' Finally, the concept of diversity forms part of the attainment target from Level 5 which states 'They begin to recognise and describe the nature and extent of diversity'. The vague nature of this statement is problematic in that it is difficult to see how 'begin to recognise', or the 'extent of diversity' will actually be determined. The proposed changes to the Primary Curriculum (2010) were less detailed than those for Key Stage 3 or, indeed, the preceding primary or secondary curriculum, although diversity was defined and migration featured as a thread within Key Stage 2. Issues of interpretation would therefore have been of even greater significance than was the case with the Secondary National Curriculum.

Diversity and National Curriculum history from 2008: a significant break with the past?

There is evidence of both continuity and change in the history curriculum. The History Working Party (DES, 1990) which led to the introduction of the first statutory orders for history certainly made reference to shared inheritances, migration, English, Welsh, Scottish and Irish perspectives in British history, together with European and world history, for example. The distance between rhetoric and practice within the context of the statutory curriculum, which emerged in 1991 together with its revisions in 1995 and 2000, was increased by teacher perceptions of content overload and difficulties in obtaining resources to support diversity. For the purposes of this chapter it is appropriate to focus on Curriculum 2000 as these orders immediately preceded the current secondary curriculum and were due to be replaced by a new primary curriculum in 2011.

The importance of history statement in Curriculum 2000 indicated that pupils 'see the diversity of human experience and learn more about themselves as individuals and members of society'. The focus statement for Key Stage 1 noted that pupils would learn about significant men, women and children. At Key Stage 2 knowledge skills and understanding required that pupils should be taught 'about characteristic features of the periods and societies studied, including the ideas, beliefs, attitudes and experiences of men, women and children in the past' (2a) and 'about the social, cultural, religious and ethnic diversity of the societies studied in Britain and the wider world' (2b). The breadth of studies included local, British, European and world dimensions as well as 'aspects of the histories of England, Ireland, Scotland and Wales where appropriate, and about the history of Britain in its European and wider world context' (8b). The last statement was vague and open to considerable interpretation. In principle these were carried through into Key Stage 3, subject to refinements, knowledge, skills and understanding requirements and the breadth of study, ostensibly to reflect progression. Both Key Stage 2 and 3 were divided into areas of study. Diversity was perhaps implicitly but not explicitly indicated in the attainment target.

What does this suggest about changes since 2008? First, the 2008 Secondary Orders are more specifically related to social, ethnic and cultural diversity and the explanatory notes define what this includes in more detail than was the case in 2000. Second, the 'Range and Content' section provides threads which define diversity more explicitly than was the case in the areas of study or general statements in the preceding order. In addition, it is appropriate to note that secondary history includes specific reference to links with citizenship, while the proposed primary curriculum included both history and citizenship within the same Area of Study.

What is the relationship between history and contemporary issues?

The use of history to support a common national identity and empire was evident in the early twentieth century. Arguably it often continued by default during the 1950s and 1960s:

> Content was largely British, or rather Southern English; Celts looked in to starve, emigrate or rebel . . . abroad was of interest once it was part of the Empire, foreigners were sensibly allies, or rightly defeated.
>
> (Slater, 1989: 1)

It provided a major focus of debate when the National Curriculum was introduced and remains the staple diet of tabloid newspaper articles lamenting students' inadequate knowledge about key dates, events and individuals in Britain's past. McGovern, a founder member of the 'History Curriculum Association', has consistently argued that children need to be presented with a body of knowledge about the past. He challenges exploring multiple perspectives and social purposes such as 'Britishness', ethnic diversity or gender as political correctness and argued for teaching landmarks in British history:

> A new generation of storybooks needs to be published to highlight the excitement of the past and its landmarks for this country and for other countries. If this leads to bias towards pride in our own national identity, so be it.
>
> (McGovern, 2007: 80)

A number of studies have questioned the effectiveness of relying on a pupils' memory of key dates and events. Wineberg's (2000) research indicated that poor memory of historical events has been an issue since the early twentieth century, regardless of the teaching approaches used. Foster *et al.* (2008) identified that history had limited impact in developing national identity:

> Students did not believe that history (beyond personal and family history) was a major factor in influencing their identity. Certainly, it would be wrong to conclude from this finding that students need a fixed, national story around which they can allegedly unite. Rather, it suggests that students require a history education that provides them with a rich and informed perspective on how the past has unavoidable influence in shaping their life and the lives of others both in the present and in the future.
>
> (Foster *et al.*, 2008: 13)

The implication of this argument is that the past is both complex and subject to different interpretations. Clearly an opened-ended and flexible framework requires the past to be seen in a more broadly based canvas which gives due attention to the way in which learning takes place. A narrowly defined curriculum consisting of key facts about a perceived common past does not meet this requirement.

History has also responded to social changes, notably in the 1970s and 1980s, exploring the experiences and issues faced by disadvantaged groups. A number of history educators provided models which related this to the way in which they approached teaching about the past. Edgington (1982) stressed that history did more than inform children about other periods and societies and that the content of a syllabus could change cognitive and affective behaviours. Goalen (1988) provided a framework for teaching history, which was intended to meet the needs of a multicultural society. Adams (1983) argued that by ignoring women's experiences textbooks were seriously distorting the past and that history is about understanding the past in all its diversity; 'history which ignores one half of the human race is bad history'. Several writers continued to argue the case for ensuring for including under-represented groups in the curriculum (Osler, 1994; Pounce, 1995; Bracey, 1995, 2008; Patel, 1997; Claire, 1996; Jackson, 1998; Grosvenor, 2000; Phillips, 2002). Phillips provided a particularly clear demonstration of how history relates to diversity by arguing that history supports identity formation and contributes to an inclusive view of society and nation together with a view of the world which looks outwards.

The distinction between teaching history as a subject and using it to address current concerns has been challenged by Lee (1991), who argued:

The reason for teaching history in schools is not so that pupils can use it for making something else, or to change or preserve a particular form of society, or even expand the economy. The reason for teaching history is not that it changes the world, but that it changes *pupils*, it changes the way what they see in the world, and how they see it.

(Lee, 1991: 43)

Lee was concerned that focusing on personal and social functions was at odds with providing a wider conception of history as a way of looking at the world:

Other historical criteria lie behind this wider conception. Pupils need to understand long-term change, to grasp the differences between short and long-term importance, to see how different kinds of significance can be attributed to the same changes in different temporal and spatial contexts. They need to examine radically different ways of life from ours, and to understand alternative individual ideas. Some ideas may be best acquired in passages of the past very clearly not concerned with issues people confront today. The distance allows judgement relatively untrammelled by assimilation to immediate prejudices.

(Lee, 1992: 23)

This argument has particular relevance when exploring diversity through history and citizenship education. Lee and Shemilt (2007) argued that using current concerns associated with human rights encouraged a deficit view of the past. They also drew on Traille's (2007) research to illustrate the danger of conflating history with identity, 'my' and 'your' histories since some black pupils felt humiliation because of the way the slave trade was taught. They questioned

Whether it makes sense to . . . contaminate 'respect for different national, religious and ethnic identities' with false pride in real or mystical achievements, relived humiliations for past failures and resentments over wrongs yet to be avenged.

(Lee and Shemilt, 2007: 17)

They also argue that the Holocaust, slave trade and empire in history could contaminate citizenship messages associated with social cohesion. They argue that history is best seen as complementing citizenship providing an understanding of how the present is the cutting edge of the past and the implications of this for challenging fixed notions of citizenship over time. In particular they stress:

The history teacher should answer for the rationality of students' conclusions but not the positions they take. We should strive to equip students with the knowledge, conceptual, and logical apparatus necessary to ensure that their decisions as citizens will be less stupid that they might have been, but we can do no more than hope their actions will also be less cruel. To expect more would be to confuse a complementary relationship with a collaborationist one.

(Lee and Shemilt, 2007: 19)

This argument has several implications. First, it is evident that history and citizenship are complementary but distinct. Osler (2009) related this issue to the Ajegbo Report (Ajegbo *et al.*, 2007) which responded to the bombings of 9/11 and 7/5. She argued that not only does history have distinctive features which separate it from citizenship but also that the report's focus on diversity and social cohesion is too narrow for it to provide a basis for understanding the past. Second, teaching which focuses exclusively on horrific events in the past is unlikely to promote either social cohesion or a well-developed understanding of the past. In history it is necessary to teach events such as slavery or the Holocaust in a broader framework. Kitson (2001) argued that the teaching of the Holocaust can be rigorous and critical as well as exploring the social and moral messages. She showed how 'diversity' can be used as a concept by examining student misconceptions such as 'All Germans were Nazis' and 'Jews were helpless victims who didn't fight back'. Equally in the DVD-Rom *Partition Remembered* (Birmingham City Council, 2009), many of the nineteen interviewees, who experienced partition, talk of good community relations before partition and relate stories of people helping each other across the religious divide. Third, it is necessary to see the past as inclusive to everyone rather than to separate it into 'my' and 'your' histories.

However, we strongly argue that students are able to identify their own culture in all its complexities through a broadly based approach to the past. Gaze (2005) argued that it is important to teach an inclusive history for students from all ethnic backgrounds – noting his shock when a young black student told him that there was no point in his studying the Second World War because it had nothing to do with him or his family. We would argue that drawing distinctions between the distinctive roles of history and citizenship strengthens the extent to which each relates to diversity in their own terms.

What is the relationship between diversity as a concept and its substantive content?

Bradshaw (2009) has provided useful insights to thinking about 'diversity' as a concept. He shows an important part of teaching about 'diversity' is supporting students who are grappling with the complexities of history, i.e. the particular and the general, similarity and difference. The article is particularly useful in that it focuses on ways in which revisiting the concept of diversity can progressively deepen pupils' understanding of its nature. However, he seemed lukewarm in supporting key aspects of substantive knowledge associated with diversity:

> It is interesting that 'diversity' immediately brings to mind for many people the notion of non-British history, or the history of diverse ethnic, cultural or religious groups, or a particular emphasis on previously under-represented groups – the working classes. Perhaps it should . . . It is necessary to reclaim the term 'diversity' from the politicians in order to bring out its meaning as the richness of the historical tapestry, the small stories, the exceptions, the variety of the past in all its fullness.
>
> (Bradshaw, 2009: 5)

We argue that this perception does not give appropriate consideration to issues such as power and inequality, together with the gaps and silences in the way that the past has been represented, which have given undue representation to some groups as opposed to others. The Qualifications and Curriculum Authority (QCA, 2005: 20) made reference to this issue:

> There has been no 'discernible change' after its complaint last year that many schools largely ignore the black and multi-ethnic aspects of British history. Too often, the teaching of black history is confined to topics about slavery and post war immigration, or to 'black history month'. The effect, if inadvertent, is to under-value the overall contribution of black and minority ethnic people to Britain's past and to ignore their cultural, scientific and many other achievements.

Overall, we agree with Claire (1996) that

> [i]n the real world everyone belongs to all three categories since each of us is male/female, and middle, upper and working class, and from an ethnic minority or the white English group in British society. In an inclusive curriculum there are good reasons for not treating race, gender and class separately, not just to match the real world but also to avoid the danger of creating hierarchies or forgetting links.
>
> (Claire, 1996: 10)

Bradshaw's reference to empire made particular reference to academic historians Ferguson (2003) and Cannadine (2001) as a means of providing diversity. Ferguson's analysis of the British Empire concluded:

> [W]hat the British Empire proved is that empire is a form of international govern-ment that can work – and not just for the benefit of the ruling power. It sought to globalise not just an economic but a legal and ultimately a political system.
>
> (Ferguson, 2003: 264)

Cannadine focused on how the British saw their empire and focused on the ruling classes. In this he argued that the expansion of empire saw social structures in Britain replicated to the rest of the world. These interpretations of empire differ radically from those presented by Said (2003), Samuel (1998) and Hall (1996), which include the perspectives held by colonized peoples. Bradshaw made reference to the contribu-tion of the empire to Britain during World War II but it is by no means clear how far he related progression to students' understanding of empire since he did not make explicit comparisons among the Roman, Norman and British empires. This leads us neatly to looking at how diversity relates to frameworks of the past.

Developing a big picture of the past: what are the implications for diversity?

A major issue confronting teachers and teacher educators is how to develop students' 'big picture' or framework of the past. The Office for Standards in Education (Ofsted,

2007) drew attention to the fragmented way in which students saw the past as a major challenge. Before considering its implications for diversity within the history curriculum it is appropriate to consider how this concern has arisen.

Rogers (1987) and Counsell (2000) argued that pupils refine their understanding of the past as they acquire new knowledge. By drawing links between past and present knowledge children are able to develop and refine their framework of the past. Shemilt (2000) argued that students have had difficulty in seeing the past as a whole. He considered that they needed to go beyond key events and distinguish between causal and logical possibilities and uncertainties about what has happened and to challenge partial histories of what took place. This was supported by the findings of a major research (Foster *et al.*, 2008) which indicated that students had difficulties in identifying past trends and development. In an interview with *The Guardian* newspaper, Foster argued that '[t]he fragmentary topic-driven nature of the English history curriculum renders the subject pointless and irrelevant to many students and educators' and that 'history would be more interesting and of greater relevance . . . if they learned it under "patterns" and "themes" that incorporate the learning of facts, dates and events' (Shepherd and MacLeod: 2008). Shemilt (2006, cited in Howson, 2007: 47) considered the use of a synoptic framework, which involved continually revisiting an initial model, as new topics and strands were taught so that the framework became increasingly sophisticated.

The following draws on recent literature connected with diversity which attempts to relate it the 'big picture of the past'. Some history educationalists have looked at different spatial dimensions to provide a broadly based framework of the past. Corfield (2009) claimed that the twenty-first century is seeing their re-emergence of 'Grand Narratives' associated with increasing concerns associated with current global issues. She argued that this needs to be reflected in history teaching by exploring the complexity and variety in the past as part of the story of human diversity. As part of a 'big picture' of the past she related this to three interlocking dimensions – continuity, gradual micro changes and turbulent macro changes within historical themes. Corfield exemplified this through a number of studies related to diversity. By drawing on the work of Sheldrake and Banham (2007) she demonstrated how a contemporary topic related to a local Caribbean community could be related to different experiences of a wide range of migrants over time – as part of Britain's big picture of the past. Corfield related this to a much bigger global narrative by the following statement:

> Continuities are often ignored or under-probed. One basic feature is the human species' propensity to travel, to settle and to reproduce, ever since our first ancestors first came 'out of Africa'.
>
> (Corfield, 2009: 57)

Several other studies relate diversity within a global framework. Chapman and Facey (2004) explored rival interpretations of the past to encourage students to consider identity issues and challenge Eurocentric perceptions. Traille (2007) argued that slavery ought to be investigated during different times and contexts and that the study of the transatlantic slave trade should include resistance to it. Gove-Humphries (2008) produced a teaching pack, *From Slavery to Emancipation*, which made reference to pre-colonial Africa, the development of the trade and the plantations, national and local links together with the range of people, black and white, operating as traders, taken as slaves and involved in emancipation.

Diversity has also been related to the dynamics and nature of historical change. Byrom and Riley (2007) used multiple narratives to develop an understanding of the complexity of relationships between Islam and the West during both the period of the Crusades and the sixteenth and seventeenth centuries and used this as a model for planning a range if themes including 'Britain – The English Empire? (National Stories): Wales, Scotland and Ireland and "Moving Stories" (Migration to and within): Prehistory, "The locals" – migration to the local area and Multicultural Britain' (Byrom and Riley, 2007: 29). Jarman (2009) explored changes and continuities in policies towards medieval Jews to determine when they were most in danger. Lyndon (2006) integrated black history within topics. For example, as part of a thematic study related to the Tudors he examined Drake's jewel, a pendant presented to Sir Francis in recognition for his work with the Cimaroons. He then related Elizabethan proclamations against increasing numbers of Blackamores to a study of Elizabethan poverty.

Some writers have considered regional diversity within Britain's 'big story'. Corfield (2009) made reference to the diverse impact the Norman invasion in 1066 and the arrival of William of Orange in 1688 made within England, Scotland, Wales and Ireland. An Irish dimension also provides opportunities for exploring diversity within our islands and has been the subject of several articles undertaken by the authors. For example, a comparison of Brian Boru and Alfred the Great was used to challenge Anglocentric approaches to the curriculum (Jackson *et al.*, 2008). Bracey (2008; 2010) used the term 'hinterlands' to show how an Irish dimension in the history curriculum could support the way in which children developed their map of the past. Here a topic such as Drogheda was explored as fully as possible within its immediate and wider context and then compared and contrasted with other contexts such the Wasting of the North or Amritsar.

There have been fewer publications and articles related to gender and class than ethnicity in recent years. Consequently, most of the literature predates current debates associated with the big picture of the past. Nevertheless, Moorse and Claire (2007) provided useful guidelines which could be related to it. They recommended teaching young pupils through the use of sources and examples which reflected both men and women. As students progressed they argued that gender should be embedded into both what was taught, the full range of second order concepts and used to 'dig deep' into the social and gendered construction of the historical record. Several publications have made suggestions about the use of content with respect to gender. Claire (1996) provided examples related to the primary history curriculum. She recommended moving beyond figures such as Boudicca when studying the Romans by using artefacts and museum images of home life to construct ideas about the lives of ordinary women. Comparable approaches were related to other periods – such as the role of women in the workforce in Tudor and Victorian periods. She also made references to teaching about different classes of women as well as their role in reform movements. Jackson (1998) related gender to developing a framework of the past in the secondary history curriculum. Overall, he provided examples which challenged simplistic perceptions of their power and role. Factors adversely affecting women's opportunities were considered, such as the growth of the medical profession. Clearly, there is scope for further studies which explore teaching and learning processes and frameworks which relate to different genders and relationships between them.

Patel (1997) noted that social class had received little attention in recent years. Successive versions of the National Curriculum have required that different sections of society should be considered. Some history educators have focused on the implications of this for teaching about the working classes with respect to the selection of content. Claire (1996) argued that teaching ought to include opportunities to challenge the view that changes have always been made by rulers and the powerful. She also indicated opportunities to explore the lives of different classes, linking this to gender within the Victorian period, for example. Jackson (1998) argued that interpretations of nineteenth-century working-class movements, such as the Chartists, as failures should be countered with those which related them to the struggle for political reform. As with gender there is scope to develop this area more fully by comparing the different experiences of different sections of society and the relationships between them over time.

The preceding paragraphs provide a range of approaches towards teaching diversity with respect to ethnicity, gender and class. The first of these has received particular attention in recent publications which will hopefully continue. However, there is a need for these approaches to be applied more explicitly to other aspects of diversity to enhance the way in which they contribute to a 'big picture' of the past. The following principles are intended to support the development of diversity in future curriculum planning.

Developing diversity within the history curriculum: suggested principles

1. Diversity within history should be seen as complementary but not synonymous with its role within citizenship education.
2. Diversity involves both the development of substantive knowledge and the development of second-order concepts.
3. Diversity should be considered within local, regional and British, European and world contexts from the distant to recent past and form part of the 'big picture of the past'.
4. Diversity should be developed as a broadly based concept within each of the above dimensions but must specifically relate gender, ethnicity and class as well as variations within them.
5. Diversity should be progressively developed as a first- and second-order concept enabling students to develop a deeper sense of period as well as the dynamics of changes affecting or restricting different people's experiences over time.
6. Diversity should provide for a more authentic understanding of the past giving opportunities to analyse different people's experiences.
7. Diversity should involve opportunities to examine evidence as well the gaps and silences in the historical record to develop an authentic understanding of the nature of historical enquiry.
8. Diversity should be taught as part of a developing framework which enables students to perfect their historical 'hinterland', exploring precedents, effects and

interpretations as well as comparing their impact in different spatial and time contexts.

Chapter summary

We have argued that diversity has a central role in the history curriculum which is distinct from but complementary to its role with citizenship. Although the term can be related to a wide range of contexts we have argued that its essential focus should relate to ethnicity, gender and class. Given the importance of these dimensions they should form central features within the 'big picture' of the past.

Recommended reading

Shemilt, D. and Lee, P. (2007) 'The new alchemy or fatal attraction? History and citizenship'. *Teaching History*, 129: 14–19.
Claire, H. (1996) *Reclaiming Our Pasts. Equality and Diversity in the Primary History Curriculum*. Stoke: Trentham.
Corfield, P. J. (2009) 'Teaching history's big pictures: including continuity as well as change'. *Teaching History*, 136: 53–9.

References

Adams, C. (1983) 'Off the record'. *Teaching History*, 36: 9–11.
Ajegbo, K., Kuwan, D. and Sharma S. (2007) *Curriculum Review. Diversity and Citizenship*. London: Department for Education and Skills.
Birmingham City Council (2009) *Partition Remembered* DVD-Rom, Birmingham: Birmingham City Council.
Bracey, P. (1995) 'Developing a multicultural perspective within Key Stage 3 National Curriculum History'. *Teaching History*, 78: 8–10.
——(2008) 'Perceptions of an Irish dimension and its significance for the English history curriculum', unpublished PhD thesis, Birmingham: University of Birmingham.
——(2010) 'Perceptions of the contribution of an Irish dimension in the English history curriculum'. *Educational Review*, 62: 203–10.
Bradshaw, M. (2009) 'Drilling down: how one history department is working towards progression in pupils thinking about diversity across Years 7, 8 and 9'. *Teaching History*, 135: 4–12.
Byrom, J. and Riley, M. (2007) 'Identity-shakers: cultural encounters and the development of pupils' multiple identities'. *Teaching History*, 129: 22–9.
Cannadine, D. (2001) *Orientalism: How the British saw their Empire*. London: Penguin.
Chapman, A. and Facey, J. (2004) 'Placing history: territory, story, identity and historical consciousness'. *Teaching History*, 116: 36–41.
Claire, H. (1996) *Reclaiming our Pasts: Equality and Diversity in the Primary School*. Stoke: Trentham.
Corfield, P. (2009) 'Teaching history's big pictures: including continuity and change'. *Teaching History*, 136: 53–9.
Counsell, C. (2000) 'Historical knowledge and historical skills: a distracting dichotomy', in J. Arthur and R. Phillips (eds) *Issues in History Teaching*. London: Routledge.

DfCF/QCDA (2010) *The National Primary Curriculum*. Coventry: DfCF/QCDA.

DES (1990) *National Curriculum History Working Group: Final Report*. London: Her Majesty's Stationery Office.

DfES/QCA (2007) *The Secondary Curriculum Review. Programme of Study: History Key Stage 3*. London: DfES/QCA.

Edgington, D. (1982) 'The role of history in multicultural education'. *Teaching History*, 32: 3–5.

Ferguson, N. (2003) *Empire: How Britain Made the Modern World*. London: Penguin.

Foster, S. Ashby, R. Lee, P. and Howson, J. (2008) *Usable Historical Pasts: A Study of Students' Frameworks of the Past: Full Research Report ESRC End of Award Report, RES-000-22-1676*. Swindon: ESRC. Available online at: http://www.esrcsocietytoday. ac.uk/ESRCInfoCentre/ViewOutputPage.aspx?data=lWEC7sNY9jlnfD32Q%2fme IPy2Z95wEGwMilPOpEWE8C3bnGeIqICC6Iy7gXA3cmLBYN5NhA9PHS4b67 goIOQ5GTjSMzl4hLgDl97Lg4lXZyBbtK%2fY3bhMT3FbVxLfbxlrtuew88%2fIRYJ 83VFoBnq%2b8A%3d%3d&xu=0&isAwardHolder=&isProfiled=&AwardHolderID=& Sector= (accessed 31 August 2010).

Gaze, R. (2005) 'Discovering hidden histories: Black and Asian people in the two world wars'. *Teaching History* 120: 46–54.

Goalen, P. (1988) 'Multiculturalism and the lower school history syllabus: towards a practical approach'. *Teaching History*, 53: 8–16.

Gove-Humphries, A. (2008) *From Slavery to Emancipation*. Available online at: http:// www.northants-black-history.org.uk/resourceDownloadIndex.asp (accessed 4 October 2010).

Grosvenor, I. (2000) 'History for the nation: multiculturalism and the teaching of history', in J. Arthur and R. Phillips (eds) *Issues in History Teaching*. London: Routledge, pp. 148–58.

Hall, C. (1996) 'Histories, empires and the postcolonial movement', in I. Chambers and I. Curtis (eds) *The Postcolonial Question*. London: Routledge.

Howson, J. (2007) 'Is it the Tuarts and then the Studors or the other way round? The importance of developing a usable big picture of the past'. *Teaching History*, 127: 40–7.

Jackson, T. (1998) 'History', in D. Hill and M. Cole (eds) *Promoting Equality in Secondary School*. London: Cassell.

Jackson, D., Bracey, P. and Gove-Humphries, A. (2008) 'Exploring significant individuals as heroes to challenge Anglo-centric norms in Key Stage 2 history (7–11)', in Y. Vella (ed.) *Transforming History Teaching–Transforming Society*. Trends: Monograph Series in Education, University of Malta, 4, pp. 19–32.

Jarman, B. (2009) 'When were the Jews in medieval England most in danger? Exploring continuity and change with Year 7'. *Teaching History*, 136: 4–12.

Kitson, A. (2001) 'Challenging stereotypes and avoiding the superficial: a suggested approach to teaching the Holocaust'. *Teaching History*, 104: 41–8.

Lee, P. (1991) 'Historical knowledge and the National Curriculum', in R. Aldrich (ed.) *History in the National Curriculum*. London: Kogan Page.

——(1992) 'History in schools: aims, purposes and approaches. A reply to John White', in P. Lee, J. Slater, P. Walsh and J. White, *The Aims of School History*. London: Tufnell.

Lee, P. and Shemilt, D. (2007) 'New alchemy or fatal attraction? History and citizenship'. *Teaching History*, 129: 14–19.

Lyndon, D. (2006) 'Integrating black British history into the National Curriculum'. *Teaching History*, 122: 37–43.

McGovern, C. (2007) 'The new history boys', in R. Whelan (ed.) *The Corruption of the Curriculum*. London: Civitas.

Moorse, K. and Claire, H. (2007) 'History', in K. Myers, H. Taylor, H. S. Adler and D. Leonard (eds) *Gender Watch. Still Watching* . . . Stoke: Trentham.

Ofsted (2007) *History in the Balance. History in English Schools 2003–7*. Office for Standards in Education. Available online at: http://www.ofsted.gov.uk/Ofsted-home/ Publications-and-research/Browse-all-by/Education/Curriculum/History/Primary/ History-in-the-balance/(language)/eng-GB (accessed 29 October 2010).

Osler, A. (1994) 'Still hidden from history? The representation of women in recently published history textbooks'. *Oxford Review of Education*, 20(2): 219–35.

——(2009) 'Patriotism, multiculturalism and belonging: political discourse and the teaching of history'. *Educational Review*, 61(1): 85–100.

Patel, L. (1997) 'History', in M. Cole, D. Hill and S. Sharanjeet (eds) *Promoting Equality in Primary Schools*. London: Casssell.

Phillips, R. (2002) *Reflective Teaching of History 11–18*. London: Continuum.

Pounce, E (1995) 'Ensuring continuity and understanding through teaching gender issues in history, 5–16', in R. Watts and I. Grosvenor (eds) *Crossing the Key Stages of History. Effective History Teaching 5–16 and Beyond*. London: David Fulton, 89–113.

QCA (2005) *History 2004/5* annual report on curriculum and assessment. Available online at: http://image.guardian.co.uk/sys-files/Education/documents/2005/12/22/History qca.pdf (accessed 31 October 2010).

——(2007) *The Secondary Curriculum Review. Programme of Study: History Key Stage 3*. London: Qualification and Curriculum Development Agency. Available online at: http://curriculum.qcda.gov.uk/key-stages-3-and-4/subjects/key-stage-3/history/ index.aspx (accessed 31 August 2010).

Rogers, P. (1987) 'The past as a frame of reference', in C. Portal (ed.) *The History Curriculum for Teachers*. Lewes: Farmer Press.

Rose, J. (2009) *Independent Review of the Primary Curriculum*. London: Department for Children Schools and Families. Available online at: http://www.catchup.org.uk/Link Click.aspx?fileticket=O0UPnzCS_zs%3D&tabid=105 (accessed 4 October 2010).

Said, E. (2003) *Orientalism*, 3rd edn. London: Penguin.

Samuel, R. (1998) *Island Stories: Unravelling Britain: Theatres of Memory, Vol. II*. London: Verso.

Sheldrake, R. and Banham, D. (2007) 'Seeing a different picture: exploring migration through the lens of history', *Teaching History*, 129: 39–47.

Shemilt, D. (2000) 'The Caliph's coin: the currency of narrative frameworks in history', in P. Sterns, P. Sexias and S. Wineburg (eds) *Knowing, Teaching and Learning History*. New York: New York University Press, pp. 83–101.

——(2006) 'The future of the past: how adolescents make sense of the past, present and future'. Paper presented at the International invitation conference: National History Standards: the problem of the Canon and the Future of History Teaching. University of Utrecht, October 2006. Cited in J. Howson (2007) 'Is it the Tuarts and then the Studars or the other way round? The importance of developing a usable big picture of the past'. *Teaching History*, 127: 40–7.

Shepherd, J. and MacLeod, D. (2008) 'History threatens to become bunk.' Crib sheet, *The Guardian*, Tuesday 15 April. Available online at: http://www.guardian.co.uk/ education/2008/apr/15/educationguardian2.educationguardian (accessed 31 August 2010).

Slater, J. (1989) 'The politics of history teaching: a humanity dehumanised?', *Institute of Education, Special Professorial Lecture*. London: Institute of Education.

Traille, K. (2007) 'You should be proud about your history. They made me feel ashamed: teaching history that hurts'. *Teaching History*, 127: 31–7.

Wineburg, S. (2000) 'Making historical sense', in P. Stearns, P. Seixas, and S. Wineburg (eds) *Knowing Teaching and Learning History*. New York: New York University Press.

Wrenn, A., Wilkinson, A., Webb, A., Gillespie, H., Riley, M., Harnett, P., Harris, R. and Lomas, T. (2007) *Teaching Emotive and Controversial History 3–19*. London: Historical Association.

Chapter 15

Citizenship and history
Uncomfortable bedfellows

Richard Harris

Introduction

Exploring the relationship between citizenship and history raises many awkward questions, both about the status and nature of these respective subjects and about the extent to which they are or should be linked. This makes writing a chapter about the relationship between these subjects challenging, but the recent introduction of the new National Curriculum also makes this a timely point to re-examine this relationship. This chapter examines what is contained in the National Curriculum, and what we can learn by examining this, before moving on to a more fundamental discussion of the nature of these two curriculum areas and how that might inform our understanding of the relationship between history and citizenship. Ultimately, teachers need to decide for themselves what the relationship between history and citizenship should be, and so this chapter aims to outline some of the issues that need to be considered.

Citizenship is not simply a curriculum subject; the creation of 'responsible citizens' is now a stated aim of the National Curriculum (QCDA, 2009), with civic participation highlighted as a measure of its success. Its status has thus become firmly established. Where this leaves history is open to debate, especially at a time when the place of history appears increasingly tenuous (see Historical Association, 2009). This chapter seeks to explore some of the issues in the relationship between history and citizenship, and may well pose more questions than answers!

The National Curriculum

There are obvious links between history and citizenship, which have been clear from the outset. The Crick Report (QCA, 1998), which was hugely influential in shaping the original citizenship National Curriculum, outlined a major role for history in supporting the development of citizenship; according to Crick (2001: xix), 'of all the other subjects History may have (should have) overall the greatest role to play'. The more recent *Diversity and Citizenship Curriculum Review* (DfES, 2007) (better known as the Ajegbo Report) also reaffirms this role. However, both see this role differently. In the Crick Report the emphasis is more on history's role in promoting political literacy, whereas the Ajegbo Report focuses much more on the development of identity. In part this is due to their conceptualization of citizenship but also the social and political context within which they were written. The Crick Report emerged at a time of concerns about political apathy, whereas the Ajegbo Report emerged in an era of concerns about 'home-grown' terrorism and fears of a breakdown in society. As such this dictates their understanding of what history can contribute to citizenship education (and implies citizenship as a subject is more open to social and political pressures).

A detailed examination of the similarities and differences between the National Curriculum in citizenship (QCA, 2007a) and history (QCA, 2007b) can provide a useful starting point for an exploration of the relationship between the two subjects. This can be done by comparing the statements which explain the importance of the subjects, the range and content, as well as the concepts and processes.

There are many similarities between the subjects which can be identified in the importance statements. For example, both subjects purport to develop young people's ability to evaluate evidence and information, be critical and present arguments. Additionally, both claim to prepare students to take part in a democratic society. The subjects entail a study of a range of beliefs and attitudes. In the citizenship curriculum it states clearly that students need to understand how society has changed, which falls firmly in the realms of history education. One area in which the subjects differ is in the subject matter. History is self-evidently rooted in the study of human activity in the past, whereas citizenship is focused on topical issues. Although even here there is an overlap as the history importance statement says history 'helps them [young people] to ask and answer questions of the present by engaging with the past' (p. 111). In some ways this is a potentially problematic statement as it could imply that all history studied should be related to the present day, which runs the risk of a 'presentist' distortion of the past. Nonetheless many teachers would argue that one of the purposes of history teaching is to understand the world in which we live now. A more fundamental difference between the two subjects, as expressed in the citizenship curriculum is the need for social action; there is an expectation that young people will become 'active' citizens.

An examination of the key concepts and processes (see Table 15.1) shows a marked difference in the conceptual approach to the subjects but a degree of overlap in the processes. History as an academic discipline and a school subject has evolved a set of 'second-order' concepts that underpin how we shape and explain our understanding of the past. Thus we look for causes and consequences, we look at change and continuity, we examine the criteria for ascribing significance to people and events. In contrast the key concepts in citizenship of democracy and justice, rights and responsibilities, identities and diversity are a mix of substantive concepts and values. In some ways this reflects the history of the two subjects. History has a tradition as an academic discipline which has evolved over a number of years, whereas citizenship is not an academic subject in the same way; it is a composite subject, drawing on a number of different sources for its subject matter, such as law and politics.

In terms of processes, there are obvious links between 'historical enquiry' and 'using evidence' in the history curriculum and the 'critical thinking and enquiry' strand in citizenship. Both expect students to carry out enquiries, using a range of sources that are subject to evaluation and analysis. Clearly there may be differences in the type of evidence used and the purpose of the enquiries but there are similarities in how

Table 15.1 The National Curriculum key concepts and key processes for history and citizenship

History	Citizenship
Key concepts	
Chronological understanding	Democracy and justice
Cultural, ethnic and religious diversity	Rights and responsibilities
Change and continuity	Identities and diversity: living together
Significance	in the UK
Interpretation	
Key processes	
Historical enquiry	Critical thinking and enquiry
Using evidence	Advocacy and representation
Communicating about the past	Taking informed and responsible action

students would be expected to work. The context for enquiry though is different. The subject matter of history is the past and, therefore, enquiry in this sense means young people have to engage with the incomplete remains of the past. This requires a different form of thinking compared with enquiry regarding contemporary issues, which are (more) likely to be sensitive and/or controversial and therefore require a more explicit handling of different opinions based upon moral values and beliefs, as well as evidence. There are also links between 'communicating about the past' and 'advocacy and representation'. Both require pupils to express their views and be able to justify them, but a much more fundamental difference between these processes is the expectation in citizenship for 'taking informed and responsible action'. This emphasizes the need for social action, underpinned by moral values. In many ways this is the crucial distinction between the two subjects; there is no requirement within the history National Curriculum for teachers to promote any form of action as a result of studying the past.

The subjects do differ widely in the specified 'range and content'. The history curriculum emphasizes themes, periods and types of history to be studied, while the citizenship curriculum is much more focused on aspects of political literacy, the legal system, rights and responsibilities and decision-making. Where the subjects converge is in the need to examine the changing nature of British society, migration and possibly the UK's relations with other countries, but, as Counsell (2002: 2) points out, '[m]ere coincidence of content is not a cross-curricular link'. Clearly there are many other areas of history that provide a context for many areas of citizenship study, but providing a context does not mean that history is actually developing meaningful links to citizenship; the following example from an Office for Standards in Education (Ofsted, 2005: 6) report makes the case clearly:

> With regard to history, for example, citizenship may draw on the past for illustration, but it is essentially about now and the future. Sometimes the two are very closely interwoven. For example, if the study of the holocaust is to have meaning, pupils must reflect on its implications for today, and 'what they can

do' when confronted with cruelty in any form, whether commonplace abuses of human rights such as inequality or new manifestations of genocide.

What this comparison shows is the ways in which the two subjects are similar but it also stresses the differences. In terms of their importance, both strive to help young people make sense of the world in which they live and provide them with the tools to do this. This is also reflected in the processes which have been identified. However, citizenship is firmly rooted in the present (although there is a need to go into the past to make sense of this) and has an explicit agenda in creating 'active' citizens; whether history shares this purpose is a moot point and will be explored further below. The subjects do have a different conceptual basis and potentially very different areas of content to study. What this comparison does not do, though, is to explain how the two subjects should come together, if at all.

What is the 'proper' relationship between history and citizenship?

Lee and Shemilt (2007) offer a helpful analysis of the ways history and citizenship could work together in the curriculum. They identify how history teachers could adopt a 'cornucopia', 'carrier' or 'complement' model to support citizenship. In the 'cornucopia' model there is little need for history teachers to engage with citizenship unless there are obvious and valid connections that could be made. In some respects this is an attractive model, which does not threaten the status quo, except it may not be a realistic prospect given the changes within the current curriculum which emphasize a more holistic approach to teaching and learning, and where citizenship is an expected aim of the curriculum. The 'carrier' model embraces citizenship more explicitly, with history being used to address specific aspects of citizenship, in terms of objectives and areas of content. This may help to preserve history in the curriculum, but at what cost? History would be seen as serving the needs of citizenship and this could result in a 'presentist' approach to the past, whereby the only topics deemed worthy of study would be those that deal directly with present issues or the historical 'message' could be distorted to fit into the prevailing mindset of modern society. The 'complement' model is the one that Lee and Shemilt (2007) appear to approve of most. It does assume that the ideals that underpin citizenship are an ethos that permeates the school and where rational enquiry and debate (seen as central democratic dispositions) are promoted. In this context history provides the opportunity for pupils to orient themselves in time and gain an awareness of how democratic institutions and ideals have developed, including their value and potential frailties. In this sense, history is the seedbed in which citizenship can flourish.

All of these models though assume a consensus about citizenship, what it is and therefore how history can support it. The problem is that citizenship is contested. Its nature and therefore its aims are hotly debated. In order to understand more fully how history could relate to citizenship we need to be aware of these debates, as different positions suggest a different relationship with history. Indeed, it is also necessary to examine what we understand by history and what we are trying to teach in history to see how different perspectives fit into differing views about citizenship. As an example, Tosh (2008: 121) argues that the most valuable role of history in schools is to provide students with the rudiments of a historical mode of thought which will make the world around them more intelligible.

Such a view downplays the role of 'content' and what students should learn in the way of substantive knowledge, but emphasizes the tools with which students need to be equipped. This seems to stress a mode of teaching where historical 'skills' are paramount, yet this may not be universally accepted as the nature and purpose of history teaching. Tosh (2008: 120–1) also argues that

> [h]istorical perspective enhances the citizen's capacity to make informed judgements about the issues of the day, to participate in public discourse, and to make intelligent use of the vote – in short, to exercise his or her active membership of the body politic.

This view offers a narrow conception of citizenship that is mainly framed in political terms, which is a model of citizenship education that would be contested by many.

What is citizenship for?

There are two broad conceptions of citizenship – namely, the civic republican ideal and the liberal tradition. There is insufficient space here to do justice to these differing concepts of citizenship (a fuller discussion can be found in Heater, 1999), so what follows is a necessarily simplified discussion. An essential difference between the civic and liberal concepts of citizenship concerns the role and relationship of the state and the individual. In the civic republican tradition, the well-being of the state is predominant, and the role of the individual is to look at ways they can serve the community. There is thus an emphasis on duties. In the liberal tradition there is a greater emphasis on individual rights, with looser ties to the state, though there is a need to promote democratic values if liberal democracy is to thrive. Both models have an impact on how history might be conceived. Thus a civic republican model *might* emphasize the importance of the 'national' story, offer stories of 'good' or 'heroic' individuals, whereas a liberal model *might* stress the development of rights, such as the extension of the franchise or the impact of protest through time. I hasten to add that these are not mutually exclusive positions; for example, both *might* emphasize the value of an approach that is grounded in evidential work and understanding how and why the past is interpreted differently. Nor do these examples convey the full extent of how history might be conceived, but it gives a sense of the different priorities that may exist or which people may adopt depending on their values and attitudes.

Though the civic republican model has its origins in Ancient Greece, it is the relative newcomer, the liberal tradition, that generally holds sway in the contemporary world. To be an effective citizen in either model though requires some form of education. Heater (1999: 164) argues:

> Citizens need knowledge and understanding of the social, legal and political system(s) in which they live and operate. They need skills and aptitudes to make use of that knowledge and understanding. And they need to be endowed with values and dispositions to put their knowledge and skills to beneficial use.

This is a useful definition, and echoes that of T. H. Marshall, who emphasized civil (largely property rights), social (mainly welfare rights) and participatory rights (via voting). The original citizenship curriculum was loosely based upon these, emphasizing political literacy, social and moral responsibility and community involvement (even though the document as written did not use these terms, it was based upon these ideas). Political literacy was seen as essential in engaging young people in action, while community involvement envisaged more voluntary activity. The social and moral responsibility strand was to foster desirable values, and emphasized responsibilities as well as rights. All three strands were interconnected. However, each of these elements are open to interpretation, which in turn impacts on how they may translate into school practice. For example, Faulks (2006) has criticized the idea of political literacy as stated in the curriculum. He rightly claims that citizenship is a contested notion, but this does not appear within the curriculum and so argues there is an emphasis on encouraging participation in the political process rather than questioning or challenging how the process operates. Whether or not this matters in the history classroom depends on your position. It is perfectly possible for history teachers to focus on the development of the political system in the UK and landmark events, such as Magna Carta, the English Civil War, the Reform Acts and so forth, without engaging in any critique of the system. In so doing they may examine causation, consequences, competing interpretations of the past, all of which are worthy elements of history teaching, but this is unlikely to be a sound form of citizenship education (even though it may provide important contextual background). Yet many history teachers may baulk at the next logical step (at least in terms of citizenship), which would be to question whether the system or society within which we live is a fair or effective one. If the purpose of citizenship education is to promote 'active' participation, then questions about the current status quo in society need to be raised, drawing on the past to explain how the situation has arisen but also provoking debate about what it could be like.

Another critic of the original citizenship curriculum is Kiwan (2008). She highlights two particular weaknesses. She agrees that citizenship has a moral angle to it, but feels the Crick Report emphasized moral values as generating respect for existing institutions and the rule of law and overlooked the development of personal values. Although the National Curriculum does mention personal values, it is not clear how these are supposed to operate in a public or political sphere. For example, there has been much talk about 'shared values' and 'Britishness', but what if these values (however they are defined) are in conflict with personally held beliefs? For example, our society is grounded in the notion of a nation state, which is effectively secular. Consequently there is a relationship between the individual and the state, which may manifest itself in some form of patriotism or loyalty to the state, and the state in turn has responsibilities to its citizens. But what happens if an individual's personal values and those of the state are in conflict – for example, where an individual belongs to a religion whose membership extends beyond the boundaries of the nation state and finds there is a tension between their religious beliefs and the actions of the secular government. Again the history teacher may be comfortable with exploring the development of Britain, as an historical entity, and perhaps to explore what 'Britishness' might be, but whether history strays into the area of personal ideas and values is another issue. A resolution may be found in Kiwan's other criticism. She argues that citizenship is also to do with the development of identity (which is defined in very broad terms) and which is absent from the original curriculum. Individuals are able to hold multiple identities, depending on context, and citizenship can help young people foster this awareness. In this case, history teachers may wish to explore ideas about identity and identity formation, which may cover personal identity.

What is history for?

As with citizenship, there are a number of different positions that people can adopt towards this question, yet it is important to pinpoint precisely what these may be and therefore examine the potential relationship with citizenship. Clearly there are numerous arguments for the place of history in the curriculum, but there is only space to consider some of these.

Let us take what may possibly be seen as an extreme position; namely, the purpose of history as a means of cultural heritage, passing on the best of what has preceded the present to act as a model for the contemporary world. Pupils would learn of the great acts of the past, see the development of key ideas such as parliamentary democracy and so forth. This 'traditional' or 'exemplary' view of the past (as defined by Rüsen, 2004) has certainly existed and sits most comfortably within the civic republican model of citizenship, being designed to foster a sense of national pride and engendering positive attitudes towards the state. The danger of such a position is that it downplays the place of interpretation within history and potentially offers a very narrow view of the past. At the opposite end of the spectrum, it could be argued, would be the argument for history as social action. For example, Banks (2006) argues that a study of the past can contextualize inequalities or problems that exist within the lives of young people. This in turn can allow young people to campaign or agitate for social change to eradicate such problems. Banks is essentially concerned with the promotion of multiculturalism and addressing racial inequalities. His context is the civil rights struggle in the US and where history is usually taught within a social studies framework, thus the lines between history and citizenship are already blurred. The trouble with such a position is its emphasis on a 'presentist' history agenda, where only issues that affect the present are studied and there is a danger that the choice of content for study may be distorted to fit such a bill. Banks does advocate an emphasis on interpretations so young people can challenge the historical story that they may be presented with, but this is essentially to ensure that they are aware of a history beyond the white Anglo-Saxon perspective.

As noted above, Tosh advocates a study of the past as a means to promote democratic modes of thought as well as providing the necessary political literacy to participate effectively in society. This chimes with much of what Barton and Levstik (2004) argue for. In terms of a history curriculum, it is easy to see how this may look, with an emphasis on political developments as intimated above. This would fit in with much history teaching that currently exists, though whether this constitutes citizenship 'training' is dubious. Citizenship is very much about the contemporary world and therefore direct links between the past and current affairs would be required to argue that this form of history teaching develops citizenship. This raises the question of the purpose for doing this; it arguably makes history more 'relevant' to young people, but at the same time are we trying to draw lessons from the past to inform our future thinking or conduct? At one level we are back to Banks' notion of history for 'social action', while it also raises a familiar question about how much we can learn from the past and whether we can use the past to avoid mistakes in the future. This engenders questions about how much we can generalize from the past. It can be argued that because history is about the particular and unique, which can never be repeated, we cannot learn any useful lessons from the past. Lee (2004), however (drawing on Rüsen), argues that history helps to orient ourselves in time and therefore informs people's judgements about potential outcomes of future actions and that a heightened sense of historical consciousness allows us to see a range of possible actions. This would entail not only a focus on developing a framework of what has happened in the past but also a focus on disciplinary aspects of history, such as working with evidence and analysing competing interpretations of the past.

Another issue debated within history is the extent to which history explicitly addresses morality and whether this is a suitable objective for history teachers, particularly with reference to teaching about the Holocaust. Short (2003) advocates using the Holocaust as a vehicle to teach explicit moral lessons and to promote an anti-racist position. Though few teachers would argue that they do not wish to produce youngsters that are tolerant of others, whether this is the realm of the history teacher is uncertain. Klaassen (2002) has shown that many teachers, not just in history circles, are uncomfortable teaching an explicit value-laden curriculum and Kinloch (2001) has argued that history needs to stick to teaching history rather than spurious moral lessons from the past. For a subject that purports to promote intellectual objective reasoning, a focus on morality promotes uncomfortable subjective and emotive concerns (though obviously the question of how objective history can be gives an additional twist to such arguments). An explicit focus on values sits squarely within citizenship education and would require teachers to be confident exploring and handling the intricacies of moral reasoning and understand how this develops in young people. Clearly history has something to contribute to the teaching of controversial and sensitive topics, but whether this is mainly to focus on the historical questions, such as why, and to contextualize events to render them comprehensible or to address the moral questions that such topics can easily provoke is open to debate.

What might it look like in practice?

As the preceding discussion indicates, there is no simple answer as to what the relationship between history and citizenship should be. There is a growing range of materials to support history and citizenship teaching, although it is important to be discerning when choosing materials as they are of variable quality. The following provide interesting examples as to how citizenship may be developed through rigorous history teaching.

The journal *Teaching History* has devoted two editions (1999 and 2002) to the relationship between history and citizenship. Both offer interesting ideas as to how the subjects can complement each other. For example, both McCully *et al.* (2002) and Phillips (2002) use historical concepts, interpretations and significance respectively to make pupils reflect on the present with reference to the past. Clemitshaw (2002) skilfully uses a local enquiry into a cemetery to develop concepts like change and continuity, and interpretations, which then leads into a citizenship focus on developing participation and responsible action.

In terms of teaching about the Holocaust, Kate Hammond (2001) and Alison Kitson (2001) offer interesting ways of addressing aspects of citizenship. Hammond looks at the moral questions that a study of the Holocaust generates and which have a citizenship dimension, but also shows how to turn these into historical questions. Kitson's article deals with issues of stereotyping and clearly has the potential to develop aspects of citizenship.

Such examples help clarify how these two curriculum areas can usefully enhance the learning experience for students, while at the same time developing key concepts, processes and knowledge in both subjects.

Chapter summary

It is important for history teachers to clarify their own position towards citizenship. To an extent this means that teachers may feel they are 'reinventing the wheel' each time they come to explore this issue, but not all wheels fit all vehicles! History teachers need to decide for themselves why history is important, what they understand about the nature and purpose of history teaching and therefore their ultimate goals for a historical education. Obviously, the National Curriculum provides a set of parameters for teaching the subject, but these are open to interpretation. At the same time teachers need to explore the same questions in relation to citizenship. Only by doing this will history teachers be in a position whereby they can identify for themselves what they see as the 'proper' relationship between history and citizenship. It is not an easy task, but, like many things in education, the complexity of the issues makes it all the more interesting.

Further reading

Barton, K. and Levstik, L. (2004) *Teaching History for the Common Good*, Mahwah, NJ: Lawrence Erlbaum Associates – provides a very detailed discussion of the different purposes of teaching history.

Heater, D. (1999) *What is Citizenship?* London: Polity Press – thorough discussion of citizenship, which provides a multifaceted explanation of the nature and meaning of citizenship.

Lee, P. and Shemilt, D. (2007) 'New alchemy or fatal attraction? History and citizenship'. *Teaching History* 129: 14–19 – this looks at alternative relationships between history and citizenship within the school curriculum.

Tosh, J. (2008) *Why History Matters*. London: Palgrave Macmillan – this provides a wide-ranging discussion about the importance of history, including its contribution to a citizenship education.

References

Banks, J. A. (2006) 'Teaching black history with a focus on decision-making', in J. A. Banks (ed.) *Race, Culture and Education: The Selected Works of James A. Banks*. London: Routledge.

Barton, K. and Levstik, L. (2004) *Teaching History for the Common Good*. Mahwah, NJ: Lawrence Erlbaum Associates.

Clemitshaw, G. (2002) 'Have we got the question right? Engaging future citizens in local historical enquiry', *Teaching History*, 106: 20–7.

Counsell, C. (2002) Editorial, *Teaching History*, 106: 2.

Crick, B. (2001) Foreword in J. Arthur, I. Davies, A. Wrenn, T. Haydn and D. Kerr. *Citizenship through Secondary History*. London: RoutledgeFalmer.

Department for Education and Skills (DfES) (2007) *Diversity and Citizenship Curriculum Review*. London: DfES.

Faulks, K. (2006) 'Education for citizenship in English secondary schools: a critique of current principle and practice', *Journal of Education Policy*, 21(1): 59–74.

Hammond, K. (2001) 'From horror to history: teaching pupils to reflect on significance', *Teaching History*, 104: 15–23.

Heater, D. (1999) *What is Citizenship?* London: Polity Press.

Historical Association. (2009) *Historical Association Survey of History in English Secondary Schools*, available online at: http://www.history.org.uk/news/news_415.html (accessed 2 December 2009).

Kinloch, N. (2001) 'Parallel catastrophes? Uniqueness, redemption and the Shoah', *Teaching History*, 104: 8–14.

Kitson, A. (2001) 'Challenging stereotypes and avoiding the superficial: a suggested approach to teaching the Holocaust', *Teaching History*, 104: 41–8.

Kiwan, D. (2008) 'Citizenship education in England at the cross-roads? Four models of citizenship and their implications for ethnic and religious diversity', *Oxford Review of Education*, 34(1): 39–58.

Klaassen, C. A. (2002) 'Teacher pedagogical competence and sensibility', *Teaching and Teacher Education*, 18: 151–8.

Lee, P. (2004) 'Understanding History', in P. Seixas (ed.) *Theorizing Historical Consciousness*. Toronto: University of Toronto Press.

Lee, P. and Shemilt, D. (2007) 'New alchemy or fatal attraction? History and citizenship', *Teaching History*, 129: 14–19.

McCully, A., Pilgrim, N., Sutherland, A. and McMinn, T. (2002) '"Don't worry, Mr Trimble. We can handle it" Balancing the rational and the emotional in the teaching of contentious topics', *Teaching History*, 106: 6–12.

Ofsted. (2005) *Citizenship in Secondary Schools: Evidence from Ofsted Inspections (2003/04)*, available online at: http://www.ofsted.gov.uk/Ofsted-home/Publications-and-research/Browse-all-by/Education/Curriculum/Citizenship/Citizenship-in-secondary-schools-evidence-from-Ofsted-inspections-2003-04/(language)/eng-GB (accessed 28 October 2010)

Phillips, R. (2002) 'Historical significance – the forgotten "Key Element"?', *Teaching History*, 106: 14–19.

QCA (1998) *Education for Citizenship and the Teaching of Democracy in Schools*. London: QCA.

——(2007a) *Citizenship: Programme of Study for Key Stage 3 and Attainment Target*, available online at: http://curriculum.qcda.gov.uk/key-stages-3-and-4/subjects/key-stage-3/citizenship/index.aspx (accessed 28 October 2010).

——(2007b) *History: Programme of Study for Key Stage 3 and Attainment Target*, available online at: http://curriculum.qcda.gov.uk/key-stages-3-and-4/subjects/key-stage-3/history/index.aspx (accessed 28 October 2010).

QCDA. (2009) *National Curriculum: Curriculum purposes, values and aims*, available online at: http://curriculum.qcda.gov.uk/key-stages-3-and-4/aims-values-and-purposes/index.aspx (accessed 28 October 2010)

Rüsen, J. (2004) 'Historical consciousness: narrative structure, moral function, and onto-logical development', in P. Seixas (ed.) *Theorizing Historical Consciousness*. Toronto: University of Toronto Press.

Short, G. (2003) 'Lessons of the Holocaust: a response to the critics', *Educational Review*, 55(3): 277–87.

Tosh, J. (2008) *Why History Matters*. London: Palgrave Macmillan.

Debating the teaching and learning of history

Chapter 16

Using academic history in the classroom

Rachel Foster

Introduction

Key content:

- justification for using academic history in the classroom;
- planning strategies for using academic history in the classroom;
- outcomes of using academic history in the classroom.

I didn't know that history was about argument.

Sometimes it is snatched conversations between student and teacher that prove the most illuminating, and the most challenging. Danny was a Year 9 student and an able historian, yet he was adamant that history wasn't for him and planned to drop it at GCSE (General Certificate of Secondary Education). I was disappointed and wanted to find out why, hence our brief conversation at the end of class. I found his comments troubling: how could a student spend three years studying history and not realize that argument is central to the discipline? To my mind, my lessons were full of argument: in the quick paired discussions where students argued about the status of a piece of evidence, or tried to decide how far they agreed with a particular claim; in the whole-class plenaries where they debated the relative importance of causes; and in their writing, where I had spent a term trying to teach them how to write analytically about the causes of World War I. But it seemed that Danny didn't *see* the argument in the same way that I did. Our discussion seemed to encapsulate a concern that plagued me as a history teacher – how to move students beyond simple narrative or formulaic structure into writing that was more analytical; in other words, a better argument. It was from this concern that my experimentation with the use of academic history in the classroom originated. My instinctive response as a historian was that the only way to help Danny to see the argument inherent in history would be to expose him to a genuine historical argument. But to do this would mean introducing Year 9 to academic history – a daunting prospect for me as a teacher, and for a class that had never read academic history before.

How and with what justification do teachers use academic history in the classroom?

History teachers and history education researchers who have experimented with or offered theories for the use of academic works of history in the classroom seem to do so for a number of different reasons. Sometimes the justification offered is extrinsic, underpinned by notions about progression and an underlying belief that exposure to academic history will in some way help students to get better at 'doing' history, understanding it as a discipline, or communicating historical knowledge. Other educators seem to offer a more intrinsic justification – that of the transformative power of reading.

Teacher educators who justify the use of academic history by appealing to extrinsic purposes do so under a number of different banners, both substantive and conceptual. One such banner is evidential or source-based. In this instance, academic texts are not used primarily to develop students' conceptual thinking about evidence, but rather are mined for substantive information or evidence. Kitson (2003), Bellinger (2008) and Jones (2009), all of whom used academic texts in this way, selected and used texts that provided intriguing or in-depth case studies. These case studies were used to build or deepen students' substantive knowledge, and to develop a rich sense of period (Jones, 2009). For these educators, the value of an academic text seems to lie in *what* it says, i.e. it is based in the substantive content of the text. Kitson (2003) and Ward (2006) went beyond knowledge-building to explore the potential of texts as sources of evidence that students used to compare and evaluate differing historical interpretations. While for Kitson (2003) the concern was still primarily with students' substantive knowledge – in this case knowledge of an interpretation – Ward was also concerned to develop students' conceptual thinking about evidence and interpretations, in particular how historians select and deploy information as evidence. However, while the ostensible purpose of using the text seems to be as an information source, there is also clearly a motivational purpose; in Bellinger (2008) and Jones' (2009) work, using an academic text was justified in part by appealing to their quality as compelling narratives and their power to fascinate students. For these educators, the value of the text went beyond *what* was said to the *way* it has been said.

Another banner under which teacher educators justify using academic history texts in the classroom is that of developing students' knowledge and understanding of historical interpretations. Some practice (McAleavy, 1993; Howells, 2005; Mastin and Wallace, 2006) explicitly seeks to develop students' thinking about interpretations as a second-order concept – this is, 'interpretations of history' in the technical National Curriculum sense of the study of subsequent interpretations. 'Interpretations' in this curricular sense means deliberate or conscious reflections on the past (McAleavy, 1993). Practitioners such as Cunningham (2001) and Shoham and Shiloah (2003) seek to develop students' awareness that there are competing interpretations of the past. Howells (2005) and Mastin and Wallace (2006) go beyond straightforward identification of interpretations into an exploration of how interpretations are constructed. Other practice is more concerned with how reading academic works of history can develop students' ability to construct their *own* interpretations. Fordham (2007) exemplifies this approach, making a persuasive case for the necessity of engaging students with historiography if they are to construct their own historical arguments.

Ward's work (2006) could be deemed to sit within both camps; going further than simply exposing students to an interpretation, she helped them to analyse its construction through the use of evidence and the historian's choice of language in his writing. The text was then used as a model to develop students' communication of their own ideas.

While these teacher educators use academic works of history in order to develop different aspects of students' historical knowledge, understanding or communication, they all seem to share a common notion of an academic text as being some kind of model. This is not to say that they all share the same curricular goals or ideas about the purpose of school history, particularly whether or not it involves students in some way imitating either the practice or products of professional historians. But there is a sense that students can get better at school history by being exposed to models of professional practice and discourse. This seems to contrast with the justification offered by Lee and Shemilt (2004) for the use of what they call 'historical accounts'. As education researchers, their primary concern is to define and construct models of progression rather than to offer practical teaching strategies for using historical accounts in the classroom. Their focus is therefore on the purpose and goals of using historical accounts, and these are informed by their underlying curricular goals as outlined in the Project Chata research; that of developing students' historical consciousness (see also Lee and Shemilt, 2004). Because their concern is with the ideas students hold about history as a discipline, how those ideas can be changed and therefore how progression in ideas can be defined, characterized and assessed, the value of introducing students to historical accounts seems to be as a tool for changing students' ideas about the discipline, rather than as a source of substantive knowledge or as a model of second-order concepts in action, mediated through distinctive language and textual style. Thus although on the face of it their approach shares similarities with the work of Howells (2005), who also wants to change students' conceptual understandings of historical interpretations by helping them to appreciate that history is consciously constructed, they actually have different end goals. Howells (2005) differs from Lee and Shemilt (2004) in so far as he wants to use students' newfound acquaintance with historical practice as a process of creation in order to support their own creation of a causal explanation.

Howells (2005) also differs from Lee and Shemilt's approach because he seems to operate with an implicit goal of using works of academic history in order to *integrate* disciplinary concepts. He cites two case studies; one in which *Time on the Cross* (Fogel and Engerman, 1974) is used to show how interpretations are shaped by the evidence base, and one in which Hutton's *Debates in Stuart History* (2004) informs an enquiry sequence that encourages students to consider how the selection of evidence can shape interpretations in response to a causal question. Hammond (2007) also has an underlying integrative purpose in her use of academic works of history. Like Howells, she used *Time on the Cross* to integrate students' conceptual thinking about evidence and interpretations (specifically the relationship between them) under the umbrella of historical methodology. This would seem to place them at odds with Lee and Shemilt (2003) whose concern with defining and measuring progression leads them to argue that it is necessary to understand how students' conceptions operate and relate to one another *before* taking a more holistic approach. They therefore explicitly argue against bundling progression in key concepts together.

Although Howells and Hammond do not explicitly state it, the way in which they use historical accounts implies an assumed goal of using them in order to piece the disciplinary strands back together.

While many teachers and researchers seem to want to pin down the benefits of using academic works of history in the classroom by offering extrinsic justifications for its use, others operate with a less tangible motivation – the belief in the transformative power of a text. This faith in the power of reading a text to change students' thinking and writing (even their world view) appears under numerous guises; sometimes it is expressed as a longing to transform students into independent learners (Helier and Richards, 2005); sometimes as a desire to share and impart a deeply held love of reading (Loy, 2008), to bring them closer to the heart of the discipline (Helier and Richards, 2005) or to expose them to a book's power *'to make us stand in a different place'* (Counsell, 2003: 2). All these appeals have the qualities of a cri de coeur – they are impassioned and rely on faith born of personal experience. This is not to say that their appeal is not well supported by empirical research attesting to the value of texts for developing students' knowledge, conceptual thinking (Andrews, 1995) and capacity to communicate (Barrs and Cork, 2001), but it is their implicit faith in the *transformative* power of a text that sets the justifications they offer apart from those offered by other practitioners and researchers. For my own experimentation with using academic works of history with my students, I was reasonably confident that I could offer a coherent, substantiated justification for how its use would benefit my students' substantive knowledge, conceptual thinking and communication skills. But underlying my consciously held justifications, and what drove my determination to persist in the effort, was the belief that if I wanted my students to understand and enjoy history as a discipline, I just *had* to get them reading.

Planning the enquiry

Choosing historians to use in the classroom

I knew that to engage Key Stage 3 students with the work of an academic historian in a meaningful way I would need to find a book that had a compelling subject matter and a clear line of argument couched in an argumentative style. I was familiar with *Hitler's Willing Executioners* (Goldhagen, 1996) from my undergraduate studies and on re-reading it felt confident that it fully met these criteria. Goldhagen's book addresses the motivations of the perpetrators of the Holocaust, interweaving powerful narrative and strong argument in a style that is provocative and engaging.

Goldhagen's book also held a distinct advantage; it had been written as a direct response to the work of another historian, Christopher Browning's *Ordinary Men* (1992), criticizing his thesis in what Birn (1998: 57) has described as *'unusually strong language'*. Browning had responded in turn (Browning, 1998), making the two historians' arguments obviously dialogic. Both historians had researched the same case study, German Reserve Police Battalion 101, yet had drawn very different conclusions from the evidence. This meant it would be possible to examine both the claims made by the historians and the evidential basis on which they made them.

The planning challenge

As so many history education experts have commented, planning any scheme of work involves walking a pedagogical tightrope – between access and challenge; fun and rigour (Riley, 2000; Byrom and Riley, 2003). Developing a scheme of work that engages younger students directly with the work of academic historians simply throws the degree of challenge into sharper relief. The tension between building motivation and accessibility while maintaining the integrity of the historians' work as far as possible was fundamental to the planning process.

An immediate decision concerned the selection of substantive content. A considerable challenge lay in the sheer size and scope of Goldhagen's thesis: *Hitler's Willing Executioners* ranges over a significant period of time, from the evolution of German anti-Semitism in the nineteenth century to the end of World War Two. Related to the scope of the thesis was its complexity and breadth. In order to understand the main tenet of Goldhagen's thesis – that the unique nature of German anti-Semitism meant that German perpetrators were willing executioners who '*kill[ed] willingly and often eagerly*' (Goldhagen, 1996: 446) and led the '*vast majority of German people to understand, assent to, and to when possible, do their part to further the extermination, root of the branch, of the Jewish people*' (Goldhagen, 1996: 454). Students would also need to understand the related claims he made about the unique nature and evolutionary path of German anti-Semitism and the nature of Germans' support for and participation in the Nazis' policies during the 1930s. Students would also need to understand Browning's claims in sufficient detail to identify the ways in which they differed from Goldhagen's. Avoiding the challenge by focusing on a single aspect of the debate would defeat the purpose of the enquiry – to expose students to the processes and products of a historical argument. Although tempting as a means of ensuring accessibility, over-simplifying the material would gut it of its power, which lay in its size and complexity. Therefore the question of how to limit the scope of the enquiry while preserving the complexity of the debate was critical to the success of my planning.

Closely related to selecting the substantive content was deciding the conceptual focus of the enquiry. While the main conceptual thrust of the enquiry appeared to be on historical interpretations, it was also clear that evidential thinking would form an inseparable part of students' conceptual thinking. In order to compare and evaluate the historians' competing claims students would need to know and understand the evidential basis out of which they arose; namely, how the nature, selection and interpretation of the available sources informed their claims. Again there was a tension between ensuring accessibility by limiting the conceptual challenge and preserving the integrity of the historians' argument.

Planning strategies

In order to limit my choices, I based my planning on the principle that the books themselves should determine the substance and conceptual focus of the enquiry. I wanted a clear rationale to guide my planning and was concerned that forcing the material into an artificial structure determined by curriculum requirements would have the opposite effect than intended: instead of making it easier to understand, it could make it unnecessarily harder.

Overview and depth

Although tempting as a way of limiting the substantial content of the enquiry, creating a scheme that was exclusively an overview or depth study threatened to create more problems than it solved. Whereas overviews can give students a big picture, setting events in their broader historical context, they also risk depersonalizing the past, robbing it of colour and human interest. Depth studies, while fascinating students with details and developing a rich, deeper period understanding, can leave students with a fragmented picture of the past. The solution lay in the books themselves, which skilfully interweave outline and depth. Part I of Goldhagen's book is a sweeping overview of the evolution of German anti-Semitism, while part II focuses on three case studies, which are used to exemplify and substantiate his broader claims. One of these case studies, the activities of Reserve Police Battalion 101, also formed the basis for Browning's book. By adhering to Goldhagen's overall structure I hoped to achieve an interplay between overview and depth that would both set the Holocaust in its broader historical context, while keeping the actions of individual perpetrators clearly in view (see Table 16.1).

Choosing a conceptual focus

While the national curriculum second-order concepts are helpful in securing rigour in planning, I felt that imposing a single concept on the material could make my

Table 16.1 Outline of the enquiry sequence

Enquiry question	What is a 'bad' history book?	
Lesson question	Aims and objectives	Content/activities
When and where was it most dangerous to be a European Jew?	• To identify patterns of change and continuity in the nature and degree of persecution of European anti-Semitism. • To characterize the nature and extent of European anti-Semitism at the end of the nineteenth century.	• Content: overview of European anti-Semitism. • Activity: living timeline.
Was German anti-Semitism 'pregnant with murder'?	• To identify Goldhagen's key arguments. • To analyse and critique the relationship between Goldhagen's claims and his evidence.	• Content: German anti-Semitism before 1933. • Activity: matching claims and supporting evidence.

(continued)

Enquiry question	What is a 'bad' history book?	
Lesson question	Aims and objectives	Content/activities
Were the Nazis' policies just 'common sense' to Germans?	• To analyse the evidence and counter-evidence used to support and attack Goldhagen's claims. • To critically evaluate the language of Goldhagen's claims.	• Content: Nazi anti-Semitic policies after 1933. • Activities: living graph; matching evidence and counter-evidence; editing an extract to modify language.
Was there ever a master plan to kill the Jews?	• To identify and characterize changes in the direction, degree and goals of Nazi policy from 1939 to 1942. • To evaluate the functionalist/intentionalist debate.	• Content: Nazi anti-Semitic policies 1939–42 • Activities: stepping stones diagram showing the size and direction of the 'steps' taken towards genocide.
In what ways were the killers of Police Battalion 101 'ordinary men'?	• To characterize key features of a typical policeman in Reserve Police Battalion 101.	• Content: Reserve Police Battalions. • Activity: creation of a picture of a typical policeman using an extract from Ordinary Men.
How far were the men of Police Battalion 101 'willing executioners'?	• To identify and compare similarities and differences between two historical accounts of the same event.	• Content: Jozefow massacre. • Activities: extended reading and comparison of Ordinary Men and Hitler's Willing Executioners.
How can we find the argument lurking in the story?	• To identify persuasive techniques used by historians.	• Content: Jozefow massacre. • Activities: extended reading, persuasive techniques bingo.
Why did ordinary men kill?	• To explain why policemen voluntarily participated in the Holocaust.	• Content: depth studies of individual perpetrators. • Activities: extended reading of Hitler's Willing Executioners and Ordinary Men.
Why do historians disagree when they are working with the same evidence?	• To critically evaluate Goldhagen's treatment of evidence. • To judge the credibility of Goldhagen's claims.	• Content: overview of Goldhagen's thesis. • Activities: re-enactment of Goldhagen's writing process.
What makes a bad history book?	• To evaluate the criticisms and merits of Hitler's Willing Executioners.	• Activities: pupils write a book review of Hitler's Willing Executioners.

planning deterministic. I wanted my lesson questions to emerge from the books themselves and the surrounding debate. This meant that although the overall tenor of the enquiry was interpretations, different conceptual lens, particularly evidential thinking, were brought to bear on the material in individual lessons. In some cases the conceptual focus was very specific to a key aspect of the debate (for example causation); in other instances, one concept was used to illuminate another.

Scaffolding

Given that the goal of the enquiry was for students to encounter the processes and products of an academic debate, students needed to engage not just with the historians' claims and evidence but also with its end product, a text. While it would have been possible to construct an enquiry that addressed Goldhagen's and Browning's claims without asking students to read the texts, I wanted students to independently read extended sections for themselves. Both books had a profound effect on me when I first read them. Much of this was to do with the immediacy and power of the story itself, but also with the authors' skills as story tellers and historians. Anger, outrage and conviction burns out of Goldhagen's prose in particular: he demands to be heard and compels a response. The intensity and immediacy of the prose inescapably draws the reader into their argument. If I stripped this out of the enquiry – if students never had the chance to hear directly from the authors themselves – it would making the teaching challenge harder by depriving me of a vital way of making it interesting.

Indeed, as my goal of supporting students into independent reading of academic history was less to do with equipping students with the vocabulary and concepts they needed and more to do with giving them the confidence and desire to read, both these things – confidence and motivation – needed to be cumulatively developed over the duration of the enquiry. The planning challenge was therefore to scaffold both individual activities and students' learning *across* the enquiry in order to gradually move them towards independent reading.

The scaffolding strategies I used had three key variables: the nature of the text used, the form in which students encountered it and the process by which they encountered it (i.e. what students were asked to *do* with the text). Scaffolding students into extended reading began with the selection of the text. My main criteria for choosing an extract was that it should be fascinating in its detail, its storytelling, its argument or its language. If I could find a text that gripped students then their motivation to read would help them to overcome the challenge the text posed.

I also considered the text's complexity in terms of ideas, language, and length. My goal was to gradually increase the complexity and length of the text that students' encountered over the course of the enquiry, slowly building their familiarity with the genre and their confidence. At a micro level, I also scaffolded students' reading by simplifying the vocabulary, sentence structure and the length of the texts. Initially, I created three or four versions of each text extract, enabling me to offer students versions that were reasonably fine-tuned to their confidence and ability (see Figures 16.1 and 16.2).

As the enquiry progressed the level of scaffolding provided through editing was slowly reduced, with each version increasing in complexity and length. By the time students were given the extended reading, they were offered only two choices, an

| Germans did <u>not</u> kill Jews because they were pressured to do so. | Germans did <u>not</u> kill Jews because they were killers by nature or personality. | Millions of Germans would have killed Jews if they had had the opportunity. |

Explaining why the Holocaust occurred requires a radical revision of what has until now been written. This book is that revision. This revision calls for us to acknowledge what has for so long been generally denied or obscured by academic and non-academic interpreters alike: Germans' anti-Semitic beliefs about Jews were the central causal agent of the Holocaust. They were the central causal agent not only of Hitler's decision to annihilate European Jewry but also of the perpetrators' willingness to kill and brutalize Jews. The conclusion of this book is that anti-Semitism moved many thousands of ordinary Germans – and would have moved millions more, had they been appropriately positioned – to slaughter Jews. Not economic hardship, not the coercive means of a totalitarian state, not social psychological pressure, not invariable psychological propensities, but ideas about Jews that were pervasive in Germany, and had been for decades, induced ordinary Germans to kill unarmed, defenceless Jewish men, women and children by the thousands, systematically and without pity.

| Anti-Semitism made Germans (the perpetrators) willing to kill Jews. | The anti-Semitic beliefs that caused the Holocaust had been present in Germany for a long time. | Germans did <u>not</u> kill Jews because they were forced to by the Nazis. |

Figure 16.1 Version 1 of an activity – pupils were offered an unedited text extract and had to identify Goldhagen's claims in the text.

Explaining why the Holocaust occurred requires a big rethink. Germans' anti-Semitic beliefs about Jews were the main cause of the Holocaust. They were the main cause of the perpetrator's willingness to kill Jews. The conclusion of this book is that anti-Semitism moved thousands of ordinary Germans to slaughter Jews. Not poverty, not being forced by a dictator, not social pressure, not personality, but ideas about Jews that were common in Germany, and had been for many years, made ordinary Germans kill thousands of unarmed Jewish men, women and children, systematically and without pity.

Figure 16.2 Version 4 (the most heavily edited version) of the same activity.

'access' version or the text itself. My goal was to encourage as many students as possible to take the plunge and tackle the full text, as about 90 per cent of them did.

The second method of scaffolding was done through the form in which students encountered the texts. Because I wanted students to make meaning from their encounters with academic historians, I knew that simply getting them to 'read' their words in the sense of making sense of the vocabulary would make nonsense of the whole exercise. If students were to encounter these historians in any kind of meaningful sense, they would have to engage with them, and that meant 'hearing' the voice of the author and caring about what they had to say. For most of the enquiry this meant me reading the text aloud to the students before they did anything with it. In one case it meant a student (a particularly skilled actor) acting the role of Goldhagen. The power of reading to students in this way is that it allows them to catch the flow and tone of the text, while helping them pass over 'sticky' vocabulary that could otherwise defeat them if left to plough through it on their own. Only when students had read several shorter extracts in this way did I give them the longest extracts to read independently.

The final form of scaffolding was through what students did with the texts. This was determined by the type of reading I wanted them to do. By limiting what students were reading for, and then supporting them in doing so, I hoped to overcome the apparent difficulty of the text by helping students to see that they didn't need to understand every word in order to *read* it. In early lessons this meant providing a lot of support to equip them to tackle the challenge head-on, for example by delineating the key ideas for them, which students then had to locate in the text, or by asking them to extract very specific things from the text. As the enquiry progressed and I moved students towards independent reading, my scaffolding strategies also evolved, and rather than showing them the challenge and helping them overcome it, I simply disguised it behind a 'fun' activity (see Figure 16.3).

The first time students independently read an extract they were simply asked to draw a picture of a typical policeman as portrayed by Goldhagen. By the time students were given the long extracts to read independently, they were familiar with the style of the prose and had been equipped with strategies to help them make sense of the text for themselves. Although I guided students' reading by asking them to read for the authors' argument and substantiating evidence, I deliberately did not go further than this. I wanted them to encounter the author's voice for themselves, unmediated by me.

Conclusion

Planning and teaching the lesson sequence was a significant investment of time and effort – what kind of experience of history did students gain from it, and how far did this serve broader curriculum goals?

Through engaging with both the processes and the products of academic history students were thinking hard about the nature of history as a discipline: about the kind of truth claims historians can make; the relationship between the kind of claims it is possible to make and the nature of the evidence base and the disciplinary procedures that govern that relationship. By directly addressing the issue of what it means and looks like to *think* and *write* as a historian the enquiry, therefore, made explicit patterns of thinking that are more often left implicit in Key Stage 3 teaching. From Year 7 I may teach students to support their points with evidence, to consider how far the evidence supports their argument and to modify their language to make it appropriate to the strength of their claims, but I struggle to help them see why it really matters that they do this. By focusing on the processes of history while

---

Goldhagen's account of Major Trapp's order:

Major Trapp assembled his battalion. The men formed three sides of a square around Trapp in order to hear his address. 'He announced that in the locality before us we were to carry out a mass shooting and he brought out clearly that those whom we were supposed to shoot were Jews. During his address he bid us to think of our women and children in our homeland who had to endure aerial bombardments. In particular, we were to bear in mind that many women and children lose their lives in these attacks. Thinking of these facts would make it easier for us to carry out the order during the upcoming action. Major Trapp remarked that the action was entirely not in his spirit, but he had received this order from higher authority.'

Some of the men testify that Trapp justified the killing with the transparently weak argument that the Jews were supporting the partisans.

. . .

Trapp also seemed to be expressing his genuine emotions. He was shaken by the order. Trapp was later heard to have exclaimed, upon seeing the battalion's doctor: 'My God, why must I do this.'

Browning's account of Major Trapp's order:

The time had come for Trapp to address the men and inform them of the assignment the battalion had received.

Pale and nervous, with choking voice and tears in his eyes, Trapp visibly fought to control himself as he spoke. The battalion, he said plaintively, had to perform a frightfully unpleasant task. This assignment was not to his liking, indeed, it was highly regrettable, but the orders came from the highest authorities. If it would make their task any easier, the men should remember that in Germany the bombs were falling on women and children.

Figure 16.3 Pupils were given extracts from Goldhagen and Browning, both concerning the same event. Pupils were asked to draw a picture showing the expression and demeanour of Major Trapp as he issued the order. They were then asked to consider why the historians had chosen to include or ignore particular details from the story.

neglecting the primary product of history – a text – they fail to see the purpose of the process or to enjoy its outcome. Asking students to consciously reflect on what history is and how it is written therefore gave them an opportunity to engage with history in a far more holistic way than a focus on a single concept normally allows. This was particularly true of the concept of evidential thinking, because students were doing it within the context of a real historical debate that gave their thinking purpose and meaning.

Although my goals were explicitly focused on helping students get better at history, this necessarily meant helping students get better at literacy. Literacy skills were inherent in activities whose acknowledged purpose was to help students think historically – reading for different purposes, identifying and extracting different types of information within a text (for example claims and evidence), evaluating the effects of tone and language, selecting appropriate vocabulary in their writing, modelling their writing on the style of another writer – students did all this and more through the different activities of the enquiry.

While clearly serving curriculum goals in terms of developing students' historical thinking an enquiry of this nature also has more intangible and broad benefits. At present, in England, only a third of students continue history past the age of 14, a trend mirrored in the school I teach in. For most of my students the enquiry was the last history teaching they would receive. What can we hope for them in terms of what an education in history can achieve? I want all my students to become critical historical thinkers, comfortable with uncertainties, alert to the complex positioning of any historical text and wary of dogmatism. I also hope that by studying people in the past, in their temporal context, they will develop a richer understanding of what it means to be a human, living in society and in time. Finally, I hope that at least some of them will be inspired to carry on reading and engaging with history beyond their formal education. Young people will surely be more likely to pick up a history book if they have the confidence to know that they can read it, and an expectation that they will find it a rewarding experience. Where will they acquire this hope and expectation, if not from their history lessons?

References

Andrews, R. (1995) *Teaching and Learning Argument*. London: Cassell.

Barrs, M. and Cork, V. (2001) *The Reader in the Writer: The Links Between the Study of Literature and Writing Development at Key Stage 2*. London: Centre for Language in Primary Education.

Bellinger, L. (2008) 'Cultivating curiosity about complexity: what happens when Year 12 start to read Orlando Figes', *The Whisperers? Teaching History 132, Historians in the Classroom Edition*.

Birn, R.B. (1998) 'Historiographical review: revising the Holocaust', in R.B Birn and N.G Finkelstein, *A Nation on Trial: The Goldhagen Thesis and Historical Truth*. New York: Metropolitan Books.

Browning, C. (1992, 1998, 2nd edn) *Ordinary Men*. London: Penguin.

Byrom, J. and Riley, M. (2003) 'Professional wrestling in the history department: a case study in planning the teaching of the British Empire at Key Stage 3', *Teaching History 112, Empire Edition*.

Counsell, C. (2003) Editorial, *Teaching History 111, Reading History Edition*.

Cunningham, R. (2001) 'Teaching pupils how history works', *Teaching History 102, Inspiration and Motivation Edition*.

Fogel, R.W. and Engerman, S.L. (1974) *Time on the Cross*. London: Wildwood House.

Fordham, M. (2007) 'Slaying dragons and sorcerers in Year 12: in search of historical argument', *Teaching History 129, Disciplined Minds Edition*.

Goldhagen, D. (1996) *Hitler's Willing Executioners: Ordinary Germans and the Holocaust*. London: Abacus.

Hammond, K. (2007) 'Teaching Year 9 about historical theories and methods', *Teaching History 128, Beyond the Exam Edition*.

Helier, D. and Richards, H. (2005) 'Do we have to read all of this? Encouraging students to read for understanding', *Teaching History 118, Re-Thinking Differentiation Edition*.

Howells, G. (2005) 'Interpretations and history teaching: why Ronald Hutton's debates in Stuart history matters, *Teaching History 121, Transitions Edition*.

Hutton, R. (2004) *Debates in Stuart History*. Basingstoke: Palgrave Macmillan.

Jones, H. (2009) 'Shaping macro-analysis from micro-history: developing a reflexive narrative of change in school history', *Teaching History 136, Shaping the Past Edition*.

Kitson, A. (2003) 'Reading and enquiring in Years 12 and 13: a case study on women in the Third Reich', *Teaching History 111, Reading History Edition*.

Lee, P. and Shemilt, D. (2003) 'A scaffold, not a cage: progression and progression models in history', *Teaching History 113, Creating Progress Edition*.

——(2004) 'I just wish we could go back in the past and find out what really happened: progression in understanding about historical accounts', *Teaching History 117, Dealing with Distance Edition*.

Loy, M. (2008) 'Learning to read and reading to learn: strategies to move students from "keen to learn" to "keen to read"', *Teaching History 132, Historians in the Classroom Edition*.

McAleavy, (1993) 'Using the attainment targets in Key Stage 3: AT2, interpretations of history', *Teaching History*.

Mastin, S. and Wallace, P. (2006). 'Why don't the Chinese play cricket? Rethinking progression in historical interpretations through the British Empire', *Teaching History 122, Re-Thinking History Edition*.

Riley, M. (2000) 'Into the Key Stage 3 history garden: choosing and planting your enquiry questions', *Teaching History 99, Curriculum Planning Edition*.

Shoham, E. and Shiloah, N. (2003) 'Meeting the historian through the text: students discover different perspectives on Baron Rothschild's "Guardianship system"', *Teaching History 111: Reading History Edition*.

Ward, R. (2006) 'Duffy's device: teaching Year 13 to read and write', *Teaching History 124, Teaching the Most Able Edition*.

Chapter 17

Highlighting evidence

Ian Phillips

Introduction

This chapter considers how sources and evidence might be used in the history class-room. This is not so much focused upon specific teaching strategies, which use evidence although some of the *Teaching History* articles referred to consider how sources and evidence might be used effectively in the classroom. Instead, the chapter seeks to develop an overview of the place sources and evidence have to play in history teaching. John Fines (1994) suggested that evidence was 'the basis of the discipline' – a view echoed by McAleavy in 1998. No one would argue that sources and evidence are at the heart of history and history teaching but it might be appropriate to reconsider the part they have to play in the history classroom, especially given the changing focus of history educators as they attempt to understand how school students can develop a more coherent overview of a period. This is referred to as developing a sense of period or big-picture history or useable historic pasts (see Dawson, 2009; Howson, 2006, 2009). With the focus on enquiries as a way of developing this coherent view of the past it would be appropriate to consider how sources and evidence might contribute to this process.

Starting points: a professional understanding of evidence

The chapter begins by considering the understanding of evidence which history profes-sionals possess (By history professional I mean anyone involved in history education from recent graduates beginning a PGCE (Postgraduate Certificate in Education) through to NQTs (newly qualified teachers), experienced teachers and history teacher educators).

The personal and professional contexts: why teachers see evidence differently

The nature of the history teachers' professional understanding – or professional craft knowledge – is further explored in an attempt to understand why school students' understanding might be different.

Changing professional dialogues: developing different methodologies

This short section considers the ways in which sources and evidence might play within an enquiry-based approach to learning history.

Micro histories: history teachers and history learners working more effectively with sources and evidence

This section considers a number of practical approaches to working with sources and evidence which might support the idea of the usable historic past.

Chapter summary

A final reflection on the relationship between evidence and big-picture history.

Starting points: a professional understanding of evidence

History graduates inevitably have an interesting relationship with evidence. Over the course of a long historical education, their awareness and understanding of evidence will have developed to relatively sophisticated levels. However, if they were to be asked direct questions about evidence they sometimes find it difficult to provide clear or precise responses. The QAA (Quality Assurance Agency for Higher Education) History Benchmark Statements suggest that history graduates should be able to:

- Read and use texts and other source material – critically and empathetically – addressing questions of genre, content, perspective and purpose.
- Understanding problems inherent in the historical record.
- Appreciation of a range of problems involved in the interpretation of complex material.
- Developing skills of a researcher: gathering, organizing, synthesizing evidence.

(QAA, 2007: p4)

When asked about working with evidence history graduates rarely employ the language of the Benchmark Statements, preferring instead to describe, in more concrete terms, what they can do with evidence – citing details of dissertations, or Special Subjects. When asked to describe the historical processes involved in working with evidence they rely on a number of stock phrases which relate to bias and objectivity. In many ways they are unconscious 'experts' as these comments from history graduates in the first term of a history PGCE course might demonstrate:

> As a graduate historian I think that the understanding you have of evidence and what you can do with it is almost subconscious. Over time you develop an innate awareness of evidence as a physical entity and an abstract idea and appreciate its significance in constructing historical accounts.
>
> (Edge Hill VLE, 2009)

And

I think you do just 'know what to do' when you approach an evidence based problem.

(Edge Hill VLE, 2009)

This comment suggests that history professionals – ranging from recent graduates to more experienced teachers – instinctively work with evidence and it might therefore be useful to consider, in a more metacognitive way, the different contexts *where* and *how*, for example, evidence played a significant role in a typical undergraduate degree course. This might help to develop an understanding of how the processes might mirror what happens in the history classroom. More importantly, it might be possible to appreciate why working with sources and evidence can be problematic. Consider these three different aspects of evidence-based work:

- Writing essays: Often these use largely secondary sources, but there is a tacit understanding that constructing or synthesizing an argument involves consulting a series of 'experts' who might also have had different perspectives. In these circumstances the synthesis or the argument involves making decisions or coming to conclusions based on an assessment of these different viewpoints. As part of the process it is important to consider the different cultural contexts of the historians whose works were consulted.
- Special subjects: Usually these involve spending a considerable amount of time working with original sources, often characterized by an almost forensic, line-by-line dissection of documents with the final examination paper intentionally vague; the 'comment upon . . . . . .' question, or a variant, remains a favourite device.
- The undergraduate dissertation: This is a significant achievement and is highly regarded. A carefully constructed enquiry, possibly based on a hypothesis which requires hard work in an archive. Initially tracking down the sources and following different trails until an argument begins to emerge The result is an original piece of history. It might be testing a national theme or event at a local level but the result is a new construction of the past, a new interpretation of history.

The personal and professional contexts: why teachers see evidence differently

There is, however, one more piece to the jigsaw: the history teacher's 'connection' to the sources and the evidence. This might appear rather trite but the 'personal connection to past events' is an essential element of undergraduate learning (Booth, 2003: p7) . He describes this as an 'emotional engagement' and believes it is a key motivational factor for history undergraduates.

It might, therefore, be possible to suggest how school history and graduate history are different and why working with evidence with school students is problematic. It is not simply about differing levels of difficulty – using harder, longer or more sources – it is the school students' cognitive maturity – how they perceive and understand the idea of evidence – which has a significant bearing on their capacity to understand. It is, however, also about processes and procedures: what students at Key Stage 3 (KS3) or GCSE (General Certificate in Secondary Education) and beyond, 'do' with evidence and how evidence might need to be more consciously integrated into teaching and learning history. With the developing emphasis on 'big-picture' history the place of evidence in the history classroom might need to be considered from different perspectives.

The earlier bullet points highlighted the professional procedures and processes: ways of working with evidence. These are not carried out in isolation but are an integral part of writing an essay or a dissertation or developing an in-depth understanding of an event or period. This explains why history professionals can talk about working with evidence being a subconscious process. Equally important are the cultural contexts within which professional historians work and develop their understanding. Booth's suggestion, referred to earlier, that there is an emotive connection is highly relevant; it enables graduate students to connect to the past whereas younger learners find it difficult to realize the significance of a source, the cultural weight or impact of a document. The 2008 Citizenship exhibition at the British Library used an incredible range of documents to 'tell the story' of the development of democratic ideas in the UK. Some, like the warrant for the execution of Charles I, might have an immediate impact with Year 8 students because the execution of the king was an intrinsically significant event. In this case the source is possibly nothing more than an artefact, a memento of the execution. In the same display case were the verbatim accounts of the Putney Debates, written in a remarkably clear and surprisingly 'modern' hand. It was easy to read Rainsborough's comment: '*[T]he poorest he that is in England hath a life to live as the greatest he; and therefore truly. Sir, I think it's clear that every man that is to live under a Government ought first by his own consent to put himself under that Government*' (British Library, 2008). In this case it is the ideas contained within the text that have a significance above the physical entity of the document itself. This is what might be meant by the cultural weight or the historical significance of a particular piece of evidence. To most school students this is just a piece of evidence, or a piece of information, which demonstrates that the world was turned upside down following the Civil War. For a historian the ideas contained within the Putney Debates have a relevance, or a resonance, beyond the Civil War and this realization, this degree of connectedness, is Booth's emotive or imaginative connection to the past. As history teachers we may not intend our source work with pupils to consist of fragmentary or isolated learning episodes but when school students do not have the contextual background it is difficult for them to make these connections and see significant links.

In the United States Sam Wineberg compared the ways that academic historians and senior high school students 'understood' evidence and the results were interesting. Wineberg found that professional historians were able to 'put emotion back into the inanimate texts that they (had) read . . .. Providing voices for the people who have been dead hundreds or thousands of years' (Wineburg, 2001: p63). The professional historians clearly had a far more informed understanding of 'the history' which gave them the bigger picture but the key factor which made their reading of texts – *evidence* – different was their significant cultural knowledge. Even bright high school students read texts in relatively uncomplicated ways seeing them simply as sources of information. The different levels of evidential understanding separating professional historians from learners, whether they be – Weinberg's senior high school students or KS3 pupils – are significant. Experience or, more properly, professional craft knowledge, which is often unstated or articulated with insufficient clarity, can sometimes make it difficult for beginning teachers to understand exactly what is happening in a history classroom, particularly where evidence and sources are concerned. This brief exploration of a graduate's experience of working with evidence might help to explain some of the difficulties beginning teachers can experience when trying to work with evidence in the history classroom. More importantly, as Ros Ashby argues elsewhere in this book, a school student's understanding of the nature of evidence and its significance is different.

Changing professional dialogues: developing different methodologies

It is instructive to follow the unfolding professional dialogues which have developed, largely in the pages of *Teaching History*, since the late 1990s to gain an insight into history teachers' thinking about sources and evidence. In many ways this has almost been a scientific process: identifying problems and difficulties, devising a series of practical measures to address some of these particular problems, and while there may have been different ideas about the place and role of evidence in school history these have become far more confident and coherent. In some ways the difficulties we had had with evidence link directly to the different or changing perceptions of the aims and purposes of school history. Working with sources and evidence was seen to mimic the work of 'real' historians. McAleavy's comments in 1998 are therefore interesting:

> By putting more emphasis on sources as the starting point for the construction of well-argued descriptions of the past we can be true also to the idea, central to the important developmental work of the Schools Council History Project, that school history can develop a methodology that is genuinely modelled on the work of academic historians.
>
> (McAleavy, 1998: p15)

The key principles here are that school history needs a methodology – modelled on the work of academic historians – but also that history is a construction and sources become the starting point for creating these views or accounts of the past. It might be that this perspective needs to shift; methodologies remain important but perhaps the model is different and a more confident community of practice is changing the emphasis or direction of school history. School history, it might be argued, has developed a different methodology or a distinctive methodology. Disciplinary structures remain important but the feature which drives the structures is that of an enquiry-based model – one that is more suited to the needs of school students and more effectively recognizes their different levels of cognitive development. Evidence instead of being *the* starting point for school history has become *one* aspect of school history. The starting point is now the enquiry and evidence becomes an integral part of that enquiry. This may be an assertion which is difficult to sustain but if we accept this changing 'role' for sources and evidence there are some important consequences. The starting point for the exploration of the past is not some challenging or puzzling piece of evidence but can begin with an equally puzzling cognitive challenge: the Enquiry Question – located within an intriguing narrative. This is contextually more accessible and means that many of the difficulties students face when confronted by evidence – it is biased, it is a (good) primary source or (unreliable) secondary source, or that it is simply important information about the past – are no longer either impenetrable barriers to understanding or repetitive and tedious tasks to be endured. Evidence becomes situated with the enquiry, almost as a case study, exemplifying an element or an aspect of the history. Where source work becomes an integral and well-integrated part of an overarching enquiry students can still acquire history specific skills, or evidence skills, but they do so, more securely within the contexts of the overarching enquiry. They can also begin to develop an understand of how accounts might be constructed. More importantly this developing understanding of evidence can help them to develop a sense of period, a more joined-up picture of the past.

Micro histories: history teachers and history learners working more effectively with sources and evidence

It matters little if students are studying history at KS3, GCSE or beyond, they have to develop particular skills; it is whether these skills are viewed as a series of isolated concrete attributes, like the ability to reverse a car around a corner. Alternatively these skills might be viewed as a series of dispositions which collectively enable you to drive a car confidently, considerately and competently; the aim is to drive a car, not only reverse around a corner. It could be a worthwhile activity comparing across the full range of secondary teaching what students are expected to know, understand and be able to do in relation to evidence.

In KS3 the relevant sentences of the Attainment Target focus on:

- investigating historical problems
- ask questions of sources
- a critical evaluation of the sources
- reach substantiated conclusions.

(QCDA, 2009)

At GCSE the emphasis is on *developing*:

- students' abilities to ask relevant questions about the past
- to investigate (evidence) critically using a range of sources in their historical context.

(OfQUAL, 2007: p6)

At Advanced/Supplementary exam level (A/S) there is an assumption that these skills, while not perhaps perfected, are at a reasonably advanced level to enable students to simply:

- analyse and evaluate a range of appropriate source material with discrimination.

(OfQUAL, 2006: p5)

Given that there exists, in theory at least, a notion of continuity between KS3, GCSE and A/S A2 history, it ought to be possible to detect a semblance of progression where students are required to do similar 'things' with evidence, where the activities appear to move comfortably from one phase to another. Unfortunately there isn't such a neat continuum. At KS3 the evidence skills are more carefully delineated and, as one might expect, there are a series of incremental descriptions of the 'things' students are expected to do. Is it possible, therefore, to suggest that at KS3 working with evidence more resembles basic skills training which can then be put to use for GCSE and A/S and A level? Probably not, and it might be less than helpful to see the development of students abilities to work with evidence in such a fixed way. This perhaps demonstrates why it is sometimes 'bad' history to use the bare-bones assessment outcomes such as Attainment Target levels to shape the substance of an enquiry. In that driving test it is important that the learner can demonstrate different competences but the examiner is forming an opinion of the abilities of the beginning driver. If we view the development and acquisition of 'evidence skills' in a similarly atomistic way students can quickly fail to see the point of the exercise. Even at KS3 joined-up thinking is important, hence the importance of the Key Concepts and in particular those of Interpretations and Significance where the purpose of the activity is to develop an understanding of how versions of the past can be constructed. In short, students as young as 12 are being encouraged to drive, albeit slowly and on private roads. Significantly in the new specifications at GCSE and A/S the message about sources and evidence are different: they are there to be used *contextually* to inform an understanding of the way interpretations and representations of the past have been constructed. Implicit in this is the notion that students at 16, 17 and 18 might, or should have, a more mature awareness of the bigger picture.

The first step, therefore, might involve getting school students to think beyond sources as information. This can appear to be complex, after all you are trying to focus, not just on what the source might say but also on what it might suggest or infer. Beyond that you might begin to consider intent and purpose. Claire Riley (1999) suggested the idea of a *Layers of Inference* model for interrogating sources. Many history departments have adopted this as a way to develop students' thinking about evidence. It provides a neat but flexible approach to source-based enquiry; students start with simple observations and basic comprehension to making inferences about the evidence. Often this is presented diagrammatically as a series of concentric rectangles with the source in the centre. The first rectangle – or layer – requires simple observation; subsequent layers develop thinking about the source at more demanding levels. The final 'layers' consider contextual issues which are not apparent in the original source but which are nevertheless important for developing what could be thought of as a complete picture. This may appear to be a somewhat formulaic way of approaching evidence-based work but what moves this beyond the 'reversing around a corner' skill is the way the layers of inference model supports more complex thinking and reasoning. As with many *Teaching History* articles, Riley was exploring her own practice and attempting to develop a more rigorous approach to teaching the big question: 'How healthy were Victorian towns? The relevant textbook enquiry was based around a number of sources which painted a series of contrasting views of towns and living conditions. The textbook way to approach this question was essentially to answer a number of largely comprehension-style questions where students drew information from the text. Such activities, if they are entirely source-based, can result in a slow, plodding, ponderous activity which highlights a number of issues:

- Nineteenth-century towns were unhealthy.
- They had high death rates caused by:
  — poor water supplies
  — inadequate sewage systems
  — housing and living conditions that were squalid and overcrowded.
- By the middle of the century reformers had identified the causes and the consequences.
- The same reformers were intent on using legislation to improve public health.

As a source-based enquiry public health may be valuable and the evidence – written and visual – can be compelling and at times suitably graphic and gruesome. The layers of inference model, however, moves students' thinking to a different level; instead of the sources simply providing information the nature of the activity enables them to develop a deeper contextual understanding into the nature of mid Victorian living conditions. Instead of viewing the bullet points as a series of pieces of information about living conditions which inevitably led to reform – the idea that there can be a number of fixed causes and inevitable results – the layers of inference model considers more personal issues, explores attitudes, values and beliefs and providing access to that idea of a sense of period.

Riley's ideas are useful for helping school students develop an understanding of the internal structure of sources and the nature of evidence; however, this is a first step. We are not only interested in helping students to analyse evidence but also we want them to do something with the evidence. In short, we are interested in helping them to develop their powers of synthesis – the ability to construct an argument. Margaret Mulholland's article (*Teaching History*, 1998) showed students what they might be able to do with their newly acquired level of understanding. The *evidence sandwich* could again be regarded as a neat trick, another isolated driving skill this time focused more upon communicating historical understanding. It could even be criticized for being limiting or constraining but it is important to be able to demonstrate that historical thinking is methodical and organized but above all purposeful. The *evidence sandwich* demonstrates to students the role and relevance of their developing evidential understanding. The origins of the article demonstrate the eclecticism of history teachers, connecting to Literacy Strategies and modes or styles of writing. Using evidence in the history classroom can take students and teachers in a number of different directions (sometimes simultaneously) but one significant way is to develop the ability to construct a historical argument. Evidence is central to the development of this 'skill' and demonstrates to students that there is more to do with evidence than simply answering a series of stale comprehension questions – or recognizing that the evidence may be biased and possibly more or less reliable. By using evidence in a rhetorical or persuasive manner, students can be helped to not simply develop a deeper or more sophisticated understanding but also to begin to appreciate how evidence is important and valuable in constructing a view of the past.

Again there is a danger that these approaches might be implemented in an unthinking way or in a mechanical, functionalist fashion. Students understand how to work the layers of inference and they know how to put the hamburger paragraph together but there are other difficulties which might arise when sources and evidence are used in what might be termed an instrumentalist fashion. School students can develop what might be considered peculiar ideas about sources and evidence; in some ways these are linked to the notion that evidence under some circumstances can't be trusted, that a cautious or critical view can sometimes be replaced by a cynical attitude – we can't really know – we can't really trust information from the past. To get over this view Byrom (1998) demonstrated to Year 7 students how evidence was used to construct accounts of the past – linking a television programme about the Peasants' Revolt to different fifteenth-century accounts surrounding the events in London which culminated in the killing of Wat Tyler and Richard II's address to the peasants gathered at Blackheath. The activity was doubly successful because the students didn't just watch the TV programme or just undertake an exercise in source analysis but carefully considered both as accounts of the past. They developed a critical understanding of the way the scriptwriters had been able to develop their narrative, considered the accuracy of this interpretation and finally when they watched the programme for a second time they were informed and critical observers and the quality of their learning was significant.

This simple but effective teaching sequence based around the critical examination of sources developed by Byrom demonstrates a different idea about the centrality of evidence in school history. In this illustration the investigation into the construction of an account was at the heart of the students' work. Their starting point was the TV narrative; their learning objective to understand the validity of one 'account' and how it came to be constructed from sources that might be contradictory, fragmentary and, to a greater or lesser degree, reliable. Exactly how this kind of source-based activity which explores the nature of evidence and how evidence can be used to put together a view of the past, or a version of the past, are exemplified by Banham (1998). The construction of enquiries which develop a dynamic, themed overview also enable students to consider aspects of a period in depth and it is these episodes – what Banham refers to as the 'evidence chicanes'. The nature of the source-based activity which in Banham's case considered the nature and the intent of the monastic chroniclers who wrote about King John in the thirteenth century helped students to understand why the monks wrote like they did. It is important for the pupils to understand the 'facts' contained in the sources but the activity also helped students develop a feel for the evidence. This it could be claimed is a part of developing that all important sense of period.

Byrom's and Banham's articles were written in 1998 but what is interesting is the way that they have anticipated some of the ideas, not only in the Mark IV (2008) version of the National Curriculum but also in the most recent versions of the GCSE assessment objectives. The idea of constructing views of the past, or understanding how these views might be constructed, becomes a significant aspect of work at GCSE and A Level – if we are to believe the 2008–9 Assessment Objectives. GCSE was formerly notorious for the way that it encouraged the sterile and ahistorical use of sources, particularly in examination papers. An entire genre of fatuous questions developed a momentum of their own; in one example pupils were presented with a photograph of a German Zeppelin taken during the First World War and asked: 'How useful is source C to a historian trying to find out about the First World War?' This provoked a series of answers relating to 'Utility of Evidence' which could be, and were, repeated like responses at a Latin mass; the words on paper might look impressive but they lacked conviction. This type of activity represented source-based history teaching at its worst, and while chief examiners were sensitive to these criticisms – the mark schemes and the annual reports of the chief examiners annually disparaged stereotypical or learned responses – it was still possible to get a grade C with this kind of performance. At KS3 it is still possible to work with evidence in a relatively fragmented or disconnected manner; the attainment target (or is it the way the attainment targets might be used?) encourages this isolated approach, measuring the extent to which students move from beginning '*to use information as evidence to test hypotheses*' to '*evaluating sources to establish relevant evidence for particular enquiries*' (QCDA, 2009). Again the decontextualized use of levels shows why isolated source-based work can be a pointless activity. Place the source work within a well-structured enquiry focused on, say, interpretations or significance and the activities develop a real sense of vitality. Students do have to develop levels of technical competence but it should come as no surprise that the more relevant or purposeful the enquiry, the more they are motivated to learn. Students do need to develop a more sophisticated understanding of evidence and once again the driving analogy is a useful device. The more technically competent you become the more you can enjoy driving. Working with sources and evidence in a more holistic way within a secure contextual framework enables students to undertake more sophisticated and more rewarding enquiries.

Chapter summary

Overviews, frameworks and useable big pictures: how might sources and evidence contribute to a more complete understanding of the past

If, as seems likely, the idea of the bigger picture, the coherent overview, is set to become a more prominent feature of history teaching over the coming years we need to be clear how source- and evidence-based work might contribute to this different emphasis. Big-picture history is not a return to simple narratives where sources and evidence are relegated to illustrative material. This view of history might be favoured by publications such as the *Daily Mail* who disparage modern students as the know-nothing victims of New Labour, when really what they mean is that they cannot answer a 20-question pub quiz focused on Imperial Heroes. Instead the community of history teachers might be seen to be responding to the more measured criticisms of Ofsted (Office for Standards in Education). *History in the Balance* (Ofsted, 2007) highlighted many of the problems which militate against developing an effective or joined-up view of the past, the History Community of Practice is reflective and self-aware and recent work by Ian Dawson (*Teaching History*, 2009) and Jonathan Howson (*Teaching History*, 2009) demonstrate this concern. Sources and evidence remain key features in developing students' historical understanding but can also play a part in making the subject rigorous but ultimately enjoyable; creating an evidence-rich environment for learners is clearly important but for this to be effective it has to be considered. Previously this might have led teachers to focus mainly on making the material accessible but the key now might be on integrating

> sources and evidence into a well-structured and considered enquiry. In this sense 'evid-
> ence skills' can be seen for what they are, not something to be developed in isolation
> but helping students to 'think with history' (Tosh, 2008).

Further reading

The *Teaching History* articles referred to in the chapter are going to offer you sound
practical advice. In terms of understanding how to make your teaching with sources
more challenging – in other words, how to avoid doing the same kind of activities
with Year 7 and with Year 9 – you should read Heidi Le Cocq's 'Beyond bias: making
source evaluation meaningful to Y7', *Teaching History*, 99, and Christine Counsell's
'"Didn't we do that in Year 7?" Planning for progress in evidential understanding',
Teaching History, 97. For more recent work on developing a sense of period and
big-picture history you should read Ian Dawson's 'What time does the tune start?',
Teaching History, 135; Ian Dawson's Thinking History website (www.thinking
history.co.uk) is also worth consulting. The final article is Jonothan Howson's
'Potential and pitfalls in teaching "big pictures" of the past', *Teaching History,* 136.
Chapter 2 by Peter Lee (Putting Principles into Practice, pp. 55–8) has a useful
introduction to student ideas about evidence in J. D. Bransford and M. S. Donovan
(eds) (2005) *How Students Learn: History in the Classroom.*

References

Banham, D. (1998) 'Getting ready for the Grand Prix: learning how to build a substanti-
ated argument in Year 7', *Teaching History*, 92: 6–15.
Booth, A. (2003) *Teaching History at University: Enhancing Learning and Understanding.*
London: Routledge.
British Library Taking Liberties Exhibition (2008), available online at: http://www.bl.uk/
onlinegallery/takingliberties/staritems/54putneydebatespic.html (accessed 5 October
2010).
Byrom, J. (1998) 'Working with sources: scepticism or cynicism? Putting the story back
together again', *Teaching History*, 91: 32–5.
Dawson, I. (2009) 'What time does the tune start?', *Teaching History*, 135: 50–7.
Edge Hill University History PGCE VLE (2009) Discussion Forum.
Fines, J. (1994) 'Evidence: the basis of the discipline', in H. Bourdillon (ed.) *Teaching
History.* London: Open University.
Howson, J. (2006) '"Is it the Tuarts and then the Studors or the other way around?"
The importance of developing a usable big picture of the past', *Teaching History*, 127:
40–7.
——(2009) 'Potential and pitfalls in teaching "big pictures" of the past', *Teaching History*,
136: 24–35.
McAleavy, T. (1998) 'The use of sources in history', *Teaching History*, 91: 10–16.
Mulholland, M. (1998) 'The Evidence Sandwich', *Teaching History*, 91: 17–19.
Office of Qualifications and Examinations Regulations (OfQUAL) (2007) GCSE
Assessment Objectives, available online at: http://www.ofqual.gov.uk/files/qca-07–
3454_gcsecriteriahistory.pdf (accessed 5 October 2010).
——(2006) Ibid.

Ofsted (2007) *History in the Balance: History in English Schools 2003–07.* Available online at: www.ofsted.gov.uk/publications/070043

Qualifications and Curriculum Authority (2007) GCSE Assessment Objectives, available online at: http://www.ofqual.gov.uk/files/qca-07–3454_gcsecriteriahistory.pdf (accessed 5 October 2010).

Qualifications and Curriculum Development Agency (QCDA) (2009), available online at: http://curriculum.qcda.gov.uk/key-stages-3-and-4/subjects/key-stage-3/history/ Level-descriptions/index.aspx (accessed 8 November 2010).

QAA (2007) Subject Benchmark Statements: History, available online at: http://www. qaa.ac.uk/academicinfrastructure/benchmark/statements/history07.pdf   (accessed 8 November 2010).

Riley, C. (1999) 'Evidential understanding, period knowledge and the development of literacy: a practical approach to "layers of inference" for Key Stage 3', *Teaching History,* 97: 6–12.

Tosh, J. (2008) *Why History Matters.* Basingstoke: Palgrave Macmillan, p. 6.

Wineburg, S. (2001) *Historical Thinking and Other Unnatural Acts.* Philadelphia, PA: Temple University Press.

Chapter 18

Literacies and the teaching and learning of history

Current approaches to reading the past

Paula Mountford

Introduction

As a result of reading this chapter you will:

- develop your understanding of the nature of literacy;
- understand the strong links between literacy, the past and the study of the past;
- reflect upon the range of 'literacies' within history, developing your thinking beyond a simple approach to reading, writing and speaking and listening begin to think about visual and ICT (information and communication technology) literacies;
- build a repertoire of scaffolding techniques that can be planned and explicitly taught to your learners;
- use the power of 'modelling' in the context of literacy to help you promote learning in history.

What is literacy?

When initial teacher education trainees are asked to define or characterize literacy a few give a rather limited answer of 'reading and writing' while the majority suggest a better and more wide-ranging answer of 'reading, writing and speaking and listening'. However, it is noticeable that small – but increasing – numbers of trainees suggest a broader range. This last group suggest, very helpfully, that any consideration of literacy must encompass 'reading, writing, speaking, listening, visual literacy and ICT literacy'. It is this wider characterization that is necessary in order to make the most of teaching and learning in history and this chapter will draw attention to the issues associated with such a position and suggest ways in which good practice may be achieved.

The above brief consideration of what trainees say is a means of beginning to clarify what is meant by literacy. This is not a straightforward matter and I would suggest that four reflections may help. First, it is necessary to have an overarching understanding of the nature of literacy and the following statement is as useful as many others in this regard:

> Literacy is the ability to read and use written information and to write appropriately for a range of purposes. It also involves the integration of speaking, listening

and critical thinking with reading and writing and includes the knowledge which enables a speaker, reader or writer to recognise and use language appropriate to different social occasions.

(Wray *et al.*, 2000: p12)

Second, it is necessary to make clear, as some of the trainees referred to above do, that literacy takes place in a range of contexts. People can and should 'read' the television, film, the computer screen and much more.

Plackett (1998) quotes Lanskhear (1987):

[The] true definition [of literacy] encompasses much more than 'basics' and may include 'new' areas such as 'computer literacy', 'visual literacy', 'media literacy' and so on.

(p44)

Literacy is not confined to the book and teachers need increasingly to respond to the needs and preferences of learners who are more used to texting than the hardbound text (Andrews, 2004).

Third, and very importantly, it is important to recognize that Plackett also notes that 'literacy is not a basic concept about functional reading and writing' (Plackett, 1998). Unless we are very careful the first two statements given above give a simplistically utilitarian view of language. It seems, if we take this view, that it is 'merely' the vehicle by which we communicate. History is, of course, portrayed and passed on through language. It is the means by which we communicate what happened in the past and allows us to create accounts of the past. But it is also intrinsically relevant to the meaning of the past. Issues about language go to the very heart of the historical process. Students and teachers of history need to not only consider the ways in which history is recorded but also to analyse the ways in which certain uses of language display or perhaps even create or help to create particular perspectives about the past.

The fourth and final point that needs to be considered in relation to a discussion about language, literacy and history is the connection that may be made between history and literature. The focus of this chapter is on literacy but we need always to be alert to the possibilities of illustrating historical issues and deepening our understanding of the past through an analysis of novels, plays, poems and other literary forms.

To some extent all of the above perspectives are recognized in National Curriculum documentation. The revised National Curriculum for history of 1999 (DFES/QCA, 1999) emphasized the importance of organization and communication in history education suggesting that students should

[c]ommunicate their knowledge and understanding of history, using a range of techniques, including spoken language, structured narratives, substantiated explanations and the use of ICT.

(p20)

The most recent version of the National Curriculum (2007) appears to have moved on considerably and is perhaps attempting to embed the teaching and learning of literacy across the curriculum and within each subject. The National Curriculum for history in making explicit the three key processes of historical enquiry, using evidence and communicating about the past shows that we are dealing with more than simple communication mechanisms. A range of 'literacies' (Strong, 1999) are at the heart of all three key processes. The section on 'Communicating about the past' states:

> Pupils develop writing, speaking and listening skills as they recall, select, classify and organise historical information, use historical terminology and language appropriately and accurately, and promote well-structured narratives, explanations and descriptions of the past. Pupils should use existing and emerging technologies where appropriate.
>
> (QCA, 2007: p114)

Locating history education within wider debates and policy initiatives about literacy

Literacy is always important to history teaching and learning and the particular importance of literacy for history education needs to be seen in its broader context. Successive governments have reinvested and reaffirmed the place of literacy within education. Some colleagues will clearly remember the introduction of *A Language for Life*, also known as the Bullock Report (DfEE, 1975), which declared that 'every secondary school should develop a policy for language across the curriculum', and the Cox Report (DES and Welsh Office, 1989), which while valuing standard forms of education also recognized the significance of students' own linguistic resources and preferences. The introduction of the National Literacy Strategy (1997), the Pilot Secondary Literacy Projects (1998–9) and other initiatives (e.g. Ensuring attainment of white working class boys in writing (2006)) have shown that this is a vitally important field. At times there have been specific policy connections made with history with key documents including *Literacy and History* (2002), *Access and Engagement in History: Teaching Pupils for Whom English is an Additional Language* (2002) and *Literacy and Learning in History* (2004). The point that simple functionality is not the sole concern of the proponents of such initiatives can readily be seen. Language, literature and literacy have been, like history, at the heart of the 'culture wars' which had cultural, political and of course educational aspects (e.g. Snyder, 2008; Hunter, 1992; Phillips, 1998) that affected English and history (as well as other subjects in England and elsewhere). As an example of the dramatic controversies during the somewhat frenzied early days of the National Curriculum perhaps Cox as the author of one of the key reports referred to above stands as the personification of those battles. Cox moved swiftly in the public consciousness from being vilified as a reactionary for his championing of 'traditional' education in the Black Papers to being labelled as a progressive for his views on language education (McCabe, 2008).

Whether what we currently have is 'progressive' or 'traditional' (and how useful those labels are) is a moot point. It seems as if the controversies over English are now more muted than they once were. For example, the fuss over Carol Ann Duffy's poem about possible knife crime (Curtis, 2008) and arguments about supposed dirty dealings in the election for the Oxford chair of poetry (Wardrop and Roberts, 2009) seem tame when compared with previous anguish. We have to reflect on the meaning of what is currently happening to know what history teachers are expected to do and are actually doing. To be specific we have to ask about the meaning of initiatives that are relevant to literacy and, as such, to history. Personal, learning and thinking skills (PLTS) are being officially promoted showing a determination to promote literacies across subjects. The guidance on seven 'Cross-Curriculum dimensions' in the National Curriculum includes 'technology and the media' in which it is emphasized that young people need opportunities to:

> access and use a rich range of technologies, including broadcast media, film, printed communications, games, web, podcasts and animation.

Through this dimension young people learn to:

- Use technology confidently and productively to find things out, try things out, develop and present ideas, and communicate with local and global audiences.
- Read, deconstruct and critically evaluate different types of media, including news, advertising images, documentaries, film and podcasts.
- Become authors of content for different types of media.

(NC, 2007)

What does the above mean? It seems that literacies are being developed within and across subjects in order to promote communication and cultural competence with explicit reference to a dynamic critical stance brought to a wide range of media. Academics, policymakers, teachers, trainees and others will need to reflect deeply on the meaning of the goals and achievements of this enterprise. We need to be alert to the full range of possibilities. Above we noted the sharply contrasting ways in which Cox's work was interpreted and we need to ask now what characterization would currently be justifiable? It would not be helpful to develop simplistic positions in which, for example, we argue that we are witnessing the fracturing of historical interpretation through a politically correct lens, and/or the reification of supposedly transferable and ultimately ahistorical skills where the absence of controversy in the drive to improve standards signals only a meek acceptance of a somewhat utilitarian approach to language. But as history specialists for whom language is an essential element of our work the need for these reflections is supremely important and entirely related to how we identify and achieve good practice. Literacy is essential, controversial and intrinsic to the work we do in our history classrooms.

Exploring the possibilities of good practice in history education

A wide range of resources are available which offer a range of ideas for connecting history and literacy from writing frames, Directed Activities Related to Texts (DARTs), note-taking grids and charts, mind maps, word games, thinking skill activities, text marking and speaking frames. But we need to go further than simply using language-based techniques. A professionally critical approach in relation to language (e.g. Counsell, 1997, 2004) allows us to mine into key concepts and processes that are intrinsic to history teaching and learning and select, design and develop a range of literacy strategies that will empower learners to work confidently and competently within these areas. We need to reflect upon and prepare our learners to read a range of historical texts from the textbook 'gobbet', as well as diary entries, newspaper articles, novels, poems and other sources. The purpose of this reading is multifaceted. Our students need to analyse, question, evaluate, reflect upon and challenge their reading. As teachers of history we need to plan to develop a range of skills that empower our learners to rise to these challenges. Our challenge as history teachers is to reflect carefully upon the wealth of suggested activities available and select appropriately the strategies and activities that will support the historical skills, knowledge and understanding we are developing in our learners. These things often happen in an integrated way with students speaking, listening, reading and writing during the same lesson or same activity which could extend over more than one lesson. For the sake of organizational simplicity I show below separate treatment of some of the key focuses for history and literacy.

Speaking and listening

Effective and engaging history teaching and learning requires teachers to create a wealth of opportunities to develop speaking and listening skills for their students. The opportunities are endless: starters, plenaries, pair work, group work, questioning activities, card sorts and thinking skills, role play and discussions to list some of the most obvious. Spider diagrams, data-capturing charts and diagrams, card sorts, thinking skills activities all can be designed and employed to create environments and opportunities for speaking and listening. The all-pervasiveness of speaking and listening is illustrated in the work of Wilkinson *et al.* (1965):

> Oracy is a condition of learning in all subjects, it is not a frill but a state of being in which the whole school must operate.

> (p44)

The National Strategy (DFEE, 1998) quoted in Grainger and Tod (2000) emphasizes the role of speaking and listening:

> Good oral work enhances pupils' understanding of language in both oral and written forms and of the way language can be used to communicate. It is also an important part of the process through which pupils read and compose texts.

> (p46)

In the revised National Curriculum documents (DfES/QCA, 1999) speaking and listening is stressed and emphasized:

> In speaking, pupils should be taught to use language precisely and cogently. Pupils should be taught to listen to others and respond and build on their ideas and views constructively.

> (p35)

So, what does this mean for good practice in history education? The Nuffield Primary History web pages (see http://www.primaryhistory.org/teachingmethods/speaking-listening-discussion-and-debate-oracy,175,SAR.html) have a wide range of useful ideas and practical examples. Clark (2001) discusses the strength of planned speaking and listening activities to support causal thinking and writing at Key Stage 3. Rudham (2001) provides valuable insights into the process of discussion in history lessons: 'The ability to clarify thoughts, to tailor the structure of an argument, to sequence ideas, to listen and recall main points, to answer questions pertinently and so on, all arise out of speaking and listening activities' (p36). I would recommend that you read (or re-read) Hunt (2000), which supports student engagement and understanding of significance. Hunt's examples from the 'Great Fire of London' (p49) and 'Reasons why the study of the slave trade and its abolition is important' (p51) would provide you with excellent starting points to reflect upon the speaking and listening opportunities. Luff (2001) gives in six bullet points a useful summary explaining why history teachers should 'focus on speaking and listening' (2001: p11) and he suggests ways of debating links between slavery and factory conditions. It is an excellent example of employing literacy skills to develop 'historically rigorous tasks and valid historical enquiry' (p10). The 'procedures' (p13) outlined in this article clearly place the activity within an historical enquiry but also provide a valuable support to teachers who want to develop debating skills within their students. The enquiry requires students to read a range of source material to build up their knowledge and understanding, to help to articulate ideas and evidence via the speaking and listening task of a debate.

Role play and drama activities could be developed to enhance speaking and listening activities within history. I recommend that you read Higgins' (2007) article which provides a very clear explanation of how to use a speed-dating format, and role-play cards to encourage investigating the thinking behind the motives of Elizabeth's suitors and Elizabeth's decisions not to marry. It explains how you would divide the group into five; one student plays Elizabeth, the other four take on roles as her suitors, 'Philip II, Robert Dudley, The Duke of Alencon and Sir Christopher Hatton' (p52). It goes on to explain how you would provide similar resources for the 'suitors', then using the format of speed dating allow Elizabeth to ask questions of each suitor in turn under time restrictions. Higgins suggests a plenary activity where Elizabeth states her choice and explains her reasoning. This approach can be applied in other ways. Higgins goes on to discuss the use of 'television trailers' (p52) for programmes such as *Casualty* and *Holby City* as the stimulus for students to work in groups, using sugar paper and pens and discussing how they might use that medium to reflect upon medicine in medieval times.

If any of these activities were used by you in a continuing professional development activity or when planning a lesson, reflect upon what you require the students to do, what you think they will learn, how you can 'scaffold' the process and support their progress. Would you automatically place your students into pairs or groups of three? Would you plan for and share a learning objective that focused on speaking and listening? Would you model the thinking behind the task? Would you be circulating the room and listening into the pupil talk? How would you 'move on' any learners who were 'stuck'? How could you capture the experience and the quality of the thinking that the speaking and listening activity helped the students to demonstrate?

Reading

History, of course, requires students to read a range of source material. You have probably used all of the following (and more): textbooks, newspaper articles, web resources, diary entries, worksheets and novels. But as I have suggested above a particular approach to reading is necessary. Counsell (2004: p1) is right to argue that, in itself, 'reading for information just won't do'. She shows that this approach to reading 'is even worse than a missed opportunity, for it undoes the history teachers' careful work of helping pupils to move beyond a concept of history as "information" and into ideas of "evidence", "source", "evidential information", or "interpretation"' (p1). She goes on to argue that 'pupils need to read texts for argument, for position, for deliberated construction, for unwitting or witting message' (p1). The key is to ensure that reading is undertaken to allow for the development of historical understanding. The connection between historical concepts (procedural and substantive) need not always be made explicitly. At times it would be unhelpful to allow the explanation of the activity to get in the way of the fun and engagement that is essential to the realization of the learning goals. But the purpose of the exercise must always be clear to the teacher and the students need ultimately to know the value of the process in which they are engaged for enhancing their historical understanding. So how can this be done? Lewis and Wray (2000) and Strong (1999, 2001) provide a wealth of activities to develop and support reading skills and as long as the connection is made with historical understanding these activities have a great deal of potential. Directed Activities Related to Texts (DARTs) are described by Strong (1999):

> [T]o help students make sense of texts in ways that are far more constructive and interesting than using simplified texts, setting decontextualised comprehension exercises or copy.
>
> (p55)

Strong summarizes a range of DARTs that include the following activities:

- **Sequencing:** Students have to order cut-up sections of text to establish meaning through structuring the text appropriately. The discussion this involves is essential.
- **Transformation:** Students have to present the text in a different form or genre (e.g. as a newspaper article, a police report, an advert, a poster, a radio report, instructions etc. This involves selecting and presenting information for a different, specified audience. Such a task may need a writing frame to support it.
- **Open-ended questions:** A few challenging questions are set for which the text offers no obvious single correct answer. Students have to consider the full text to deduce their answers. The reasons for coming to their decision are central to group feedback on answers.
- **Flowcharts/diagrams/drawings:** Students are asked to make visual representation of some of the information in a text.
- **Interrogation:** In groups, students formulate the questions that need to be answered in order to understand the text.

- **Highlighting text:** Students are asked to highlight or annotate parts of a text that relate to particular issues or aspects.

(p57)

There is much more that can be done in connection with reading for historical understanding. Using the five Ws and H (Leat, 1998) you can support your class to engage with written texts and visual images. The question stems: Who? What? Where? When? Why? and How? can be used by pairs or small groups to formulate questions to interrogate the text or visual image. This activity works well with paragraphs, longer texts, newspaper articles or a range of visual sources. It allows focused discussion about the questions to ask; it then requires students to use the questions to engage with the text and discuss possible answers and value of the questions asked.

The above approach complements that adopted by a range of practitioners who work with children of various levels of ability. The Nuffield Primary History Project has developed a text breaker (see below) that encourages students briefly to review the main features of the text and then gradually to develop a precise focus on historical understanding. I am not entirely convinced that it would be necessary always to follow the sequence of activities for reading nor to concentrate on the identification of grammatical terms as shown in the text breaker but it does provide a useful guide for decoding historical texts.

A General structure of text
- outlines
- features

B Words and phrases
- concrete nouns
- abstract nouns
- adjectives
- verbs
- adverbs
- pronouns, etc.

C Ideas
- main ideas
- sequence of ideas
- hierarchy of ideas

D Genre and register
- author's intent
- language used: tone, conventions
- audience

E Historical and other concepts
- time: dates, periods, sequence
- terminology: war, Reformation, valour
- cause/consequence: reasons, situations, significance, results

- interpretations
- evidence and enquiry
- writing.

Writing is clearly an essential part of the historian's repertoire and teachers need to make full use of the potential it offers. This can be done by recognizing its formative value as well as its capacity to illustrate the achievement of understanding. In 1997 SCAA (School Curriculum and Assessment Authority) usefully suggested that

> writing should not just be seen as an outcome. It is a pedagogical tool. Writing can be seen as a means to an end in helping pupils to see the organizational demands and problems at the heart of any attempt to communicate the results of historical study. Writing tasks can be used to lead pupils into the higher-order thinking necessary both for historical enquiry and for the acquisition of knowledge.
>
> (p5)

In part the process of leading students to achieve high standards is to ensure that they can take notes effectively. Curiously this important skill is often not taught explicitly:

> The ability to make notes from a variety of sources is an important skill in gathering information and one that is increasingly relied upon as pupil's progress through the educational system. It is still rare, however, judged on informal questioning of students of all ages, to discover any to whom note-taking has been actively taught. Most pupils appear to somehow 'pick it up' or 'work it out for themselves'. There are, however, many ways in which teachers can assist their students to become more efficient and effective note takers.
>
> (Lewis and Wray, 2000: p46)

Most trainees will have already received a good deal of advice from their own universities where note-taking is increasingly taught (e.g. see http://education.exeter. ac.uk/dll/studyskills/note_taking_skills.htm). But it will be important that note-taking is not seen as an end in itself. A review of the many excellent activities on the site www.thinkinghistory.co.uk shows that a key to success is to link the notes that you require of students to the purpose of the exercise. Once this is done there is a reduced possibility of filling pages of exercise books with dates and names that mean little or nothing. Better to follow the advice of Counsell (1997) who suggests card-sort activities (a form of note-taking) as a staging post towards 'analytical and discursive writing'.

It is essential that students are encouraged to write for a purpose. In order to help them achieve the goal of understanding and practising history at higher levels writing frames are useful devices. Lewis and Wray (2000) described their work on the EXEL (Exeter Extending Literacy) project:

> The template of starters, connectives and sentence modifiers which constitute a writing frame gives children a structure within which they can concentrate

on communicating what they want to say, rather than getting lost in the form. However, by using the form children become increasingly familiar with it.

(p92)

Banham and Dawson (2000) with their very striking references to the analogies of 'hamburger paragraphs' (in which layers of text show features such as point, evidence, explanation) and the 'History Grand Prix' in which students are encouraged to explain history in clearly structured ways using evidence and focusing on key concepts.

Much of the work that is connected with writing history can be developed with an explicit appreciation of the writing of others. But this needs to be handled with care. Many teachers have dabbled in using either extracts or whole novels to support student learning, and as an inspiration to write historical fiction. This activity ranges widely from Roman slave stories to Victorian child labourers to First World War Tommies. All too often these accounts are superficial and formulaic. Counsell (2004) describes them as 'cold floorboard syndrome' (p56). A simple storytelling approach (perhaps from a teacher who is searching for a homework 'filler' task that students will do but from which they will not gain much) is best avoided. It is far better to be ambitious and focused in use of literature. The work of Martin and Brooke (2002) is quite useful in this context. They suggest that

> [w]riting and studying historical fiction can help to achieve that elusive balance between different historical perspectives, encouraging greater emphasis on the social, cultural and aesthetic aspects of a period in a rigorous and engaging way.
>
> (p30)

They argue that historical fiction can 'develop students' understanding of history' (p31) with progress being made in the following areas: 'enquiry, interpretation, communication and knowledge and understanding of characteristic features' (p31). Martin and Brooke (2002) advocate a focus on plot, the construction of a 'story recipe that provides a creative constraint' (p31), a focus on setting. They recommend that 'students need to have acquired a very strong visual image in their head' (p32). Their work is developed further in the book *Write Your Own Roman Story* (Brooke *et al.*, 2001). Their work, although dating from 2001, is a perfect example of cross-curricular working encouraged by the new National Curriculum (2007).

English and History teachers can collaborate to plan for really valuable cross-curricular experiences for Key Stage 3 or 4 learners. This is a project that could be developed on a trainee's main placement, within an NQT (newly qualified teacher) year or as a high-level structural collaboration between experienced heads of departments. The CPD potential for you and your department is enormous. Cross-curricular collaboration is a key focus within the new National Curriculum (2007). It is not something new but it is challenging, time-consuming and complex to build relationships and pedagogical understanding across subject areas. Is it an idea already embedded with the school action plan? Or the department's action plan? Does your mentor or your department have experience of collaborating with English and drama?

Chapter summary

- Students and teachers of history need to use a wide-ranging characterization of literacy(ies) including the understanding of the issues associated with new technologies.
- There is strong official support for history teachers to engage with literacies and, in order to fully understand the nature of officially perceived possibilities of such work, a wide-angled view of the National Curriculum and other initiatives should take place (including, for example, a focus on cross-curricular matters).
- A critical approach should be adopted in which literacy is both the tool to understand the past, a means by which the business of reading and writing the past is illuminated (i.e. the connection between literacy and procedural concepts of history), and a way in which skills can be used to represent the past to others.

Further reading

Counsell, C (2004) *History and Literacy in Year 7*. London: Hodder Murray. A very valuable overview of ideas, issues and suggestions for practice.

Martin, D. and Brooke, B. (2002) 'Getting personal: making effective use of historical fiction in the history classroom', in *Teaching History 108*. London: Historical Association. A good practical guide to what can be done in the classroom.

Department for Education and Employment (DfEE) (1975) *A Language for Life (The Bullock Report)*. London: DfEE. One of the modern classics about language and literacy. Fundamental ideas that shaped policy and which have long-lasting significance.

Wray, D., Medwell, J., Fox, R. and Poulson, L. (2000) 'The teaching practices of effective teachers of literacy', *Educational Review*, 52 (1). A research-based account of what teachers do.

References

Andrews, R. (ed.) (2004) *The Impact of ICT on Literacy*. London: RoutledgeFalmer.

Banham, D. and Dawson, I. (2000) *King John: Pupil's Book: A Key Stage 3 Investigation into Medieval Monarchy (This is History)*. London: Hodder.

Brooke, B., Martin, D. and Dawson, I. (2001) *Write Your Own Roman Story*. London: John Murray.

Clark, V. (2001) 'Illuminating the shadow: making progress happen in causal thinking through speaking and listening', *Teaching History 105*. London: Historical Association.

Counsell, C. (1997) *Analytical and Discursive Writing at Key Stage 3*. London: Historical Association.

——(2004) *History and Literacy in Year 7*. London: Hodder Murray.

Curtis, P. (2008) 'Top exam board asks schools to destroy book containing knife poem', *The Guardian*, 4 September.

Department for Education and Employment (DfEE) (1975) *A Language for Life* (The Bullock Report). London: DfEE.

——(1998) *The NLS Framework for Teaching*. London: DfEE.

Department for Education and Skills (DfES) (2004) *Literacy and Learning in History*. London: DfES.

Department of Education and Science (DES) and Welsh Office (1989) *English for Ages 5–16* (The Cox Report), London: HMSO.

DFES/QCA (1999) *National Curriculum*. London: HMSO.

Grainger, T. and Tod, J. (2000) *Inclusive Educational Practice Literacy*. London: David Fulton Press.

Higgins, C. (2007) 'Speed dating with Queen Elizabeth. Role-play activities to engage and challenge young learners', *Teaching History 128*. London: Historical Association.

Hunt, M. (2000) 'Teaching historical significance', in J. Arthur and R. Phillips (eds) *Issues in History Teaching*. London: Routledge.

Hunter, J. D. (1992) *Culture Wars: The Struggle to Define America*. New York: Basic Books.

Lanskhear, C. (1987) *Changing Literacy*. Buckingham: Open University.

Leat, D. (ed.) (1998) *Thinking Through Geography*. Cambridge: Chris Kington.

Lewis, M. and Wray, D. (eds) (2000) *Literacy in the Secondary School*. London: David Fulton.

Luff, I. (2001) 'Beyond I speak, you listen, boy!' Exploring diversity of attitudes and experiences through speaking and listening', *Teaching History 105*. London: Historical Association.

McCabe, C. (2008) 'Professor Brian Cox: English scholar, poet and editor of 'Critical Quarterly' whose Black Papers sparked debate on education', *The Independent*, 29 April.

Martin, D. and Brooke, B. (2002) 'Getting personal: making effective use of historical fiction in the history classroom', *Teaching History 108*. London: Historical Association.

National Curriculum (NC) (2007) Available online at: http://curriculum.qcda.gov.uk/key-states-e-adn-4/cross-curriculum-dimensions/index.aspx (accessed 23 July 2010).

Nuffield Primary History, available online at: http://www.primaryhistory.org (accessed 5 October 2010).

Phillips, I. (2008) *Teaching History: Developing as a Reflective Secondary Teacher*. London: Sage.

Phillips, R. (1998) 'Contesting the past, constructing the future: history, identity and politics in schools', *British Journal of Educational Studies*, 46(1): 40–53.

Plackett, E. (1998) 'What literacy means', *English and Media Magazine*, 39: 43–6.

Qualifications and Curriculum Authority (QCA) (1999) *Improving Writing at Key Stages 3 and 4*. London: QCA.

——(2007) *History. Programme of Study for Key Stage 3 and Attainment Target*. Available online at: http://curriculum.qcda.gov.uk/key-states-3-and-4/subjects/key-state-3/history/index-aspx

Rudham, R. (2001) 'A noisy classroom is a thinking classroom: speaking and listening in Year 7 history', *Teaching History 105*. London: Historical Association.

SCAA (1997) *Extended Writing in Key Stage 3*.

Snyder, I. (2008) *The Literacy Wars: Why Teaching Children to Read and Write is a Battleground in Australia*. Sydney: Allen & Unwin.

Strong, J. (1999) *Literacy at 11–14*. London: Collins Educational.

——(2001) *Literacy Across the Curriculum*. London: Harper Collins.

Wardrop, M. and Roberts, L. (2009) 'Ruth Padel quits as Oxford University's Professor of Poetry amid "sex smear claims"', *Daily Telegraph*, 26 May.

Wilkinson, A. (1965) 'Spoken English', *Education Review*, occasional publication, no. 2, University of Birmingham, School of Education. In Grainger, T. and Tod, J. (2000) Inclusive *Educational Practice Literacy*, London: David Fulton Press.

Wray, D., Medwell, J., Fox, R. and Poulson, L. (2000) 'The teaching practices of effective teachers of literacy', *Educational Review*, 52 (1).

Chapter 19

History teaching and ICT

Terry Haydn

I always start off by saying, don't go anywhere near a computer, unless there are these rare occasions where using a computer helps you to be able to do something. If you haven't got a good idea in the first place, just shoving up a PowerPoint isn't going to do the job.

—Advanced Skills Teacher, advice to student teachers,
OECD case study

Introduction

Given that there are many demands on their professional time, how much time should history teachers invest in the development of their ability to use information and communications technology (ICT) effectively in their teaching? Given the range of ICT applications and resources now available to the history teacher, what are the most intelligent and productive avenues of ICT to explore in terms of 'pay-off' for the time and energy invested? And what are the 'key variables' in terms of factors influencing the extent to which history teachers become accomplished users of new technology? This chapter draws in part on the experiences of the author as a history teacher and history teacher educator, and in part on recent research on how teachers learn to use ICT effectively in subject teaching.

How important is the ICT 'agenda' for history teachers?

One of the ironies of the above quotation is that the Advanced Skills Teacher in question is exceptionally accomplished in his use of ICT to enhance teaching and learning. His teaching sessions on global citizenship often have a powerful and inspirational influence on learners in terms of the impact both on their thinking on global citizenship issues and on their motivation to explore the use of ICT in their own teaching. The quotation does, however, make the (perhaps obvious) point that there is no automatic 'dividend' to be gained from using ICT in teaching. An Ofsted (Office for Standards in Education) report on the use of ICT in history classrooms found that lessons where new technology was used were on average less satisfactory than lessons without ICT (quoted in Harrison, 2003). Is there anyone reading this page who has not, at some point, been severely bored by a PowerPoint presentation? Other negative aspects of ICT use in history teaching include 'Encarta Syndrome' (copying and pasting without reading or understanding), an increase in didactic 'teacher-led' pedagogy ('Look what I can do with a whiteboard!'), the distracting influence of multimedia effects, slowing down of content coverage, unfocused and unproductive 'pinball-style' browsing of the internet, meretricious and low-value games and quizzes and loss of sequential narrative (Laurillard, 1998; Tufte, 2006; Walsh, 1998, 2006). It has been argued that 'it doesn't matter whether history teachers use ICT in their classrooms . . . what does matter is that history is still on the school curriculum and that it is well taught' (quoted in Dickinson, 1998: 16). The annual Schools History Project Conference would appear to bear out this assertion: each year there are many inspirational sessions given by leading-edge practitioners which make little or no use of ICT.

And yet, for all the reservations about access issues, unreliable equipment, commercial hype and the gap between claims made for ICT and what is standard practice, most people reading this chapter will have encountered some educational uses of new technology which have had a positive impact, which made a point in a particularly powerful and effective way, or enabled them to learn or do something more quickly and securely than would have been the case without the aid of new technology. Most people who have worked in teacher education for a number of years have encountered some teachers and some departments who have managed to transform pupils' attitude to learning through the use of ICT, or pupils' ability to learn for themselves or to learn collaboratively using ICT, or to express themselves digitally in a fluent, powerful and accomplished manner.

I would argue that it is still possible to be a competent history teacher without making extensive use of ICT. But I also believe that if history teachers do not consider the possibilities that new technology offers them, they are missing out on some opportunities to teach more effectively and vividly through the skilful use of 'impact' resources (see Haydn, 2005). ICT can also add to the variety of learning approaches which can be used with pupils, and it can help in getting pupils to engage with history outside taught sessions.

What does it mean 'to be good at ICT' as a history teacher?

A recent survey of the views of experienced teacher educators and school-based mentors attempted to elicit views about 'what it means to be good at ICT' as a student teacher (OECD, 2009). The outcomes of the UK strand of the survey suggested that perhaps the most important facet of ICT competence was thought to be the ability to *apply* ICT in a way that improved learning outcomes. It was interesting to note that out of 52 respondents only one defined competence in ICT in terms of a list of technical things that teachers should be able to do. It was acknowledged that basic technical competence was an 'entry-level' factor to developing the capability to use ICT effectively in subject teaching, but advanced levels of technological expertise were not generally regarded as an influential factor in ICT capability. Having an up-to-date awareness of the range of ICT applications and resources which might have the potential for use in subject teaching was mentioned as a factor which was likely to contribute to progress in becoming good at using ICT, but it emerged as much less important than teachers having good ideas about 'what to do' with ICT applications once they had learned how to use them:

> If they're creative people then they will have a go and they will look for . . . ways of making it relevant and exciting and interesting, and try things out, even they don't always work, it's about them thinking about what sorts of things you can do with Twitter, or PowerPoint or whatever.

> It's certainly not about how much they use ICT – PowerPoint and whiteboards often don't add value to pupils' learning . . . it's about them coming up with some good ideas that work to improve lessons.

> It's not good enough to put a tick, can use PowerPoint, tick, can use Moviemaker . . . it's about how well they can use it . . . whether they can use it in a powerful and effective way.

> It's actually about creativity and flair in thinking of how best to deploy ICT.
>
> (OECD, 2010)

Becoming good at ICT is partly about discerning which applications seem likely to have the potential for high 'pay-off' in terms of enhancing learning in history, and which are tangential or irrelevant – and then having the intelligence and application to go on to devise or acquire worthwhile things with ICT.

One further facet of progression in ICT which emerged from the study was the extent to which student teachers possessed the skills to be able to involve pupils in using the ICT software or application, independently and usefully, in terms of their learning. In this model there might be thought to be several levels of capability:

1. awareness of the application and of the fact that it might be used to develop pupil learning;
2. ability to use the application;
3. ability to use the application (to some good learning purpose) in a classroom context (with real, live children);
4. ability to get pupils using the application autonomously and usefully.

Given the limited curriculum time available to many history teachers in terms of timetabled lessons, and recent developments with the internet, virtual learning environments (VLEs), and Web 2.0 applications, this last step opens the door to pupils being able to continue to engage with the subject, and with the work being undertaken in the classroom, outside timetabled lessons, in a wider range of ways than has been traditionally available in the form of reading and written assignments. There are now many history departments where the majority of pupils spend more time learning history outside the classroom than in taught sessions. As well as potential advantages in terms of pupil engagement with the subject, it can be helpful for pupils to be able to express themselves 'digitally', and can help to avoid over reliance on handwritten tasks that are one of the things that puts some pupils off the subject (QCA, 2005). As on experienced mentor pointed out, '*Some kids are still having to*

*do fairly dull worksheet exercises for homework, others are being told "Make a website on
. . .", or "Do me a film trailer on . . .". There is no question in my mind which of these
types of homework is best for pupils' learning"* (quoted in Haydn, 2010).

Why do some history teachers become more adept users of ICT than others?

Another key variable which emerged from the OECD study was the 'ability to learn'
of student teachers themselves. Student teachers generally receive the same course
inputs relating to ICT, and yet some make more progress than others in terms of
maximizing the potential of ICT to improve teaching and learning in history. It was
felt that although school experience and having a mentor who was a good 'role model'
for ICT were also 'key variables', part of the explanation lay in student teachers'
perseverance, commitment, professionalism and ability to be 'a good learner':

> They all get pretty much the same input . . . at least in the taught course at the
> university . . . and yet some of them get much further in their use of ICT than
> others and it doesn't seem to be just about which schools they have gone to for
> their placement. There are psychological and attitudinal factors at work here . . .
> it's about attitudes to risk and new experiences, about initiative and perseverance.
> Some of them are full of good intentions but don't stick at it and move on with
> things . . . They say 'That's great . . . that's really interesting . . .', and then go
> away and forget all about it.
>   Some of them are full of good intentions but never get round to it . . . others
> are very dogged and persevering . . . 'I'm going to stay behind in school every
> night this week until I can do this' . . . you need to get across to students these
> points or they think of it just in terms of being good or bad at ICT as a sort of
> genetic thing.
>
> (OECD, 2010)

As well as devoting time to ICT, the ability to work collaboratively with others, to
'sub-contract' ICT agendas, and share resources and ideas were seen as factors which
influenced how accomplished students would be by the end of the course.

Lessons learned

There is now a substantial body of research and inspection evidence about the use
of new technology in schools. The following section is an attempt to distil some of
the key findings which have emerged from the lessons of the past decade in relation
to the use of ICT in subject teaching and in history teaching in particular (see, for
example, Barton and Haydn, 2007; BECta, 2008; JISC, 2008; e-help, 2009; Ofsted,
2009; Walsh, 2005).

It's as much about pedagogy as technology

Being good at ICT is often considered in terms of technological proficiency. This
chapter argues that it is more about teachers' pedagogical skills in using ICT. Most of

the PowerPoint presentations that are stultifyingly boring are dull not because they do not use advanced sophisticated technical features of the application but because their authors have lost sight of how to engage the audience with the ideas and content of the presentation. Walsh (2006) makes the point that classroom response systems can be used for batteries of dreary multiple-choice factual retention tests, or for the provocative and thoughtful promotion of argument and debate, problematizing the issues involved and getting learners to question their assumptions about historical issues. Learning to use ICT in teaching is an interesting (and complex) process because it involves some elements that are rather like 'training' (being instructed in the correct way to do something), and some that are 'educational' in nature, where reflection, and a consideration of possible alternative approaches are required.[1] Effective *classroom application* of ICT involves high-order thinking, creativity and imagination, not just technical capability.

Moving beyond PowerPoint

The past few years have seen a massive increase in the number of classrooms in the UK which are equipped with data projectors, and nearly all schools now possess some form of VLE. If there is such a thing as a 'killer application' in ICT (in terms of an innovation which radically transforms teachers' practice), it is perhaps the data projector. In many ways, this has been a positive development in terms of the ease and convenience with which teachers can incorporate ICT as a component of a lesson, compared with marching the class down to a computer room for a 'set piece' ICT lesson. However, this development has not been unequivocally positive. Lodge and Hodge (2008) make the point that unlimited access to 'easy' technology can make teachers lazy, and there is evidence from the recent OECD study of some teachers becoming over-reliant on particular forms of ICT, and, in particular, drifting into the habit of having the data projector and PowerPoint or the data projector and interactive whiteboard on all through the day, right through every lesson. The sheer ease and speed with which it is possible to 'knock up' a PowerPoint presentation may also mean that some teachers stay within this 'comfort zone', rather than exploring the possibilities of exploring other ICT agendas with the potential to enhance learning in the history classroom. Several respondents in the OECD survey saw this as being unhelpful, not just in terms of varying ways of using ICT but also in terms of students being able to develop teaching skills that did not depend on new technology:

> I'm making them deliberately do without ICT . . . which is quite interesting because I got them storytelling and they couldn't do it, because they had to use themselves . . . so I think, you know, so I think I probably have to keep a wary eye on that, because they forget how to do the simple things.
>
> Some people get complacent and just shove up a succession of lazily put together PowerPoints instead of exploring the wide range of other ICT applications which can be used in history classrooms – digital cameras, sound files, Web 2.0 apps . . .
>
> (OECD, 2010)

The need to use ICT in a way that involves pupils actively in learning

The use of PowerPoint and interactive whiteboards can be very teacher-centred, with the emphasis on the teacher controlling and manipulating the presentation software in a way that increases didactic teaching and reduces active pupil participation in the lesson, leading to what has been termed 'passive engagement' on the part of the learners. 'Active learning' in this context does not necessarily mean moving around, group work, etc.; just some windows of opportunity to do more than listen or write things down. This is where developing pupils' ability to use ICT to express views, respond to questions or create digital content can be invaluable. As Hadfield *et al.* (2009: 15) point out, '[p]roviders and schools should be aware of the digital habits and skills of their pupils. ICT interventions should build on these skills to engage pupils and motivate them to voice their views and create their own content.' Texting is now an important component of the cultural literacy of many young people, but the potential to draw on this form of literacy still tends to be under-explored by many teachers (JISC, 2008). When using ICT via the data projector and presentation software, whether it be PowerPoint, the interactive whiteboard or other programs, it can be helpful to give some thought to what the pupils will be doing while the presentation software is being used (not least, 'are they being made to think?').

There is no necessary correlation between the expense and sophistication of new technology applications and their potential for being useful for enhancing teaching and learning in history

There are now several very expensive ICT applications in schools, including interactive whiteboards, e-portfolio software, and classroom response systems. However, this does not mean that attention should focus exclusively on these 'Rolls-Royce' technologies, and some teacher educators and mentors have questioned the utility and value for money of some of these applications, and raised the question of whether there is pressure on teachers to make use of them simply because so much money has been invested in them (OECD, 2010).

The potential of these applications should be considered, but it is also worth exploring applications which are not expensive investments. Walsh (1998) pointed out that the simple word processor is a very useful instrument for helping pupils to organize their thinking in history. The websites of Doug Belshaw (http://dougbelshaw.com), Andrew Field (www.schoolhistory.co.uk), Dan Moorhouse (www.schoolshistory.org.uk), Russel Tarr (www.activehistory.co.uk), John Simkin (http://www.spartacus.schoolnet.co.uk) and Neil Thompson (www.keystagehistory.co.uk) offer a range of suggestions of software and websites that are both free and useful to history teachers. The 'keepvid' site is a very useful tool for downloading moving-image clips onto your own storage devices so that you can use them when you want (http://keepvid.com). The simple memory stick is another application that has transformed teachers' ability to store, accumulate and deploy high-quality 'impact' resources – but some history teachers make more effective and discerning use of them than others.

Social bookmarking sites such as Delicious (www.delicious.com) allow you not just to tag your own bookmarks but also to access the 'archives' of other collectors of history resources on the internet (see, for example, the collections of Russel Tarr, http://delicious.com/russeltarr). Many history teachers now use clips from YouTube, but fewer use the facility to access the collections that have been built up by history teachers with a particular interest in web resources (see, for example, youtube.com/dmoorhouse1973). The Historical Association's website now features 'webtrails', which provide access to collections of articles on particular key concepts (http://www.history.org.uk/resources/secondary_resources_61.html). Some history teachers make more effective use of this digital community of practice in history education than others.

The importance of preparing, refining and adapting web-based resources

Although the internet offers an enormous quantity and range of resources to the history teacher, it is unusual to find resources that are 'shrink-wrapped' for the perfect lesson. Most inspirational teaching requires meticulous and thoughtful preparation, adjustment to the context of the lesson and the learners and careful reading of the instructions relating to how the resource might best be deployed (for a powerful demonstration of this, see the extract from Walter Lewin's lecture at http://www.youtube.com/watch?v=AaALPa7Dwdw&feature=fvw; for a history specific example, see the 'Battalion 101' materials at http://www.keystagehistory.co.uk/free-samples/battalion-101.html). Ian Dawson's site (www.thinkinghistory.co.uk) contains many excellent ideas for classroom activities in history, contributed by some of the most talented history teachers in the UK. But it does take a few minutes to read through the materials in order to develop a clear understanding of what is involved, and how exactly to prepare for and carry out the activity. The internet is a wonderful source of ideas, and it often reduces the time required to put together a lesson 'from scratch', but it does not obviate the need for teacher mediation of the resources.

Hard choices

Table 19. 1 contains a list of some ICT applications or 'agendas' that are of potential relevance to history teachers.

The proliferation of ICT applications which have been developed over the past few years means that there simply aren't enough hours in the day to develop advanced skills in the use of all these applications. There are now dozens of Web 2.0 applications which have the potential to be used in history lessons (for a list, see http://www.uea.ac.uk/~m242/historypgce/ict/welcome.htm). There are hard choices to be made in terms of which ICT agendas will be most helpful in improving pupils' learning. Given the importance of *applying* ICT expertise in teaching, it is probably better to explore some of these agendas in depth, rather than acquiring superficial acquaintance with all of them. The following is a list of tentative suggestions for ICT agendas which I would consider to be of relevance to most history teachers.

Your digital archive and its deployment in your teaching

To what extent do you make good use of ICT to get hold of high-quality 'impact' resources? How good are your 'collections' – of visual images, moving-image extracts, (digitally available) newspaper articles, web interactivities, maps, documents, ideas for lesson activities from history websites? And what proportion of your collections are translated into classroom teaching activities which improve pupils' learning? There is a danger of simply building up a massive pile of digital 'stuff' which does not get 'processed' into high-quality teaching activities.

How good is your use of presentation software (e.g. PowerPoint)?

How to make PowerPoint (or alternatives) less boring is an issue for most history departments given the number of classrooms that are now equipped with data projectors and the fact that PowerPoint is one of the most commonly available forms of presentation software in schools. Some suggestions for effective use of PowerPoint can be accessed at http://www.uea.ac.uk/~m242/historypgce/ict/welcome.htm.

To what extent to you exploit the potential of Web 2.0 applications for improving teaching and learning in history?

In the recent survey of student teachers' use of ICT (OECD, 2010) Web 2.0 applications emerged as one of the facets of ICT that leading-edge practitioners in ICT felt had most potential for improving teaching and learning. Wikis in particular evinced very positive comments (see, for instance, Russel Tarr's use of a wiki at www.history-wiki.wikispaces.com). You should at least explore what might be done with wikis, blogs and podcasts before deciding which ICT agendas to explore and

Table 19.1 History and ICT: what is there to think about?

Twitter	Using history websites	Digital cameras	Image editing packages
Word-processing exercises	Data-handling packages	Using maps and animations	Desktop publishing
Presentation software	Mind-mapping software	Storyboarding software	Website design
History forums	Scanners	Digital video editing	Camcorders
Interactive whiteboards	Data projectors	Wikis	Blogs
Podcasts	Other Web 2.0 applications	Flash animation	Audacity
Digital sound recorders	Hot potatoes and similar (quiz design)	RSS feeds	Classroom response systems

develop. In addition to wikis, blogs and podcasts, there is now a wide range of other Web 2.0 applications which have the potential to provide different learning experiences for pupils in history (see http://www.uea.ac.uk/~m242/historypgce/ict/welcome.htm for a list of some of these applications and a short description of what they can do).

How good is your use of digital video editing in your teaching?

Digital video editing emerged as another application which many leading-edge users of ICT mentioned as having considerable potential for enhancing pupils' experience of school history, whether it was the teacher using it to make arresting 'hooks' for lessons or pupils using digital video editing to make short documentaries or film trailers. The development of user-friendly packages such as Windows Movie Maker has reduced the amount of taught time which needs to be devoted to acquiring the skills to edit digital video. For some examples of what can be done with digital video editing, see Richard Jones' former departmental website at www.internationalschool-toulouse.net/, and the documentary made by his pupils at the International School, Bratislava, at www.internationalschoolhistory.net/BHP/index.htm.

How helpful is your use of the VLEs which you have access to?

Most schools and educational institutions now have a VLE. Some of them are not fully developed, others are rich in information about courses, syllabuses, resources, etc., but are largely in the form of what has been termed 'shovelware' (ways of shovelling information round the system). In an analysis of 'traffic' on VLEs and other communications platforms, it was found that only 16 per cent of all exchanges could be said to be 'learning dialogue' which offered the opportunity to change respondents' minds or reconsider their opinions and positions; 84 per cent of content was factual information, statements of opinion or emotion which actually closed down learning exchanges and possibilities, or were 'cut-and-paste' exercises without real engagement with learning possibilities (McFarlane, 2009). But there were some instances of 'learning dialogue' which offered the opportunity to change respondents' minds or reconsider their opinions and positions. Given the potential of VLEs to get pupils learning outside of taught sessions, it is worth thinking about the extent to which you are making good use of the potential of VLEs, and the extent to which learners contribute to the VLE to argue, discuss and debate history.

The use of ICT to develop pupils' information literacy

As Reuben Moore (2000) and Ben Walsh (2008) have argued, helping young people to make mature use of the internet and developing their ability to handle information intelligently should be an essential part of a historical education for children growing up in the twenty-first century. Building up an 'archive' of internet sources which raise issues of reliability can be particularly helpful in this respect. Walsh's article provides a number of sources which are useful for helping teachers to develop pupils' skills of information literacy, and it can be helpful to build up your own archive of resources which address the issue of reliability of information.

The use of data-handling activities

Data-handling activities can be invaluable for giving pupils an understanding of the ways in which historians use data and can help to develop genuine skills of historical understanding and insights into particular facets of the past. It is one of the areas where ICT unquestionably makes it easier to explore and interrogate large datasets. An excellent introduction to the use of data-handling activities in history can be found in Walsh (2005). The chapter includes details of usable datasets which are available on the internet. Another good example of online datasets which can be used to explore historical hypotheses can be found on the Historical Association's website (http://www.history.org.uk/resources/secondary_resource_1572,1590_11.html).

What to do with interactive whiteboards?

Some history teachers think interactive whiteboards (IWBs) are a wonderful asset; others think that they are expensive and not particularly valuable. The answer to this conundrum is to have an open mind and find out for yourself through dialogue, research and experimentation. As in other facets of ICT, decisions about what facets of ICT to invest time in can also be influenced by context – for instance, access to IWBs and working with colleagues who are accomplished in the use of IWBs (a range of resources and ideas about using interactive whiteboards in history can be accessed at http://www.uea.ac.uk/~m242/historypgce/ict/welcome.htm).

Using the internet to support historical enquiry

It is widely acknowledged that just telling pupils to find something out on the internet is not a good use of precious curriculum time. However, in the longer term we do want pupils to be able to use the internet intelligently and autonomously. History departments need to have a 'long-term plan' to work towards pupils' being able to conduct their own enquiries on the internet. Over the course of their school careers, pupils should move from working with fairly tightly designed 'webquests', structured by the teacher, to enquiry questions which allow for more learner thought and choice over pathways through the enquiry (see Dan Lyndon's webquests at www.webquests.comptonhistory.com, and guidance on web debates at http://www.history.org.uk/resources/secondary_resource_1572,1794_11.html).

Of course, these points do not constitute a comprehensive agenda for the exploration of ICT; they are just examples of the sort of areas which history teachers should consider, along with thinking about whether it is worth developing your own website, how much time and effort to invest in using an interactive whiteboard and so on. The ability to use ICT is of course no longer an optional competence for teachers. Four of the 33 standards required to obtain Qualified Teacher Status (QTS) in England relate to ICT (TDA, 2007). However, the question, 'To what extent am I making the most of the potential of new technology to improve my teaching?' is one that I think anyone involved in history education should ask themselves.

Chapter summary

There is much to be said for getting pupils to engage in data-handling activities, providing opportunities for them to express their views and ideas digitally, and using ICT to support 'dialogic learning' in the form of discussion, argument, debate and the possibility of changing and developing pupils' thinking about aspects of the past. However, I still believe that the biggest single advantage that ICT offers for enhancing teaching and learning in history is the opportunity it affords for getting hold of powerful resources for teaching and learning in history; to use Ben Walsh's phrase, 'building learning packages' (Walsh, 2003). The internet has massively increased the resources available to history teachers, but one of the big variables relating to history teachers' use of ICT remains the extent to which they take advantage of digitally available materials to build up powerful archives of resources, and the extent to which they possess the energy, imagination and intelligence to process and adapt these resources into high-quality learning experiences for their pupils.

There is usually no substitute for investing time and thought in ICT agendas. Learning out how to use applications and web resources is often less influential and time-consuming than working out what you can do with the applications and resources to improve your teaching once you have figured out how to access them and use them.

There are different strands involved in becoming 'good at ICT' as a history teacher and different ways of using ICT in an accomplished way. Some history teachers become technically expert in using quite complex and sophisticated ICT applications, such as web design, Flash animation and other web interactivities. Others concentrate on less complex applications and use their initiative and judgement to collect 'gems' from the resources available on the internet. I believe that any intelligent and diligent history teacher can become 'good at ICT'.

Further reading

- The e-help website (http://e-help.eu) has seminars conducted by many of the leading-edge practitioners in history and ICT. The text versions of the seminars are a quicker way of finding out about these facets of ICT use as not all the video files have been edited.
- There are many excellent websites for history teachers. A list of some of them can be accessed at http://www.uea.ac.uk/~m242/historypgce/ict/welcome. htm, but it can sometimes pay to systematically and extensively explore one good website to get ideas about the wide range of ways that ICT can be deployed to teach history. The National Archives Education site (www.nationalarchives.gov. uk/education) is particularly good in terms of instructional design and breadth of coverage. Ian Dawson's site (www.thinkinghistory.co.uk) is also an excellent site for accessing the ideas and resources of many expert history teachers.
- The Historical Association's website (www.history.org.uk) has improved enormously in recent years. As well as providing access to past issues of *Teaching History*, there are sections on e-cpd for history teachers (full access only to members of the Historical Association).
- Ben Walsh's book *Exciting ICT in History*, (2005, Network Educational Press) remains a useful introduction to the range of ways in which ICT can be used

by history teachers, but it understandably does not include the most recent developments relating to Web 2.0.

- If you want help on the technical aspects of using ICT, Johannes Ahrenfelt and Neal Watkin's book *Innovate with ICT* (2008, London: Continuum) offers valuable advice in how to get going and make more effective use of a wide range of ICT applications.
- Because it is difficult to comprehensively explore all aspects of the use of ICT in history teaching within one chapter, I have put further information on my course website at http://www.uea.ac.uk/~m242/historypgce/ict/welcome.htm.

Note

1 In England, the terms 'initial teacher education' and 'initial teacher training' in practice mean the same thing. Higher education institutions tend to prefer the term 'initial teacher education' and politicians and some policymakers tend to use 'initial teacher training'. While there might be some important philosophical issues around this distinction (most parents in England are fairly comfortable about the idea of 'sex education', but might be less sanguine about 'sex training'), to all intents and purposes, the two terms mean the same thing in terms of the English system of teacher education. However, in relation to the issue of teachers learning to use ICT, the distinction between education and training is perhaps not just a philosophical or semantic one. There is a case for arguing that effective preparation of teachers to use ICT requires elements of both training and education. Training generally implies the teaching of protocols, and instructing learners that there is a correct or effective way to do something. Being able to use ICT effectively in teaching generally requires 'a sense of audience', imagination, creativity and judgement, in addition to the ability to 'work the technology'.

References

Barton, R. and Haydn, T. (2007) 'Common needs and different agandas: how trainee teachers make progress in their ability to use ICT in subject teaching', *Computers and Education*, 49: 1018–36.

BECTa (2008) *Web 2.0 Technologies for Learning at KS3 and KS4 – Project)Overview*. Available online at: http://partners.becta.org.uk/index.php?section=rh&catcode=_re_rp_02&rid=14543 (accessed 3 December 2009).

Dickinson, A. (1998) 'History using IT: past, present and future', *Teaching History*, 93: 16–20.

e-help (2009) European history e-learning project. Available online at: http://www.e-help.eu/ (accessed 3 December 2009).

Hadfield, M., Jopling, M., Royle, K. and Southern, L. (2009) *Evaluation of the Training and Development Agency for Schools for Schools' funding for ICT in ITT projects*. London: TDA.

Harrison, S. (2003) 'The use of ICT for history teaching: slow growth, a few green shoots. Findings of HMI inspection 1999–2001', in T. Haydn and C. Counsell (eds) *History, ICT and Learning in the Secondary School*. London: RoutledgeFalmer, pp. 38–51.

Haydn, T. (2005) *History, ICT and Impact Learning*. Online. Available online at: http://www.uea.ac.uk/~m242/historypgce/ict/impact_learning.htm (accessed 3 December 2009).

——(2010) In Press. 'What does it mean "to be good at ICT" at school and university?', in G. Baker and A. Fisher (eds) *The Meeting of Minds: Mapping the Pedagogical Interface between Arts Academics and Schools*. London: Continuum.

JISC (2008) *Great Expectations of ICT: Findings from the Second Phase of the Report*, London: JISC. Online. Available online at: http://www.jisc.ac.uk/publications/documents/great expectations.aspx (accessed 22 September 2009).

Laurillard, D. (1998) 'Multimedia and the learner's experience of narrative', *Computers and Education*, 31: 229–42.

Lodge, J. and Hodge, V. (2008) 'Presentation and pedagogy', paper presented at the 4th ESCalate ITE Conference, University of Cumbria, Carlisle, 16 May.

McFarlane, A. (2009) 'Thinking with content', paper presented at the CAL 09 Conference, Brighton, 24 March.

Moore, R. (2000) 'Using the internet to teach about interpretations in Years 9 and 12', *Teaching History*, 101: 35–9.

Ofsted. (2009) *The Importance of ICT*. London: Ofsted.

OECD. (2009) ICT in initial teacher education project. Available online at: http://www. oecd.org/document/13/0,3343,en_2649_35845581_41676365_1_1_1_1,00.html (accessed 3 December 2009).

——(2010) *Case Studies of the Ways in Which Training Providers in England Prepare Student Teachers to use ICT in Their Teaching*, Paris: OECD. Available online at: http://www.uea.ac.uk/~m242/historypgce/ict/welcome.htm (accessed 3 December 2009).

QCA. (2005) *Pupil Perceptions of History at Key Stage 3*. London: QCA.

TDA. (2007) *Professional Standards for Qualified Teacher Status*, London: TDA.

Tufte, E. (2006) *The Cognitive Style of PowerPoint: Pitching Out Corrupts Within*. Connecticut: Graphics Press.

Walsh, B. (1998) 'Why Gerry likes history now: the power of the word processor', *Teaching History*, 93: 6–15.

——(2003) 'Building learning packages: integrating virtual resources with the real world of teaching and learning', in T. Haydn and C. Counsell (eds) *History, ICT and Learning in the Secondary School*. London: Routledge, pp. 109–33.

——(2005) *Exciting ICT in History*. Stafford: Network Educational Press.

——(2006) *Beyond Multiple Choice*. Available online at: http://e-help.eu/seminars/ walsh2.htm (accessed 3 December 2009).

——(2008) 'Stories and their sources', *Teaching History*, 133: 4–9.

Chapter 20

Educational visits

Helen Snelson

Introduction

Key content:

- Why educational visits are a vital part of education.
- How historical visits help students make progress with the key concepts and processes of history.
- Making visits an integral part of the history programme of study.
- Guidance on the planning of safe and successful visits.

Why educational visits are a vital part of historical education

Somehow it is accepted wisdom in schools that fieldwork is vital to progression in geography, but the same consensus does not exist for progression in history. History teachers can find themselves having to justify the need for an educational visit both to sceptical members of leadership teams and to colleagues reluctant to release students from their lessons. Therefore, any chapter on educational visits for the use of history teachers needs to start with a rehearsal of the arguments as to why educational visits are a vital and integral part of historical education and not just a bolted-on extra; nice but not essential.

It may be necessary to start with a justification for educational visits per se. Recently, there have been several ministerial statements making it clear that current education policy regards educational visits as beneficial to learning and as an essential part of the curriculum. For example, speaking at the awarding of the Council for Learning outside the Classroom's first Quality Badges for educational providers, the Children's Secretary said he wanted to see as many children as possible taking part in learning outside the classroom as part of their school lives (DCSF, 2009). That said, the initiative 'Rarely Cover', designed to reduce teacher cover of other's lessons as part of the teachers' workload agreements, resulted in many secondary schools reducing educational visits as far as possible in September 2009. It is to be hoped that this will be a temporary solution as other procedures are developed, but it is certain that staff will have to justify taking students out of school very clearly and persuasively.

So, why are educational visits so beneficial? If this chapter had been written five years ago it would no doubt have talked in some depth about theories of learning styles and how visits could meet these needs. In vogue in the British education system, such theories espouse the view that children have different preferred methods of learning and that effective teaching should recognize and seek to reach these different styles (DCSF, 2008). However, in recent years these theories, and the models developed from them, have been called into question (Revell, 2005). Nevertheless, while education and psychological research may not currently provide a robust defence, the professional judgement of experienced teachers tells them that the variety of stimuli made possible by an educational visit does add value to learning.

For example, educational visits can contribute to the development of the personal, learning and thinking skills (PLTS) required for success in learning in ways not easily replicated in the classroom. These PLTS are identified as independent enquiry, creative thinking, reflective learning, team-working, self-management and effective participation (QCA, 2008b). Well-planned educational visits can require students to do the following:

- Plan and carry out investigations to reach substantiated conclusions. For example, the teacher may structure a visit around a historical enquiry such as: 'What evidence can we find at York Minster about the religious beliefs of medieval people in England?' This would require students to study the structure, history and contents of the cathedral as a historical site in order to make inferences about the past using the evidence before them. It may also include input from experts on site.
- Respond to their surroundings by questioning, forming hypotheses, making connections and finding solutions. For example, during a visit to the Cabinet War Rooms and Churchill Museum, students could be challenged to put together their own interpretations of Churchill by selecting from the diverse evidence presented. Students would be required to think about what the evidence was revealing to them and build up a persuasive, well-substantiated narrative.
- Assess their own work, receive feedback, evaluate experiences and communicate their learning. For example, students returning from a visit to the D-Day beaches could be challenged to present the visit and their learning to other students. This process would require them to select the salient points of their learning and decide what was of most relevance to their peers.
- Work collaboratively, supporting others and taking responsibility, while behaving appropriately in unfamiliar environments. This is a skill area which visits can develop more quickly and effectively than the classroom environment. The visit selected depends on the needs of the students. For example, some students will find the experience of being away from the classroom for a short time a challenge. Others may be stretched to work at the edge of their comfort zone by more extensive travel. In all cases prolonged time away from the familiar environment brings to the surface teamwork challenges for students which, if well managed by staff, are great opportunities for personal growth.
- Organize their time, take the initiative, respond flexibly to changing circumstances and manage risk. Educational visits require students to look after their own equipment, be punctual at meeting points, make judgements which concern

their own safety – for example, in crossing roads. As with the teamwork point, above, development of self-management is accelerated by prolonged time away from the familiar classroom environment.

- Discuss, persuade, advocate and negotiate. For example, students can be required to put together a marketing strategy for an English Heritage site and put their case to an on-site expert for funding for their project. Being at a site increases the resources available for student use and provides a 'real-life' feel for the task.

Of course, other subjects can also argue that their educational visits provide opportunities to gain the personal, learning and thinking skills, so why should the history department be given permission to take students out of school? Helpfully, the Key Stage 3 Programme of Study for History in the National Curriculum for England, which came into force in the maintained sector in September 2008, states that students should have the opportunity to: 'Appreciate and evaluate, through visits where possible, the role of museums, galleries, archives and historic sites in preserving, presenting and influencing people's attitudes towards the past' (QCA, 2008a). It is, therefore, expected by Ofsted (Office for Standards in Education) that schools will be making every effort possible to enable students to make educational visits connected to their study of history.

Such visits bring the subject to life and enhance progression in the key concepts and processes. As a result they also increase uptake at GCSE (General Certificate of Secondary Education). (The latter is not perhaps part of the argument put forward to justify taking a visit, but it is a reason to have the argument!) Table 20.1 gives specific examples of how visits can aid progression in the key concepts and processes in ways which are not easily replicated in the classroom.

Although the National Curriculum has divided the study of history into key concepts and processes, all history teachers are aware that disaggregation of the discipline can be carried too far. History is greater than the sum of its parts and educational visits provide excellent opportunities to enable students to see how the component parts of the discipline fit together. Table 20.1 gave examples of how visits can enable progression in each of the key concepts and processes, but a well-planned visit, while clearly focused, should not be too tightly prescriptive in its aims and timetable so that unexpected and unplanned learning is squeezed out. Once students are outside the classroom their responses are much harder to predict. Much of the learning which takes place on school visits is unquantifiable and unknown; we should celebrate this and be flexible enough to accommodate it. Visits are a holistic experience, giving students the opportunity to enjoy the discipline of history and 'join the dots' of its component parts.

This assertion is borne out by speaking to A-level history students who have experienced several years of educational visits. Such groups always make similar comments when asked about their perceptions of the benefits of visits to their historical learning. For example, classroom learning is made more interesting, makes sense and is easier to remember; it's easier to understand change and continuity; it's easier to understand what sources are and how interpretations are formed. Their overall sense is that educational visits have added breadth as well as depth to their historical learning.

The National Curriculum 2008 also requires cross-curricular working and sets out several cross-curriculum dimensions, the first of which is identity and cultural

Table 20.1 Specific examples of how visits can aid progression in the key concepts and processes

Key concepts	
Chronological understanding	Art galleries are excellent places to develop chronological understanding beyond the basic counting of time. Teaching students to orientate themselves in the history of Western art brings a potentially dull concept to life and gives a framework for understanding turning points, trends and terms (such as Renaissance and Modern) which is remarkably accessible and to which other historical learning can refer.
Cultural, ethnic and religious diversity	The artefacts and objects in museums can make very clear the diversity of experience of a single time or place. For example, by careful selection of artefacts to focus upon as evidence, the Docklands Museum of London engages students with the incredible diversity of London's population and its trading links across the ages.
Change and continuity	A visit to a local town centre, cathedral or other significant building enables a study of change and continuity of use, which includes the visual impact on the environment and a chronological context. Students can make connections between past and present more easily.
Cause and consequence	Battlefields offer a chance to explore cause and consequence within a clear framework and to demonstrate the linking of factors which is often problematic for lower-achieving students.
Significance	Military and civilian cemeteries are excellent places to explore the concept of significance. Pupils can engage more easily with the complex issues concerned, such as resonance with the present and the nature of remembrance and its purpose.
Interpretations	Museums such as Imperial War Museum North wear their interpretations on their sleeve. This transparency is particularly helpful to enable pupils to understand the impact of, for example, selection, ideology and the present on historical interpretation.
Key processes	
Historical enquiry	A visit to a historical site set in the context of an enquiry can allow students to develop the enquiry in ways which particularly interest them. For example, a visit to a castle as part of an enquiry into the role of castles in the Middle Ages allows scope for students to pursue a specific, independent interest, for example, in building techniques or living conditions.
Using evidence	A visit to a local archaeological site to ask the experts can be followed by the use of archives, photographic evidence and census material to enable students to be more independent in their enquiries and use a wider variety of evidence.

(continued)

Key processes (cont.)

Communicating about the past	Visits give so many opportunities for purposeful communication of historical learning. For example, students can make digitally produced tours of a local area with commentary to inform tourists about a theme from local history.

diversity (QCA, 2008c). Educational visits provide an outstanding opportunity for cross-curricular work while maintaining the integrity of each academic discipline. For example, a cooperation between RS and History resulted in a day at the Wilberforce House Museum in Hull. Students spent the morning using the museum's collection to put together a debate on the abolition of the transatlantic slave trade. In the afternoon they continued to use the collection to design a campaign for a charity working to raise awareness of people-trafficking in the UK today. The complementarity of both content and skills was very explicit and the study of both subjects was enhanced.

Finally, it is always a good idea to offer sceptical colleagues the chance to be staff members on visits. Colleagues are frequently surprised by the amount of work involved, the quality of learning that takes place, the impact on themselves and, above all, the responses of students. Experienced teachers are full of examples such as hearing a lower-ability student in Tyne Cot Cemetery, Belgium, announce: 'I understood before, but not like this.'

Educational visits as an integral part of the history curriculum

A wide range of historical visits are undertaken each year. Figure 20.1 lists some of the types of visit that take place. The needs of particular groups of students should be the key determinant in choosing a type of visit.

Very rarely do effective educational visits stand alone; they are usually clearly bedded into the history curriculum and their outcomes explicitly assessed. Sometimes this may be very straightforward – for example, attending a local evening lecture on an A-level topic – the information from which is then used in written responses. However, visits are usually part of a skilled curriculum planning process. Two case studies can illustrate this point.

Coursework projects	Local history
National collections	Special exhibitions
International travel	Cross-curricular
Competition prizes	University-linked
Lectures	Debates
Cultural centres	

Figure 20.1 Examples of types of historical visit.

Case Study 1: a Year 8 local history visit to an archaeological dig

The overarching enquiry was 'What was it like to live in York in the early twentieth century?' The key concepts and processes focus was the use of historical evidence to understand diversity of experience. The archaeological site was yielding evidence of life in what had been one of the materially impoverished areas of the city and was used for this section of the work. Prior to the visit, students examined the photographic evidence available from the local archives and read extracts from Rowntree's sociological survey *Poverty: A Study in Town Life* (Rowntree, 2000). This gave them a general introduction to the lives and living conditions of poorer citizens at the turn of the last century. The visit was conducted by an archaeological education officer, with whom the staff had worked prior to the visit. She used the photographs from the preparative lesson and showed the students the parts of the site shown in this evidence. She then allowed the students to handle a selection of artefacts dug up at the site and questioned them about what they could learn about people's lives from these. During the visit the students also became acquainted with the street names of the area. The following week in class, extracts of the census were used to find out who lived in the houses previously seen in the photographs and at the site. Following further work to build up a picture of life for more affluent citizens, students were able to understand why evidence for their lives survives to a greater extent than that of less wealthy citizens. Students went on to produce a museum display case titled 'Life in York in Edwardian times' and were assessed on their understanding of diversity and use of a range of historical evidence to illustrate their claims.

Case Study 2: an A-level study visit to Berlin

This example was planned with the German Department in a school and also gave opportunities for students to experience the culture of the German capital. The planned historical learning was to enhance the students' understanding of the A-level unit 'From Defeat to Unity: Germany 1945–1991'. A walking tour of the centre of Berlin was scheduled for the first day, to encourage students to engage with sites as evidence and to consider interpretations, as well as to familiarize them with key locations and their role in key events. For example, the site of the Neue Wache was used alongside photographs of it since the time of the Kaisers and an article about its effectiveness as a memorial. Students could see for themselves the different incarnations of the building and experience the contemporary memorial, while starting to engage with the debates relating to significance, diversity and interpretation which are involved in decisions about commemoration. Careful attention was paid to the balance and ordering of visits to sites. It would be very easy to encourage students to develop a distorted understanding of life in the former German Democratic Republic (GDR) by visiting only the former Stasi HQ and Hohenschönhausen Prison. Consequently, a visit to the GDR Museum took place before these visits. It is full of artefacts and objects providing an overview of everyday life in the former GDR, thus providing a context and a contrast to the specific focus upon the oppression of the Stasi. The option of a guided tour at Hohenschönhausen was taken up after a pre-visit revealed that the tours given were both very informative and also transparent about the nature and extent of evidence available to construct the narrative being used. In the later stages of the visit, pupils used recording equipment to hold 'voxpop' interviews with members of the public in Alexanderplatz. Their brief was to ask people for their memories of the two Germanies before the opening of the Berlin Wall and their opinions about the impact of the fall of the Wall on Germany. Adopting an approach which constantly flagged up the interpretative nature of the sites and memories as historical evidence fed into discussions both in Berlin and back in the classroom. Students were explicitly encouraged to introduce the issues raised into their written work.

Ideally, visits should be timed to best enhance learning, but the timing of visits is not always under the control of the visit leader. The A-level study visit to Berlin described in Case Study 2 had to take place in holiday time halfway through the course of study. In many schools, activity weeks are set aside for the purpose of educational visits. While these serve to minimize the disruptive impact of visits on other lessons, they can also limit learning. For example, an activity week at the end of the summer term precludes effective follow-up work in class. If ideal timing is not possible, then planning must take place to structure lessons and the visit itself, in order to maximize the learning opportunities in the time available.

While it is sometimes possible to require and enable all students to take part in an educational visit, it is frequently the case that educational visits are optional; not least because they can involve financial cost. The ethical issues involved are not within the remit of this chapter and are usually the subject of whole-school policies. However, there are ways in which the learning of all can be enhanced by a visit undertaken by a group of students. One successful model is to require students on a visit to prepare a study session for students who have not been on the visit. This requires students to question, analyse and evaluate their experiences, in order to present them clearly to their peers. This model is enhanced by the use of ICT (information and communications technology). Students can record experiences for feedback in class using visuals and sound and engage in dialogue with students back in school while they are away. Simple blogging sites allow question and answer sessions to be set up as a visit is in progress. Of course this can be extended to family members with ease. The result is a greater degree of reflection by all concerned and the greater integration of the visit into the history curriculum.

Guidance on the planning of safe and successful educational visits

A common news item: 'A culture of fear has grown up around trips, with anxious schools avoiding taking children out of the classroom because of the perceived possibility of legal action if something goes wrong' (*The Guardian*, 2009). It is the case that processes and procedures are much stricter than they were 20 years ago. It is also the case that serious accidents on school visits remain very rare. Teachers can draw on a lot of support and expertise to help them plan safe and successful educational visits.

Planning visits

Successful visits require clear educational outcomes. The purpose and outcome of the visit must be clearly thought through. This sounds obvious, but it is the section that can easily get less attention compared with the safety planning and organizational detail. Prioritize it, make time for it and think about:

- Which year group does a visit best suit and what timing would fit the programme of study?
- What is the concept and process focus to be?
- How is the visit to be embedded into the students' curriculum?
- How can robust cross-curricular links be drawn out?
- What prior learning is required?
- What differentiation issues need to be considered?
- How will activities undertaken progress students' learning towards the outcomes?
- What resourcing and organization is required to ensure successful outcomes?
- How will outcomes be assessed?
- How can the visit help progress the learning of students not able to go on the visit?

It is important to use imagination and have a clear focus upon students' needs. Many destinations offer 'off-the-shelf' packages, some of which are very good. However, teachers should assert the needs of students, being clear and demanding with requirements. Museum staff are delighted to work with teachers with a vision of how the visit will progress their students' learning. Providing an Educational Visits Coordinator (EVC) approves, there is no reason why an overseas visit cannot be organized 'in-house'. This approach improves flexibility in planning and delivery, reduces the cost considerably and does not always involve more work.

However, the practical organization involved in making visits possible is demanding, involving organization of pupils, parents, colleagues, travel firms, transport, venues and oneself. Good judgement of one's own experience and capabilities is vital. As a useful rule of thumb, no one should lead an educational visit without having been a supporting member of staff on an equivalent visit.

Also vital is the ability to seek and take advice. Every school has an EVC and before you undertake any organization, you must speak to her/him. S/he is the expert on all the processes required to make sure that visits take place safely, with

---

Visit planning checklist

Outline proposal to formal approval
- Collect Visits/Activities Off-site document from Educational Visits Coordinator (EVC).
- Read Notes and Guidance in the document, the Local Authority (LA) Code of Practice, Guidelines for Educational Off-site visits and Activities and check www.visits.n-yorks.net/training.htm.
- Complete 'Outline proposals' section.
- Ensure provider has completed an LA 'Form for Completion by Tour Operators and Providers'.
- Receive EVC approval in principle.
- Complete 'Cover requirements' and submit form to cover administrator.

- Receive cover approval.
- Complete 'Accounting and insurance' and discuss any financial assistance for students with the bursar.
- Receive confirmation accounting and insurance requirements met.
- Read and complete 'Risk assessment', consulting EVC for information and advice as required.
- Complete 'Other requirements for residential/overseas visits' (if applicable).
- Return document to EVC for approvals to be arranged, no later than the date agreed in Section I.
- EVC returns document. Check relevant approvals are complete and all signed.

Pre-visit planning, organization and administration
- Target students.
- Contact parents/guardians about acceptance/non-acceptance.
- Obtain fully informed written parental consent.
- Collect deposit/payment (as applicable).
- Book transport/accommodation/activities (as applicable).
- Full details of visit/activity published and students briefed on expectations/requirements.
- Parents meeting at least 4 weeks before departure (residential trips only).
- Obtain student contact/medical/dietary information, attach copies.
- Obtain staff contact/medical/dietary information, attach copies.
- Collect passport copies for overseas visits and attach copies.
- Inform staff of any disruption to lessons via the staff bulletin.
- Put a list of students involved on the noticeboard in the staff room.
- Contact Canteen if taking more than 20 students off-site.
- Brief staff on visit and ensure they have all paperwork, including contact/medical/dietary copies and laminated card with contact numbers.
- Complete 'Checklist'.
- Sign the document and get head teacher signature.
- Copies of completed document and attachments to Senior Management Team (SMT) on duty, EVC and reception. Original document and attachments taken on visit/activity.

During and after the visit
- Ongoing risk assessment/contingency management.
- Log any incident/accidents and inform SMT contact if necessary.
- Report to SMT on arrival at activity destination (overseas visits).
- Report to SMT on duty on return to school.
- Complete evaluation form and send to EVC with original documentation and any completed accident/incident forms.

Figure 20.2 Example of visit planning checklist.

managed risk and without causing organizational problems. The EVC will explain what steps you need to take to fulfil the school's requirements and be there to advise you at any stage. To give a sense of the range of organizational measures required, Figure 20.2 is an example of a checklist from a school's visit planning document.

Most local authorities now also produce websites dedicated to support and advice for teachers organizing visits.

Risk assessment and management

Risk assessment and management are at the heart of the organization of safe educational visits. Bad press includes: 'Teachers also claim that the amount of time taken up dealing with health and safety concerns is a deterrent' (*The Guardian*, 2009). However, teachers are very good at taking care of students; they should always be assessing and managing risk and have good support networks in place to support them, as outlined above. A safe visit requires the following essential ingredients:

- competent leadership and management
- plenty of staff
- staff who can work together as a team.

An A-level residential visit to Paris by train and metro
A. Group Management
Risk 1) Students getting separated from the group/lost while moving
(Risk level – high)
Management of risk:
- Students and parents briefed on responsibility and listening at pre-visit meeting
- Students reminded on visit about meeting points, listening, metro station procedure, road safety, phones on, etc.
- Students briefed at each meeting and travelling point about destinations and meeting points
- Counting groups system in place
- Each group member has a list of others' mobile numbers, including staff
- Students briefed to stay in groups of minimum of four when not with staff
- Students given emergency numbers and told to carry at all times
- Students and staff get enough breaks/sleep to avoid overtiredness.
(Risk level – low)

Year 9 day visit to Holocaust Memorial Centre by coach
A. Group Management
Risk 1) Students getting separated from the group/lost while moving
(Risk level – medium)
Management of risk:
- Letter to parents asks them to reinforce message given to students before the visit at the student meeting about listening carefully to instructions
- Students asked before they get off the coach at the service station to check their watches, stay in groups of minimum of four and to repeat back the return time to the coach that is given out
- Staff count students back onto the coach.
(Risk level – low)

Figure 20.3 Extracts from risk assessments.

Recommended staff–pupil ratios are available from EVCs, but there are other considerations. For example, if a particular pupil has special needs which will require staff attention, or if the visit is to take place over several days staff will need to take breaks, or if the visit involves the use of public transport higher levels of supervision are required. Taking as many staff as possible is always recommended.

A school visit is not the place for staff to get to know each other. The leader must ensure that all staff can work together well and know and are happy with their roles. When an emergency happens, there is no time to sort out staff competence and ability to work together.

The EVC is the point of contact for specific risk assessment processes and procedures, including incident and accident reporting, but general principles apply. First, the process of risk assessment is more important than the finished document. It is not acceptable to download generic risk assessments from providers. Managing risk is an active process which starts with good planning, and must be communicated to staff, parents and pupils. Second, inexperienced staff can make the mistake of viewing risk from the perspective of the site rather than from that of the students. The same riverbank holds different risks for a group of Year 7 students than it does for a group of A-level historians with Duke of Edinburgh awards. Finally, educating students to manage their own risk is essential if they are to learn to keep themselves safe. There is no such thing as 'no risk'; it has to be managed. Failing to make a professional judgement about the amount of risk your students can safely manage leads them to miss out on opportunities to grow in independence. Figure 20.3 gives examples of short extracts of risk assessments which clearly show the student-centred approach.

Chapter summary

- Educational visits are a 'Good Thing'!
- They enhance learning and thinking skills and deepen and broaden historical understanding.
- Visits are an essential part of the curriculum and not an optional, they should be firmly embedded in the history curriculum.
- Visits must have clear aims and be carefully planned, staffed and managed in conjunction with EVCs and other participants.
- Students enjoy visits – they fire the imagination and promote independence.

Further reading

Council for Learning Outside the Classroom at www.lotc.org.uk
www.teachernet.gov.uk/visits
www.educationalvisitsuk.com/index.htm
TDA (2008) www.ttrb.ac.uk/ViewArticle2.aspx?ContentId=15851 (accessed 17 October 2009). For an introduction to some of the theories on learning see article on gifted and talented education at the teacher training resource bank.
Teaching History 126, March 2007, focuses upon educational visits

References

DCSF (2009) www.dcsf.gov.uk (accessed 17 October 2009).

TDA (2008) www.ttrb.ac.uk/ViewArticle2.aspx?ContentId=15851 (accessed 17 October 2009).

Guardian, The (2009) 'Teachers put off school trips by litigation fear', Saturday 3 October 2009.

QCA (2008a) http://curriculum.qcda.gov.uk/key-stages-3-and-4/subjects/key-stage-3/history/programme-of-study/index.aspx (accessed 12 November 2010).

——(2008b) http://curriculum.qcda.gov.uk/key-stages-3-and-4/subjects/key-stage-3/history/plts-in-history/index.aspx (accessed 12 November 2010).

——(2008c)   http://curriculum.qcda.gov.uk/key-stages-3-and-4/cross-curriculum-dimensions/index.aspx (accessed 12 November 2010).

Revell, P. (2005) 'Each to their own', *The Guardian*. Available online at: www.guardian.co.uk/education/2005/may/31/schools.uk3 (accessed 17 October 2009).

Rowntree, B. S. (2000) *Poverty: A Study of Town Life*, Centennial edition, Bristol: The Policy Press.

Chapter 21

Assessment

Joanne Philpott

> Assessment in education must, first and foremost, serve the purpose of support-
> ing learning.
>
> —Paul Black and Dylan Wiliam, *Inside the Black Box*

Introduction

This chapter will consider the purposes of assessment and its many facets in a history classroom. It will focus on the competing purposes of assessment and what this can mean to each of the groups involved and consider the differing approaches to assessment of historical learning. The chapter will address how a teacher can maximize the information provided from assessing pupil learning and reflect on how to feed forward information to the pupil in order to ensure assessment has a significant impact on pupil progression. The roles of day-to-day, periodic and summative assessment are explored in depth and the role of feedback and intervention are considered in relation to using assessment for learning with reference to school-based experiences.

The purpose and nature of assessment in the history classroom

Assessment is a fundamental aspect of history education. It is an opportunity for the teacher to determine and reflect on pupil learning and progress. Assessment allows the teacher and pupil to consider progress to date and the steps a pupil needs to take in order to get better at history. The teacher can make use of this information to inform their planning and personalize the curriculum to the needs of each pupil. Assessment should be regular, encompass a variety of learning styles and provide prompt and accessible feedback for the pupil to make use of. History educators have strived to remain at the forefront of development in assessment, especially in times of curriculum change such as in the 1990s with the publication of the original version of the National Curriculum and more recently in 2008 with the revised National Curriculum.

Assessment in education refers to the evaluation of a pupil's achievement on a course over a given period of time. Highlighted by the work of Black and Wiliam (1998) assessment was, in many educational institutions, considered to be a conclud-ing activity to a unit of learning, with the sole purpose of measuring achievement. This approach to assessment is commonly known as summative assessment and is often considered to be a one-way process arguably done *to* pupils rather than *with* them, marked by the teacher using a grade or numeric score. Driven by the work of Black and William and the Assessment Reform Group since 1998, assessment has undergone dramatic change both in its purpose and its methodology in the classroom.

In recent years, teachers have aimed to make assessment more purposeful in its nature through its integration into the series of learning journeys upon which pupils and their teacher embark during their history curriculum. Ian Phillips (2008: 122) defines this style of formative assessment as 'the day-to-day evaluation of student progress, it is a process which is part of teaching and learning, and integral to the lesson.' Assessment therefore needs to have clarity of purpose if it is to be useful to pupils and teachers and the following section of this chapter will consider the different purposes of assessment for history teachers and their pupils.

Who assesses pupil learning?

At Key Stage 3 (KS3) pupil learning is assessed through teacher assessment. Teacher-based judgements are often moderated within departments to ensure consistency across pupils, classes and schools. At Key Stage 4 (KS4) and Key Stage 5 (KS5) external assessors take responsibility for the final summative outcomes of pupil learning through examination and coursework while teachers maintain responsibility for assessing the progress a pupil is making across the course. The pupil is able to assess their peers and their own work when offered the necessary support structures and success criteria. Peer assessment is a staged process which needs to be planned for across the academic year. Once pupils have acquired the necessary skills to undertake peer and self assessment, pupils become better equipped to identify the requirements of different aspects of historical understanding and analysis and are able to progress further.

Why does assessment take place?

There are four key groups involved with assessment and the purpose of assessment is different for each group, though there are some overlapping features. These are listed below and are all vital within the assessment process. It is important to remember that when assessing a pupil's progress a teacher needs to be aware of their different audiences yet purpose must remain intrinsically driven by the desire to help pupils get better at history.

The teacher:

- to monitor progress
- to set work-related and personal targets
- to measure learning and understanding
- to move students forward
- to maximize student potential.

The pupil:

- to evaluate their progress
- to work towards and meet targets

- to maximize their own potential
- to be rewarded for their success
- to move forward in their learning.

The parent:

- to be informed of their child's progress
- to increase home–school communications
- to offer guidance on how to support their child's learning
- as part of whole-school attainment and progress.

The school:

- to inform others of a pupil's progress
- to support intervention where necessary
- to monitor departmental and whole-school targets.

What do history teachers assess?

History teachers assess pupil learning and progress in historical understanding making use of their professional judgement and guidance from statutory requirements. At KS3 this means assessing learning in historical concepts, range and content and the processes by which the understanding of the former have been demonstrated. This is measured through teacher assessment making use of departmental mark schemes and more formally using the National Curriculum Attainment Target and Level Descriptor. Pupils who choose to study history at KS4 usually follow a GCSE (General Certificate of Secondary Education) course will discover that the assessment objectives have become more prescriptive but are fundamentally the same as those at KS3. Defined by Qualifications and Curriculum Development Agency (QCDA, 2002) the assessment criteria are generic and apply equally to every history syllabus. A system of levels translates into a final grade awarded through a combination of controlled assessment and external examination. In GCSE specifications (revised 2009) Assessment Objective 1 requires assessment of pupils to recall, select and communicate their knowledge and understanding of history while Assessment Objective 2 focuses on their ability to demonstrate their understanding of the past through explanation and analysis of concepts and key features of a period. Assessment Objective 3 requires pupils to understand, analyse and evaluate historical sources and interpretations. At A level or level 3 equivalents the assessment objectives remain fundamentally the same but with increased challenge and rigour.

What forms does assessment of historical learning take?

How to create assessment fit for the purposes set out in this section will be explored in more detail in Section 2 of this chapter. In brief, assessment of historical learning can be achieved through a variety of methods and approaches but most importantly should be an integral part of effective teaching and learning and be inextricably linked to the curriculum. Much assessment takes place in day-to-day teaching where learners receive immediate feedback on their understanding of the specific aspect or topic being explored and where teachers adjust their short-term planning in line with learners' needs. At other times, teachers need to stand back and reflect on the learner's overall performance across their historical learning by drawing on a wide range of evidence. Finally, at regular and planned intervals assessment will be used to measure attainment at the end of a unit of learning via internal or external specifically designed assessment tasks.

Creating assessment opportunities in the history classroom

In order to explore the means by which the many purposes of assessment can be achieved it will be useful to determine some degree of classification. Recent development work in assessment by QCDA has attempted to do this by identifying three types of assessment: day-to-day, periodic and transitional. Table 21.1 is adapted from QCDA National Curriculum website (2008), and summarizes the key features of each type of assessment.

This section will consider each type of assessment in turn and consider approaches to teaching and learning to maximize historical learning for pupils.

1 Day-to-day assessment

Day-to-day assessment refers to the evidence gathered by teachers of pupil achievement and progress on a lesson-by-lesson basis as demonstrated through interactions, observations and ongoing assessment. In every lesson a teacher should aim to observe, listen, engage with and respond to pupil learning. Such regular involvement with pupils may not appear to be assessment in a conventional form yet it is from such interaction that teachers construct a professional judgement of a pupil's historical understanding and determine the small steps the pupil needs to take to make progress. In departments where there is an emphasis on summative assessment tasks, the day-to-day class work and homework can reduce in importance and rigour for the teacher and child and progression across a unit can be limited through the devalued status of the work undertaken. By making greater use of day-to-day class work and homework for day-to-day assessment of historical learning, the value and profile of such work increases for both the pupil and the teacher. As a lesson-by-lesson record of pupil

Table 21.1 Key features of assessment types

Day-to-day	Learning outcomes shared with pupils Peer- and self-assessment Immediate feedback and next steps for pupils
Periodic	Broader view of progress for teacher and learner Using national standards in the classroom Improvements to curriculum planning
Transitional	Formal recognition of achievement Reported to parents/carers and next teacher/school May use tests/tasks from national sources

work, the exercise book or folder rises in status by being the primary portfolio of learning. This is not to suggest that every aspect of a pupil's bookwork is levelled or graded; instead, each outcome of pupil learning is commented upon by the teacher through praise and guidance. This enables the teacher to gain a holistic view of the learning of the pupil.

When considering oral and active learning it is neither practical nor beneficial to log the contribution every child makes each lesson. It is the expertise of the teacher in their professional capacity that enables them to be able to build an understanding of a child's strengths, attributes and areas of challenge based on relationships built within the classroom. Yet there are means of recording some of their more pertinent actions or comments and thus recording your assessment of the pupil. Photographing and videoing lesson activities can prompt teacher and pupil memory of the learning that took place during the lesson and a brief note in the mark book or a scribbling on a sticky-note will suffice to remind the teacher of a valuable contribution made by a pupil. This is particularly effective when images of photographs are the lesson plenary, printed for pupil annotation or form part of a class display.

There are attributes which contribute to the value of day-to-day assessment as an effective means of evaluating pupil progress and achievement. First, the lessons have to have value as indicated through clear and mapped lesson objectives and outcomes. In other words the lessons need to centre on a clearly communicated historical learning focus which contributes to a shared learning journey. Second, pupil outcomes benefit from being referenced to shared task criteria; the more comprehensible the task criteria the more straightforward the feedback, target setting and opportunities for peer and self marking. Third, inbuilt opportunities for non-written learning outcomes allow pupils to demonstrate their learning in ways that will at times prove non-threatening and at other times create challenge depending on the pupils' learning preferences. For example, Fullard and Dacey (2008: 25–9) demonstrate the value of oral assessment in their causal reasoning and evidential thinking unit of work on the English Civil War, with the day-to-day learning preparation materials for the final outcome forming part of the evidence for assessment. They allow for a range of learning styles and place importance on learning made along the journey to the final outcome.

The strength of many day-to-day learning outcomes is that they cannot be measured numerically and can only be judged by how far they contribute to pupils' ability to conceptualize or make use of historical processes. In this regard day-to-day learning outcomes are part of the necessary formative building blocks to move learning forward. Thus day-to-day pupil work is worthy of teacher comment and guidance and rarely of grades and marks, if pupils are to meet some of the desired purposes of assessment as outlined in Section 1.

2 Periodic assessment

Periodic assessment was brought to the education community's attention in 2007 through the QCDA/DCSF (Department for Children, Schools and Families) initiative known as Assessing Pupil's Progress (APP). The notion of periodic assessment, however, is not new and the process of teachers making use of collections of pupil work to evaluate progress has been used in some departments and schools for many years. In 2009–10, APP was being developed (under the labour administration) in the foundation subjects as a tool to view pupil progress, by periodically making use of collections of day-to-day learning, in order to make interim judgements on pupils' progress using a wide range of evidence taken from a variety of classroom contexts. The assessment of learning is completed by the teacher through evaluation of a collection of pupil learning; the teacher forms a judgement of how far the work meets the intended outcomes and what the individual pupil needs to do in order to improve next time.

This form of assessment works hand in glove with day-to-day approaches to assessment and encourages the teacher to move away from single assessment tasks. Progress can be more easily ascertained through a more holistic view of pupil learning. The editorial of *Teaching History 131 (Assessing Differently edition)* comments that the tension created through the competing demands of assessment has resulted in school curricula 'transformed into hierarchies of tiny increments and stages, filigreed ladders that pupils must ascend and know they are ascending, regardless of whether these reflect the depth, complexity or richness of the discipline and how pupils learn within it' (TH 131, 2009: 2). The periodic approach to assessment attempts to overcome these tensions and encourages teachers and pupils to recognize the integral nature of the many facets of historical learning.

Burnham and Brown identified the atomized nature of assessment in 2004 in their groundbreaking article Assessment without Levels (Burnham and Brown 2004). Burnham and Brown began their planning for assessment by focusing on what they were hoping to achieve and for whom and how the assessment should be useful. Using day-to-day assessment strategies Burnham and Brown argued they were able to assess their pupils' learning, amend planning based on pupil understanding and work towards a final outcome which had value and meaning to the pupils in their classes. Their pupils build a series of formal, informal and day-to-day assessments which provide teachers with a full picture of a pupil required to make a judgement.

Such day-to-day and periodic judgements as identified by Burnham and Brown encourage pupils, teachers and departments to make use of prior learning, to reflect on the historical complexity of what they are being asked to do and how to make use of this in future learning. This is often referred to as 'Assessment for Learning' and has become commonly known as a process undertaken in partnership by teachers and pupils to enable pupils to understand the learning process they are involved in and how to get better within that process. In 2003 the Assessment Reform Group published their research-based Principles of Assessment for Learning. They are summarized as follows:

- is part of effective planning
- focuses on how students learn
- is central to classroom practice
- is a key professional skill
- is sensitive and constructive
- fosters motivation
- promotes understanding of goals and criteria
- helps learners know how to improve
- develops the capacity for self-assessment
- recognizes all educational achievement.

In 2003, the KS3 National Strategy identified Assessment for Learning in six key areas of classroom practice; they are:

- objective-led lessons
- making use of summative data
- use of criteria
- oral and written feedback
- peer and self assessment
- target setting
- questioning (added in 2006).

This is an all-encompassing agenda. History teachers and departments cannot ignore the importance of assessment for learning in moving history teaching and learning forward. Assessment for learning is the most critical tool in developing and personalizing an individual child's route through school. It is through using a range of assessment for learning approaches that a teacher and student come to a purposeful understanding of the individual's learning needs.

Assessment using day-to-day and periodic approaches is purposeful, informative and thus powerful for the pupil and teacher. My approach to periodic assessment was heavily influenced by involvement in the APP pilot and KS3 Exemplification of Standards Project (Freeman and Philpott, 2009: 4–13). After reflection on the project it became apparent that the greatest impact on effective periodic assessment came from a planned conceptual progression map with clearly defined learning outcomes to support assessment for and of pupil learning (see Figure 21.1). Together pupils and teachers follow a sequence of learning which aims to ensure pupils are able to connect together the lessons along the learning journey and make use of feedback in a formative manner. The sequence of learning is set out in Figure 21.1.

1. The learning journey of a unit of work is shared with the pupils at the beginning of the unit and pupils complete each enquiry from the scheme, making use of shared task criteria for their learning outcome.
2. The teacher marks the pupil work for each enquiry and feeds back to the pupil using the progression map for guidance.
3. Pupils are given time to employ next step targets derived from the progression map during the feedback lesson (a lesson where time is allocated for pupils to refer to feedback) and are referred back to the targets when completing a conceptually similar task.
4. Prior learning from across the unit is made use of in the final task .
5. Evidence of pupil learning from all of the enquiries, is used as a collection to form a best fit periodic judgement of the pupils progress in historical understanding.
6. Pupil progress is reported as levels for tracking purposes and with next steps targets for future pupil progression.

Figure 21.1 Progression map.

Table 21.2 Key areas of assessment for learning

Objective-led lessons	As defined through planned enquiries
Making use of summative data	For tracking and targets at the end of the unit
Use of criteria	Shared with pupils for the learning outcome of each enquiry
Oral and written feedback	Through day-to-day class work and homework making use of the progression map
Peer and self assessment	Pupil can log where they have met their targets and use the task criteria for peer assessment
Target setting	Fed back to pupils regularly making use of the progression map
Questioning	As part of day-to-day teaching and learning

When reflecting upon the 2003 KS3 National Strategy identified Assessment for Learning in six key areas of classroom practice, it is possible to identify how this approach to periodic assessment meets the approach previously outlined and is shown in Table 21.2.

3 Summative and transitional assessment

The term 'transitional' refers to assessment that provides a formal recognition of achievement and can be used to inform others; for example, an end of KS level or a GCSE (General Certificate of Secondary Education) grade – a level of grade which should mean the same to any teacher, parent or employer across England and Wales. Transitional in this context of assessment can also mean summative assessment. Summative assessment is often derived from milestone tasks which demonstrate that a particular point along the learning journey has been reached and enable a teacher to measure a pupil's progress against agreed standards within any Key Stage. They often form the basis of a pupil's termly (or more frequent) tracking data and in many instances such pieces of work can also be formal assessments such as an end of unit exam or piece of coursework.

Summative assessment tends to be completed at the end of a unit of learning, has an agreed mark scheme, provides a pupil with a grade or level and can (but does not always) provide next-steps learning. Examples of learning outcomes may be a piece of extended narrative or analytical writing such an article or essay, or a series of questions demonstrating evidential analysis; even presentations or more creative outcomes such as museum displays and websites can be used as a summative assessment of pupil learning. Table 21.3 charts the summative assessment used in KS3 at Dereham Neatherd High School – each has its own mark scheme and is completed at the end of a unit of work. Day-to-day tasks from the scheme of work contribute to a pupil's ability to complete the final task. The strength of a summative task is in demonstrating what a pupil has learned over a period of time; their weakness is that they provide a snapshot of learning rather than a holistic view as can be seen through periodic assessment. It is worth noting, however, that a pupil's termly reported level

Table 21.3 KS3 milestone tasks with assessment focus

Year group	Topic	Concept	Task
Year 7	Roman Norfolk	Diversity	Leaflet
	Medieval lives	Change and continuity	Essay
	Native Americans	Significance	Extended project
Year 8	Monarchs through time	Change and continuity	Living graph
	French Revolution	Causation	Mind map
	Glorious Revolution	Significance	Flow chart
	Industrial Revolution	Diversity	Essay
Year 9	Slave trade	Causation	Presentation
	Holocaust	Interpretations	Essay
	World War I	Significance	Magazine article
	World War II	Interpretations	Museum display

at Dereham Neatherd is based on a periodic judgement towards which summative assessments contribute, thus avoiding the difficulties raised by Burnham and Brown regarding levelling individual pieces of work.

Information gleaned from assessments provides valuable insights into the relative strengths and weaknesses of a pupil's historical understanding. This information, as already stated, usually forms the basis for tracking data and reporting to parents. School data tracking systems are used to measure teacher and departmental performance and are an important aspect of a school's self-evaluation and local authority and Ofsted (Office for Standards in Education) inspections. Increasingly departments and schools make use of their data tracking systems for pupil intervention and targeting as well as to monitor teacher and departmental performance. At a class-based level assessment data can perform the same function though with a greater emphasis monitoring educational progress of the pupil than on teacher monitoring. The overuse of data should in itself carry a large educational health warning and data should not be collected for the purpose of creating charts and spreadsheets displaying artificial or linear rates of pupil progress. Data should be collected with the purpose of recording a pupil's progress and alerting the teacher to anomalies in the expected rate of pupil progress.

Take, for example, Class 9Y who have been periodically assessed once per term using day-to-day and summative tasks. The majority of pupils have made some progress across the terms; a few pupils have not moved forward; others have made an increased rate of progress and a small number have achieved less well in the second term than in the first. The classroom teacher can explain this based on the conceptual basis of the work, such as an increased emphasis on significance and interpretations or evidential understanding, areas which many pupils find challenging or it may be linked to the learning styles employed in the second term. Such information encourages the teacher to reflect on which areas of the history curriculum may need readdressing or will require a different pedagogic approach in the coming term. The discrepancies within the data may alert the teacher to the need for closer analysis of the pupils who stood still or regressed as well as the pupils who made a significant improvement. At this point the teacher will benefit from returning to the individual pupil's evidence

Assessment is an integral aspect of teaching and learning and can be approached through a variety of methods. It is of fundamental importance to determine the rationale for and focus of historical learning within a given unit of study and the role assessment will play within this rationale. The use of day-to-day, periodic and summative assessment in achieving this aim can then be mapped and planned for through progression charts, mark schemes and task criteria. In turn the outcomes and experiences of the classroom inform teachers' planning in order that history teachers can focus on helping pupils get better at history. Through careful interplay of the differing approaches to assessment a holistic judgement of a pupil's historical understanding can be reached and formatively used to move a pupil forward in their historical learning journey.

Figure 21.2 Intervention map.

of learning and undertaking closer scrutiny of the strengths in a pupil's work or the areas that were previously targeted and progress failed to be made.

Using assessment data and its accompanying information, the teacher may decide to adopt intervention strategies with a number of pupils in Class 9Y. Figure 21.2 shows how a simple assessment traffic-light system can support a teacher's knowledge of their pupils and trigger a series of intervention strategies to improve historical understanding. While such a system is applicable to any subject, within a history classroom subject-specific targets or a subject report can ensure that a pupil is being given the best possible opportunities to become a better historian. A pupil who has achieved beyond expectation may need to be stretched and challenged using differentiated materials and extension tasks. A pupil falling below target may simply need a word of encouragement or, on closer evaluation, may need support in their understanding of sense of period or use of significance criteria. A pupil significantly below target may have difficulties with the conceptual level of the tasks undertaken and so may benefit from a more personalized curriculum or one-to-one intervention. If assessment is an opportunity for the teacher to determine and reflect on pupil learning and progress as well as allow the teacher and pupil to consider progress to date and what the pupil needs to do to get better at history, the effective collation and analysis of assessment data is a useful tool to benefit this process and, therefore, the historical understanding of all pupils.

Bringing it all together

Let us consider a case study from *Teaching History* that exemplifies how history teachers are able to shape their practice of assessment using day-to-day, periodic and summative approaches, while maintaining the purpose, rigour and creativity they expect from their pupils. Matt Stanford (2008: 4–11) wanted to develop his pupils' sense of period and their cultural understanding of the past, but saw limitations in having the traditional essay as the final product of their enquiry. Stanford identified the purpose and rationale for his assessment and designed a unit of study and final assessment task fit for purpose. He wanted to maintain rigorous historical learning yet offer pupils a creative outcome to their learning. Using a series of mini-enquiries to support the overarching enquiry Stanford was able to employ a range of learning styles to address historical concepts and support progression across these concepts. Having identified the conceptual focus and planned for progression with a clear learning outcome, Stanford was able to assess pupil learning on a day-to-day basis. The mini-enquiries demanded use of prior learning, thus providing value and relevance to the day-to-day learning and subsequent feedback, following concern that previous day-to-day 'tasks I had asked them to complete were completely undermined and devalued by the lack of recognition they received' (Stanford, 2008: 5). From the series of mini-enquiries pupils produced a collection of work Stanford would be able to periodically assess (though he does not indicate whether pupil collections were used in this way within his article). Finally, Stanford's pupils were able to make use of day-to-day learning in a final task with a shared mark scheme to support next-steps learning. Stanford demonstrates the importance of determining a clearly defined purpose of assessment when embarking upon a unit of work and knows how assessment will support pupil learning rather than drive it. Stanford's work demonstrates an appreciation of assessment in its holistic rather than piecemeal form through the use of day-to-day, periodic and summative approaches to assessment.

Chapter summary

Through a combination of theoretical discussion and practical examples this chapter has aimed to clarify the complex nature of assessment. This chapter has considered why teachers assess and the forms assessment can take. It has also addressed the issue of how to make effective use of information gleaned from assessing pupil learning to enhance pupil progress. All these issues are worthy of consideration within an individual, departmental and whole-school context. The application of these approaches to assessment cannot operate in isolation and will be influenced by individual school circumstances and will need to be considered in terms of whole-school ethos. Fundamentally, however, the response to and application of ideas from this chapter should be steered by individual philosophy of history teaching and how it can be used to help children progress within their history learning.

Further reading

Black, P., Harrison, C., Lee, C., Marshall, B. and Wiliam, D. (2003) *Assessment for Learning Putting it Into Practice*. Berkshire: Open University Press.

Burnham, S. and Brown, G. (2004) *Teaching History 115, Assessment Without Levels edition*.

Stanford, M. (2008) *Teaching History 130, Picturing the Past edition*.

Philpott, J. (2009) *Captivating Your Class, Effective Teaching Skills*. London: Continuum.

For more information on assessment at KS3 in the National Curriculum go to http://curriculum.qcda.gov.uk/key-stages-3-and-4/assessment/index.aspx (accessed November 2009).

References

Assessment for Learning: 10 Principles Assessment Reform Group (2002). Available online at: http://www.assessment-reform-group.org/CIE3.PDF (accessed November 2010).

Black, P. and Wiliam, D. (1998). 'Assessment and Classroom Learning'. *Assessment in Education*, 5(1): 7–71.

Black, P. and Wiliam, D. (2006) *Inside the Black Box: v. 1: Raising Standards Through Classroom Assessment*. NFER Nelson.

Burnham, S. and Brown, G. (2004) *Teaching History 115, Assessment Without Levels edition*.

Freeman. J, and Philpott, J. (2009) *Teaching History 137, Marking Time edition*.

Fullard, G. and Dacey, K. (2008) *Teaching History 131, Assessing Differently edition*.

Phillips, I. (2008) *Teaching History, Developing as a Reflective Secondary Teacher*. London: Sage.

Stanford M. (2008) *Teaching History 130, Picturing the Past edition*.

Teaching History 131 (TH) (2008) *Assessing Differently edition*.

Chapter 22

Fortified silos or interconnected webs

The relationship between history and other subjects in the curriculum

Alan Sears

Introduction

This chapter will:

- examine the phenomenon known as 'curriculum wars' and how these wars play out within the area of social education and between social education and other areas;
- discuss possible interconnections between history and other school subjects;
- argue that history has an important contribution to make in developing understanding in a range of curricular areas;
- show some practical ways that connections can be made between history and other subjects in the curriculum.

'Tories herald new curriculum wars' (Mansell, 2009) screamed a recent headline in *The Guardian*. While this declaration refers to conflict over the nature of the curriculum in a particular time and place – England in 2009 – Steiner (2007) points out that so-called 'curriculum wars' have been going on in Western societies for at least '24 centuries'. These battles centre on questions around content (what should be taught?), sequence (in what order or to what ages should particular material be taught?) and method (what is the best way to teach the curriculum?). The skirmishes have included how to deal with questions of creationism and intelligent design in science classes, the use of calculators in maths, the best ways to teach young children to read, and how to deal with issues of sex and sexuality in health education. The fights over these issues are often vociferous and, as the headline above implies, extend well beyond the community of professional educators.

The field of social education generally, and history education in particular, has often been at the centre of the conflict. One front is the war in the battle to secure space in the curriculum; a fight social studies and history have generally been losing vis-à-vis other subjects perceived to be more relevant and important such as literacy, maths and science. More damaging perhaps than the war between history and other subjects has been the civil war that has raged within the field of social education more generally – the conflict which Evans (2004) calls 'the social studies wars'. A key front in these wars has been the battle between history and citizenship for dominance in the social education of students. A number of articles and books have been written about these conflicts which have spanned the globe and included battles about curriculum standards in the USA, Aboriginal history in Australia and Canada and the treatment of World War II and its aftermath in the curricula of Germany and Japan, just to name a few (Nash *et al.*, 1997; Cole, 2007; Clark, 2008).

It is well past time to end both the inter-subject war and the civil war within social education. Elsewhere (Sears, 2011) I show how the latter in particular is largely built on false premises and has been destructive for both sides. In the remainder of this chapter I will both show how history has important areas of connections to other subjects in the curriculum and explore in detail some of the particular connections between history and citizenship education. My argument is that we should be seeking to build interconnected webs between and among subjects rather than constructing fortified silos of disciplinary solitude.

Connections between history and other subjects

While the connections between history and citizenship are perhaps the most obvious ones, there are important associations that can be made between history and other subjects in the curriculum as well. Traditionally curricula and many schools (especially secondary schools) are organized around distinct subjects or disciplines. One feature of the curriculum wars is that the boundaries around these subjects are often fiercely guarded and teachers and curriculum planners rarely collaborate across disciplinary lines. They often know very little about other subject areas and are suspicious of them. This kind of suspicion is evident between history and citizenship in England. Reacting to recent calls for more attention to history in the citizenship curriculum (Ajegbo *et al.*, 2007) leading history educators in England wondered if this rapprochement might prove to be a 'fatal attraction' for history, arguing that 'attempts to deliver the citizenship programme of study in history classrooms should never compromise history's integrity or sacrifice purposes and objectives particular to history education' (Lee and Shemilt, 2007: 14).

While I am in sympathy with the idea that the major disciplines have something unique and important to contribute in terms of both content and processes to the education of students, there are significant possibilities to enhance these contributions through cross-disciplinary teaching. One of the most significant possibilities for connecting history to work in other areas is to recognize that academic disciplines and school subjects have histories of their own and that understanding these histories helps build the kind of critical understanding of subject matter generally advocated in curricula around the world. Writing about mathematics, for example, Jankvist (2009: 237) argues that history has a role to play both as 'a tool for the actual learning and teaching of mathematics' and 'as a goal in itself'.

As a tool, history can demonstrate to students that the concepts and processes they struggle to learn were not arrived at quickly by mathematicians either, but often took years to work out. An understanding of the fluid and shifting nature of particular topics can help students cognitively as they develop their own understandings of the subject matter. As a goal, history helps students to understand the contextual situatedness of the discipline. Students will come to understand maths as

> a discipline that has undergone an evolution and is not something that has arisen out of thin air; that human beings have taken part in its evolution; that

mathematics has evolved through many different cultures throughout its history and that these cultures have had an influence on the shaping of mathematics and vice-versa; or that the evolution is driven by internal and external forces.

(p. 239)

Howe (2009: 397) takes up the same theme with regard to teaching science. He argues that contemporary science curricula call for students to develop an understanding of the nature of science as a discipline. This is important because it helps 'students develop their understanding so they will become critical consumers of the very scientific knowledge that increasingly impacts their daily lives.' He contends that teaching the history of science is the key way to achieve this as it fosters an understanding that 'there are historical, cultural, and social influences on the practice of science.' Howe goes on to suggest that students study critical episodes in the history of science engaging with questions such as: 'How was the scientist's work influenced by the culture in which he/she operated? What ramifications may his/her conclusions have on sociological or political policy? Did any issues of ethics or values come into play with the historical episode?' (p. 401).

The work of popularizers of the history of science such as Stephen J. Gould (1981, 1989) and Bill Bryson (2003) make it clear that understanding the historical contingency of scientific exploration, including how cultural context impacts the way scientists work, is essential for understanding science and critically engaging with the scientific issues that confront contemporary society. Science often does not progress in neat, logically coherent ways and its findings are often oversold. In the words of one population geneticist from Oxford, 'you can trust the studies well enough, generally speaking. What you can't trust are the sweeping conclusions that people often attach to them' (quoted in Bryson, 2003: 465). It is absolutely essential that students develop an understanding of what scientists have discovered, how they came to their findings, and how those findings are then used in debates about public policy. The history of science is an obvious vehicle for developing these understandings.

Religious education is another subject with a vital connection to history that works both ways: history is deficient without attention to religion and religious education is deficient without attention to history. Gates (2007) points out that many Western societies have basically expunged attention to religion from the curriculum (and other areas of public life) to their great detriment. He and others (Noddings, 2008) argue that religion is a persistent and influential force in contemporary society and that religious literacy is vital for effective citizenship and social cohesion.

One aspect of religious literacy is understanding the role religion has played in the development of contemporary society. Unfortunately, one of the outcomes of aggressive secularism in much of the democratic world has been a purging of religious ideas and topics from history curricula. Noddings (2008: 387) argues this has been the case in the USA, writing that 'the ignorance of Americans on religious matters is appalling.' She contends the failure to accord balanced treatment to religious ideas, movements and people impoverishes the history curriculum. She writes, 'we simply excise a substantial part of our own history when we omit discussion of religion' (p. 370).

While it is true that a comprehensive and critical approach to teaching history requires consideration of religion, it is equally true that a thorough approach to religious education requires substantial attention to history. In accordance with the work of Noddings discussed above, Gates (2007: 61) makes a compelling case that 'critically appreciative attention to religion is a precondition for any education, religious or secular, which claims public sponsorship in a democratic society.' The trouble is, however, when it is dealt with in the curriculum religion is often treated with kid gloves. Courses in world religions 'often concentrate on famous leaders, ritual practice, significant dates, costumes and celebrations. They avoid the critical discussion of beliefs and refer to religious wars and persecutions with delicacy, often treating them as anomalies' (Noddings, 2008: 370). The application of ideas and approaches consistent with the work in historical thinking discussed above would bring a more critical and balanced treatment to religions and religious history.

The three subjects discussed above – maths, science and religious education – are offered as examples of the kind of relationship that can be developed between history and any discipline. They all exemplify the dual approach outlined by Jankvist of using history as both a tool – a way to better learn the subject matter of the other discipline – and a goal – a way to historicize the other discipline so as to better understand it as an historical entity that has shaped and been shaped by the society in which it exists. It would be very beneficial for teachers of history and other subjects to explore together how they might develop these two aspects of connecting history and other disciplines in their schools.

Besides citizenship, the subject with most obvious links to history is literature. Like the other subjects dealt with above, literature has its own history that can be interesting to study in and of itself. More important is the contribution literature and literary forms can make to developing an understanding of history. Space does not allow for a comprehensive treatment of this topic but a few examples will be explored here.

The narrative form is basic to both history and literature and can be a powerful tool for engaging students in historical study. Colleagues and I (Clarke *et al.*, 1993; Clarke and Smyth, 1993), for example, developed a project aimed at teaching ancient and medieval history to primary school students using stories as the central vehicle for engaging students with the long ago and far away. Primary social studies had long been trapped in a Piagetan framework that assumed the inability of young children to deal with the abstract nature of historical study and focused instead on the consideration of what were assumed to be more concrete and immediate themes and topics: family, neighbourhood, community, etc. Our work built on both emerging critiques of Piaget and a growing body of scholarship demonstrating that 'the narrative form is amenable to children's ways of thinking' and 'germane to history'. We also argued that using story forms 'allows teachers and children to cross over the traditional disciplinary divisions' (Clarke and Smyth, 1993: 76).

Working with teachers and librarians we developed units around a dozen stories covering eras and societies ranging from Bronze Age Greece (Jason and the Argonauts) through fifth-century China (The Monkey King) to medieval Arabia (Sinbad the Sailor). Teachers were provided with both a children's and adults' version of the story and a range of supplementary materials dealing with the history, geography and cultural features of the relevant times and places. They began their teaching with the story and used that as a base for a more comprehensive historical study. Even teachers who 'initially doubted their ability to bring unfamiliar subjects to their students found that the story was an excellent vehicle, bringing meaning to an otherwise abstract study' (Clarke and Smyth, 1993: 78).

Similarly, fiction can be employed in a number of ways to engage older students in the study of history. As we did with primary students, stories can be used as a means to capture interest and immerse students in the issues surrounding historical times and places. The award-winning Australian novel *The Secret River* (Grenville, 2006), for example, ranges from early-nineteenth-century London to the fledgling colony of New South Wales in Australia and deals with issues of social class, crime and punishment, prisoner transport, colonialism and Aboriginal–White contact. The richly described settings and complex character development draw one into long-ago places quite effectively and could serve as a springboard for more analytic consideration of the topics addressed in the work.

Period literature can also be used as a primary source for more fully understanding particular times and places. The work of Ivan Turgenev (1994), for example, provides a first-hand description of country life in Russia at the critical juncture when serfs were being freed and revolutionary movements gaining steam in the mid to late nineteenth century. His short stories (Turgenev and Freeborn, 1967) explore the lives of serfs, village folks and nobles and the interactions between and among them. If one wants to understand what a Russian nihilist of the 1860s was like there can be no better source than the novel *Fathers and Sons* and the character Yevgeny Bazarov. The novel could be read in its entirety but any of the long dialogues between Bazarov and the aristocratic Pavel Petrovich Kirsanov are highly illustrative of the divisions in Russian society at the time.

The range of possibilities for using historical fiction or fiction rooted in a particular historical context are limitless. There are important things to keep in mind when using narrative fiction in a history class, however. One is that the very things that make narrative so powerful as a teaching tool – the way it resonates with how people think and describe their own experiences and the way it draws us into the time and place – are the things that potentially make it dangerous for the study of history. A story well told has the potential to reinforce the ideas that history is a single, linear story. As Barton (1996: 403) points out, '[h]istory isn't a story; stories are simply one way of talking about the past, and any single story invariably involves selection, simplification, and distortion.' Teachers using fiction to engage students' interest in history or immerse them in particular times and places will also have to develop activities to help students interrogate those powerful accounts.

A second concern is that fiction is simply not history in the disciplinary sense, and its authors are not bound by the conventions of evidence and argument that regulate the practice of historians. One way to deal with this concern is for teachers to explicitly raise questions of sourcing when considering fictional accounts. Sourcing is a key component of the critical reading of text and involves evaluating the reliability of a text through asking questions like: Why was the text produced? What is the perspective of the author and how has that shaped the text? How does the information or perspective presented fit with what we know of the time and place from other sources? Where there are differences, how can I ascertain which sources or accounts are reliable? As Martin and Wineburg (2008: 305) point out, sourcing is something sophisticated readers regularly do unconsciously and 'is key to understanding how knowledge is made in many disciplines but is especially important in history.' Helping students develop their abilities to source is a central component of virtually all approaches to teaching historical thinking and that kind of critical reading is very useful for literary studies as well.

Finally, a way to employ historical fiction in the teaching of both history and literature is to have students write it. Seeking to write fiction that is true to what historians know of a time and place and yet includes literary devices and techniques not usually used in historical writing has great potential for developing students' understanding of both disciplines. It will also contribute to undermining the subtle power of fiction described above as students learn about the ways in which fiction writers select material and shape their stories to reflect particular rather than universal perspectives.

Connections between history and citizenship education

Civil wars are reputed to be the most vicious and there is some evidence that this is true in the battles between history and citizenship (Sears, 2011). These two subjects have obvious areas of overlap but often defend their disciplinary boundaries quite fiercely. Similar to the discussion of the relationship between history and religious education earlier in this chapter, I argue that history needs to be more focused on its role in educating citizens and citizenship needs to be understood in its historical context.

Keith Barton and Linda Levstik (2004), two eminent history educators from the USA, concur contending the central purpose of history education is to foster good citizenship. For them history does this through promoting 'reasoned judgment' (p. 36), 'an expanded view of humanity' (p. 37) and 'deliberation over the common good' (p. 38). They call on history teachers to recognize the civic purposes of their subject and teach it accordingly. Promoting reasoned judgement, for example, would involve asking students to make judgements about historical events and persons; promoting an expanded view of humanity implies considering the histories of groups and nations different from our own; and promoting deliberation over the common good necessitates asking students to consider how historical study might inform debates about current policy and practice.

Concomitantly, a comprehensive consideration of citizenship must include attention to history. Democratic ideas have evolved (largely as the result of struggle) across time and context from Ancient Greece to the present and to be fully educated about those ideas students have to know something about this long struggle. Part of what is wrong with contemporary approaches to civics and citizenship education is their disconnection from this historical context. Paying attention to the history of specific state contexts is also important in citizenship education because, while there are common or generic aspects to democratic citizenship that exist across jurisdictions, it is most often lived out on the ground in specific contexts that give it both form and function. A combination of factors including history, geography and demography work together to produce quite distinctive versions of liberal democratic citizenship across countries, even those with relatively similar political heritages such as Britain, Canada and Australia.

First steps in building connections on the ground

While the curriculum wars rage particularly at the level of policy and curriculum planning, often what separates subjects at the level of the school is simply benign ignorance. Teachers of various subject areas are not so much hostile toward other disciplines as ignorant of possible areas of overlap or simply too busy to think about collaborative planning with colleagues from other disciplines. The most effective way to initiate work together is to begin with small steps between individual teachers in particular schools rather than by policy fiat from above. Some things that might foster collaboration include:

- Ask for help rather than offering suggestions. People often respond much more positively if they are asked for their input than if they feel they are being told what they should do. The possibilities here are virtually endless. A history teacher teaching about the Renaissance might approach a science teacher and ask him or her to make a presentation to their class about key scientific advancements of the period and how they shaped our evolving understanding of the natural world. A religious education teacher might be asked to speak about the conflicts between scientific and theological assumptions of the period and the teacher of literature might be asked to highlight two or three pieces of literature that represent key trends in the era. All of these would enhance students' historical understanding of a particular time and demonstrate to them the interconnections between and among academic disciplines. These requests might come with offers to reciprocate where the history teacher can visit the other classes to help put topics being studied there into historical context. Students of physics, for example, could be engaged in thinking about the wider social impacts of the work of Copernicus and Galileo and how the reaction from the church shaped they way they went about conducting and sharing their work.
- Start small and build from there. Being asked to do one or two class presentations is far less daunting than planning collaboration across the curriculum for a term. Where there is success in collaborating in small areas, teachers might attempt greater integration. For example, teachers of history and literature who have done guest presentations in each other's classrooms might want to collaborate on a unit centered around a particular event or era. They might, for example, study World War I with a particular focus on how it has been portrayed in poetry and fiction. A key historical question for this kind of study might be something like, what insights can we gain into to mindset of the period through the literary works? From a literary perspective one could ask, how did the events of the period shape the themes and forms employed by novelists and poets?
- Ask students to make explicit connections between and among the courses they are taking. One of the most notoriously elusive goals in education is knowledge transfer; that is, the application of knowledge learned in one context to another context. Much of the evidence available indicates that for transfer to take place teachers have to explicitly structure activities to make it happen. History teachers can give students assignments that ask them to integrate learning from other subject areas. For example, they might ask students to investigate the religious institutions and beliefs prevalent in a particular time and place and write an essay

or make a presentation about how those shaped relevant historical events. The great debates within German churches in the 1930s about how to respond to the Nazi government provide substantial material for developing both religious and historical understanding not only of that period but also of the more general question of the relationship between church and state.

- Schools might foster cross-disciplinary work by organizing events and assemblies around particular themes. One theme that cuts across a range of subject areas is developing cross-cultural understanding and respect for multiple perspectives. This is relevant to curricula in citizenship, history, literature and religious education. Work in historical thinking places a significant emphasis on understanding the Other, albeit a historical rather than present Other. The past has been described as a 'foreign country' (Lowenthal, 1985) and research indicates that many students see residents of that country 'as inherently inferior and ignorant' (Lévesque, 2008: 162). This is exactly the kind of understanding, or misunderstanding, about which those interested in contemporary approaches to multicultural education and religious education are concerned. Through addressing the procedural concept of historical empathy or perspective-taking, history educators advocate developing students' understanding of and empathy for 'conflicting belief systems, and historical actors' differing perspectives' (Seixas, 2006: 17). It strikes me that the two projects – developing complex historical and contemporary understanding of difference – are entirely complementary. Students in a school might be asked to construct a profile of their community including the history, literature and religious traditions of its constituent groups.

When seeking to collaborate with colleagues it is important to be able to demonstrate to them that interdisciplinary work will not detract from meeting the prescribed outcomes for their subject area. Particularly in systems where there are relatively high-stakes exams, teachers will be concerned about straying too far from the prescribed curriculum. Consistent with Howe's (2009) conclusions about science discussed above, I believe student achievement on important outcomes can be significantly enhanced through this kind of collaboration but teachers cannot be expected to take that for granted.

The point in all of these examples is that individual teachers or school staffs can foster interdisciplinary collaboration at a local level in spite of the curriculum wars that might be raging elsewhere in the education system. These collaborations are not designed to weaken or displace any of the subjects involved, but rather to enhance their scope and help students make useful connections between and among them.

Conclusion

The curriculum wars described above have often been vicious and destructive both to the individuals involved and to the curriculum itself. As Macintyre (Macintyre and Clark, 2004) points out, they have more to do with vanquishing the enemy than seeking understanding. The overheated rhetoric employed and sweeping, simplistic ideas touted as solutions to our educational dilemmas have not served educational reform very well. It would be far better, as Macintyre (Macintyre and Clark, 2004: 243) argues, 'to seek understanding'; to seek for ways to build complimentary relationships between and among curricular subjects to the benefit of all. In this chapter I have tried to establish a foundation for seeking understanding and collaboration between history and other subjects in the school curriculum.

Acknowledgements

I would like to acknowledge the research assistance provided for this chapter by Cynthia Wallace-Casey.

Further reading

Keith C. Barton and Linda S. Levstik (2004) *Teaching History for the Common Good.* Mahwah, NJ: Lawrence Erlbaum Associates.
Kieran Egan, Maureen Stout and Keiichi Takaya (2007) *Teaching and Learning Outside the Box: Inspiring Imagination across the Curriculum.* New York: Teachers College Press.
Alan Sears (2010) 'Historical thinking and citizenship education: it is time to end the war', in Penney Clark (ed.), *History Teaching and Learning in Canada: A State of the Art Look.* Vancouver: UBC Press.

References

Ajegbo, S. K., Kiwan, D. and Sharma, S. (2007) *Diversity and Citizenship Curriculum Review.* London: Department for Education and Skills.
Barton, K. (1996). '"Everyone knows what history is . . ." Research, instruction, and public policy in the history curriculum'. *Theory and Research in Social Education*, 24: 391–415.
Barton, K. C. and Levstik, L. S. (2004) *Teaching History for the Common Good.* Mahwah, NJ: Lawrence Erlbaum Associates.
Bryson, B. (2003) *A Short History of Nearly Everything.* Toronto: Anchor Canada.
Clark, A. (2008) *History's Children: History Wars in the Classroom.* Sydney: University of New South Wales Press.
Clarke, G. and Smyth, J. (1993) 'Stories in elementary history and social studies'. *Canadian Social Studies*, 27(2): 76–8.
Clarke, G., Sears, A., Smyth, J. and Easley, S. D. (1993) 'Voyages in primary social studies: a story-based approach'. *Thresholds in Education*, 19(4): 13–16.
Cole, E. A. (ed.). (2007) *Teaching the Violent Past: History Education and Reconciliation.* Lanham, Maryland: Rowman & Littlefield.
Evans, R. W. (2004) *The Social Studies Wars: What Should We Teach the Children?* New York: Teachers College Press.
Gates, B. (2007) *Transforming Religous Education.* London: Continuum.
Gould, S. J. (1981) *The Mismeasure of Man* (1st edn). New York: Norton.
——(1989) *Wonderful Life: The Burgess Shale and the Nature of History.* New York: W.W. Norton.
Grenville, K. (2006) *The Secret River.* Edinburgh and New York: Canongate.
Howe, E. M. (2009) 'Henry David Thoreau, forest succession and the nature of science: a method for curriculum development'. *American Biology Teacher*, 71(7): 397–404.
Jankvist, U. (2009) 'A categorization of the "whys" and "hows" of using history in mathematics education'. *Educational Studies in Mathematics*, 71(3): 235–61.

Lee, P. and Shemilt, D. (2007) 'New alchemy or fatal attraction? History and citizenship'. *Teaching History* (129): 14–19.

Lévesque, S. (2008) *Thinking Historically: Educating Students for the Twenty-First Century.* Toronto: University of Toronto Press.

Lowenthal, D. (1985) *The Past is a Foreign Country.* New York: Cambridge.

Macintyre, S. and Clark, A. (2004) *The History Wars* (New edn). Melbourne: Melbourne University Press.

Mansell, W. (2009) 'Tories herald new curriculum wars'. *The Guardian*, 20 October. Available online at: http://www.guardian.co.uk/education/2009/oct/20/curriculum-debate-syllabus-lacking-content (accessed 5 October 2010).

Martin, D. and Wineburg, S. (2008) 'Seeing thinking on the web'. *History Teacher*, 41(3): 305–19.

Nash, G. B., Crabtree, C. and Dunn, R. (1997) *History on Trial: Culture Wars and the Teaching of the Past.* New York: Knopf.

Noddings, N. (2008) 'The new outspoken atheism and education'. *Harvard Educational Review*, 78(2): 369–90.

Sears, A. (2011) 'Historical thinking and citizenship education: it is time to end the war', in P. Clark (ed.), *History Teaching and Learning in Canada: A State of the Art Look.* Vancouver: UBC Press.

Seixas, P. (2006) 'What is historical consciousness?', in R. W. Sandwell (ed.), *To the Past: History Education, Public Memory and Citizenship in Canada.* Toronto: University of Toronto Press, pp. 11–22.

Steiner, D. (2007) *Curriculum Wars: Ancient and Modern.* Available online at: http://educationnext.org/curriculum-wars/ (accessed 4 December 2009).

Turgenev, I. S. (1994) *Fathers and Sons.* New York: W.W. Norton.

Turgenev, I. S. and Freeborn, R. (1967) *Sketches from a Hunter's Album.* Baltimore: Penguin Books.

Index

Note: page numbers in **bold** refer to figures and tables.